THE COLLECTION

THE COLLECTION

———

PETER ACKROYD

*Edited and with an Introduction
by Thomas Wright*

Chatto & Windus
London

Published by Chatto & Windus 2001

2 4 6 8 10 9 7 5 3 1

Copyright © Peter Ackroyd 2001

This selection, editorial apparatus and the Introduction
copyright © Thomas Wright 2001

Peter Ackroyd has asserted his right under the Copyright, Designs
and Patents Act 1988 to be identified as the author of this work

First published in Great Britain in 2001 by
Chatto & Windus
Random House, 20 Vauxhall Bridge Road,
London SW1V 2SA

Random House Australia (Pty) Limited
20 Alfred Street, Milsons Point, Sydney,
New South Wales 2061, Australia

Random House New Zealand Limited
18 Poland Road, Glenfield,
Auckland 10, New Zealand

Random House (Pty) Limited
Endulini, 5A Jubilee Road, Parktown 2193, South Africa

The Random House Group Limited Reg. No. 954009
www.randomhouse.co.uk

A CIP catalogue record for this book
is available from the British Library

ISBN 0 7011 7300 9

Papers used by Random House are natural,
recyclable products made from wood grown in sustainable forests;
the manufacturing processes conform to the environmental
regulations of the country of origin

Typeset by Deltatype Ltd, Birkenhead, Wirral
Printed and bound in Great Britain by
Clays Ltd, St Ives plc.

To the memory of George Gale

Contents

III Lectures, Miscellaneous Writings, Short Stories
Lectures

Miscellaneous Writings

Short Stories

Acknowledgements

I would like to thank the staff of The London Library and of The British Library (in particular, that of The Newspaper Library at Colindale) for their assistance during my research for this anthology. I would also like to express my gratitude to my agent Giles Gordon, to Penelope Hoare of Chatto & Windus (both of whom provided information for my introduction), to Christopher Sinclair-Stevenson and to Howard Davies, the copy editor of this book. I am also indebted to Alan Bun and Mick McGinnegan for their help in tracking down some of Mr Ackroyd's articles, and to Mark Amory, literary editor of the *Spectator*, who very kindly allowed me to photocopy Peter Ackroyd's *Spectator* contributions at the magazine's offices in Doughty Street.

I would like to thank News International Newspapers Ltd for its permission to reproduce the pieces that appeared in *The Times* and the *Sunday Times*, the *New Yorker* for allowing me to include the article on Walter Pater, the *New York Times* for its permission to reprint four book reviews, and the *New Statesman* for allowing me to reproduce the short story 'The Plantation'. Peter Ackroyd's *Spectator* articles are reproduced courtesy of the *Spectator*.

The following articles, which appeared in *The Times*, are reproduced from manuscripts and typescripts rather than from the published versions: 97, 98, 100, 101, 102, 103, 104, 106, 108, 109, 110, 112, 113, 114, 115, 117, 118, 119, 131.

Thomas Wright
London, 2001

Editor's Preface

In one of his reviews Peter Ackroyd remarks that a 'visionary is also a prodigal'. This could certainly be applied to Ackroyd himself. During the last twenty-eight years he has written almost a million words in the form of reviews, lectures, introductions, short stories and miscellaneous writings, in addition to over twenty published works of poetry, criticism, drama, fiction and biography. As one critic put it, Ackroyd, like a character in one of his own novels, seems to have become imbued with the energy of his native city or to have been granted, by some Faustian bargain, a sense of time that ordinary mortals cannot comprehend.

From his vast body of work I have compiled a volume that is approximately 150,000 words in length. As well as choosing the pieces that I personally found most interesting and entertaining, I have had three main aims. First, I have tried to include articles in which Ackroyd addresses what I believe to be the principal concerns of his writing, such as the limitations of the scientific or materialistic vision of the world, and the various ways in which the past may animate the present. In adopting this approach, I have attempted to do justice to the variety of Ackroyd's preoccupations and interests as well as to the complexity of his ideas. Indeed, I hope that he emerges from this volume as a less familiar and more complicated figure than the 'Cockney visionary' of popular perception.

Second, I have chosen writings that reveal Ackroyd's characteristic critical attitudes. These include his emphasis on language and style over the 'content' of books, and his tendency to place apparently modern literary trends in the context of older traditions. Ackroyd brings such concerns and ideas to bear upon even the shortest television review, and this confers a degree of coherence on the heterogeneous contents of this volume. In this sense, to use a distinction he makes in one of his *Spectator* pieces, Ackroyd is a 'critic' rather than a 'reviewer': although he is sensitive to the particular qualities of the work under review, typically he will place it within his own order or system. In this anthology I have tried to offer the reader a clear picture of Ackroyd the critic. To this end, I have decided to include a number of pieces in which he discusses the criticism of writers such as V. S. Pritchett, Roland Barthes, F. R. Leavis and Harold Bloom, and defines his own position in relation to theirs.

My third aim has been to select pieces that relate to Ackroyd's own novels and biographies. I have chosen a number of articles and lectures in which he comments directly on his own work or discusses the genres of historical fiction and biography. I have also selected a number of reviews in which, to borrow a phrase from Ackroyd's article on Virginia Woolf's essays, he seems to be 'expounding the artistic principles that inspire his own work'. *The Collection* can therefore be read as a companion volume to Ackroyd's novels and biographies.

The editorial procedure for this volume should be mentioned at this point. First I gathered together material of roughly 300,000 words in length from Ackroyd's miscellaneous writing; then, with the help of Ackroyd himself, I made my selection. Where it has been possible to do so, I have reproduced final manuscript versions of articles rather than published texts, as Ackroyd's copy was, of course, sometimes altered by editors. I have indicated the instances in which I have used Ackroyd's manuscripts in the Acknowledgements.

It has been necessary for me to make certain changes to some of the pieces. In almost thirty years of journalism and occasional writing, it would have been impossible for Ackroyd not to have reused his favourite phrases and analogies. The most obvious of these repetitions have been silently removed. In addition, my copy editor Howard Davies has made all of the pieces consistent in matters of copy style.

I have classified the articles first by genre, and then arranged them in a broadly chronological order. Needless to say, this book does not have to be read straight through from cover to cover. In my introduction I have tried to place the articles in the context of Ackroyd's career as a writer and in the context of the various publications in which they appeared.

Thomas Wright
London, 2001

Introduction

Peter Ackroyd was born in London on 5 October 1949, the only child of Graham Ackroyd and Audrey Whiteside. His parents separated soon after his birth and he was raised by his mother and grandmother on a council estate near Wormwood Scrubs prison in west London.

In his early years he was exposed to two great influences on his vision of the world: Catholicism, the faith in which he was brought up by his mother, and the city of London, the streets of which he would explore with his grandmother. According to his mother, Ackroyd was a precocious and ambitious child. He read newspapers at the age of five, wrote a play about Guy Fawkes at nine, and dreamed of becoming a famous tap dancer or a great magician. Having attended the local primary school in East Acton, at the age of ten he was awarded a scholarship to St Benedict's, a Catholic public school in Ealing.

In 1968 Ackroyd entered Clare College, Cambridge. At Cambridge he decided to be a poet and in 1971, his final year, he published *Ouch*, his first volume of poetry. He left the university having achieved a 'double First'. From 1971 to 1973 Ackroyd was a Mellon Fellow at Yale University. In America he met poets such as John Ashbery, wrote a play (now lost) entitled 'No', which was entirely made up of quotations, and finished the polemical prose work that was eventually published in 1976 as *Notes for a New Culture: An Essay on Modernism*.

On his return to London in 1973 he wrote to all the newspapers and London literary magazines offering them his services. George Gale, then editor of the *Spectator*, was one of the few people who replied. Ackroyd went to see Gale at the magazine's office at 99 Gower Street and was given some books relating to Wyndham Lewis to review.

Two days later Ackroyd returned with a 1500-word article. Impressed by the review (it was eventually published on 9 June and is the first item in this volume) and by Ackroyd's professionalism, Gale interviewed him for the then vacant post of literary editor. During their conversation, Gale asked Ackroyd if he had any personal problems. When Ackroyd confessed to 'a bit of a drinking problem', he was appointed literary editor on the spot. According to Simon Courtauld, author of *To Convey Intelligence: The Spectator 1928–1998*, alcohol played a significant role in the life of the magazine, even in its pre-Doughty Street days.

At the age of twenty-three Ackroyd thus joined the small permanent staff of the *Spectator* (in the early 1970s the magazine employed four or five people). He became the youngest literary editor in the history of the *Spectator* and also the youngest in London at the time. In the book reviews he wrote almost every week during his five years at the post (a selection of which are reproduced in this anthology), he frequently alluded to his age and lack of experience. '[This book] reminds me of my schooldays back in 1967,' he remarked in one; 'I am practically uneducated,' he commented in another. Indeed, his journalistic persona was that of an energetic and mischievous young man who was never afraid to take on the elders who, to adapt one of his own phrases, he certainly did not regard as his betters.

With an incisive style and a mordant wit, Ackroyd challenged the great and the good of literature. In one review he dismissed the late poetry of Auden as 'dreadful stuff'; in another he accused Nabokov of 'playing with himself' in print. Of Ted Hughes' *Gaudete* he wrote, 'there isn't a good line in the book', and his comment on a novel by Yukio Mishima was: 'This is not writing, this is Barbara Cartland – and Barbara Cartland at least has the courage not to commit hara-kiri over it.' With acerbic epigrams such as these Ackroyd attempted to write the epitaphs on a number of reputations. He seemed to relish the occasions when he could point out that literary emperors such as Larkin, Castaneda and Pynchon were not wearing any clothes.

In the London literary world of the 1970s Ackroyd was therefore something of a gadfly who might be compared to Gore Vidal or to the anonymous reviewers who write for *Private Eye*. He emphasized his status as an outsider by frequently attacking conventional literary criticism. On the one hand, members of academia (or 'modern Grub Street' as he called it) were censored for being the slaves of ideological fashion and for being too scared to make qualitative judgements. On the other, he attacked 'the baa-lamb reviewers' of the national newspapers and described most literary journalism as 'rubbish . . . written about rubbish'.

Ackroyd's later journalism is neither as eccentric nor as abrasive as his writing for the *Spectator*. One reason for this is that in the mid-1970s the *Spectator* commanded a relatively small circulation of just over 10,000 copies a week. From its position on the margins of the world of London journalism, it could be outspoken and provocative. In his history of the *Spectator*, Simon Courtauld suggests that the most important editors of the magazine in the 1970s encouraged their contributors to be forthright. Courtauld describes George Gale (editor 1970–3) as a gruff 'maverick' figure and tells us that Alexander Chancellor (editor 1975–84) aimed to produce a 'civilized and slightly anarchic' magazine. Ackroyd's journalism can therefore be seen as part of the magazine's prevailing tone. It comes as no surprise to find his reviews alongside articles by equally challenging and idiosyncratic writers such as Auberon Waugh, Christopher Hitchens, A. N. Wilson and Germaine Greer.

After *Ouch* (1971), Ackroyd published two volumes of poetry in the 1970s: *London Lickpenny* (1973) and *Country Life* (1978). His verse has been compared to the work of other 'Cambridge Poets' of the period, such as Nick Totton, Ian Patterson and John James. These poets, who knew each other at university, created a poetry that has been described as 'avant-garde': it lacks a central perspective and a single style or tone, and it has no subject other than language or the process of poetry itself. By what Ackroyd describes as a miracle of 'generational taste', they all admired the work of John Ashbery and Frank O'Hara, and despised what they regarded as the more conventional productions of poets such as Larkin, Plath and Hughes.

Ackroyd's own practice as a poet and this 'generational taste' informed many of his *Spectator* reviews. He frequently criticized poets who, in his opinion, fulfilled popular notions of the 'poetic' and who used language as a transparent tool through which 'life' and 'experience' could be represented. In contrast, he praised writers such as J. H. Prynne and his fellow 'Cambridge Poets', whose language divests itself of signifying force and either returns to a state of play or becomes a magical agency that creates rather than reflects reality. Ackroyd thus used his position at the *Spectator* to promote the work of his favourite poets and his friends (he also commissioned reviews from some of them). His articles might be described as an ambitious Poundian bid to create among general readers the taste by which their poetry, and his own, might be judged.

The *Spectator* reviews also reveal evidence of Ackroyd's work as a critical theorist. In his extended polemical essay *Notes for a New Culture* (1976) he identified two antithetical cultural forces: 'humanism' and 'modernism'. Put simply, humanistic authors, for Ackroyd, were primarily concerned with the 'content' of writing and with the representation of 'reality', while modernists regarded language as an autonomous sign system. Ackroyd argued that, since the 1930s, humanists had dominated English criticism and literature; he suggested that this accounted for their 'impoverished' and 'dispirited' state.

Ackroyd's animosity towards humanistic authors can be found throughout this anthology and, in particular, in those writings in the *Spectator* where he characteristically criticized works in which, as he put it, 'sheer "content" usurps the higher claims of style, form and technique'. This obviously included all 'realistic' writing and any work that attempted to convey a 'message'. In contrast, he commended books in which 'life is kept at a respectful distance' and in which language becomes the 'main character'. This did not mean, however, that Ackroyd encouraged English writers simply to imitate French modernists such as Robbe-Grillet. He suggested instead that they should try to avoid the 'weary conventions' of both realism and experimentalism and search for some way of going beyond them.

Ackroyd's term of literary editorship came to an end in 1979, at which date he became the *Spectator*'s film critic and joint managing editor. He held the latter position until 1982. During his years as literary editor he had tried to make the book pages as eclectic as possible by commissioning articles from a wide variety of reviewers such as Roger Scruton, Robert Skidelsky, Joyce Grenfell, Richard Shone, J. H. Prynne and Brigid Brophy.

The large body of film criticism that Ackroyd wrote for the *Spectator* between 1979 and 1987, a sample of which has been reproduced here, is also informed by his attitudes to literature. Ackroyd would, for instance, criticize 'realistic' directors who, in his view, confused filmic reality with that of the world. Typically, he focused on style rather than content, and mastery of cinematic technique was always his criterion of quality. Peter Greenaway was thus praised for creating works that had the 'logic of the visual imagination' and Spielberg was rated above more 'intellectual' or apparently 'significant' directors such as Bergman and Tarkovsky. Such directors, Ackroyd argued, had essentially 'literary' or 'theatrical' imaginations and in consequence sometimes forfeited the effects that made cinema unique.

As a critic of film Ackroyd was as much of a 'maverick' as he had been as a reviewer of books. He attacked eminent directors with his savage wit (Fellini was described as an 'Italian Ken Russell' and as 'more of an interior decorator than a director'). He ridiculed the pretentiousness and solemnity of newspaper film critics, and he was always at pains to distinguish himself from them. He made a point of watching films with a normal audience rather than at special showings for journalists, and in his last *Spectator* article on film in 1987, he expressed great pride at the fact that no quotations from his reviews had ever appeared on promotional posters.

During the period of his association with the *Spectator* (1973–87) Ackroyd also wrote a number of miscellaneous articles. George Gale commissioned him to write several pieces on the 1973 election, and sent him to Tripoli to cover the war between Israel and Egypt. Under Alexander Chancellor's editorship, Ackroyd wrote travel pieces as well as investigative articles on English prisons and on poverty. A small selection of these occasional writings has been included in this book.

Ackroyd established his reputation at the *Spectator*. His journalism attracted the attention of Nikos Stangos at Thames and Hudson, who commissioned him to write his first commercial books: *Dressing Up: Transvestism and Drag: The History of an Obsession* (1979) and *Ezra Pound and his World* (1980).

In 1981 Ackroyd completed his first novel *The Great Fire of London*. Giles Gordon, who had recently become Ackroyd's literary agent, offered it to Christopher Sinclair-Stevenson, then managing director of the publishers Hamish Hamilton, who published it at the beginning of 1982. David Roberts of the Rainbird Publishing Group then commissioned Ackroyd to write a short life of T. S. Eliot for its series of illustrated biographies. As Ackroyd wrote a far longer study of the poet than Rainbird wanted, they passed the book on to Hamish Hamilton, then a sister company, who published it in 1984 as *T. S. Eliot*. Along with the Eliot biography, Ackroyd began to write a novel about Oscar Wilde. When he had finished *The Great Fire of London* Ackroyd had had no idea of what to write next and it was Giles Gordon who suggested the subject of Wilde. Before embarking on his research for the novel Ackroyd had never read a book by Wilde or even seen *The Importance of Being Ernest*. With typical energy, he immersed himself in Wilde's work and produced a fictional autobiography that was published by Hamish Hamilton in 1983 as *The Last Testament of Oscar Wilde*.

Ackroyd's *Spectator* writing was remembered long after he had embarked upon his career as a novelist and biographer. When Francis King reviewed *The Great Fire of London*, he remarked that it was brave of such a notoriously caustic critic to publish a work of fiction.

Even in 1990, in his review of *English Music*, D. J. Taylor recalled the 'slashing articles' Ackroyd had written in the 1970s. Owing to the demands on his time, Ackroyd left the staff of the *Spectator* in 1982 to become a full-time writer. Although he received a small advance for the biography of Eliot, he needed to support himself by writing as much freelance journalism as he could. Thus it was that, between 1982 and 1986, he wrote, in addition to his film criticism and the occasional book review for the *Spectator*, regular book reviews for the *Sunday Times*, and twice-weekly television reviews for *The Times*. Even by his own standards this was a particularly prolific period of his career. In some weeks, no less than five articles would appear under his name.

Ackroyd was commissioned to write book reviews for the *Sunday Times* on a regular basis by its literary editor Claire Tomalin. His reviews for the paper (a sample of which have been reproduced here) are neither as aggressive nor as idiosyncratic as his *Spectator* writings. He had less control over the kind of books he could review (there are, for example, far fewer pieces on poetry) and over the size of his articles, which tend to be shorter and of a uniform word length. He was also writing for a larger and a different kind of audience: while *Spectator* readers probably enjoyed his outspokenness, readers of the *Sunday Times* may have looked for other qualities in his reviews.

From around 1982, Ackroyd's approach to reviewing seems to have changed. He tended to write short discursive essays on the subject of the book under review rather than to engage in a lively dialogue with its author. He also used his reviews as an opportunity to air his opinions on literature and other cultural issues. In other words, he no longer wrote as a full-time critic of fiction and of the contemporary literary scene, but as an established author of prize-winning novels and biographies. (*The Last Testament of Oscar Wilde* won the Somerset Maugham Award in 1983. *T. S. Eliot* was awarded the Whitbread Prize for the best biography of 1984; it was also joint winner of the Royal Society of Literature's William Heinemann Award.)

Although Ackroyd rarely referred directly to his own books in his reviews, they offer us numerous insights into his intentions as a writer. It is interesting, for example, to read his comments on works of historical fiction such as Michael Moorcock's *The Laughter of Carthage* (see page 160). Ackroyd's remark that Moorcock had transcended the orthodox categories of 'realism' and 'fantasy' in the book throws light on his own aims. From this, and other comments, it is clear that he regards historical fiction as a way of bypassing and rising above the 'weary conventions' of realism and experimentalism he had described in his *Spectator* reviews. Equally revealing is his comment: 'the reason that [Moorcock] can see the past so clearly is because he sees the present equally clearly: when he is writing about the one he is at the same time writing about the other'. This echoes a number of statements Ackroyd has made about his own novels.

In 1982 Ackroyd's friend, the critic and novelist Bryan Appleyard, recommended him to John Higgins, then arts editor of *The Times*, as a television reviewer. From 1982 to 1986 Ackroyd wrote over two hundred television reviews for this newspaper. A few of the most characteristic pieces have been selected for this volume, such as his reviews of documentaries on different areas of London and his spirited criticism of a number of scientific programmes, together with some of his funniest and most personal reviews. His comments on Quentin Crisp and Kenneth Williams are very entertaining, and it is hard to imagine any other reviewer comparing members of the cast of *EastEnders* to stars from the Victorian music hall, or advising its script-writers to introduce more Cockney rhyming slang. These pieces display Ackroyd at his most witty and relaxed. Having watched a programme at the offices of *The Times*, he would dash off his article in the space of a few minutes.

In 1986 Ackroyd, who had just received both the Whitbread Prize and the Guardian Fiction Award for his novel *Hawksmoor* (1985), became chief book reviewer of *The Times*, a position he still holds at the present date. His predecessor, James Fenton, decided to leave the post in the spring of that year and Ackroyd was approached by the paper's then literary editor, Philip Howard. As chief book reviewer Ackroyd has written over 350 reviews of books about topics that range from sewage to Mrs Humphry Ward, often treating those subjects on which he himself has written such as Dickens, Oscar Wilde or the history of London. As Ackroyd has established himself as one of the most popular contemporary novelists dealing with historical subjects (*Hawksmoor* was followed by *Chatterton* (1987), which was short-listed for the Booker Prize, *English Music* (1992), *The House of Doctor Dee* (1993), *Dan Leno and the Limehouse Golem* (1994) and *Milton in America* (1996)) he has also been asked to review numerous historical novels.

With the publication of *Dickens* (1990), *Blake* (1995) and *The Life of Thomas More* (which was awarded the James Tait Black Memorial Prize in 1998), Ackroyd also became renowned as one of the most accomplished contemporary biographers. In consequence, he has been given many literary biographies to review, and his comments on works by biographers such as Michael Holroyd and Jenny Uglow throw considerable light on his own practice. His repeated argument that it is through style alone that the biographer can convince the reader of the veracity of their narrative is, for example, illuminating in this context. His suggestion that the structure and style of a biography should somehow embody its subject is also consistent with his own approach. In *T. S. Eliot* (1984) he frequently parodies his subject's prose and *Dickens* (1990) is written in imitation of a nineteenth-century novel.

Although Ackroyd's book reviews have become less abrasive with time, the style of his articles for *The Times* is almost as distinctive as the style of his writing for the *Spectator*. In a review of Borges' *The Total Library* he remarked that 'the essay is so personal . . . a form that, to trust its efficacy, you must trust the voice behind it. It is a matter of tone.' Ackroyd's own tone is impatient, authoritative and at times almost Johnsonian in its imperiousness. 'Good criticism,' he characteristically comments in a review of Edward Said's *Beginnings*, 'is not as good as good fiction or good history. That is all there is to be said.' He writes with fluency and gusto; he can also be very amusing. 'There are occasions,' he remarks of Harold Bloom, 'when he might be a sports reporter, rather than a literary critic'; and in his review of several books on Auden he muses: 'Those were the days when it was a pleasure, rather than a painful duty, to be homosexual.'

Ackroyd's style can also be intimate and personal but it would perhaps be wrong to read his journalism as strictly autobiographical. Ackroyd himself frequently criticizes journalists who make 'the cardinal mistake of using the first person singular' and who publish extracts from their diaries instead of book reviews. In his biography of Eliot he commented that the poet's critical works are 'dramatic monologues no less rigorously "worked up" than his poetry', and there is certainly a sense in which Ackroyd, in his own reviews, is playing the part of the authoritative critic. It is also interesting to note the way in which Ackroyd's style changes according to the author he is discussing. His articles on Wilde are witty and epigramatic; when writing about Auden or Truman Capote he cannot resist the temptation of 'camping it up'. Ackroyd's gifts as a mimic are therefore on display in his journalism as well as in his novels and biographies.

The first lecture reproduced in this volume, 'The English Novel Now', is the transcript of a radio talk given in 1981; all of the other lectures were written and delivered between 1993 and 1999.

'The Englishness of English Literature' was the Leslie Stephen Lecture for 1993, given by Ackroyd at Cambridge University on 22 October of that year. In it he adumbrated a specifically English tradition of writing whose representative authors focus on the external aspects of the world and delight in the scenic and the theatrical. In many of his reviews Ackroyd alludes to this tradition: in one, for example, he argues that nonsense literature is an essential part of 'the English Genius. It is related to that heterogeneity within a literature where matters oratorical, poetical and farcical can all be fastened together.' It is of course a tradition to which Ackroyd's own work belongs and in this sense the lecture could be read as an exercise in self-definition.

In this lecture Ackroyd developed the ideas he first explored in his novel *English Music* (1990), itself described by reviewers as an 'essay on Englishness'. It could also be viewed as Ackroyd's response to the hostile criticism levelled at that novel by certain reviewers, who complained of what they regarded as the novel's 'nationalistic' and 'reactionary' flavour. In his lecture, Ackroyd was at pains to demonstrate that his idea of a national tradition is neither elitist nor some literary equivalent of little-Englandism. Many of the arguments contained in this lecture inform Ackroyd's forthcoming non-fictional work 'The Origins of the English Imagination' (to be published in 2002).

In his lecture Ackroyd associated this English tradition with a Catholic culture that has been forced underground since the Reformation and with a sensibility that is particular to London. Ackroyd explored the London origins of this tradition and sensibility at greater length in his LWT London Lecture for 1993, 'London Luminaries and Cockney Visionaries', which was given on 7 December at the Victoria and Albert Museum and televised on 19 December. By 1993, Ackroyd was popularly regarded as a 'London novelist' and as something of a 'Cockney Visionary' himself. With the exception of *First Light* (1989) and *Milton in America* (1996) all of his fictional works have been set in London. It is, as Ackroyd puts it, the 'landscape of his imagination'; it might also be described as the informing presence of his novels as their plots seem to emerge spontaneously out of the streets of the city. Ackroyd's imaginative history *London: The*

Biography was published in 2000; the city also provides the background to his earlier biographies. In these, each of Ackroyd's subjects is described as having been created by London; in turn, he suggests that they recreated the city in their works. Thus Blake's vision of the world was shaped by the sounds and sights of the city and in his works he reinvented it as 'Infinite London'.

Blake was the subject of Ackroyd's next lecture, which was delivered as the 'TLS Talk' in the winter of 1995 at the Tate Gallery, and in February 1996 at Gresham College. 'William Blake, a Spiritual Radical' explored Blake's radicalism in the context of late eighteenth-century London and hailed him as the great prophet of the new millennium. For Ackroyd, Blake was a man who attempted to find an 'alternative source of power' to conventional science and who tried to invent a language and a mythology with which to describe the spiritual forces at work within the fabric of material reality. Certain critics have described Ackroyd's own endeavour as a writer in exactly these terms.

In 'All the Time in the World' (Writers and the Nature of Time), a lecture written for the Chicago Literary Festival in 1999, Ackroyd discussed his own writing more directly and at greater length than he had done on any previous occasion. In it he not only commented upon *The Plato Papers*: *A Novel* (1999), the fictional work that he had just published, but also upon his earlier writings. It represents the clearest statement of his aims as a writer and contains some of his most illuminating comments on his novels and biographies.

Although those who attended these lectures may recall the occasional joke or aside that is not contained in the texts reproduced here, and although several repetitions have been removed, they are accurate transcriptions of what Ackroyd said on each occasion. They have not been rewritten for publication; as a result, they are necessarily less elaborate than the other writing contained in this anthology. Their style is direct and their tone intimate: reading them it is easy to hear the voice in which they were delivered and to imagine Ackroyd's performance on each occasion. That Ackroyd regarded his lectures as performances was apparent to his audiences. During 'The Englishness of English Literature' he played the part of the provocative and aggressive orator; his Blake lecture was delivered with all the fervour and grandiloquence of an Old Testament prophet.

'London Luminaries and Cockney Visionaries' has never been published in its entirety (except as a limited edition pamphlet); 'The Englishness of English Literature' has only ever been printed in an academic journal. 'William Blake, a Spiritual Radical' and 'All the Time in the World' (Writers and The Nature of Time) have not been previously reproduced.

The last section of the book, 'Miscellaneous Writings', comprises pieces dating from every period of Ackroyd's career. A number of pieces in which Ackroyd comments on the subjects and the writing of his novels and biographies, are included. None of these revealing articles has been reproduced since their original publication. Most of them have been taken from *The Times*; others are prefaces to special editions of Ackroyd's works.

I have also selected the 'Manifesto for London' that Ackroyd wrote during the run up to the recent mayoral election, and his introduction to one of Frank Auerbach's catalogues. Ackroyd has written a number of articles on art over the last decade, his art criticism including essays on London painting and the work of artists such as Stephen Harwood and William Blake, as well as reviews of several exhibitions. His article on Auerbach has been chosen for this anthology as it is his most characteristic piece. Also included here are a number of reviews that Ackroyd has written for American publications such as the *New York Times* and the *New Yorker*.

Finally, I have reproduced three of Ackroyd's four published short stories. 'The Inheritance', published in the *Spectator* in 1979, is Ackroyd's first work of fiction. In it he rehearsed some of the techniques that he would employ in his novels. Part of the narrative is set in Borough in south London, an area to which Ackroyd returns in his first novel *The Great Fire of London*. Similarly, 'The Plantation House', which dramatizes the way in which the past may influence the present, reads like an Ackroyd novel in epitome. Ackroyd wrote these short stories for his own pleasure some time before they were published. None of them was commissioned.

In conclusion, Ackroyd's own attitude to his journalism and his miscellaneous writings can be mentioned. Ackroyd is often disparaging of journalists and journalism; in one review he quotes with obvious approval Cyril Connolly's statement that in the world of newspaper reviewing 'nothing is secure or certain except the certainty of [the reviewer] turning into a hack'. He can also be deprecatory when commenting on his own journalism. In his valedictory film piece for the *Spectator*, for example, he remarked that he always left journalism for Sunday because it is a 'day of rest'. To use a cliché often employed in this context, Ackroyd sometimes regards his journalism as something he does with his left hand.

Yet, while Ackroyd clearly considers his journalism and his miscellaneous writing as less important than his other work, it is, I believe, valuable both in itself and as a supplement to his novels and biographies. At a time when many book reviewers use their personal emotions as a test for what is and what is not good literature, and in which much academic writing is as unreadable as it is unread by the general public, it is refreshing to read well-written criticism that is informed both by a coherent theoretical standpoint and a broad literary culture. Ackroyd's critical writings are always entertaining and stimulating and his sensitivity to literary excellence is rare.

It is also interesting to read the pieces included in this anthology in relation to Ackroyd's novels, biographies and other works. Ideas, analogies and even entire phrases can sometimes migrate between the separate parts of his oeuvre. A curious example of this is to be found in his enthusiastic review of Simon Callow's biography of Charles Laughton, which was published in *The Times* in 1987. Towards the end of this article, he quotes Dickens' phrase: 'the more real the man, the more genuine the actor'. Uncannily, it was this very phrase that became the opening line of the one-man drama, *The Mystery of Charles Dickens*, which Ackroyd wrote thirteen years later in 2000. The play was performed by Simon Callow.

I
Writings for the *Spectator*
1973–1987

Book Reviews

Wyndham Lewis: Fictions and Satires
R. T. Chapman

Unlucky for Pringle
Wyndham Lewis

Wyndham Lewis is, as they say, an enigma. He has been generally considered to be an exponent of modernism, but his own writing is strongly traditional. He might be either philosopher or artist, or both. And he has that quite un-English virtue of quantity without the sacrifice of quality. When faced with mysteries such as these, the critic will invariably turn to the more obvious productions of the writer which, in the case of Lewis, happen to be his opinions. He has been called a propagandist and a polemicist, and has as a consequence been relegated beneath the 'big three': Joyce, Pound and Eliot. He has been seen as a literary mosquito or, worse, as an entrepreneur. Certainly Lewis had that distaste for human beings and that capacity for intrigue which is common to certain literary types, but his role is a much larger one than is commonly assumed. His polemics, against Bloomsbury for example, were pronounced from a thorough if militant understanding of British culture. Lewis saw himself as a keeper of the faith, and there is a spirit and range of inquiry within his writing that has been seriously undervalued. These two books emphasize that range.

Lewis's life, like his writing, was perverse and disordered. In his early career, he was poor and he was an artist, and consequently liked to make friends. He moved from group to group, and from opinion to opinion, until he was enough master of the situation to found his own movement. These were the days of Vorticism, and of self-confessed publicity. For Vorticism was one of the most formative events of his life, and its magazine *Blast* has had few rivals in spleen and effectiveness. No writer, however, can survive for long within a group and Vorticism suffered from a surfeit of talent and nerves. But it was unique with the presence of people like Gaudier-Brzeska and Pound, and with its recognition of contemporary European culture as something other than impressionism and the motor car.

But this flair for seeing what was vital, in cubism and in German expressionism, has been misunderstood; Vorticism has been labelled as 'avant-garde' and 'modernist' and quickly forgotten. It suggests Europe and revolution and ugly murals upon buildings. But the central fact of Vorticism, and one that connects with the whole tenor of Lewis's work, is that it represents an informed and spirited return to what Lewis saw as the native tradition of English culture. Lewis was actually against modernism in its conventional form: 'We are against Europeanism, that abasement of the miserable intellectual before anything coming from Paris.' And this tone is refreshing, especially in our time when 'structuralism' is fast becoming the new orthodoxy within the universities of England.

Lewis saw his art and his writing as a return to the centre of the English tradition. Whether this tradition is real or not is not the point; it became the value from which Lewis could direct his satire and polemic. It represented a standard against which the prevailing forces of constraint and academicism could be placed. He put his finger on the disease within English culture, and constructed a cure. It was a major effort and one that found him few friends. Although it was ultimately unsuccessful, it changed the face of English culture. And in these times, when an American provincialism and cult academicism are our sole resources, the nerve and spirit of Lewis deserve to be honoured.

But Lewis is by no means an entirely satisfactory writer. There is something too heated and assertive about his writing, and it often suffers from an excess of point. He knows what he is saying, but not whom he is saying it to. There are certain writers who can connect the movement of their literature with philosophical or political statement, but the balance in Lewis's work is unsteady. It is like that of a bright young man who will sometimes moralize without having a morality.

Something of this emerges from Robert Chapman's critical study. The book traces very carefully the progress of Lewis towards more and more dogmatic and sententious statement, and towards the idea of himself as Swift or Juvenal lashing the follies of the age. Chapman shows that this entails a loss of subtlety in Lewis's later work, a retreat into a kind of hardness and fantasy that are incongruous with the poetic vigour and detail of his earlier writing.

But Chapman generally refrains from making critical judgements about the quality and development of Lewis's writing – it is not quite the thing nowadays to judge – and traces instead the 'ideas' or symbols which occur in it. The book is both critical history and commentary, and it covers that fashionable notion of 'dialectic' which Chapman discovers in Lewis's work, a dialectic between mind and body, between ideas and human existence. There is nothing particularly surprising about this – the divorce between idea and reality is clearly the foundation of any satiric work – but the themes of Lewis are discussed by Chapman with tact and expertise. The case for Wyndham Lewis as a satirist could not be better made, although I suspect that there is more to be said.

Chapman also conveys well the atmosphere of those times, which now seem so distant. It is extraordinary, at this late date, to read of the excitement and interest which artistic manifestos and exhibitions aroused. Even the daily press – even, I might add, the *Daily Express* – took an intelligent if slightly haughty interest in the ideas of 'the artist' and the welfare of his art. There was a kind of cultural health in London, a sense of intrigue and novelty that has now been dissipated in our more populist time. But if Chapman evokes the spirit of London, he also brings home the courage of the middle-aged Lewis in standing apart from it, and the denigration which he had to endure because of his stand. After his attachment to Vorticism, Lewis seemed to step apart from the literary and cultural world. His refusal to entertain a fashionable socialism in the thirties made him a target for liberals and intellectuals alike. He became a solitary man, for hell has no spite like a liberal intellectual scorned. He was detested for his principles, and the cultural establishment never forgave him. The satire came from a real wound.

I suggest there may be more to Lewis than this paranoid, satirical persona. And it is this further element which emerges in the collection of Lewis's published and unpublished short stories, *Unlucky for Pringle*. They range from 1914 to the 1950s, and they present a miniature history of Lewis's art. The short story form is a difficult one to master, especially for a propagandist and satirist. But this is its advantage for seeing Lewis entire. For it evokes the more imaginative areas of his writing, and excises that moralizing and tendentiousness of which he is capable. Although Lewis did not see life whole, he saw it clearly and steadily; *Unlucky for Pringle* is a surprisingly fine book.

Lewis had an eye for the dotty and the deranged from the beginning of his writing, and it is simply his analysis of their moral condition which changes. The progress of his writing never did run smooth, and his position as both moralist and imaginative writer becomes more and more difficult to sustain. In the stories of the 1950s which are reprinted in this volume, the prose has become a heavier thing. Lewis comes to dwell more and more upon mental and moral deformity, on what is unlucky or odd. The humour vanishes. In 'Doppelgänger', the story of the cuckolding of an ageing poet, the descriptions of mood and conversation are still sharp but the action and narrative are tendentious and simplistic. Lewis's imagination has become vulgar, as if a bright young man has been undeceived by 'life' and yet has nowhere else to go. In the later work of Lewis, it is the moral which is the thing. And this 'lonely old volcano', who once had so much to say in a divided culture, was left to cultivate his own opinions.

9 June 1973

2

English Literature and Irish Politics
Matthew Arnold

It is odd that Matthew Arnold may be the last great English critic. The stock image of the man is something like the eminent Victorian, the Inspector of Schools, that melancholy and forbidding figure who might have sat for Lear's Dong with the Luminous Nose. And it might have seemed odd to his contemporaries. At university, he was notorious for his fastidious dress and his wit. He was always laughing. Later, of course, he was to gain notoriety through his melancholy and haunting verses. But there is nothing that seems to fit the image of the great critic, none of the personal magnetism of Johnson or the representative quality of Boileau. He was and is something of an outsider, and it is just one more paradox that it is an American publisher who is providing us with the scholarly and definitive edition of his prose.

This present volume is the ninth, and the extraordinary length of the complete series is bringing home the range and variety of Arnold's writing. There are essays in this volume on poetry, on the laws of copyright, on schools and on Ireland. But to say that they are various is not to say that they are also eclectic. There is a sustained manner and tone throughout the essays which identifies them and lends them substance. I have just read, for example, essays on Wordsworth, Keats and Byron: poets who were close to Arnold, and whom he might have been expected to treat in a partisan spirit. But they are final and consummate appreciations. There is a tact and a responsiveness within them that actually improves upon the essays of Samuel Johnson. Arnold's criticism has such an instinctive force that it is as if he were essentially writing of himself. But it evades mere self-absorption by that central instinct he had for what was and was not valuable. These essays are undeterred by literary fashion; Arnold saw things whole, and in a clear light.

It is this steady attention to principle which marks Arnold's strength as a critic. There is a constant moral (but not moralistic) attitude – poetry as 'a criticism of life' – which saves him from being simply a contemporary force. There is nothing garish or pedantic about his writing. It is just and it is public. It manifests a kind of cultural health.

It is this cultural health which is the context of Arnold's variety of concerns, and the title of this volume – *English Literature and Irish Politics* – is a clue to the range of his writing. It also suggests their connection. For him, literature, education and politics were of a piece. They were susceptible to thoughts and to judgement on the same grounds. It was always his aim to see the object clearly, an attitude struck in the essays here on the future of liberalism and the state of Ireland: 'To look things full in the face and let them stand for what they really are . . .', and Arnold's thought is neither reactionary, nor revolutionary. It is conservative in the sense that it appeals to principles, and liberal in the sense that it is not blinded by them. His was the 'disinterested play of the mind'. Not our fashionable and humanitarian liberalism, but one committed only to lucid argument and to 'civilization'. But it is at this point that we become dissatisfied.

His comments on the Irish question, for example, are eminently sane and just but, like all of his contributions to political debate, they were ignored. His play of the mind seems peripheral, and perhaps suspect. It is possible that he realized this himself, and certainly he was aware of the limitations of his writing. His endemic melancholy may be in part a realization that his 'principles' were imaginary and ineffective. There is a certain emptiness, for example, in his continual looking back at a classical past and at an imagined European spirit. Life and politics continued its dirty and irrational way, and Arnold remained the stranger, the scholar gypsy. These volumes from America demonstrate that the writing is a whole, but that Arnold was not a whole man. We should thank the Michigan press for their scholarship, and for their bringing Arnold into the light he so respected.

23 June 1973

3

Forewords and Afterwords

W. H. Auden

For the poet, the discipline of prose writing is necessary but subsidiary. It demands too much assertion, it confesses too much. It is difficult, then, to be both poet and critic but actually far more difficult to be both poet and reviewer. The critic – like T. S. Eliot – will be forming a description of his poetry in the criticism he writes. But the occasional reviewer is prohibited from any grand design; he writes to a stated length and to a deadline. He writes, honourably enough, to earn a living.

Mr Auden's *Forewords and Afterwords* is a collection of just such reviews. It ranges over his favourite interests of poetry and opera, religion and sex. We have grown accustomed to this, but the speed with which this collection was assembled underlines the familiar obseisance with which his work is treated. But before we accept the work, we should see it for what it is. There are obvious comparisons. Where Eliot pares down his critical range in order to create the vocabulary of a new tradition, Auden is personal and eclectic. Where Wallace Stevens attends continually to the precepts of his chosen art, Auden's references to poetry are random and occasional. It is a criticism that is at once strongly individual, and yet with a total effect that can be disconcertingly impersonal and bland.

Despite the general opinion, it is an advantage to know a great deal before setting about the task of reviewing. This is not a question of fact and detail, but rather an instinctive rightness of emphasis – the ability to set the context for a particular work without making that context too obtrusive. Auden has this gift of unobtrusiveness but his perspective is one of personal temperament rather than of cultural history. There is a weakness here, of course. For in areas which have some connection with his life and needs, Auden writes with an unerring directness. But in intellectual and doctrinal matters, he sometimes comes unstuck.

In the essays upon classical culture and upon existentialism, for example, Auden tends to summarize an argument without comment; he gives a potted cultural history which is neutral and occasionally tedious. And he gives the disconcerting impression of possessing only information which comes from the book under review. This is a perfectly proper means of reviewing (and one more difficult than people imagine) but in Auden's work I expected something more, a personal colour and an original argument. It is not unjust here to refer to certain of Auden's poems: there is that same facility for presenting an argument rhetorically without any personal involvement in its content or its implications.

But, also with the poetry as with the prose, the hallmark of Auden's manner is a certain down-to-earth tone, an ability to see the human truth of situations and the refusal to be fooled. In the best of these reviews there is this tone. I can think offhand only of a trivial but illuminating example – when Auden describes the tortured antics of a Russian aesthete, he comments, 'No Englishman could possibly do such a thing.' It is a voice, at once accurate and ironic, that cannot be easily described; it is, as Auden says of that of another poet, one that can only be imitated or quoted.

For it is the voice of a particular civilization that connects these reviews. It is a voice that celebrates the instinctive and permanent forces of human community and the necessity to be decent and a good sport. It can, of course, become uncomfortably bland, but it has great force when it evokes themes which interest Auden deeply. I am thinking here, for example, of the essays about Tennyson and Dag Hammarskjöld. It is a voice that seems strongest in one of the finest essays of the book, 'As It Seemed to Us'. And it is not coincidental that this last is also the most autobiographical of the collection, for this is the root of Auden's achievement as a prose writer. In those essays that are purely formal and argumentative, there is an absence of point that manifests itself in the abstractness and imprecision of the writing.

I only labour this point to underline that Auden is a great reviewer despite himself. Or, rather, despite his professed opinions. For the constant theme of these reviews is that the life of the writer is coincidental and irrelevant. The corresponding interest is, naturally, in the technique of writing rather than in self-expression or the bugbear of 'experience'. But it becomes obvious from a reading of this book that the best writing of Auden emerges in those reviews which have a personal and instinctive origin. It is in this sense that Auden remains a reviewer rather than a critic. He does not have the theoretical exactness of a great critic, but he has that flair and virtuosity which are the hallmark of a fine journalist.

7 July 1973

4

Gravity's Rainbow
Thomas Pynchon

Americans are not known for their reticence, and American critics will not murmur when a roar will do. So it is that *Gravity's Rainbow*, apocalyptic enough as it sounds, should be recommended by the man from the *New York Times* as one of the five books to take to the moon (there, of course, its seven hundred pages of fine print might conceivably float free) and by the man from *Saturday Review* as an advance 'beyond' *Moby Dick* and *Ulysses*. Why any reasonably intelligent critic would think that there is a point 'beyond' the two, and that even if there was it was necessary to reach it, is 'beyond' me. But there it is, on the cover of this gargantuan obelisk of a book. Of course, the American critics have always had a penchant for the Great American Novel, one which would somehow fabricate both a history and a culture in one volume, and their eccentric ravings can be dismissed as the foibles of latter-day Romans looking for a Greece. But it amazes me that a reputable English publisher can reprint their gush, and add some of his own to boot. According to the blurb, Pynchon has been greeted as 'more bizarre, complex, obscene, difficult and stunning than anything since James Joyce'. Hail fellow, well met kind of prose, and of course I am pleased to note that it is now considered an advantage to be both difficult and obscene – not to say complex and, I would add, an excruciating bore.

I have sat and slept through this novel for five days, and words would fail me if logorrhoea were not so catching. As it is, I am compelled to clutch at straws and cannot do better than to employ the fiercely inventive and prodigiously intricate language of the blurb itself. I hope you'll pardon this lack of editorial control, but exhaustion makes strange bedfellows. *Bizarre*, yes, *Gravity's Rainbow* has its twists and turns. It is ostensibly a picaresque version of the last days of the Second World War; rash as it is to attempt a precis, there is a small interior landscape which has all the characteristics of a mirage among deathless wastes. Those mythical beasts, American servicemen, figure roundly in the narrative: not least among them Slothrop, Tantivy, Teddy Bloat and Pirate. There is Kevin Spectro, the homicidal quack who calls all his patients 'Fox' and dreams of violating young girls, and there is Roger Mexico, a young statistician who dreams of nothing more vulgar than predicting the laws of rocket-strikes. Unfortunately, the above-mentioned Slothrop has a certain, scatalogical gift of prophecy and can intuit the destruction before it actually arrives. This has made him the object of suspicion and research, under the trained eye of one Pointsman – a Pavlovian of excruciating proportions who is a member of the Abreaction Research Facility (ARF, get it?). These creatures of fancy are all ensconced within the 'White Visitation', a propaganda station beamed at Europe and beyond.

But the world is Mr Pynchon's oyster, and his private war radiates through time and space with as much subtlety as a stain. Occupied Holland, where Hansel and Gretel never had it so good, and pre-war Germany, the factotum of seances and poverty are relentlessly exposed; similarly, the African tribe of the Zone-Hereros and the Kirghiz peasants of Central Asia are given the old historical one-two and are drawn into a cultural design as breathtaking as it is irrelevant. For the central portions of the narrative seem (and in a narrative of such staggering insouciance, 'seem' is to be believed) to be devoted to the wanderings of Slothrop. His psychic gifts render him the conventional outcast, and his later days are spent in the solitary track of the Rocket. I have to admit defeat at this point, and confess that I had no idea who or what the Rocket was. It may have been of such heavy symbolic intent that it went completely under my head, and I had to be content with the incidental detail of Slothrop's trips. He is lost and found in Zurich and Argentina, pursued by agents and triple-agents in a bewildering variety of guises. The Rocket is eventually fired, but not before the future has become a mechanical nightmare of considerable proportions. Yes, I would say it was bizarre.

Complex, that is, full of unnecessary and self-conscious involutions and neologisms. At first I entered what I thought to be the atmosphere of the novel, a subterranean world full of shuttered rooms, but I came to realize that this was the effect of the style itself. It is a crammed and choking prose, replete with images and allusions that slide out of one consciousness and into the next. It is, of course, a very deliberate rhetoric which is supposed to replace the conventional pieties of realistic narrative but it succeeds only in murdering them. It is the definitive Orwellian newspeak, and one which relies heavily upon James Joyce's – what Pynchon would no doubt call – kollidoscrape. See, I can do it too. Experiment is the easiest kind of writing.

But Pynchon is not, in fact, in an easy relation to his material and there is a continuing, perplexing amalgam of what purists call language and reality. Joyce created a style, and Pynchon merely borrows stylistics. His prose does, occasionally, take off in a lyric song and this is when he is at his best. Passages of natural description and urban blues are the finest in the book, and I was left regretting that Pynchon was not simply an old-fashioned 'beat' writer who could fashion a private rhetoric out of the surface of language. Instead, he invades his narrative with an irony which is anxious as much as it is dead-pan, and leaves it in the throes of self-doubt.

Obscene, yes, there are passages of remarkable and highly wrought obscenity within the narrative. And it doesn't surprise me one bit that during these moments of climax – of a myriad form, incidentally – Pynchon should let fall his experimental prose and return to occasionally plain Anglo-Saxon syllables. It suggests to me that the message may be more important than the medium and, if this were the case, why has he draped a perfectly good adventure within opaque and distant folds? The obscenity is, for all you censorious majority, pure obscenity and has no redeeming features of art or significance. This is not altogether a surprise in the context of *Gravity's Rainbow*, but it does suggest the central problem of the narrative. It is discontinuous and indirect, and we are prevented from observing anything other than the odd dash of local colour.

Difficult, possibly, but do you remember that statisticians' dream: the chimpanzee which, if put in front of a typewriter, would eventually produce the works of Shakespeare verbatim. This has always struck me as an unlikely story, but even more so in these late days when a critic would prefer to praise the chimp's first efforts as 'difficult' and forget about the rest. This is not, in fact, a terribly 'difficult' book. It has its ups and downs, but nowhere reaches the level of experimentation of a Joyce or Sarraute. It remains gloomily and sullenly ensconced within the realistic tradition, making an occasional foray into the wastes of surrealism and neologism but always returning to that bankrupt heritage which it carries as a dwarf would carry a blind giant.

Stunning, rarely, but it would be unfortunate to leave this novel on a note of unrelieved criticism. Thomas Pynchon has obviously taken great pains over the book, and presumably a great deal of his time. I salute his craftsmanship and dedication, and I only suggest that he fashion it to more immediate and less apocalyptic ends. I had the uncomfortable feeling that there was a grand symbolic design which I was continually missing, and if this is the case I blame Mr Pynchon. He has written a novel which would deter and baffle any but the most avid research student pursuing a thesis. *Gravity's Rainbow* becomes a specimen of Eng. Lit. as soon as it comes off the presses, and this is the heart of my suspicion of it. When the novel becomes the Great Novel without a tincture of self-doubt then the climate of writing becomes very unhealthy indeed. I might put the same point differently by noting that Pynchon offers us the rhetoric and the appearance of grandslam, ring-a-ding real thing but does not provide the substance. It is as if his entertainment were more *theatrical* than anything else, and that what is on stage is the Life and Tragical Death of the Serious Work. Unfortunately, the wake has turned out to be a little too long.

17 November 1973

5

Chimera

John Barth

There is nothing particularly ignoble in a novelist being self-conscious about his craft, but when he imposes these trifling concerns upon the poor reader it becomes a matter of public concern. Mr Barth, a Professor of English and winner of the National Book Award, has chosen to do just that in *Chimera*, a tripartite beast, a novel within a novel within something else on the Chinese principle that a great many boxes are better than a hat. It begins well enough, with a sort of highbrow camp as Barth narrates the narrations of Dunyazade narrating the narrations of Scheherazade (known as Sherry to her handmaidens) to Shahryar. But after that I got them all mixed up, mere pips, as Omar Khayyam might say, squeaking in the bowl of night. These particular Orientals come, in fact, from some pot-pourri known as *The Thousand and One Nights* which Mr Barth thinks of some cross-cultural importance and of which he proceeds to make very heavy weather indeed.

It seems that, behind the seven veils, Sherry is looking for a key. Being something of an Ur-structuralist, she comes to realize that looking for the key is in fact the key itself. Mr Barth then appears in the most inappropriate form of genie, and proceeds to tell her the whole tedious story of *The Thousand and One Nights* which he has already read in a later existence. It is all an intolerable mish-mash, and should have remained in the misty land of faery, were it not for people like Mr Barth who have an intolerable urge for systems and meanings. The more unintelligent reviewers will no doubt be taken in by the novel's fanciful contemporaneity, and will talk about its 'stark presentment of the boundaries of fiction', 'medieval simplicity' and such like, and this may well be Barth's intention: there is no doubt that perspectives appear and disappear as if by magic, and that the prose has its glancings and twinklings as it continually evades the issue (whatever the issue may be). But Barth is trying to spin gold out of the pointless questions which pursue formalists and aestheticians, and he does not realize that the pointlessness becomes all the plainer in a fictional guise.

The offence is compounded by Barth's incursions into classical mythology, in the second and third sections of the novel, which are entitled 'Perseid' and 'Bellerophoniad'. When an American writer touches upon such matters I feel a *frisson* on behalf of centuries of classical scholarship; Americans, being a poorly educated race, take the Greek myths far too seriously and become either pompous or heavily jocular about them. Professor Barth has naturally gone for the jocular 'angle', and has recounted the unutterably boring mythic lives of Perseus and Bellerophon in a suburban demotic that relives the boredom of the original while increasing its capacity to irritate. In the beginning there is darkness, as Perseus recounts his chequered career to Calyx, who knows the stories already and is thus in the same unfortunate position as the reader. The assiduous handmaiden has actually completed a series of wall-paintings on that very subject, and is clearly reluctant to have her work spoiled by the real thing. This framing device is a pretty conceit (Barth is continually wreaking fantasy upon his fantastics) but it does not save the narrative itself from an intolerable slackness, which became all the more evident when I ceased to wonder who was addressing whom.

The matter is not settled in 'Bellerophoniad', when Barth becomes even more self-conscious than the conventional experimental novelist and turns his fables into an elaborate apologia for his own apparently miserable and wasted life. At one point he elevates the novelist (i.e. Barth) into a vatic role, and at the next he belabours himself with a dutiful and tedious modesty. Once you mix this sort of thing with a Bellerophon of a more than baroque complexity – he is preparing a career based upon a reading of the preceding 'Perseid', setting out a plan for the story he is in fact already telling etcetera – you have a narrative that will not stay still under the reader's gaze. But this complexity is so much a matter of the technical surface of the prose that it takes only a conscious effort of the mind to see through it and, underneath, to find lurking that most fabulous and archaic of mythical beasts, the labyrinth that goes in all directions at once and leads nowhere at all.

20 July 1974

6

Napoleon Symphony

Anthony Burgess

Yes, Mr Burgess is fluent and fanciful and inventive; he is even occasionally fertile. He tells us so himself, in a 'verse epistle' to the reader. And the problem with this book is the temptation to put everything in inverted commas. Its title bears some allusion to the *Eroica* (so the publishers are kind enough to tell me), although the Elizabethan analogy between language and music seems a singularly pointless one at this late date. Certainly the writing has an artificial pace reminiscent of some of the more *troppo* passages of *opéra bouffe*, but Mr Burgess's diction has a generally squelchy quality which one does not associate with anything in particular: 'He hovered voluptu- ously on the promise of a sneeze but, a strong man, would not yield.' I like that 'hovered', even though it is supposed to be comic.

The secret life of a hero is one of those incurably romantic themes which will remain novelettish despite all attempts to enliven it. And Burgess certainly tries. There is, however, a rule in fiction that there are only a finite number of plots but an infinite number of novelists, and Mr Burgess contrives a rhetorical garishness by shifting the surfaces of his writing around like toy bricks: there are many different voices, letters, dead-pan narrative and a number of poetic intervals (although Mr Burgess is by no means a poet).

The novel opens with Napoleon winning battles for the Directory while his wife, between bouts of Bonaparte, is pining for a guardsman. Any novelist's pen would go out to her. We are then treated to Napoleon's Egyptian campaign, with some conventional moments of disease and/or terror. Eventually Napoleon is crowned Emperor, although Burgess never seems quite sure how he made it, and becomes 'N', that formal yet abstract force which heaved its way out of Russia. 'Let the picture,' as Burgess says in one of his less self-conscious moments, 'be painted in tears.' And Napoleon ends in exile, with doctors squabbling over his corpse.

It is not a particularly pretty story, but in *Napoleon Symphony* the hero is the quintessentially romantic figure whose tears can kill little children in the street, and the one who goes amongst his people in disguise. He is the hero who strives for the vainglory of nations before the growing power of the *Volk*: 'I had not yet got down to calling it anything,' Talleyrand smiled, 'but since you press me, I will launch the term *master race*.' There are a great many of these nudges and winks to posterity and a strain of what one might call *contretemps* runs through the novel: 'This is the nineteenth century, not the eighteenth', and so on.

This is, in fact, a conventionally imagined book which makes use of the iron disunities of our time and which whips up its language to a frenzy for no particular reason. Mr Burgess employs a variety of styles in an excessively self-conscious way, with the result that any dialogue between recognizable human beings seems a trifle cracked. There are some allusions to *The Dynasts* and some odd quotations from Gerard Manley Hopkins, and the literariness of the whole narrative is merely confirmed by a pastiche of *Ulysses* (Burgess seems to have some proprietorial claim to Joyce, although it is difficult to see any similarity) which sets all of the preceding narrative at an aesthetic distance. You could no doubt call the novel a 'sport', Mr Burgess being fanciful and inventive and outrageous, but it is only what the closing epistolary verse would call an 'orthodox success'. We are not particularly amused.

28 September 1974

7

Some Little English Versifiers

Love or Nothing
Douglas Dunn

Printed Circuit
Andrew Crozier

Wound Response
J. H. Prynne

Since there is not one good poem in this *Poetry Supplement*, and since it has been distributed for Christmas in the same spirit as other people give scarves or bottles of gin, it might be charitable to ignore it altogether and to discuss the poets of Zambia or of the Windward Islands. But there are no less than six poetry reviewers and two poetry editors in this collection (if they had not between them devalued poetry beyond the point of endurance, they would make up the 'establishment') and, as a case history, the pamphlet is worth brief comment.

Mr Larkin, in his role as taxidermist, has brought together some specimens of language from which all invention has gone; the poems deal 'wryly' with certain rural or domestic interiors, and within this small space they specialize in that nerveless monotone which passes nowadays as the English 'tone':

> She was a small dog, neat and fluid.
> Even her conversation was tiny:
> She greeted you with *bow* never *bow-wow*

No, this is not a poem by Norman MacCaig in praise of one of his contemporaries. He has entitled it, in that 'wry' British way, 'Praise of a Collie' and, like some of the other Aesopian gems in this collection, it would show to best effect upon a chocolate-box. We could even create a chocolate montage from some of the livelier moments in the book:

Arnold was John the Baptist, coming late
Before he came, the country and the town
From harvest time to ailing in November
Made scientific sense not destiny
It is unbearable – well, almost so.

You will notice the common movement of line in these five separate poems, and the fact that their regular rise and fall cannot disguise the flatness of the language. There is a toneless objectivity in the verse which can salvage only the husks of meaning; it is dead poetry because it is predictable poetry, with a conventional language unerringly creating conventional themes. The only way of making this kind of verse readable is to press it into external shapes, and there is a marked preponderance of tiny forms throughout the volume. But they are all smooth and alike; their language has become that worn coin which is passed from hand to hand. How are the poets in Zambia doing nowadays?

Of course the confluence of poetry reviewers in the anthology may help us to appreciate the recent acclamation of Douglas Dunn as a great poet and the new bright hope of English verse. In *Love or Nothing* Mr Dunn certainly satisfies the conventional notions of what is 'poetic' and what is not. He concerns himself with certain private and domestic themes ('wryly', of course) and he uses external forms to mark the boundaries of what can reasonably be said in a poetical manner. The effect is that of a thin and single voice which is conscientious without being adequately self-conscious. Given the fact that the inherited poetic language has become somewhat strained at this late date, Mr Dunn's tone is necessarily over-emphatic; he uses a great many adjectives where none would do, for all the world as if he were trying to write prose:

sleep walking in plastic darkness

and

Wrecks of many seas
Here by the silent shipyards.

He is forced back upon a flat and denotative language, of points rather than themes, of 'content' rather than expression, and it is one which

can be rescued from prosiness only with the aid of external and
rhetorical gestures:

> The white moon opens over a ridge of bracken
> Spilling its prodigal rays into the eyes

Now where have I read that before? Where the line is not controlled by
an obvious movement of this kind it becomes flaccid and tedious:

> Old cities and shipyards,
> Belfast, Glasgow, fervent closures
> Of protestantism dispensed with –

and so on. At the centre of this poetry, and that of Mr Larkin's
anthology, is a language that has become so fatally weakened that it
can only reflect certain domestic truths and social aphorisms. It has lost
its inheritance, it has abandoned all pretence to inventiveness, and so it
has resigned itself to being parochial. But the effort to make virtues out
of this necessity is one that has largely been lost.

But there is an English poetry which has risen above all that fiddle,
and two recent books mark a distinct change of emphasis and of
direction. Mr Crozier, in his new collection,* dispels that quaint
illusion (shared by many of our 'established' poets, of course) that
contemporary poetry is necessarily obscure:

> Carelessness
> Can pull down in an hour what enterprise
> Has taken years to build. A tenor of
> I will not pass this way again
> Much to the delight of the audience.

Mr Crozier has created a poetry which is open in the sense that it does
not rely upon the trickeries of regular forms or a heightened 'poetic'
language – which is a more schematic way of saying that it is not tied
to a romantic notion of the self and a no less romantic (or 'wry')
objectivity. It is a quiet and even poetry, and within the unforced
texture of the work there is created that illusion, indispensable to the
best poetry, of the familiar being made new again:

* *Printed Circuit* Andrew Crozier

> If you get lost
> Bid me despair and I'll despair
> Under that Cypress tree. The gates are all
> Suspended. Straw-hatted they sigh and glug
> Their Turkish coffee at home
> Once more, and done up neatly.

There is no generalized 'meaning' to be divined from the poetry; the lines have not been pressed and flattened into the service of a particular 'point', but create their own space and their own activity. The whole thus becomes more than its parts, setting up a novel relation between the language and our preconceived idea of it:

> We are reminded by the frightening
> personal resemblance of this work detached from experience.

J. H. Prynne's poetry, especially in this most recent volume,* is less open to the casual reader; he has been accused of obscurity (which means simply that poetry reviewers never take any trouble over their reading), but his is a difficult poetry only in the sense that there is a new quality in its language, a power which is undoubtedly *there* but one which has yet to be brought to adequate recognition:

> The apple cap sinks down to your faint hopes,
> sprawled in the sun on the grassy hillside,
> shirt over the soft
> haemal arch. By this vane in the ground
> the roots start to sicken,
> snow normal to zulu time stuns soft news
> of choice all over the earth.

The uses of formal harmony make this a special kind of language, it is clearly 'poetry', but its procedures come from a language and a range of reference which are very different from the inherited modes within Mr Larkin's anthology:

> The brietal perfusion makes a controlled
> amazement and trustingly we walk there, speak
> fluently on that same level of sound;

* *Wound Response* J. H. Prynne

> white murmur ferries the clauses to the true
> centre of the sleep forum.

The poetry here has slipped out of the demotic and domestic bonds which have trammelled English poetry for many years, and it realizes a new force which can lend even the most apparently conventional lyric a fresh access of strength:

> O lye still, thou
>
> 　　　　　　　Little Musgrave, the
>
> grass is wet
>
> 　　　　and streak'd with light

The resonance of this suggests that Mr Prynne is connecting, by indirection or by design, with the indigenous wealth of the language – a wealth which has not been inflated because it has hitherto remained concealed. He would certainly not be in place among the thin lines of the *Poetry Supplement*; by bringing into harmony the varieties of technical and moral vocabulary which have been previously separate and alienated, he creates a poetry which may bring the whole soul of man into activity. Naturally reviewers and editors cannot be expected to notice such things.

4 January 1975

8

The Collected Poems, 1956–1974

Edward Dorn

Edward Dorn is one of the two or three best American poets now writing; if I add that he is also one of the two or three best poets writing in English, I shall no doubt be accused of that snivelling abasement before American culture which is current in certain circles. The truth is that American culture consists of no more than two or three good poets, a number of florid and over-praised novelists, a moribund art industry and a non-existent theatre. Some civilization.

But Dorn *is* very much an American poet, and he has created a distinctively American idiom. He has published seven books of shorter poems, all of which have been collected here, and a long sequence – *Gunslinger*, not printed here – which is arguably the finest long poem to have been written in America in the last thirty years. It is also a specifically American work, using a dissonance which jars the European ear and a melodramatic virility which used to be characteristic of 'the frontier' myth. The poems here show this language in the making; the earliest in the book are placed within that blank landscape, and within some long, emphatic lines which go right back to Whitman:

> and dust masking the hedges of fields she knew
> in her eye as a vague land where she lived,
> boundaries, whose tractors chugged pulling harrows
> pulling discs, pulling great yields from the earth
> pulse for the armies in two hemispheres, 1943

But Dorn sometimes makes his points too well:

> In America every art has to reach toward some
> clarity. That is our hope from the start.

English poets have also practised clarity, with varying degrees of success, for some centuries now; in fact, it is a general mistake of American writers to confuse clarity with sincerity. As Dorn puts it:

> It is a *real* mystique, not a
> mystique. A mystique of the real.

Statements like this, which have nothing very much to do with his achieved poetry, have often led to Dorn being confused with such poets as Robert Creeley or Gary Snyder; they also believed in 'the real' but for them it was all mixed up with a tacky orientalism and a wheedling, hysterical adolescence. Clap your hands if you still believe in Allen Ginsberg.

From the start, Dorn had too firm an ear and too clear a vision to become involved with all that fiddle. The 'real' in his early poetry is natural without being in the least sentimental, and this book marks the strength of his poetic progress from collection to collection – until he can now turn his poetry to a reality both more public and at the same time more intractable. The language is harder, the rhythms less fluent, and the whole exercise more individual than his earlier work:

> Bent in the dim light
> of that specific cabin space they had,
> those unlucky children, a meal
> of various cereal dumped on the market
> to make room for vaster crops next year
> a thing they couldn't have understood
> or that charity is quite often
> a device to prevent spoilage.

This is, if nothing else, a poetry of statement and with verse like this Edward Dorn has become the only plausible, political poet in America. Political poetry has nothing whatever to do with the extent of the poet's political knowledge, his *savoir faire*, or even the 'side' he takes; it has to do with the quality of his response to public situations, not whether that response is 'right' or 'wrong'. Dorn has created a lyrical, descriptive language which can effectively convey that quality:

> the arrow of the art passes through our centers
> and it used to leave us amazed at the rapport
> of our mutual singular disaffection.

What the 'real' comes to mean for Dorn is the identity of the speaker and what is spoken, with something like an Orphic spirit, and in a culture which depends for its most splendid effects upon various forms of separation – the television and film, the astronauts in their space modules – this stance is in itself very much a political one. And this sense of connection – whether it be between the self and its proper place, or between the object and its exact role – leads Dorn to some very clear observations:

> All the children
> were taught the pledge of Allegiance, and
> the land was pledged
> to private use, the walnut dropped in the
> autumn on the ground
> green, and lay black in the dead grass in the
> spring.

This is a direct but not an unmusical language; its harmony comes from the specific depth of the words, rather than from assonance and polyphony: in other words, the lines cling to a simulacrum of truth, to a true and local voice.

The 'truth' of poetry can sometimes, of course, be painfully banal and there are certain poems in this collection which are marred by amateur historicism and by a rhetorical use of the language of economics. But it can also hit its mark:

> England beware
>   the cliff of 1945
> turns a natural insularity
> into a late, and out of joint
> naturalism of inbred
> industrial indecision.

Dorn's proper achievement has been to create single-handedly a language of public reference, and to have brought within the sphere of expressive language and poetic experience objects and feelings which had been, literally, *unimaginable* in those terms. It is in this context that he is one of the masters of our contemporary language.

10 January 1975

9

The Decay of the Angel
Yukio Mishima

If the publishers are right and this is the 'climax' of Mishima's work, I am very grateful to have missed all of the other novels, and if he is indeed 'the most dynamic and outspoken writer of post-war Japan' then that crowded and polluted people should learn to concentrate on making pen batteries. *The Decay of the Angel* is extremely scrutable; it is novelettish to a degree, and is full of those Oriental gnomic utterances which are an infallible sign of simple-mindedness. The novel opens with sixteen-year-old Tōru Yasunaga looking romantically out to sea, and with seventy-six-year-old Shigekuni (which must, as it turns out, be the Japanese for Sugardaddy) Honda doing the same thing in a slightly more symbolic manner. Mishima actually goes so far as to call the sea an 'infinity' which, unless he has suffered a great deal in translation, must be as ludicrous in Japanese as it is in English.

There is a great deal of tatty philosophizing throughout the book, no doubt because it is much easier to philosophize than it is to write a novel: 'If seeing is a meeting between being and being, then it must be the facing mirrors of two beings.' And Mishima has learnt Sartre's lesson that bad philosophy is the essential prelude to even more ragged romanticizing: 'Occasionally he would let a soft smile float to his lips, but it had in it nothing of sympathy. It was the final sign rejecting humanity, an invisible arrow released from the bow of his lips.' This is not writing, this is Barbara Cartland – and Barbara Cartland at least has the courage not to commit *hara-kiri* over it.

Discerning a plot beneath all of this overwriting is like trying to do a crossword in dark glasses. Honda decides to adopt Tõru for reasons which are only made clear in Mishima's earlier novels, but it has something to do with beauty and evil and the fact that Mishima has absolutely nothing to say. Tõru, with a mixture of vanity and guile, becomes the master of Honda's life but tries, in a moment of self-recognition which romantic novelists like Mishima call 'blinding', to kill himself. The story does not get much further than this since Mishima steers his characters into endless and ostensibly lyrical ruminations about the meaning of it all (I began to suffer from this myself). He even goes so far as to repeat in detail twenty-five pages of Tõru's adolescent diary – perhaps not realizing that it *is* adolescent. Writers, like water, find their own level.

But no doubt everything is meant to be symbolic. Tõru suffers noticeably from the 'five signs of decay' of an angel, there is some debased neo-Platonism littering the narrative, and an emphasis upon reincarnation which suggests to me a very easy way of keeping the same characters in different novels. All of this makes for an imperfect melodrama, in which every action is unlikely but thoroughly predictable. Plot, character and interest are superseded by reveries full of fury but signifying nothing – as if there were a James Baldwin struggling to get out of Mishima's self-consciously and phonily masculine frame. His is a portentous and empty book.

25 January 1975

10

Look at the Harlequins!
Vladimir Nabokov

Mr Nabokov clearly thinks of himself as a very good, if not a great writer; having been praised by sycophantic American reviewers, and having been read by a small percentage of the American middle classes, he has come to the blinding conclusion that the important thing about Nabokov's writings is Nabokov himself. This is the common strategy of second-rate writers, and in *Look at the Harlequins!* Nabokov has forestalled the judgement of whatever thin cultural history is written of our time and has composed his own literary history. This is the novel to end all of Nabokov's novels – or at least one hopes so.

'The Narrator' of the book is Vadim, an emigré writer with pretensions and Nabokov in his own coy and conventional way lists the man's 'other books' on the fly-leaf; this parodic solemnity gives you a sneak preview of a meta-novel in the making. Vadim starts his unreal life in the Easter term of the Cambridge year and 'over lunch at the Pitt' – a Cambridge club which only emigrés could take seriously – there are hints of Nabokov's adamantine tricks to come: 'Ivor Black wanted Gogol's Town Mayor to wear a dressing gown because "wasn't it merely the old rascal's nightmare and didn't *Revizor*, its Russian title, actually come from the French for dream, *rêve*?" I said I thought it was a ghastly idea.' Ghastly indeed, but this does not prevent Nabokov from pursuing it like a crazed lepidopterist. When Nabokov mentions any writer, of course, he is really discussing himself, and this little vignette will give you some idea of the *festschrift* to come.

The narrator turns out to be of the *soi-disant* school and is very much like those other personae whom Nabokov heaps upon himself in an effort to keep warm: Vadim is of Russian stock, he travels to Paris and then to an American university, he writes for emigré journals and throughout it all exhibits an obsession with himself which I could not share. He hates the ticking of clocks, and the smell of other people's bodies: anything and anyone, in fact, who could interrupt his contemplation of his own self-sufficiency. So it is that he marries disastrously and is left with one daughter who, quite naturally, disowns him. But all of this is merely the technical surface of Vadim's misery, since he suffers from a peculiar neuralgia which prevents him from locating his body within the abstract categories of space: this precipitates a seizure, and the novel ends with the notion that this is really about a displacement of time rather than of space. It would be a cute way of disowning these memoirs, were it not incomprehensible. Meanwhile, Vadim has become a popular and respected novelist, although there is no clue for aspiring authors about cause. The messages received about his great works make them seem uniformly tedious and self-indulgent; but this may be how reputations are made – Nabokov, after all, should know.

What we have, as always, is a magical mystery tour into the purlieus of Nabokov's greatness, and in *Look at the Harlequins!* he presses his search into himself with even greater fervour, daring to go where no man has gone before. He drops a host of tiny allusions and coy hints about his previous novels, and there are a great many characters and situations which have an unmistakable air of *déjà lus* about them. There are two explanations for this: it may be that Nabokov is fascinated by his own work, and so continues to harass and worry it in order to extract some key or secret code which will justify it all; or, more probably, it may be that his talent has long since atrophied and he is condemned to the constant reworking of his original material, to press some scent out of the already heavily pressed flower.

But to offer *Look at the Harlequins!* as another and a different novel requires the help of two overweening assumptions: the first is that the readers will be so familiar with the range of Nabokov's work that they will pick up the allusions which fly towards them. This is, of course, an unwarranted assumption. The second is, that Nabokov is a great enough writer to be able to afford the luxury of such self-indulgence. To put it more crisply, are his novels good enough to be remembered? No. He simply takes part in more and more elaborate exercises in self-justification and, if you forget the rhetorical tricks which have endeared him to the American critics, there is not and there never has been anything of great import in his writing.

This is principally because Nabokov is a rhetorician rather than a creative writer. He has mastered all of the technical tricks of the novel, and he has invented a few of his own, but the heart of the matter has consistently eluded him. So he is forced to recapitulate the themes and the appearances of his earlier fiction, a fiction composed of fancies rather than imagination, and will never develop its substance. As grand-aunt Baroness Bredow puts it to the narrator of this latest effort: 'Trees are harlequins, words are harlequins,' which is fine for a baroness but not for a novelist. Nabokov's prose is self-indulgent without being self-conscious, with that sweet and soft texture which is an infallible sign of something slightly 'off'. Nabokov says of another emigré writer that he employs 'pretty prose and borrowed poetry', and that is exactly what is wrong with his own weak and derivative prose. When a novel strives too hard to become literature, it falls into literariness. Nabokov's words are hollow and external, and he lays them on with a very flat trowel. All that is left is a solemn persona playing with himself and that – of course – leads to blindness.

19 April 1975

II

Tales of Power
Carlos Castaneda

'Do you know that one moment can be eternity?' says Don Juan to Carlos Castaneda, with the same breathless originality you would expect from Julie Andrews singing of similar things in *The Sound of Music*. Yes, I have heard such things about 'eternity' before, but it comes as a counter-cultural shock to see them repeated in a book which is supposed to be expanding the mind rather than filling it with ancient clichés: 'Things are real only after one has learned to agree on their realness.' This is an important point, of course, and it will no doubt be met by a reverent silence among the student population of America and their professors of sociology, anthropology and con-temporology. But for the rest of us, average and unenlightened as we are, what is trite remains trite even when it is announced in solemn and pietistic terms.

For those of you who have not been following the series, Carlos Castaneda is on a magical mystery tour in search of that perennial illusion which always appeals to faddists, 'the totality of oneself'; his guide and perfect master is Don Juan, who says a great many perfect things about the 'ultimate nature' of reality. Castaneda is continually being surprised, agitated and amazed and, I would have thought, is an easy lay for any sorcerer with his eye on the main chance. Their relationship is much like that of Don Quixote and Sancho Panza, except it is Panza who insists on tilting at windmills. After a great many feats of prestidigitation and levitation, Castaneda is carried over the threshold of his perception and is left to jump, literally, into the dark.

There has been some minor controversy over the authenticity of Castaneda's works: are they factual or fictional, and is Castaneda now a perfect 'warrior' or is he what he may always have been: a businessman? These are not interesting questions. The books themselves have to be central, so are they worth reading? *Tales of Power*, despite the astonished and revelatory terms in which it is couched, simply repeats most of the truisms of conventional religious literature. Although Castaneda's mysticism is neatly packaged, and tricked out with some charming Mexican expressions, the experience itself and the account of that experience stay very close to the stereotypes:

> We are boundless. The world of objects and solidity is a way of making our passage on earth convenient. It is only a description that was created to help us. We, or rather our *reason*, forget that the description is only a description and thus we entrap the totality of ourselves in a vicious circle from which we rarely emerge in our lifetime.

The fact that Castaneda is always dragging in this hoary seventeenth-century concept of 'reason', and that he even manages to include something known as the 'will' as well, suggests that initiation is not what it used to be. Castaneda merely regurgitates the conventional mystical attitudes, but at this late date they are simplistic and confused.

But the perfect warrior is no slouch, and he has used all the paraphernalia of a false culture to prop up his archaic points. Castaneda caught the counter-culture just at its tumescence and he purveys his mysticism in a fashionably Amero-Indian setting and with a liberal sprinkling of hallucinogenic drugs. Fashion, it seems, can make masters of us all and that image of the warrior – determined, self-sufficient and full of power – is one that will appeal to middle-class youth and to their academic fellow-travellers. The secret of popular success is to say conventional things so baldly and so often that the ignorant and the innocent will assume them to be original. I would rather read Thomas Traherne than Carlos Castaneda, but then tradition is an acquired taste, and you cannot expect readers or publishers to look beyond a fast buck and a fast success.

The narrative itself is winsome to a degree. The improbabilities and the coincidences are so brazen that I can only assume the book is factual, but Castaneda and his perfect master are so fatuous that they resist any attempt to look at them sympathetically as recognizable human beings. Mysterious looks are always being given and cryptic things are often being said – 'Somehow you would have found me,' says Don Juan as he magically turns himself into Greta Garbo.

So the prose of Castaneda's revelations is turgid and inept, and his characters are sheer cardboard, but it must also be said that he is a dab hand with the sublime and the beautiful, and I suspect that his books sell to that vast bulk of the reading public who prefer shivers down their spines to anything more substantial. If he had not made his pile out of pop religion, he would have been a very good writer of ghost stories or the more gory kinds of comic strip. When he gets down to the direct transcription of places and situations, his prose comes alive and takes on a very subtle and artificial directness – and it is only when he goes on about enlightenment that the prose becomes the flaccid bearer of cliché. But I suppose the critics will still praise him for his inane ramblings about essence and one-ness, and that illusion which all good fiction should destroy – the illusion that the world has a perceptible form, a glowing essence to which poor humankind can connect – will be perpetuated and will remain a source of grief and embarrassment to those who are silly enough to fall for it.

10 May 1975

12

Verse, and Worse?

Striking the Pavilions of Zero
John James

The Mountain in the Sea
John Fuller

High Pink on Chrome
J. H. Prynne

Pleats
Andrew Crozier

There is a great divide in English poetry, not that you would notice it if you read the literary weeklies and the intellectual monthlies. Here, to begin with, are two books: John James's *Striking the Pavilions of Zero* – a somewhat odd and abstract title, perhaps – and John Fuller's *The Mountain in the Sea* which has a more familiar and a more 'poetic' sound to it. Mr James's book is published by a small press; its design and its typography are unfamiliar, and it has a colourful print on its cover. Mr Fuller's book is produced by a large London firm of publishers, and its cover is the simple and standard one they use for their poetical products – the point being, no doubt, that no one could possibly buy one by accident. Mr James's book has a note: 'Some of these poems first appeared in *The Anona Wynn Collection*, *The Curiously Strong*, *The Park*, *One*, *Second Aeon* and *Sesheta*.' Mr Fuller's acknowledgements are: '. . . some of these poems first appeared in *The Cellar Press*, *Encounter*, the *Listener*, the *New Review*, the *Observer*, *Outposts* and the *Times Literary Supplement*.'

And there you have it: the great divide. On the one side, magazines which are not the staple diet of the 'reading public' and poems which are not read or discussed by our poetry 'critics', whoever they may be nowadays. On the other side, the familiar parts of the literary soft machine. John Fuller's poems have become a standard feature of the cultural prints, and you will generally find them tucked away at the bottom of a column. You would find it much harder to come across the collections of John James, or of Andrew Crozier, or of Jeremy Prynne but all the fuss about *Poetry* not being read (even the literary editor of *The Times* has been raising his voice for the proper distribution of *Poetry*) is not about these poets at all; it is only about the John Fullers, the Douglas Dunns and the Vernon Scannels: in other words, *Poetry* in its familiar and domestic guise, that English *voice* – that *tone* – we have come to know and love.

John James has, quite deliberately, moved out of this context. *Striking the Pavilions of Zero*, in other words, breaks up the conventional, formal limits of 'the poem', it attends instead to the discrete line of the verse – that single, specific instance and its possible harmonies. John Fuller, in *The Mountain in the Sea*, adheres strictly to small forms in which the lines are, characteristically, a vehicle for gnomic 'thoughts' and wry 'feeling'. But to press poetry into the service of reflection and observation is to make it, I think, inexpressive:

> Here warmth is transmitted.
> Your idle hand reaches
> And grasps a myriad boulders
> Of impossible size.

And it is this monotone which characterizes the volume. James's freer use and more open development of the language allow for a much greater range of effects, whether it be the cocky insouciance of his English manner:

> & if there did happen to be a bullet amongst us
> it would never find anywhere to go

(and how refreshing it is to come across a hard Englishness in a poetry untouched by grandfather Larkin and the rest of the gang), or the soupiness of his lyricism.

Mr Fuller's poetry, where every word is heavy with the weight of implied reference, cannot quite manage this variety of tones. It is significant that the best poems in his book – like 'Wild Raspberries', for instance – are attractive simply because they have a momentum which breaks free of syntax and small form:

> A roofless ruin, luminous under sprays
> Like faery casques or the dulled red of lanterns
> Where the flame is low and the wax runs into the paper . . .

I could put it another way by noting that, ordinarily, Mr Fuller employs the same syntax and the same range of voices as the current social novel in England; the problem with the now sacrosanct division of prose/*Poetry* is that it reduces the difference between them to the level of simple content and treats only in passing the language which is actually being used. Where the novel concerns itself with the romance of individual life, Mr Fuller concerns himself with the romance of pre-individual life: the mountain, the sea, ancient settlements and the other poetical emblems of early twentieth century verse. John James, meanwhile, is using the language in ways that disorder its familiar patterns; his is a poetry of abstract statement, moody description, polemic and satire, all taking their place within the free fall of his verse. The idea of a poem's *movement* is therefore much more important to him than it is to Fuller, since it suggests those qualities of change and fluency which are at the centre of his design:

> It's only a game but oh so steadfast we keep on
> passing the brink of an elegant nothing though
> sometimes something in us makes everything tremble
> & then the world doesn't exist anymore
> or else we're mistaken & it merely makes a different sound

Mr Prynne's latest volume, *High Pink on Chrome*, is 'difficult', which is simply to say that he is using a vocabulary and a poetic method which have still to be learned by those who read poetry and those who profess to read poetry. In this new book, a series of phrases (not, emphatically not, a series of 'images' or a number of thoughts) are pressed into tightly constructed forms by the power of an imagination which changes the surface of language:

> And yes, substance has no
>   contrary among things that are:
> what we must is the dream of
>   a sharper cold, and she knows
> that also. As all things pass
>   to and fro in the world, from
> one hand to another, belayed.

The form here is not engineered by its content, as it is in the poetry of Mr Fuller, but by the proper limits of expression; in this volume, notations of physical collapse, and presentations of the English landscape and its seasons, are transformed by Prynne's dazzling and authoritative uses of the language. The poem becomes an emblem, attracting and dispersing several variants of poetic writing within a small space. This concision sometimes makes for harmony and for 'romance':

> And take her softly, in fear for
> sanity at the open window, light
> slanting in through the limes

but the romance is continually being undercut by irony:

> Over the rosy hedges the passions
> in their circuit feel for the safe
> edge of the hoop, their votive antiphon . . .

It is rather as the metaphysicals did it, and Prynne has the same intensity of reference and that same heat in the language. By refusing to become a readily accessible and intelligible writer, he has ensured that poetry can no longer be treated as a deodorized museum of fine thoughts and fine feelings; he is creating instead a complete and a coherent language.

Of all the poets here under review, Andrew Crozier is the most theoretical in his approach to the language of poetry; he is not an 'experimentalist', thank God, and the *avant-garde* has been dead for some years now. In fact, his latest volume, *Pleats*, is on the face of it a detailed and somewhat mundane transcription of the facts of daily life:

> Prudently I retired
> for the time being
> like a dotted line
> leading to bed.

Small facts and apparently trivial events (going to sleep, getting up, going shopping) are presented within a direct and unembarrassed prose which puts to shame those self-conscious practitioners of Marxist or 'oral' poetry who try to write a common language and end up by spinning a particularly offensive rhetoric. Mr Crozier is not of that company, since he has a very clear notion of the language, and of the way in which poetry can mediate between the word and the world.

The objects of the world find their proper place in Mr Crozier's calm and collected lines, and they are not wrenched out of shape by the poet's preoccupation with some external 'meaning' or with some ideal order into which both poetry and the world might fit. Crozier's poetry has no internal momentum which imposes itself upon the objects within it; it moves rather by a process of accumulation and constant reinvention:

> together again while you and I
> set off around the pond talking
> about ducks and the volume of foliage
> on a summer branch which dips
> toward the water to be reflected
> in words that condense like the image
> of each leaf shifting over the others

Mr Crozier is a 'mystical' poet in the sense that it is only language which can interpret and irradiate the world – not by substituting itself for it, but by dwelling within it. Language, thus broadly expressed, precedes form, content and meaning.

20 December 1975

13

The Auden Generation
Samuel Hynes

There are two distinct versions of the thirties. There is the orthodox view of it as part of the ongoing history of English taste, with poems and novels which have led naturally to the great literary achievements of the Arts Council. Many of the shining knights of the thirties, after all, live on – mostly in villas in southern France, but they do live and sometimes add lustre to the literary journals. The other version is a little more convincing – it is, quite simply, that English culture in general, and English poetry in particular, started to go badly wrong in the thirties, and that they have never recovered. Mr Hynes's concise and elegant study of that decade treats these matters only indirectly, but he does in passing suggest a third version of the period under review: he discusses the writers of the thirties (and particularly those middle-class poets who were grouped around that doyen of the middle class, W. H. Auden) in the context of technical and formal innovation. Hynes's subject is 'specifically the growth of literary forms' and, Mr Hynes suggests, it was in that sense that Auden and his university friends were making it new. They were a very self-conscious generation with, as Auden put it, 'an altering speech for altering things'. All poets with an eye to the main chance say such things, but there was something in the air of the period which made it seem more than usually appropriate. Even T. S. Eliot was impressed by all the publicity, and he dismissed the great modernist works of the twenties (including his own) saying it was as if 'the intellectual and artistic output of the previous seven years had been rather the last efforts of an old world than the struggles of a new'.

It must have been a very brave, or very harsh, new world to have impressed such an ironist. And Eliot would no doubt have appreciated the fact that this dawning world should have had, in retrospect, such timid and traditional chroniclers. This is Mr Hynes's story, and he tells it very well. From his account, the thirties are part of some other and distant culture; the self-images of the age – mountain climbing, the Truly Strong Man, the quest, History – are all but incomprehensible now. It was a time when poetry was taken seriously. It was a time when young writers were not wholly at the mercy of publishing economics (there was no end of arcane and theoretical titles). And since literary matters were not in those days conducted at the level of TV book programmes and *Guardian* profiles, there was a real and consistent questioning of civilized values – What is the role of poetry? What is the significance of documentary techniques? What does 'realism' really mean? Questions which nobody would now understand or, if they did, would care to answer. So the thirties was a period of intense activity, and as a consequence most of the written work has that winning combination of vitality and clumsiness. But were Auden and his gang really making it new, as they insisted they were? And, if so, why did their poetry age so rapidly into the magazine verse of the forties and fifties?

Mr Hynes does not address himself directly to such questions, but in this exhaustive survey he implies the answers. That generation grew up in the shadow of great events. Such was the preoccupation of writers like Auden, Spender and Day-Lewis with public causes that they felt they could safely lay aside the modernist works of Pound, Eliot and Joyce in order to confront politics head-on, to make public and polemical statements. But they did this from a position of relative naivety and, it must be said, relative security – so they were at the mercy of political theories, of which there was no lack, and wholly in the grip of the peculiar, myth-making habits of young poets. Mr Hynes is an acute judge of such matters and describes precisely the wayward progress of these innocents at home; but he should not take so much at face value. He documents Auden's political beliefs (or the lack of them) and his poetic development (or the absence of it), but it must also be remembered that Auden was a very sharp operator indeed. He found a publisher and he found an eager audience by playing to the gallery; he never ceased to do so, and this is part of the legacy of the thirties. Given this combination of myth-making and fraudulence, much of the verse of the thirties now seems dull; like all other matters, politics cannot be handled directly in poetry without becoming rhetorical or meretricious.

But, since it *was* a matter of rhetoric, the political mood did not last long; it did not even survive the period which Mr Hynes covers in his book. The main transition, as he describes it, is one from left-wing polemic and political activity to the middle-class delights of what had really always been a solid and comfortable poetry: 'The men who had been sentimental Marxists in their youth were in their thirties, were reviewing for the *Daily Telegraph* and writing books on commission.' So, having entertained a middle-class audience with their rhetoric, they could now begin to live comfortably off the proceeds. Or, as Spender put it more diplomatically, 'poetry is not the same as action and a poem is not the same as a political thesis'. But this magnanimous gesture on the part of the thirties poets, this solemn return to their true calling, is not quite the formative act of an Eliot or a Joyce. It was rather a return to an easy and empty art. Having failed to qualify politically, they decided to 'make do' artistically.

Mr Hynes does not make any final judgements of this kind, but he does prepare the way for them when he documents the conventional origins of that brave new poetry of the thirties: 'So one might say that most of the contributors to *New Signatures* were already Hogarth "house pets" . . . Nothing could have been more conventional or less revolutionary than the way in which these young reputations were launched.' And for all those protestations about an 'altering speech', the actual poetry remains conventional and readily accessible. The achievements of Eliot and Pound were ignored; European modernist movements were not understood; the language was never developed beyond a dull, referential level which is still the standard for established English poetry. The thirties poets, in other words, represented a return to English provincial life. They were parlour poets, and they exploited what seemed at the time to be a particularly modern form of parlour rhetoric. As Hynes puts it, 'New poets become a renascence when a public wants and needs a renascence, and Spender and his friends were celebrated almost before they were published because they seemed to offer new responses to new problems.'

And at least, one might add, there was then a public which actually cared about such things. The problem with the thirties is now simply one of senility: our new literary giants have never left that parlour. The publishers of books of verse and the editors of literary magazines, who were for the most part weaned on that notion of English taste, are still printing imitations of the manner which Auden and Spender introduced. But now, forty provincial years later, there is no public left to care. Mr Hynes has provided a precise and thoughtful book, but the real history of English taste has yet to be written.

19 June 1976

14

Thought, Words and Creativity

F. R. Leavis

In this latest book, Dr Leavis forgoes his recent polemical essays and reverts to the works of D. H. Lawrence. Since Dr Leavis is the last critic which this country or its universities will produce, his decision – at the age of eighty – to go back to the works of our greatest modern novelist is a significant one. He returns to the major texts of Lawrence in order to elucidate and to sustain what have now become Leavis's major concerns: 'life', 'thought' and 'civilization'. To wrench these terms out of context is to do great violence to the actual subtlety and complexity of Dr Leavis's language, which works characteristically by suggestion and by a gradual accumulation of meaning. And this latest book is indeed, in this sense, the most difficult. But it is difficulty of a fruitful kind. His tone has remained caustic; he makes established persons feel uneasy.

Thought, Words and Creativity is, as its title suggests, a more 'abstract' study than the earlier *D. H. Lawrence: Novelist*. The book has a convincingly theoretical cast as Leavis proceeds at once to discuss Lawrence's 'vital intelligence', that 'living integrity as the actual principle of life'. It is easy to jib at these captivating but ostensibly meaningless formulations (we prefer books on *Shelley and Harassment*, we even prefer Oxford academics enthusing over Ted Hughes) but to treat them as propositions – to be verified by analytical methods – is to miss the significance of Leavis's tone. He is a critic who proceeds by indirection to the heart of his design, a writer who prefers the constant accretion of sense, the steady construction of meaning which is only significant when seen *as a whole*. That is why this book continually turns back upon itself, why it repeats certain phrases of Lawrence over and over again, why it returns to certain central distinctions and never rests in any final conclusions. *D. H. Lawrence: Novelist* was longer but sharper; it had more verve, and more *brio*. It knew its enemies, but it knew its strength. In this book, Leavis leaves to one side the polemical material of the earlier book in order to concentrate upon the one, salient thing: the language of Lawrence. And that, even in extracts, is still a marvel to read.

After the opening chapter, from which the book takes its title (and which was first published in the *Spectator* in a slightly different form), Leavis begins with an analysis of the relative failure of *The Plumed Serpent*. What he says here is essentially a preparation for the later chapters, since it gives the first inklings of what Lawrence meant by 'Art-speech is the only speech'. Dr Leavis then goes on to investigate *Women in Love*. His method is one of a generalized but authoritative going-over of the text, quoting a passage and then eliciting its assumptions before proceeding to another extract, the insights of which are employed to add to and sustain earlier ones. Although he would no doubt resent the notion, Leavis comes in some places close to the descriptive methods of Martin Heidegger in a work like *The Essence of Poetry*. Leavis uses a no less abstract and theoretical prose which is no less firmly based upon concrete models, Lawrence's words being employed in much the same way as Hölderlin's lyrics. Certainly Leavis's study of *Women in Love* is less localized than it was in his earlier book, but there Middleton Murry acted as Leavis's foil and here he is engaged only with the writing itself. The prose may be less sharp, but it has more resonance:

> . . . the creativity threatened by industrial civilization, with its power to mechanize what lives in it or by it, depends on the robustly individual human being – the profound creative individuality that can draw on the source that lies deep down, uncontrolled by the ego, and is the source of spontaneity.

This is not negligible or inarticulate writing, however fashionable it may now be to sneer at it; and if literary criticism can ever lay claim to moral seriousness, then it is indisputably from passages of this kind.

But it seems to me that Leavis is our last critic. Humane criticism has now played itself out, and has become a vehicle for such external pursuits as sociology and anthropology. The new positivists have taken over in the universities, with their creepy Francophilia. And even among the admirers of Leavis, the particular emphases of his language have turned into a prescriptive moralism which does violence to proper criticism. For despite Leavis's attention to the 'words on the page' (an abstraction which has been widely misunderstood and abused since its formulation), he is constantly and irritably reaching beyond the text – to grasp and elucidate 'truths' which, I believe, literature neither creates nor reveals. After a discussion of *The Rainbow* in this book, for example, he goes beyond the unnatural boundaries of the fiction: 'But we didn't create ourselves; and the sole access to the promptings to be gathered from the unknown – from which life and creativity enter us – is by the well-head, which is deep below our valid thought.' Creativity here, and by implication the works of language which are created, is seen as deriving from a context beyond the confines of literature and of language.

Both the strength and the failure of Leavis's mature criticism rest in his constant attempt to find 'values' – whether spiritual, moral or humane – in literature which are simply not there to find. Is literature 'thought about life', as Leavis insists, or is it thought about language?

Or, to put it in the context of another of Leavis's terms, is there actually a 'reality that transcends language' and, even if there is, can such a thing be elicited from a reading of Lawrence's fictions? Language is thus seen as embodying truths, and, however 'concrete' and however 'actual' it may be, it becomes a form of rhetoric used for external and utilitarian ends. This cannot, I think, be right – and this is partly the reason why Leavis has returned so insistently and so creatively to Lawrence's texts, teasing out of them confirmation and sustenance. He mistakes their nature, and so will often become over-emphatic in their defence. His urgency and his moral fervour reclaim the finest spirit of our literary humanism, but his fervour serves to confirm, too, the pressures under which it is legitimately giving way.

But again, and it bears repeating in the face of so much bland and meretricious opposition, Leavis is a great critic precisely because he refuses to recognize this. He is uniquely responsive because he is so emphatic about the nature of the object at hand. That is why he is so exactly right about 'the failure of civilization'. At certain points in this study Leavis discusses such periodicals as the *English Review* and *The Calendar of Modern Letters*, and the unacknowledged theme of this book is 'the disappearance of an educated, reading public'. Given the current contempt for standards evinced by such state organizations as the Arts Council it is difficult not to assent – 'And to destroy the educated public is to kill English literature – past literature as a living influence, and the possibility of significant new creation in the present.' I do not think that Leavis's conception of 'literature' is a just one, but that does not deflect from the rightness of his judgement in these matters. It is the mark of a great critic that he can wield irreconcilable or insupportable beliefs into judgements of the widest significance and validity; so that uncertainties of critical response can lead to the major certainty of the central, human response. Dr Leavis has, more than any other English critic of this century, made that mark.

28 August 1976

15

W. H. Auden: Collected Poems
Edited by Edward Mendelson

Now at last we have the great poet, caught by Edward Mendelson in what is a work of enormous scholarship and love. The volume of Auden's achievement defies immediate critical analysis: seven hundred pages of fine print, 400 poems and some of them very long indeed. But who would be foolish enough to see it as a 'mirror' of our times? There is not one poem in this book which does not contain a beautiful or an unusual line, but there are very few which do not seem abrupt, flawed or unfinished.

They are all, unmistakably, the work of Auden. No poet of his generation acquired such a familiar tone, that raffish poise between schoolboy and schoolmaster, and no poet acquired it so quickly and with such considerable success. Even the early poems have a developed tone and syntax which Auden was never completely to abandon:

> It is time for the destruction of error.
> The chairs are being brought in from the garden,
> The summer talk stopped on that savage coast . . .

The poet springs up fully armed, and although there are some faint traces of early poetic influences – of Yeats and Eliot particularly – they are either skilfully concealed or else charged with irony and bathos. But no poet as receptive as Auden to the prevailing climate will want to escape his time completely. There are other influences at work, and Auden started writing in that odd and heady period when the works of Freud and Marx were becoming fashionable; at a time, then, when nebulous concepts and vague forms of intellectual discipline were placed in the service of romantic mythologies which were no less potent for seeming 'scientific'. Auden's is an art which, from the beginning, used instant methods to achieve vaguely intellectual, quasi-romantic effects.

Even in his earliest poetry, Auden had a taste for gnomic utterances enhanced by emphatic rhythms, for pen-portraits, for short moral lessons, for poems filled with arguments which were never quite as coherent as his rhymes suggested. Auden was, in other words, always a rhetorician, aware as any poet of the truth-giving powers of language but, like any rhetorician, also a formalist prepared to meddle with those powers. He always chose the right tone for the right message, and for the right audience.

English poetry had not behaved in that way since the eighteenth century (Auden's argumentative Muse was the perfect accompaniment to a new Age of Prose) and his effect was enormous. He gave other poets the itch to generalize – to say the right things for the wrong reasons – but he also gave them a highly private language which defeated them. He encouraged smartness and glibness in poets who were not quite as smart or as articulate as he. He encouraged overstatement, and the history of recent years is littered with the inflated corpses of dead poems. With his rhetorical ability to employ different forms for different occasions – with 'Songs', 'Lullabies', 'Letters' – he indirectly turned light verse into something of a poetic fetish, and it has remained an alibi ever since for weak or vacillating poets. More importantly, Auden's rhetoric fatally weakened the language in any hands other than his own: he taught poets to use the language as a vehicle for their consciences, or as the blunt instrument of their 'tone'. Despite his often expressed and boring concern for poetic form, he actively encouraged poetic licence of the most dangerous kinds.

All this was to be expected. A poet who finds his style early in his career is bound to create considerable difficulties for himself and for others; so was there anywhere for Auden to go after the audacious and considerable verses of his youth? This edition gives some sense of continuity, if not of development. Auden's early hard lines soon disappear; the enthusiastic employment of forms and conceits continues, but now with too much ease and fluency. The struggle to find 'an altering speech for altering things' has been won, but at great cost. A sort of monumental calm descends over Auden's poetry in the forties. Where in his early poetry he gave his general statements a concrete etymology, in his later poetry that happy union of the actual and the ideal, that line which crosses precariously between the particular image and the general intent, becomes too stylish and too explicit. His poetry becomes a manual of dexterous techniques. All the work has been done, and he need only stand back and let the verse create itself in a succession of jokes, imprecations and subordinate clauses:

> As I stand awake on our solar fabric
> That primary machine, the earth, which
>   gendarmes, banks
>   And aspirin presuppose
> On which the clumsy and the sad may all
>   sit down . . .

As always, the tone remains easy, the enjambements assured. In the poems of what might be called his 'middle period' – 'In Praise of Limestone' being a sufficiently familiar example – a number of clauses, each containing an ascertainable and readily comprehensible image, are linked loosely together within the harmonics of an established tone. Nothing is disordered; nothing can go wrong. In the end, though, this 'tone', that particularly English quality which Auden ended up by calling 'common sense', came to dominate whatever Auden had to say. When Auden's poetic strategies became clear, his forms became harder and more predictable, his range of subjects more solipsistic and quirky. He either had something, or nothing, to say. What he actually said it *with* was of lesser consequence, and so he was always seduced by a trite phrase or an easy rhyme:

> Admirer as I think I am
> Of stars that do not give a damn
> I cannot, now I see them, say
> I missed one terribly all day . . .

His easy success, and his late decline into amusing doggerel, are part of the same movement. His is a case of the individual talent, to use an antique distinction, which matures at the expense of the tradition. So it is that early influences in his work are minimal or concealed and that, in his later poetry, the language degenerates and the 'I' becomes at once more insistent and more precarious. As his messages and private codes deserted him, so his language became drained and lifeless. Politics was an early and useful disguise but, when that failed him, he turned for an alibi to that most unpoetic of pursuits, Religion.

When Auden 'got' religion, he explicitly devalued poetry: 'That love, or truth in any serious sense/Like orthodoxy, is a reticence . . .' And of course 'Anything will do for children/Made in God's image . . .' Poetry becomes a pastime, a series of Horatian exercises to keep one's end up – rather like doing crossword puzzles. 'So thinking he returned to duty, reclaimed by the actual world where time is real and in which, therefore, poetry can take no interest.' There are some things, then, which are either unsayable, like 'love' and 'truth', or else not worth the trouble of saying. And so Auden slowly pushed himself and his art into a corner – 'About the House', as it turned out. This may seem strange after the heady political commitment of his early years, when poetry was an instrument of belief, but it was natural for him to abscond from History in order to nurse his private pleasures. Poetry was always concerned with instruction or with entertainment – always, in fact, with something other than itself. Auden's progress from politics to quietism, from Marxism to Religion, is not the progress of a poet but of a moralist.

And so in his late poetry there is the same easiness and fluency, but now they have been entrusted to those small topics which Auden came to celebrate: occasional feasts, limericks, moral homilies, private musings on the weather or the state of his domestic life:

> as if you didn't know
> that in a permissive age
> so rife with envy
> a housekeeper is harder
> to replace than a lover . . .

It is dreadful stuff, and only in the context of over-ambitious American rhetoric and tawdry English poetasting would his last poems seem interesting. But he had once been a strong poet, and to the end he remained a significant 'case'. His real measure has yet to be taken; it is the major merit of this painstaking and thorough edition that, perhaps despite himself, Mr Mendelson has taken the first step in the re-evaluation of Auden's flawed but notable achievement.

18 September 1976

16

Ezra Pound: The Last Rower

C. David Heymann

It is natural and just that Ezra Pound should baffle his critics. He is the greatest poet of the modern era, he was also a rabid anti-Semite who became either clown or traitor. The distinction, however, interests only biographers or liberals – the life is now unimportant and only the work remains. Mr Heymann concedes his special interest in the subtitle of his study, 'a political profile'. But although this suggests a unity of purpose if not of design, that obvious division between the life and the work is everywhere apparent and never resolved.

Pound was always possessed by the idea of himself. As a young poet he was no better than many of his contemporaries but, unlike them, he had an immense power of will which he was not slow to exercise. He was self-conscious enough to see himself as a cultural force, and he had determination enough to make himself one. His conspiratorial instincts gave him the authority with which to press the claims of Eliot and Joyce, while providing him the incidental pleasure of offending the literary establishment – then, as now, worthless. When he left London for a greener Paris, London ceased to be the literary capital of Europe and has never been since.

Mr Heymann deals with these matters carefully and well, but he is clearly more interested in Pound's sudden involvement with public affairs, and particularly with the simplistic doctrine of Social Credit. Pound assumed that he could extend his conspiratorial perceptions – he was always eager to discover the 'secret history' of human affairs – into political and social matters, but he failed. He was effective within a literary culture for one essential reason: he had a superb ear for the language, which he could instinctively trust and which always substantiated his judgements. But he had no such solid and incontrovertible perception in political matters, and his sharpness quickly degenerated into vituperation and, eventually, into a form of paranoia.

All the evidence which Mr Heymann has accumulated, from diaries and letters, suggests that Pound started to go 'mad' in the mid-thirties when he was living in Paris. A poet goes 'mad' when he misjudges his tone, and then the language turns against him. Pound's pushy, pseudo-Western barbarisms had revalued the European tradition. There are a great many virtues in being practically self-educated when confronted by a literary establishment which, for all its learning, cannot tell a good poem from a bad. But that blunt and hectoring manner could not and did not work in political and economic affairs. Pound had turned without pausing from aesthetics to morals, and the same voice will not do for both. As long as he confines himself to the role of money and the elements of Social Credit, the collapse of his language is not immediately noticeable; money, for Pound, assumes much the same role as poetry – being an emblem of moral behaviour, a token of a nation's value rather than the value itself. But that same tone could not sustain his political and social concerns, where the moral life of a civilization is directly concerned. His vigour turned into rigidity, his sharp language into a monstrous rhetoric:

> a dung flow from 1913
> and, in this, their kikery functioned,
>   Marx, Freud and their american beaneries
> Filth under filth . . .

From Heymann's careful documentation of the period before the war, it is clear that Pound was no mere eccentric dazed by events. From the beginning he was closely involved with Fascism and quickly became one of its more ferocious publicists:

> What I am ready to fight against is having ex-European Jews making another peace worse than Versailles . . . Roosevelt is more in the hands of the Jews than Wilson was in 1919 . . . But you let the Jew in and the Jew rotted your Empire . . . I am not arguing. I am just telling you, one of these days you will have to start thinking about the problem of race, breed, preservation.

Thus Pound broadcast from Italy to the Allied nations. Mr Heymann has collected a great deal of such material, and a picture of Pound emerges as a sycophant, a self-publicist, a bore continually bombarding the Italian authorities with absurd proposals, a collaborator whom even the Italians sometimes despised: 'It is an eccentric plan conceived by a foggy mind, lacking all sense of reality.' Even later, when the

Allies were methodically destroying Italy, Pound saw the futility of his efforts but did not renounce his grandiloquence. He was, he said, 'the last American living the tragedy of Europe'.

All this persiflage neglects, of course, the paradoxically fine poetry which Pound was writing during these years, a poetry which will survive when the work of his saner and more respectable contemporaries has been forgotten. Although Heymann has written a conventional biography, Pound's language keeps breaking in, and a critical study ought to complement the political one. Here is a note which Pound wrote from the mental hospital, St Elizabeth's, where he was incarcerated:

> grey mist barrier impassible (*sic*)
>   ignorance absolute
>
>   anonyme
> futility of might have been
> coherent areas
>
>   constantly
>   invaded
>
> aiuto

This is not even good verse and, more importantly, it was not meant to be. Pound had devalued speech by his constant rhetoric, and for a while language repaid him when he lost control of his words – he, 'the lord of his work and master of utterance'. His daughter Mary saw it clearly, and makes more sense of some of the *Cantos* than many critics: 'He was losing ground, I now see, losing grip on what most specifically he should have been able to control, his own *words*.' When Pound denied his vocation, when he became a traitor to himself, the aesthetic consequences were as inevitable and as severe as the public ones.

But Ezra Pound never lost his self-possession. Mr Heymann, in the aftermath of Watergate, has been given access to Pound's FBI files and has come up with some inadvertent comedy as Pound faces his attorneys, judges and psychiatrists on his return to America as a traitor: 'He is abnormally grandiose, is expansive and exuberant in manner . . . he is, in other words, insane and mentally unfit for trial.' More stupidity from a Dr Overholser: '. . . it is quite obvious that the man has always been unusually eccentric through the years. He has undoubtedly a high regard of his own opinion . . .' It is the great merit of this book that Heymann brings together for the first time all of the official papers, and so gives a solid sense of the wall which was gradually being built around Ezra Pound. He was imprisoned in St Elizabeth's in 1946 and released, after a decade of protests, in 1958. He was then writing some of the outstanding passages of the *Cantos*; when he arrived in Italy from America, he gave the Fascist salute. Then in Mr Heymann's phrase, 'the great silence descended in the summer of 1961'. But Pound did not retreat into wordlessness before he had marched at the head of a neo-Fascist rally in Rome. The contradictions remain, and confuse the biographers.

But it is possible that Pound's frantic activities are merely part of his ceaseless, futile attempt to give his life the resonance and self-certainty which his language possessed from the start. The finest poet will, ideally, look for the symmetry between word and meaning, the ideal union which imparts 'meaning' to life, and life to the language. Poets are alone in their constant attempt to return to the paradisaical myth of that time when name and essence were one. That paradise haunts both Pound's life and his work. He had tried to bring the word and the meaning, the name and the object, together in an enormous synthesis – but this is never possible in a world of rhetoric and lies, of bad verse and worse men. And so he abandoned speech, the message of that world, and made the best of a now broken language:

> That I lost my center
>   fighting the world.
> The dreams clash
>   and are shattered –
> and that I tried to make a paradiso terrestre.

25 September 1976

17

Yeats

Frank Tuohy

Biography is a substitute in this country for critical thought. If it is done at all, it should be done quickly. Unfortunately, Yeats is a gift to the prolix biographer: he was what he seemed to be. He was all personality and no character. Most good poetry springs directly from false emotion, and so Yeats was doubly blessed with his Irish grandiloquence and his natural propensity for rhetoric. But Frank Tuohy has written a brief and astute biography, cutting through the flummery in ways that our better known and more long-winded biographers might study.

The facts of Yeats's life are amply documented elsewhere, and Tuohy has shifted the conventional balance somewhat by dwelling upon Ireland and Yeats's Irish context; it is as if that nation's appalling history were the ventriloquist for those rotund stanzas, those souped-up images, those magnificent hyperboles. Jack Yeats had said of his son, and of the Pollexfens from which he came, 'to give them voice is like giving voice to the sea-cliffs'. The absurd histrionics of the father are an apt prologue for the son's career. Yeats was tone-deaf, and suffered from defective sight: the landscape he conjured up, that 'Ireland' he suffered like a bad tooth, was a convenient camouflage for his persistent self-absorption. He discovered another particle of himself in every poem that he wrote.

So it is a little wayward of Mr Tuohy to concentrate upon the external events of Yeats's life, when such matters as theosophy and Irish politics were part only of the great swooping homewards of Yeats's egotism. He had what Conor Cruise O'Brien has more circumspectly called 'pride and prudence'. He attached himself to the Golden Dawn because it made complex events blindingly simple, while appealing at the same time to his anti-Englishness (the 'occult' has always been used by gifted poets as a way of kicking against the established pricks). Yeats treated political matters as a branch of aesthetics, and his involvement with Fascism in the thirties was, in this sense, predictable. It appealed to his temperament, to that early desire to 'hammer my thoughts into a unity', and that was enough.

All great poets are authoritarians – whether it be Pound's Fascism, Eliot's royalism or Auden's early Marxism. Politics are merely a form of gratification for the troubled self, thus acting as a substitute for poetry when the verses run dry. The passion for social order is particularly strong in Yeats, and it is the merit of Tuohy's biography that he documents this while at the same time providing an entertaining but convincing picture of the eccentrics, madmen and knaves who inhabited Yeats's Ireland. He is also a sharp judge of literary matters when he cares to be, as with this comment on some of Yeats's more obscure stanzas: 'How can one suspend disbelief when one has no clear idea what is being believed?' That could have been engraved on the stone in Drumcliff churchyard.

23 October 1976

18

The Autumn of the Patriarch
Gabriel García Márquez

Márquez, despite a critical reputation hovering somewhere between Joyce and Nabokov, is not a 'difficult' novelist by any standard. There is much less in his work than meets the horrified eye, as it swivels over acres of close print, over sentences which arch and loop through clauses and subordinate clauses, over an 'I' which can change into a 'he' or even a 'you' at a moment's notice, and over time-scales which shift continually and inexplicably. But all this is an illusion. It is hard to think of a more orthodox novelist, or of one who uses so many conventional tricks to make so many conventional points.

For an apparently 'revolutionary' writer, it is odd how smoothly *The Autumn of the Patriarch* slips into the usual fantasies of power. The patriarch himself is General Rodrigo de Aguilar, a standard South American dictator who has ruled, it seems, from the beginning of time over a country which has become the natural prey to fantasies and illusions of an alarming kind. Nothing seems real any more, except the shapes and sizes of the general's obsessions. These are all carefully detailed as the novel shifts forwards and backwards through innumerable atrocities, miracles and governmental crises. Two thousand children are murdered, whole settlements are razed to speed the general's progress, his licensed butcher tortures and beheads thousands of presumably innocent people, and finally the sea itself vanishes. The only figure to emerge from this gloom relatively unscathed is the general himself; his death, differently described, opens each section of the narrative, his fears are romantically evoked, his physical presence drooled over.

It might be, of course, that the book itself is another of the general's fantasies: there are concubines everywhere, the general's physical double (who is eventually murdered) is a perfect ingredient in a paranoid's vision, and all madmen linger upon the panorama of their death – especially when it is accompanied by general decay. Without his obsessions to unbalance the narrative, in fact, no particular incident stands out from the run of corruption and failure. Everything is simply part of the weightless procession of the novel's rhetoric. Rhetoric is, after all, simply the pomp and circumstance of language – and so it is inevitable that a narrative of this kind should take as its real subject the glorious and diverse appearances of power, everything that is easy and hollow. The book is the equivalent of a bad film stunningly photographed.

Márquez actually manages to turn murder and torture into aesthetic phenomena: '. . . lulled by the sound of the trail of yellow leaves of his autumn of pain which had begun forever that night with the smoking bodies and the puddles of the red moon of the massacre.' All the emphasis of the sentence is upon the general's private suffering, and none at all upon the public killings. It might be possible to make a political point here about the nature of Márquez's real allegiances, but I won't. The critical point, in any case, is less libellous. His prose is descriptive and never active; it is all adjectives and no verbs. It acquiesces in what it describes simply by embroidering; it doesn't alter the perspective by definition or analysis. This makes even the characterization of the general a relatively easy matter – he has, it seems, a fixation upon his mother and a pressing need to replace love by power. Everybody has said that, and most have said it better.

And so although other critics have dwelt lovingly upon the novelty and the difficulty of Márquez's 'vision', it is all familiar enough. Woolf did it; Firbank did it better; Joyce never stopped doing it. Márquez's is the pop version, and so it is readily accessible to journalists and academics. The journalists swoop upon his South American connection as though this were some guarantee of his good intentions; the academics admire anything which is twenty years out of date, and which has to be translated. No doubt Márquez, already one of 'the great writers of our time' according to the blurb, will get his Nobel Prize.

30 April 1977

19

The Castle of Crossed Destinies
Italo Calvino

People play card-games with each other because they enjoy winning, but one plays cards with oneself only out of necessity. Patience, as its name suggests, is positively Buddhist in its emphasis on vacancy, and absolute boredom. The Tarot, a gaudy set of cards generally used for prophecy, is more complicated. One look at the eerie figures of the pack – the Popess, the Page of Coins, the Hanged Man – is enough to make it clear that these emblems are so embellished and so abstracted that they have become religious figures of unusual power. But the cards also represent early forms of narrative – the story of the past as well as of the future – and it is in this sense that Italo Calvino has used them in his latest book.

His narrative is plain enough to begin with: 'In the midst of a thick forest, there was a castle that gave shelter to all travellers overtaken by night on their journey . . .' The castle itself is in a state of shocking disrepair, and all of its inhabitants are mute – European critics will be asking themselves, is this an allegory for the state of the novel? Perhaps it is. In any case, the only way in which the travellers can communicate is through the cards of a Tarot pack. They use the fantastical set painted by Bonifacio Bembo for the Dukes of Milan, and their stories take on in turn the weird and evocative colour of these representations. The first of them, 'The Tale of the Ingrate', seems at first to admit of a literal meaning. But very quickly any one-to-one relation of the picture to the story gets lost in a maze of possible but conflicting interpretations. As the cards are laid down upon the table, other stories begin to interesect with the first until there is no knowing where one begins and the other ends.

By the time the book is finished, and Calvino has changed the venue of the rituals to a tavern, the possibilities seem exhausted. By some chance juxtaposition all of the familiar narratives have come forward: Hamlet, Oedipus, Lear, Parsifal, Macbeth, Roland and Faust jostle among the columns of gold and green. So the stories of the Tarot are at least as familiar as the emblems of religious painting, in the sense for example that 'Saint George can be painted without believing too much in him, believing only in painting and not in the theme'. And Calvino believes in his writing, not in the stories; as a consequence his prose has a peculiarly weightless quality which the translator, William Weaver, has beautifully evoked. Calvino just concerns himself with the various orders and sequences which he has so assiduously and so obsessively created out of the cards. But by establishing such a distinctive set of relations, by forming circles and squares and double axes, the threat of disorder is – to use the old phrase – always on the cards: 'Roland descended into the chaotic heart of things, the centre of the square of the cards and of things, the point of intersection of all possible orders.' It sounds like a very long novel.

In fact it is as if the necromancer and the clairvoyant, by using the Tarot, can achieve what the novelist always fails to:

> . . . our elderly neighbour, now that he finds a deck of tarot in his hands, wants to compose again an equivalent of the Great Work, arranging the cards in a square in which, from top to bottom, from left to right and vice versa, all stories can be read, his own included.

But the Great Work slips away so easily, since the cards themselves are signs to be read only in relation to each other. They are, literally, 'about' nothing: 'The kernel of the world is empty, the beginning of what moves in the universe is the space of nothingness . . .'

Some of the stories in the book culled from this knowledge are very elegant, and Calvino's fables seem to be perched precariously beyond the confines of ordinary narrative. In his previous book, *Invisible Cities*, a traveller returns with stories of eerie and enormous cities which bear some relation to those we know but somehow exist outside ordinary time and space. And so it is in this book: the fables which

Calvino has rescued from the ultimate chaos of Tarot-playing are strange mixtures of the ancient and the modern, of solemn mythical personages and Calvino himself, pictured as the King of Clubs and clutching a gigantic pencil. The intervention of this card into the game allows Calvino to enter his main theme, which is the fortune of writing.

He should, in his picture, have been blindfolded – at least temporary blindness would have saved him from the glare of the scattered cards. A random inventiveness will easily collapse, one picture changing into another picture. But there is no way of telling 'his own' story, since each person's narrative becomes mingled with all the others, and there is no one smart enough to trace it back to its origin. If the Tarot represents all possible lives and possible fates, then the narrator will eventually come to a complete halt: '. . . objects and destinies are scattered before you, interchangeable and unchanging, and he who believes he makes decisions is deluded.'

And so *The Castle of Crossed Destinies* is elegant, tightly con-structed and totally self-enclosed. The only thing to do is to pack up the cards, leave the castle which may or may not represent the novel, throw out the Tarot pack which is pretty but in the end stale and pointless, forget about religion and all of its pagan substitutes, and begin another book. And this, I imagine, is what Calvino is now doing: '. . . to begin writing again as if I had never written anything before.'

14 May 1977

20

Gaudete
Ted Hughes

God knows I must be a weak little helpless person, but I can't take all this suffering any more. Every time I open Ted Hughes's latest book, there is something about testicles, bone tissue or vomit. It's like watching *General Hospital*. And quite frankly what adds to my guilt about this cowardice is the fact that Hughes is only doing it for my *benefit*. He's not doing it for fame or for the money – his royalties are probably going to some important Wildlife Fund – he's only doing it to *help* us. There he is, hunched over his electric typewriter, the hair falling across his burning eyes, muttering all those Anglo-Saxon rhythms in his rugged regional accent: he has taken all the suffering of the world upon his shoulders and is offering it to us, for only £4.50! This is what life is all about! It's magnificent! He must be the greatest poet of his age!

At least that is what the newspaper reviewers have been saying for some years now, ever since I was a boy and Ted Hughes was telling us the real truth about pigs, crows, elephants and jaguars. The reviewers liked him so much that even the academics felt they were missing something: he was put on the syllabus. But nothing could have prepared them for all the marvellous new anguish which Hughes has discovered; suddenly, with *Gaudete*, we are in man's country again where the true violence is. We began with *Fantasia*, and now we've got *The Exorcist*. Here at last it all hangs out, all the 'buckets of fresh blood', 'organs of horrific energy' and 'uncontrollable eyes'. Michael Winner would love this book.

Gaudete is really just an old-fashioned hymn in praise of violence. Here we have the famous poet, the unacknowledged legislator of his race, writing about men and women as though they had just stepped out of Pavlov's cages for a quick stroll around the cemetery. On the first page a Reverend Lumb finds himself in a mass grave, among eye-pits and animal tendons and lizard figures; from pages 23 to 131 his demonic double assaults a number of parishioners in a number of ways; on page 35, Major Hagen clubs his pet labrador to death; on page 45 a young girl hangs herself; and on page 132 there is an orgiastic ritual, Hollywood-style, in the basement of the local church where the ladies seem actually to be imitating Hughes's earlier poems by putting on animal masks. At last Hughes has learnt the lesson: suffering and pain are always boring, unless they can be made shocking.

In fact I think Ted Hughes simply wants to entertain us with some ordinary sex and violence, and it's rather unfair of his publishers to break the book up into a number of incomplete lines and describe it as 'a strange and powerful new poem'. Poetry it isn't:

> Lumb's face
> Contorts, transforming
> To a grotesque of swollen flesh

> A glistening friar-fat
> Gargoyle of screaming or laughter . . .

Something has obviously gone wrong. Hughes was able to drag all those dumb animals into his act because they couldn't fight back. But it is one thing to treat animals as though they had human characteristics, it's quite another to treat human beings as if they were animals and reducing them, like a butcher, to lumps of tissue, bone, blood and sex. When a writer is possessed by images of gratuitous violence and sexual mayhem, he is forced to reduce both his language and his theme to lumpish vehicles of his obsessions. For all the reviewers' talk about 'apocalypse' and the 'human condition', it's really as if Ted Hughes had just rifled through a bestiary to pick up his characters. When a man talks about love, and ends up by writing pornography, it has to be assumed that his writing has failed him. And here it has: there isn't a good line in the book.

In fact the writing is so consistently heavy-handed, so trite and so clumsy that it has taken Hughes's rather elderly admirers a real effort of will to admire it. But they have managed the trick in the past: heavy writing can always be mistaken for serious writing, just as rhetoric can generally pass for poetry in a poor light. But surely not this time:

> Warms his calming hands
> Beneath her amply stylish coat.
>
> Her nerve-harrowed face
> Crisping towards a coarse harvest handsomeness
> Rests on his shoulder . . .

It all sounds as if it had been lifted from a handbook for poets, a thesaurus of phrases only to be used in a real emergency. I was trying to remember when I last came across verse of this kind, and then it came to me: William McGonagall! Our taste in suffering may have changed – Hughes was called a 'survivor poet' and the poet of apocalypse, whereas Mr McGonagall specialized in train crashes on a large scale – but the clumsy rhetoric is much the same. *Gaudete* is a modern, and much longer, 'Tay-Bridge Disaster'. The prose is tired and hectoring, the verses are flaccid, and the lines so loosely arranged that they flop on top of each other.

I do hope schoolmasters and provincial lecturers wake up to all this before our young people get the notion that suffering is somehow 'important', and that the worship of pain is the only true worship. Bad poetry can be corrosive, at least for a while.

11 June 1977

21

A Victim of the Aurora
Thomas Keneally

Although the publishers describe this remarkable novel as 'Thomas Keneally's first detective story', it effectively marks the demise of that debased and flatulent genre. The villain, after all, is 'the aurora' itself and the victim is never specified; it might even turn out to be the novel itself. It is set at the close of the sticky Edwardian era and so, theoretically, it might be described just as easily as a historical novel – but, like all of Keneally's work it actually subverts European history (Keneally is an Australian writer, and this plays a large though unacknowledged role in his writing) by bringing to it alien and more vigorous perceptions. A group of Edwardians are travelling to the Antarctic on the New British South Polar Expedition; the King dies when they are isolated on the ice, and so in a sense they become the last Edwardians on earth, persisting in rituals which have already become outmoded. In Keneally's hands the historical novel is redeemed as the raw materials of the past are turned into a kind of fable.

These blinding metaphysical matters don't mean that Keneally is forgetful of technical considerations. He astutely aligns the imaginative content of historical fiction with the pert structure of the detective thriller, and by conflating them creates a new thing. Victor Henneker, a homosexual journalist who is reporting on the Expedition, is brutally murdered and left on the ice – and the narrator sets out to uncover the identity of the murderer. A conventional detective thriller would, at this point, assume that murder is as much part of the orderly business of life as cooking or making the bed: it has to be assumed that murders are rational, because they are always solved by the use of reason. Crime has its cultural codes and conventions, and if they were ever to be broken, it would be difficult to know what 'crime' actually was. An act becomes a 'murder' only when it fits neatly into an ordered scale of human behaviour.

But nothing is ordered at the Pole: these rather prim Edwardian gentlemen are surrounded by packs of ice whose natural processes remain mysterious to them, above their heads gleams the aurora itself which defies their powers of observation and description, they discover a sodomite among them, and then they learn that they are being watched by a castaway from an earlier expedition who has abandoned human habitation but who invades their lives like some inescapable wraith. They are, in other words, marooned; and when their world of domestic ritual – it's all very much like a small public school – and scientific observation is shattered by the murder of Henneker, they must all assume that some external force is responsible. Crime, and madness, have to be banished if they are to preserve their own sanity: '"I won't admit to them how Victor died. It is information that would make us barbarians." I felt a rush of panic at being elected to this inner committee of three. "Why?" I asked, "Why plague *me* with the truth."' But when the narrator assiduously follows the normal rules of detective fiction, the consequences begin to corrode the safe world which such fiction must always adopt.

But this is not a weak-kneed or vapidly ironic handling of the techniques of English fiction – that kind of novel is only being written by teachers of English in provincial universities. Thomas Keneally is a powerful and subtle writer, whose simplicity of style must never be confused with simplicity of meaning. He actually uses the Polar Expedition as a way of breaking several historical codes, as the Edwardian age vanishes as mysteriously as the aurora itself.

That age was, if you like, the age of appearances, of decorum. And so it was also the age which enshrined shame as one of its driving principles. Shame is that which must be concealed and, in this way, it acts as a moral force – as a fuel which can only be burnt up by effort and aspiration, rather than a set of obsessions which can be exorcised by analysis. All of the characters in this book suffer from varieties of guilt, but they expiate it in the endless cataloguing of Antarctic life, and in restless voyages across the ice.

The book is full, then, of extraordinary images and implications. In all of Thomas Keneally's work there is an attempt at what I have called the subversion of received European history by rendering it both more exactly – his sense of place is remarkable – and more luridly. It is part of the strange darkness of the Australian imagination. The colour, the vivid imaginings, the rhetorical simplicity of his evocation of the past have to do with Keneally's own manner, but also with a quality in Australian writing: its bleakness and its blank pessimism. And so the image of the Antarctic castaway is the most powerful in the book. He suffers, too, from a peculiarly advanced form of guilt – 'You see, it's a . . . a . . . an unclean practice what I've done. It needs very special acts of purification' – but he vanishes before he can be exorcised.

Madness is not that easily expiated; the more these Edwardians turn away from it, the closer it will eventually come to them and then they will have to deal with it madly. Although Victor's murder is technically solved, its reverberations continue. The final solution of the crime is terrible in itself and terrible in its implications. It is the strength of this book that both possibilities are brought into the light: 'It was the act that rendered the condition of the century terminal. Nothing ever since has surprised me.'

3 September 1977

22

Sade, Fourier, Loyola
Roland Barthes

There is a sentence of Nietzsche which hangs over French criticism: 'I fear we are not getting rid of God because we still believe in grammar.' Roland Barthes has altered the perception a little and now it seems, after reading his books, that we won't be rid of sex until we stop believing in language altogether. It can become an incestuous and ridiculous exercise, this pursuit of metaphors and analogous myths, but Barthes' writing is so clear and bracing that he manages to avoid the preciosity of which some of his English imitators are more than capable. Despite his daunting reputation, he writes the crispest prose of all those French 'post-structuralists' – Lacan and Derrida, to name thirty-four – who have woken up to find themselves famous in the Anglo-Saxon world.

Sade, Fourier, Loyola was published in France six years ago, and so it arrives here in translation with some of its bloom rubbed off. It is a witty and colourful book (comparing him with our resident academic critics is like comparing Velázquez with a street artist), and readily accessible to anyone who has the faintest notion of recent French criticism. The book traces the work of the title's three 'founders of language' – not those mythical Amazonians who uttered sounds and found them harmonious, but three despised and excessive votaries of the written word who liberate language from its solid referential powers by isolating it, by revealing it, by taking pleasure in it. Barthes has a simple formula: 'Not to tell, but to tell that one is telling'. And so the written word, when it has been fully revealed, cannot be scrutinized for moral soliloquies or for doctrinal comfort – the sole pleasure is the pleasure of the text. In *Sade, Fourier, Loyola* that idea of pleasure is extended.

On the face of it the three of them – the bad, the mad and the sad – have little in common except that for Barthes they are 'logothetes' or creators of language. The central fact of Sade's work is not its sexual or violent content, which suffers from *politesse* and is truly monotonous, but its language, which is continually interesting. Sex in fact becomes an imitation of language, since it is treated rhetorically: the oratorical and erotic codes 'form one same line, along which the libertine travels with the same energy'. A society which bans Sade's work is mistaking its nature because the books are strictly fabulous, impossible, unrealistic: 'Sade radically contrasts language with reality or, more precisely, he places himself at the sole instance of the "reality of language".' Just as sex is for Sade an exercise in methodology so Ignatius Loyola's *Exercises* mechanizes the devotional life, making it in a sense an adjunct to language. Loyola invents a grammar for deciphering the will of God and loads the devotee with the same constraints which Sade prescribes for his orgies: solitude, a set of fixed physical and mental gestures, a codified life of discipline and reason. As language loses its powers of reference, human beings are reduced in the same process to neutral and colourless ciphers.

In the work of Fourier, too, which Barthes sees as 'pure language', as lacking content, the social world is divided and arranged. In the utopian community of Harmony, pleasure is triumphant – the sea will be made of lemonade – but this pleasure can only be the result of calculation. The human community will be divided into a series of 'phalansteries', in which people with similar temperaments and needs will be distributed and combined. No doubt it is madness; Fourier's work destroys and reinvents everything; it has no recognizable relation to anything we know. Or it is, as Barthes would say, a triumph of language devoid of any political, scientific or theological content. To live in Harmony, of course, would be a hell as disagreeable as Sade's pits of perversion. It seems that language can only flourish, or be redeemed, in texts that obsessively constrain, codify and mechanize the human world. Perhaps only the obsessed – the obsessional neurotics, as the jargon goes – are in a position to understand language, since for them it is the only free and private space which remains.

This is where doubts about the Barthian analysis begin to grow. Although his identification of pleasure with the use of language leads to some extremely sharp and perceptive statements ('. . . neologism is an erotic act, which is why it never fails to arouse the censure of pedants'), his own work is, like that of Sade or Fourier, impossible. He is an inventor, not a critic or an exegete. He is a fabulist, ironically concealing himself by creating a number of theatrical arguments, a series of tableaux which are in fact created in his own image as much as that of the books he is ostensibly reading.

Throughout *Sade, Fourier, Loyola* he is recording his own journey through 'pleasure' (sexual, religious and literary enjoyment are all factitiously and, I suspect, too ostentatiously aligned), and his own anxieties about it. He protests too much about *jouissance*. By relentlessly defending the status of pleasure without responsibility (since responsibility is, after all, the moral *content* of pleasure), he is in no position to recognize permanent comfort in the content of language. It can be very reassuring to find meaning in our words – either as a political narrative, which confirms or revises our sense of ourselves, or as a story in which the ordinary self can be suspended as long as the narrative may last. To deny this is to deal in fables – and some of them privately inspired in ways that Barthes himself would probably not acknowledge.

15 October 1977

63

23

Joyce's Voices
Hugh Kenner

Professor Kenner has been serving up portions of James Joyce for many, many years; this time 'the voices', next time the ears or perhaps the nail-parings. But since the prose of *Ulysses* and *Finnegans Wake* resembles the American language in its infinite malleability and ultimate blandness, it is appropriate that it should have been finely ground in the mills of transatlantic exegesis. These republished lectures, though, are less exacting; apart from some interesting but inconclusive speculation about Joyce's muddled sense of his own identity (the syntax of his private letters is obscure, often to the point of illiteracy) and about the precise size and location of Leopold Bloom's non-existent watch, Hugh Kenner limits himself to a graceful and predictable tour round the estate.

The follies and gardens are, in this case, the words of *Ulysses*. Professor Kenner restates the fundamental, obvious but often unacknowledged fact about the book: it is made up of writings, not speech. Its world (although in truth there is no 'world', only a succession of sentences) exists through the mediation of language; *Ulysses* is part of the history of style, and can't be excavated by literary archaeologists in search of meanings, allegories or values. In literature such 'things' are quite properly reduced to words. Kenner makes the useful point that this represents the collapse of naturalism, of 'evidence carefully marshalled' by the narrator; just as Joyce perverts the role of the 'detached observer' of conventional fiction – there are an embarrassment of 'voices' in the text – he destroys the primacy of 'meaning' and of 'truth' as *the* characteristics of fiction. Things only exist in the context in which they are perceived – and for the novelist that can only mean the words on the page. There is no world waiting sullenly to be charted, no essential purpose to explicate, no significance to impart.

And so the characters of *Ulysses* are forced to play roles, uneasily adopting myths in order to explain themselves, continually announcing themselves to the world with rhetorical flourishes or baroque literary devices. In every case the reader will be forced against what Kenner calls the 'sheer stylistic arbitrariness' of it all. But it's necessary to be cautious at this point, since it is very easy to become fixated with 'style' – and with it the implication that there is some residual content to be unearthed if only we knew the place to dig. When Kenner talks about 'a contrast of textures' rather than 'a contrast of knowledges' we can forgive him the gracelessness of his phrases but not the inconsequence of his thought. *Ulysses*, more than any other contemporary novel, has represented to us the fact that there are no 'knowledges' recumbent in some timeless limbo, waiting to be woven into the 'textures' of language. The texture of language is precisely the knowledge that it carries, just as 'understanding' cannot be imagined outside the physical processes of the cerebellum.

As a proponent of style, however, Professor Kenner is singularly careful about his own. He specializes in dazzlingly modest exegesis, and tries very hard to combine the rigour of the Anglo-Saxons with the rhetoric of the French. There are tacit obeisances through the book to Derrida and even, perhaps, Lacan – Kenner is now a professor at Johns Hopkins University, where the more grandiose critical tools are now the new instruments of obfuscation – but the text of *Ulysses* itself is, happily, never deformed or concealed in the process. Just as Joyce reintroduced rhetoric and myth to the domestic Edwardian world of his contemporaries, so Kenner is able to add a kind of Thomas Rymerian lustre to the tarnished vessels of literary criticism.

9 September 1978

24

A Lover's Discourse
Roland Barthes

La Rochefoucauld penetrated the heart of the mystery: 'Some people would never have been in love, had they never heard love talked about.' *A Lover's Discourse* investigates this paradox; how can individual human beings suffer the invasive powers of 'love' (so violently that the lover may even kill himself or the loved one) when the moods and codes of love are so impersonal, so familiar and so hackneyed? Even its most potent images tend to be trite, reflecting not the agony of the individual spirit but the blandishments of commercial entertainment. I am convinced that the lover's experience of loss and separation, for example, is coloured by those scenes of parting obligatory in the war films of the late forties and early fifties: the train pulling out of the platform, the wife or lover left behind, running after the train, the face behind the carriage window, the smoke and, sometimes, the rain. The lover will cry over this popular representation just as forcefully as he will lament his own condition; he may even insert himself into the scene in an act of vicarious homage, metaphorically standing on the platform as the train – the train 'of his life', as he might put it – pulls away from him. And yet why is it that he will willingly enter the banal and abstract repertoire of love's images, when his own plight must seem to him to be unique?

Roland Barthes dwells on this question here by considering, in a number of short essays, the vocabulary of love; words which haunt the lover – waiting, embrace, exile, silence, gossip, will-to-possess – are presented alphabetically to give at least the illusion of random objectivity. Physical sex is, literally, unspeakable and in its place M. Barthes unfolds its rhetoric; the lover, in the peculiarly vulnerable position of being 'in love', reaches out for these words as a camouflage and a defence, a carapace which does not have to include self-knowledge. Clichés, such as 'I am lost without you', are his one precious possession because they allow him to rise above any proper consideration of his own position. These words and phrases have existed before, and will exist after, the lover's predicament – and yet they can be used to sanction, justify and even explain that predicament. That is why the language of love is both so bland and so plangent, so familiar and yet so powerful, infinitely analysable in its shallowness; it is both a social artefact and a register of intimate feeling.

And so by tabulating this vocabulary of desire, intimacy and absence M. Barthes provides a complete and 'objective' picture of love, seen from a distance like some planet wandering towards earth; although we know that it may destroy us, we see it whole. But, in contrast, love's career follows a predetermined course: the first sight, the capture, the familiarity, and then the days of boredom, incomprehension and anxiety as the original image of the loved one fades. M. Barthes explores the stages and the declamations of this process, where the words are always fresh and yet always the same:

I make myself cry, in order to prove to myself that my grief is not an illusion: tears are signs, not expressions. By my tears, I tell a story, I produce a myth of grief, and henceforth I adjust myself to it . . .

A Lover's Discourse is a kind of mercurial elegy; in keeping with the simultaneously private and universal context of love, the book is both elaborately individual – with the syntactical ellipses and *longueurs* of Barthes' prose – and at the same time entirely anonymous. Anybody might have written it because it can, by its very nature, only repeat what has been said before, endlessly. As if in recognition of this, Barthes employs quite freely the words and sentences of other writers; and, since the roots of French theory (whether in Sartre or in more modish figures like Lacan) have always been orthodox and occasionally sentimental, it's quite natural that Barthes should want to use *Werther* as his principal source.

But the book is also the result of a private collusion, between the lover – the 'fragments' of whose 'discourse' are here exhibited – and the loved one who is called 'X'. Some extraordinary passion leaks through Barthes' lucid prose. But the impulse towards fiction, which is the conventional way of presenting such intractable material for public consumption, has become for M. Barthes the impulse towards organization. He is a novelist who cannot bring himself to write a narrative; the horror has been systematized alphabetically; his only real characters are his words. Instead of delineating his misfortune in the discursive terms of prose narrative, Barthes quarantines the signs and codes of love and covers them with ice – he isolates and sterilizes these words so successfully that their internal relations, which ordinarily are blurred by conventional ways of seeing, become clear. And 'love' itself is transfigured in the process:

For a hundred years literary madness has been thought to consist in Rimbaud's 'Je est un autre': madness is an experience of depersonalization. For me as an amorous subject, it is quite the contrary: it is becoming a *subject*, being unable to keep myself from doing so, which drives me mad. *I am not someone else*: that is what I realize with horror.

31 March 1979

67

25

Chaucer's Knight: The Portrait of a Medieval Mercenary

Terry Jones

Yesterday's heroes become, of course, today's villains or nonentities; every one of them, from Errol Flynn to Scott of the Antarctic, is so investigated and analysed that only the siftings of ordinariness remain. The quondam 'pillars' of the so-called 'establishment' are, in their turn, discovered to be treacherous or corrupt little men. And now Terry Jones, in *Chaucer's Knight*, has taken that paradigm of noble virtue – the 'verray parfit, gentil knyght' of *The Canterbury Tales* – and shown him to be a brutal and untrustworthy mercenary, a kind of fourteenth-century Callan devoted to looting and killing.

It had to happen. Literary scholarship is not an occluded science, an activity reserved for the cloister. It provides an image of the age's grimace – it has, in fact, become an activity too topical to be left to the scholars. And so it is pleasant to see Mr Jones, a member of the Monty Python team, rushing into print, wielding footnotes and brandishing authorities to prove that the Knight was a 'male chauvinist' and a social climber. It may not be a very complex theory, but it is an unusual one. And Mr Jones is pugnacious – and convincing – in its defence. He takes all of the accepted interpretations of *The Canterbury Tales* and discards them, shred by shred. It is always good to find an interested reader who is ready, and able, to puncture received academic wisdom: 'The claim by Muriel Bowden,' he writes, 'that Chaucer uses "worthy" to mean "brave" in his translation of Boethius's *De Consolatione* is based on a misunderstanding of the Latin *valentia*.'

Solemn observers might mutter something about the decline of our culture, in which television comics can inherit the mantle of scholarship and, what is more, wear it with some aplomb. And students yet to be born will read Jones's description of Chaucer, as 'a concerned, committed writer', and date it with uncanny accuracy to the period of the late seventies. But, for the moment, Mr Jones's book is entertaining and, to some extent, plausible.

In less concerned and committed times than ours, of course, the Knight was seen as a chivalric emblem, embodying truth and steadfastness, honour and virtue. Such abstractions were once useful and effective (in swaying, for example, the more gullible sections of the population) – and, since literary criticism tends to reflect life rather than literature, the academics enshrined them in their textual apparatuses. But now all knights, and abstractions, are diminished; Mr Jones has written a plain man's guide to the nobility. The Chaucerian paradigm is described as both greedy and treacherous; an opportunist who participated in massacres; a pirate who pillaged even Christian cities; a mercenary bought, even, by the Arabs. It sounds too bad to be true, but there is a great deal to be said for Jones's version. His analysis of Chaucer's text is painstaking, his pursuit of the historical examples is thorough, his conclusions appropriate if somewhat pedestrian. The new Chaucer is cynical and sarcastic, an exploder of myths, a natural democrat who despises tyrants and those men, like the Knight, who serve them for money.

But the old Chaucer was, in fact, a poet – no doubt able to hold various incompatible theories at once, and engaged upon a long poem that brings together several kinds of language, like a sequence of notes played on the same piano. Terry Jones may be able to prove to his, and even our, satisfaction that the Knight of the *General Prologue* is a common mercenary; but it does not necessarily follow that Chaucer is therefore engaged in parody or satiric description at his expense. Chaucer is not Plautus, nor is he Lytton Strachey. To see him only in this context is to flatten his language until it becomes the blunt instrument of 'realism'; Chaucer's Knight can be both virtuous and treacherous, mercenary and chivalrous. The language of poetry is not the language of exposé.

The Knight's Tale suffers, for similar reasons, in Jones's hands. This elaborate narrative of Palamon and Arcite fighting over Emily, with Theseus deliberating in the background, has previously been seen as a flawed and mercurial courtly romance; Jones describes it as 'a barrack-room brawl dressed up in the fine rags of pageantry' and, later, as 'long-winded, sententious waffle'. All this on the assumption that the Knight is an uneducated barbarian – and that Chaucer is being covertly witty. It would be the merest truism to note that the tale can soar above its teller. But even if the poem were a hymn to tyranny, as Jones claims, it would not, for that reason, be less powerful or less beautiful. The either/or approach to literature tends to neglect the genius, and look for the reporter or the ideologist. Chaucer's poem might be mimetic, farcical and idealized within the space of fifteen lines – and so, of course, might the Knight himself. And, at this point, criticism ought decently to bow out.

19 January 1980

Essays

26

The Slow Death of Academic Literary Criticism

At a time when frenzied letters are being written to *The Times* about the state of contemporary art criticism, it is as well to remember that there are far more severe critical problems elsewhere. Literary criticism – to take the most important but least discussed example – is now all but paralysed; this has nothing to do with book reviewers, who perform a useful public function and who, in any case, would never aspire to the dizzy ranks of 'the critics'. I am referring to those critics in the universities, who publish long articles in specialized journals, who write books about Henry James or Samuel Johnson; who, in short, are a cut above Grub Street and its environs. There has been nothing original from them in ten years. I have yet to read a contemporary academic critic who could write more intelligently, or read more carefully, than a good book reviewer. And I have yet to meet one who was not a willing slave to whatever ideological fashion currently holds the academies in thrall.

Cambridge University is a case in point. It was here that the 'study' of English literature was established, and where it has now degenerated into a number of academic squabbles over one trend or another: leading to confusion among the students and a general failure of nerve among the staff. Cambridge had, until recently, been the quiet home for liberal, humanist critics who wrote essays about *The Tempest* and, as far as I know, never did harm to a living soul. But their humanism got sloppier and sloppier, and the atmosphere changed. Socialism and sociology became fashionable, and there was a spate of Marxist critics who discussed books as though they were an adjunct to social theory. And now the French, or at least the disciples of the French, have arrived, armed with texts and meta-texts, ready to swear that theirs is the only way to read books. And when everyone else has lost their nerve, what could be more attractive than a fearfully rigid and complex set of instructions on how to read and how to write? For beleaguered academics, who don't know what they're doing or why they're doing it, it comes as an unexpected blessing. Why, it's like having Anglo-Saxon on the syllabus again.

This is, of course, an abbreviated history but something very much like it is the context for two books by two academics: *Explorations* by L. C. Knights and *The Unnatural Scene*, a study of Shakespeare's tragedies by Michael Long. There is one thing in these books which runs deeper than any differences of tone and method, although both men might deny it – it is Cambridge. The books are conceived, born and nurtured within that atmosphere, and it shows.

The central problem can be stated quite simply: what is this 'literature' which we take for granted, and what are its particular characteristics that make it susceptible of being taught and lectured upon? These questions lurk somewhere in most books of academic criticism, with the nagging doubt – that perhaps, after all, English literature is not really a university discipline – which must continually be allayed. So Mr Knights, in this civilized collection of essays upon a variety of literary topics, feels constrained to describe literature as a 'form of knowledge' and as 'an irreplaceable way of arriving at truths that are of the highest importance to us'. People who might then ask, what are these 'truths', need not stay for an answer because there isn't one. 'Truth' and 'knowledge' are suggested and never defined; they lend a spurious force to the critical argument, without at any time illuminating it.

Of course literary academics have always relied upon this imprecision to bolster their claims for their study, and in fact clumsiness and confusion can often be mistaken for virtues; it is the peculiar characteristic of literary studies that it can make large claims for itself as a 'form of knowledge' at the same time as it rejects any generalized or specialized investigations as being not concrete, not finely rendered, not humane. But the problem is larger than this. To describe literature as a form of knowledge, and then to leave the matter as vague as Mr Knights does, is to make a hostage to ideological fortune. A 'form of knowledge', which actually has no form whatever, is woefully ill-equipped to resist the blandishments of whatever sociological, ideological or critical fashions drift upon the scene. So it is that Marxism, structuralism, formalism, practical criticism, and even plain, old-fashioned humanism are purveyed in turn, according to the particular college, the politics and the age of the tutor, and the intelligence of the student.

Mr Knights is, I suspect, a plain old-fashioned humanist himself; his ideology comes out of Coleridge and Arnold and it is one that asserts such things as the 'unity' of a creative work and – more importantly – its moral usefulness. As Knights says, 'what, to put it crudely, its uses – moral, educational and even political – are'. Or, to put it even more crudely, if students come up to Cambridge to study literature, and I am being paid to teach them literature, well goodness me, it *has* to be useful. If it were not, the English faculty would fall like a pack of cards.

There is a larger point here, too, but it is difficult territory to cross within a short article: however much lecturers may discuss subtle moral complexities and delicacies of response, and however much Mr Knights may apologize in his book for seeming too 'cut-and-dried', to draw moral lessons or moral exempla – which, however refined and carefully phrased they may be, is exactly what academic critics try to do and like to do – is to devalue the written language and to turn it into a simple vehicle for the communication of certain human truths and human values. As Knights says of *The Tempest*, 'It helps us to face with something that is neither wistfulness nor despair the intractability and the limitations of life.' No wonder the academies are in confusion when literary critics can indulge in trite sermonizing, when a play is used as an anodyne, and when criticism becomes some sort of adjunct to moral philosophy. As long as creative writing is seen in this context, it remains subservient to any bright new entertaining theory which is imposed upon it; it is given no form of its own.

Michael Long is not a humanist, as far as one can tell these days, but he has adopted a quasi-scientific vocabulary which is very closely aligned to Knights's more urbane style. In Mr Long's book, there is again that constant emphasis upon the usefulness of what he and his colleagues are doing: 'making the experience of his [Shakespeare's] tragedies a kind of training in keenness of feeling, refinement of emotional response'. There was a time when only priests and psychologists performed this impractical task. And for Long, again, literary criticism becomes a vague substitute for sociology and ethical theory: 'The plays contain a finely realized understanding, basic to their tragic vision, of social distance and stratification systems, of ethnocentrism . . .' Poor Shakespeare; for Knights he becomes a theologian and for Long he turns into a sociologist. And creative writing, when seen in such aesthetic and moralistic terms, falls bound and gagged into the hands of academics with a job to do. No wonder that literary studies are falling apart; the sooner, the better.

6 March 1976

27

The Future of English Prisons

Prisons have, in a sense, survived by accident on the weary complicity between society and its outcasts. But the prison system has failed to halt the rise in crime, overcrowding has now stretched prisons beyond tolerable limits, and social changes have shattered the conventional features of prison life, producing bewilderment and frustration, forcing everyone in the prison service to re-examine the nature and usefulness of prisons as they now exist. Deterrence, containment, rehabilitation, retribution: which code-word will make sense of this huge and increasingly outmoded social institution?

In this context it is significant that, in my conversations with prison staff, the word 'punish' was rarely used. I would try to introduce it into conversation, only to be waylaid by 'man management', 'retraining', 'rehabilitation' – the bureaucratic language of power. 'The punishment stops at the court,' one prison governor explained, 'here we have to deal with the whole person.' Punishment, as a concept or as an actual presence, has been removed and in its place has been installed 'treatment' – a sometimes haphazard and often amateurish philosophy of personal development.

But although prison staff are not always the best people to supervise or assess such putative treatment, this is the point at which a prison acquires its identity. Regimes differ according to the nature of the 'treatment' proposed. Prisons are closed and secretive societies because it is only under these conditions, of complete submergence in the system, that the arduous processes of self-assessment and rehabilitation are supposed to do their work. Secure walls envelop the prisoner with society's will:

The ideal point of penalty today would be an indefinite discipline:

an interrogation without end, an investigation that would be extended without limit . . . the calculated leniency of a penalty that would be interlaced with the ruthless curiosity of an examination.

Michel Foucault, *Discipline and Punish*

Governors talk about 'my' prisoners. They are the property of the state and its representatives. They are there to be observed, tested, educated, put to work, trained to be better citizens. I also use them for my own purposes when three inmates are, at my request, brought into talk to me for the purposes of this article. It is always a question of 'them' and 'us'. And so the failure of the prison system is endemic; because of its nature, and because of the demoralizing effect it has upon its inmates, it can never hope to fulfil what is required of it – to make offenders in some way more responsible and self-reliant. It takes away the faculties and potentialities which it is supposed to be encouraging. 'You've only to look at the dark rings under everyone's eyes here,' one 'lifer' told me, 'to see how much frustration and tension you have to cope with here.' 'Banging up' – the locking away of inmates – is clearly an inefficient way of dealing with those who are unstable and weak. And since the vast majority of the prison population are drawn from the industrialized working class, inveigled into crime through social and economic circumstances rather than through any innate criminal predisposition, the forced proximity of such offenders is unlikely to have a salutary effect.

Under these circumstances, rehabilitation is a largely meaningless concept. I have yet to meet a prisoner who didn't treat it as a joke: 'They don't teach you to regret what you've done – they teach you not to get caught again.' It may also be that rehabilitation fails because it is placed in too narrow, or conventional, a context. In the nineteenth century, religious exhortation was seen as the key to the reformation of the prisoner; now it is work – 'productive', meaningless labour. One inmate is drilling holes in metal shelving; another is stencilling a sign saying 'HM Borstal'. 'I like my prisoners fit or dead,' one affable governor told me. No doubt the results of this forced labour are sometimes beneficial: the prisoner who is binding a copy of Sir Leon Radzinowicz's *The Growth of Crime* might join a firm of bookbinders on his release but, since he was by trade an interior decorator, this seems unlikely.

Coldingley Prison was built, in 1969, as an 'industrial prison' where 'the working day and the forty-hour week are declared to be inviolable'. It is efficient, profitable and well administered. One prisoner called it 'hell'; another was less flattering.

It should not be made a burden or imposed as a task. Whatever is so proposed presently becomes irksome: the mind takes an aversion to it, though before it were a thing of delight or indifference.

Locke, *On Education*

One prisoner at Coldingley worked in a large laundry, as part of an assembly line. Did he intend to work in a laundry on his release? He assumed I was joking. Most prisoners will, of course, go back to what they know best:

One of the main research projects at Coldingley is . . . to test the central idea or belief upon which the Coldingley regime was based – that of work having a rehabilitative effect upon prisoners. The reconviction studies to date indicate that there is no significant difference either in reconviction rate or speed of reconviction between Coldingley men and similar men in other prisons.

Coldingley – an Industrial Prison (Home Office pamphlet)

But industrialized labour is, nevertheless, declared to be 'inviolable'; although it has no tangible or beneficial effect upon prisoners, it is still considered to be the most salutary and important aspect of 'outside' life to be copied 'inside'. In this sense the prison system is a paradigm of modern society, since it represents that point at which social conventions are concentrated and enforced. The three regular features of prison life – the cell, the workshop, the hospital – are a microcosm of the ideally efficient, technocratic state (just as schools, hospitals and factories resemble prison life in certain of their aspects). For good or ill, prisons are not separate places but the invisible centre of a network of relationships which cover the whole of society. That is why no one can imagine a society *without* prisons. How we deal with our prisoners is, in one sense, a measure of how we deal with ourselves – hence prison reform has as long a history as prisons themselves. They have the unenviable task of being both the punitive element of the State and the keeper of its conscience.

Given this unfathomable but ineluctable necessity, it may be impossible (and perhaps even dangerous) to change the general nature of the prison regime. But it should at least be possible to remove those specific abuses which make life intolerable for both staff and inmates. It's clear, for example, that the Department of Health and Social Security should make specific provision for offenders who are mentally ill or emotionally disturbed; the prisons cannot cope with them. I have walked around the psychiatric ward of one prison hospital – the inmates are curled up in a self-induced stupor, locked behind bars which should not be there. It is important, also, that the secrecy which surrounds prison life should, as far as possible, be lifted. Prisoners are not bacilli to be sealed in tight containers. The whole system of parole needs further investigation since it contains elements of injustice and arbitrariness which are alien to the concepts of English law.

But the major and immediate effort should be directed towards alleviating the appalling overcrowding in the local prisons of this country – which, essentially, means a thorough examination of the status and the conditions of the petty offenders who make up the bulk of the prison population. Most attention has, in recent years, been given to the peculiar needs and problems of 'lifers' – murderers, rapists, terrorists, violent criminals and so on. They tend, after all, to be the more interesting 'cases', and their confinement constitutes the one unchallengeable function of the prison system. But in the process petty offenders have gone by default; they go out and come back through the prison gates in ever increasing numbers. They are the children of the prison system – the detritus of the 'social dustbin'.

This endless recycling process will have to be short-circuited if prisons are ever to have the space and the resources to deal with those men and women who must be contained for very long periods. Various short-term measures have been suggested to diminish overcrowding and the incidence of recidivism; an increase of remission on short-term sentences from one-third to one-half, better after-care facilities, and so on. But the radical answer to overcrowding, recidivism, and the consequent institutionalizing effects of prison life, can only lie in the decriminalization of many petty offences and the extensive use of non-custodial sentences. Magistrates keep on sending people to prison who should not, or need not, be there. Criminal laws have not yet been adjusted to the available social solutions, and the prisons of this country are being crippled by the system of which they are the foundation. This is not a particularly 'liberal' or 'soft' response to crime; it is the most practical way of dealing with a prison system which has now been stretched beyond the limits of its tolerance, and of coping with people whose lives have been unnecessarily destroyed in our name. The alternative is more overcrowding, and therefore more security, and therefore more repression – until, finally, the explosion.

Certain images remain. 'What do you miss most?' I asked one man who had already been in prison for seven years. 'What everybody does. Love and affection.' He is now on day-release: 'And how did you feel when you first stepped outside?' 'I couldn't help smiling.' 'Come and have a look at this boy,' the assistant governor told me – even the most well-intentioned gentlemen sometimes treat prisons as zoos – and so I peered through a small hole in the cell door. A young man was lying face down on his bed. He was not asleep. He lifted his head wearily, gazed at the offending eye, and laid down his head on his bed again. In Wakefield prison, an old mulberry tree stands in the middle of a courtyard. It was around this tree, many decades ago, that women prisoners would walk in exercise. Hence

> Here we go round the mulberry tree,
> The mulberry tree, the mulberry tree . . .

Just behind this tree there stands a large, white building. It is now a segregation block, where violent prisoners are taken out of the sight and hearing of the other inmates, but until recently it housed a Control Unit – where, it was alleged, the more recalcitrant prisoners would spend long periods in conditions of extreme hardship and even of sensory deprivation. It was closed after 'unfavourable publicity'. It is disquieting to meditate upon these two images, and the historical connection between them. Together, the women trudging around the tree and the violent or unstable men locked in brilliant white cells, they evoke the futility and failure which mark the penal history of this country:

> A Jayl is but the world's Epitome
> There ye contemplate how to lie
> I'th'Grave, before ye come to die

Advice to the disconsolate Gentlemen-Prisoners (1673)

3 February 1979

28

England's New Client State

It is strange how the most important concepts are often the easiest to dismiss. Poverty is said to be 'relative' – implying that it can be neglected in order to concentrate on real and absolute issues, such as pornography and law-and-order. Poverty is a 'state of mind' – suggesting that money is unnecessary for health or happiness. Poverty is 'cultural' – meaning that it is indigenous to certain social or geographical areas, and therefore can safely be ignored by those on the outside. And yet, without anybody really noticing, over the last ten years the nature of poverty has changed significantly; and 'the poor' have become a silent emblem of the ways in which the state has altered its relationship to all of its citizens.

A street in Newcastle without trees, but it looks more denuded because there are no cars; half of the houses have corrugated sheeting where their windows should be – these are the ones about to be demolished, but there are others which are still inhabited. There are piles of rubbish outside number fifteen, the plastic garbage bags knocked over and gnawed open by stray dogs. Inside the walls are patched with damp and there are transparent plastic sheets, instead of glass, over some of the windows; there is no carpet on the floor, and the furniture is second-hand, scuffed. Mrs Simon has three small daughters; her husband abandoned her eighteen months ago, and can't be found. For her own upkeep and that of her children, she receives altogether in supplementary benefit £29.00 per week – for gas, for electricity, for food, and for clothing. Of this the amount she receives for each of her children is £4.40 – in other words each child is to be clothed, fed, and kept warm on 63 pence per day.

The poor tend to be invisible; in the same way that passers-by will automatically avert their eyes from tramps and vagrants who haunt the cities, so the vast army of the needy and the deprived are ignored, reduced to living precariously off the margins of the state. 'There will always be poverty' or 'the poor are always with us': the public catchphrases are a way of noting that, in the last analysis, such people don't matter. And this is, in a sense, the proper definition of poverty:

the poor are those people who are excluded from the ordinary human life of the community.

Statistics may, however, be more precise. Let us accept the conventional definition of poverty as the basic level of supplementary benefit – the last resort which the state offers, the money given to those people who have no source of income and no likelihood of getting one. A married couple receive £3.61 per day, and an allowance is given for each child – 94 pence a day is provided, for example, for children between the ages of eleven and twelve. It is difficult enough to envisage many people surviving on such meagre resources. But by the end of 1976 (the last year for which there are reliable figures) there were seven million people living at or below this income. And there are indications that these figures are rising continually. There were in 1974, for example, 1,410,000 people with incomes actually below that level – but by 1976 there were 2,280,000. There are, in this country today, 1½ million children living on the poverty line – and more than half a million now living below it.

It is easier, of course, to ignore or to fail to comprehend the nature of the society in which we live; it is often more natural and pleasant to do so: after all, why wake the sleepwalker? The spectacle of politics, and all the talk about 'issues' and 'personalities', is more familiar and therefore more reassuring. And, in order to mask the realities, we resort to the myths which are assiduously propagated by the public media.

The principal myth concerns 'the scrounger', the wastrel who lives in ease off the money of the taxpayers. Although such people exist, there are cases where the label seems peculiarly inappropriate. Mrs Ford had been living with a man for six weeks; he was unemployed, although no longer receiving unemployment benefit. The woman claimed the ordinary benefit for herself and her four children – approximately £33.00 per week – although, according to Social Security rules, the man should have claimed it on her behalf. At this point the bureaucracy of the state moved in; a young official of Social Security, having been 'tipped off' about this lazy and extravagant couple, came round and tore up Mrs Ford's benefit book in front of her. There was no money for two weeks; this was over the Christmas period. In April, a fraud officer asked Mrs Ford to sign a document admitting her culpability in not informing the officers that there had been a man in her house. She signed; she was taken to court and fined a total of £300, to be paid at the rate of £2.00 per week – or, in other terms, what

Social Security calculations assume will maintain a small child for three days. Three months later Mrs Ford went into hospital as the result of a bad pregnancy (unfortunately her baby died), and during that period she failed to maintain the payments of her fine. A warrant is now out for her arrest.

Perhaps this family should learn to stand on its own feet, and become more responsible for its own welfare. The man could try harder to find a job, although an unemployment rate in the area – Newcastle – of 17 per cent might make this difficult. Mrs Ford could send her children into care, and also get herself a job. By such means we might rid the nation of one of its scroungers, and the taxpayers might sleep a little easier in their beds. The reality of the matter is, however, also reassuring: the government has estimated that, in 1976, fraudulent benefit claims amounted to £2,170,907; on the other hand, the amount of benefit which was not 'taken up' (i.e. which should have been claimed, but wasn't) came to £250,000,000. The taxpayer is, in fact, making a kind of profit out of the poor.

But if 'the scroungers' can make headlines, it is altogether easier to ignore those seven million people who live at or below the poverty line. But society is, in fact, often best understood by looking at its victims; and if we care to look at the nature and the character of these people, certain pertinent facts emerge which concern the development of the whole community. There are of course those categories of the poor which never change, the 'outsiders' with whom society has never learned adequately to cope – the very old, the disabled, the homeless and the vagrants. But, over the last ten years, there has been a change in the nature of poverty which has yet to be adequately recognized. There has been a disturbing increase, for example, in the number of single-parent families: mothers with small children, without husbands or whose husbands have deserted them, who cannot survive and bring up their children without state intervention. In addition, the difficulties of single-income families on low pay have become far more acute; this group obviously includes those men and women who work for less money than that provided by the government in supplementary benefit, but it also includes those middle-class families whose previous affluence has been dissipated by inflation and by the unequal fruits of 'wages policy'. One man, a government scientist in his fifties, wrote to me that:

We are in the same house, but my mortgage is showing signs of extending to infinity. We pay what we have to pay and go deeper into the red . . . we have not had a holiday for five years . . . we do not eat out, even on anniversaries . . . We do not entertain because of the disreputable state of our house, and we are fast losing contact with all our friends.

And then of course, as a third growing category of the poor, come the unemployed, the ghost in the machine. What each of these three groups has in common is the fact that they cannot fight back or, in the language of cliché, 'stand on their own feet'; they are all peculiarly vulnerable to social and economic forces over which they have no possible control.

Mrs Cunningham's husband deserted her, and she has been left to bring up three children. She works part-time, and receives enough state benefit to bring her income to the level of the poverty line. The family 'manage', in the sense that the children don't go hungry or remain unclothed, but as a poor person Mrs Cunningham lives in a kind of exile from the ordinary life of society. When her husband deserted her, she was at first afraid to claim any state benefit; she was even afraid to leave the house for fear of seeming what in fact she is – emotionally and financially alone, helpless. The only life outside her family is that of work; she never goes out at night, and cannot afford the fares to visit old friends. When her colleagues at work go out to cinemas or parties, she is always somehow excluded. Perhaps it is because she is a single parent (although she is still young and attractive); perhaps because they know that she couldn't afford a ticket to the cinema, or clothes for a party; perhaps because they know that she could never reciprocate their hospitality (living now in two rooms with three children) and wish to spare her any possible embarrassment. All of these explanations are likely but, effectively, poverty has turned her into a non-person. She has become invisible, except to the children who depend on her for everything – which, under the circumstances, can only amount to very little.

Mr Johnson, with a wife and four children, works in the tailoring industry and earns £52.00 per week; he has a family income supplement of £9.00. It is plausible enough to maintain that this is sufficient to 'get by' – if to get by means to stay alive – but it places enormous material and emotional pressures upon the family. Although the problems of isolation are not so acute as they are for single-parent families, Mr and Mrs Johnson have not had a holiday in thirty years, and they have not been to a cinema or pub since their marriage. The diets, for themselves and for their children, will be of the most rudimentary kind: meat of any sort is a rarity. And under these conditions of 'relative' deprivation, such obvious items as shoes will be a luxury almost impossible to afford.

In some ways it is the children who suffer most: 'I feel more sorry for them than I do for myself.' They ask for things which they cannot possibly have; the need to claim for free school meals, in the classroom every morning, marks them out as different. And they themselves come to realize the difference: some of their friends will shun them, their clothes are all second-hand and reflect the second-hand status which has been foisted upon them. And such children, because of their relatively poor education and the fact that they have to leave school early in order to ease the burden on their parents, will often themselves be doomed to a life of low pay. This has become known as 'the cycle of deprivation'.

Although the life of the Johnsons is not one of squalor, it is one of dinginess, of making do with their lives within a small and confined space, unable to see any way out of their situation. Feelings of helplessness can become very acute. Mr Johnson once worked through his annual vacation in order to pay for his son's school blazer; the extra money which he earned rendered him ineligible for his usual rent rebate from the council. The 'poverty trap' is not just a social scientist's hypothesis: Mr Johnson was actually worse off than before as a result of working harder. These are the facts of the matter: a man who has been working all his life is now unable to live with his family on anything but a level of daily, worn subsistence.

The situation is worst of all for the long-term umemployed. They are treated, both by Social Security officers and the public media, as second-class citizens in some way responsible for their own indigence. They are never, for example, allowed to move on to the higher, long-term rate of supplementary benefit to which everyone else is entitled. 'It was as if,' one man who has been unemployed for five years told me, 'a huge stretch of water separated me from everyone else.' His children sat around white-faced. Although the affluent see poverty as an inescapable and incurable social disease, it is most often seen by those who experience it as a stigma – the unemployed tend to be both more assertive and more anxious, self-justifying and insecure in equal measure. A new identity has been forced upon them, and they have become reliant upon the state for their most basic needs.

This is a humiliating and dangerous position – all the more so because it is one in which most of the poor now find themselves. They are becoming the children of the state. Just as the administration itself creates poverty through its deflationary policies, so the poor are becoming more and more reliant upon its bureaucracy. They have become institutionalized just as surely as if they had been given a uniform and number. And with the economic recession in the West, and the decline of heavy industry in Britain, the number of the unemployed and those on low pay will continue to grow: in other words, the army of the poor grows larger all the time and there is no prospect of any change in their condition. When I earlier described the poor as the silent emblems of our society, I meant something quite specific: we are now creating, amongst us, a client state. The state has intensified poverty, and maintains it with its bureaucracy. The Supplementary Benefit scheme was established in 1966 as a subsidiary or 'back-up' system, a haven of last resort for those who could not claim National Assistance. It now controls the livelihoods of five million people, and is growing all the time.

Like all bureaucracies, it has of course become more complex and remote. But, since it is after all a 'welfare' bureaucracy, there are a large number of social workers who try and ensure that the system works for the benefit of those embroiled within it. The system *itself*, however, is rarely challenged. Although there are endless complaints about the obstructions, the petty humiliations and even brutalities involved in claiming Social Security, nothing is done to alter the essential nature of the system. Such complaints reminded me forcibly of the way in which prisoners discussed their goalers; and, in fact, similar conditions can be said to apply. Since the growth of education is paralleled by a diminution of resources in the United Kingdom, we have the paradox of the poor being more aware of the hopelessness of their condition and yet at the same time more dependent upon the state; they are both more articulate and yet more helpless, more bitter and yet more resigned. This is also the case in the vast institutions of the state – in prisons, in hospitals and in asylums. It is perhaps significant that the majority of the poor, like prisoners and the inmates of hospitals, take tranquillizers in order to survive from day to day. It is certainly true that no one has yet adequately grasped or recognized the nature of the new helot classes – suspicious, more sophisticated – which are being created in our advanced, benevolent, technological society.

For romanticists, of course, this new reality of poverty is uninteresting; it is not as picturesque, for example, as Asian slums. Children may be wearing second-hand shoes, but they are not going barefoot to school. They are eating beans on toast five days a week, but their bellies are not swollen. The poor may not be able to afford the bus-fare, let alone a ticket, to the cinema, but they are not rioting in the streets. Sheer material want and privation have indeed vanished – affluence has become picturesque instead. Our society offers, through advertisements and the blandishments of the commercialized media, the future as a realm of limitless possibilities for further consumption; to be denied the very things which society declares to be most important – this is the nature of poverty in contemporary Britain. The poor are the shadows which society casts; they are always forced to be takers and never givers; they tend to be fearful, guilty, isolated, unwilling to peer into the future.

Poverty is indeed a 'state of mind' and it is indeed 'relative', but in all cases it now means much the same thing – to be at the mercy of forces over which you have no control. The best definition of poverty is that condition of being trapped, unable to move in any direction – and, in our time, to be trapped by the state. That is why the only solutions to poverty are assumed to be managerial ones – the nature of being poor is that you are there to be helped and/or manipulated. The manipulator himself, whether it be a Social Security officer, businessman, politician or social worker, leaves himself out of the equation. The poor are always 'out there'; they are, by definition, those people who have been exploited so successfully that they are now quite without power. With the rapid growth in their numbers, and the nature of their maintenance and control by the engines of the bureaucracy, they have become an image of the new citizens which our advanced society is creating. It is happening under our noses, and yet we still prefer not to look.

21 April 1979

29

California Dreaming

Los Angeles and San Francisco

The screen-writer, one of 'the fifteen best in Hollywood', was getting nervous. We were lunching in La Dome, a Hollywood restaurant apparently carved out of green ice-cream, with an Englishman, a 'mini-mogul'. The mini-mogul stared distractedly out of the window whenever talk of the writer's project came up; he jumped up and went out to the lavatory when a 'pilot' was mentioned. The screen-writer began to shake visibly, and took a handful of pills out of his wallet: blue ones, pink ones, yellow ones, enough to kill an elephant. The mini-mogul cackled ecstatically and called to the waiter: 'Can we have a glass of water for Mr Frankenthaler's pills, please?' He was beginning to enjoy himself; I swam into view. 'And so is that all you do, then, sit in London and write *books*?' 'Well, I work for a magazine called the *Spectator* as well.' 'Oh, the *Spectator*. I came out here to get away from all that crap.' The screen-writer began to relax; the mini-mogul was having a good time. 'Come on, let's go shopping. I want to buy you something American.' I now have a silk cowboy shirt, bearing a legend of fearsome obscenity. But I was a late arrival; Nathanael West had discovered Hollywood much earlier, in *The Day of the Locust*: 'It is hard to laugh at the need for beauty and romance, no matter how tasteless, even horrible, the results of that are. But it is easy to sigh. Few things are sadder than the truly monstrous.'

The people who come to Hollywood are pursuing an idea – of money, of power, of 'stardom'. 'Yes,' a young man said to me at a party, 'the people who are interested in the future come to California. We create the fantasies for 98 per cent of the planet.' He was an executive, he was a success, he was 'into psychic technology'. As we spoke, a cabaret magician was performing to disco music; the guests – relatively incurious about each other – stamped and whistled as red and blue doves appeared and disappeared. Even when these people relax, they need to keep their illusions. And the need runs very deep. At a beach club in Santa Monica, two elderly couples were sitting in their cabin; there was a large mirror on the far wall and, with their backs turned away from the beach, through that mirror the four of them looked at the reflection of the sea. It was exotic and it was also chilling, another reminder of why it is that Disneyland is the Holy City of California. Among the plastic trees and the humanoid dogs and ducks, a new world is being created: 'We are now entering Tomorrowland. The world of the future where man's anxieties have passed.' And the ride only cost fifty cents.

In this process, this striving towards illusion, the human personality becomes a blurred thing, something to be instantly transformed – a kind of television image. It has been said that nothing is real in Los Angeles until your agent and your psychiatrist have agreed that it is so. For certain reasons, which remained curious and inexplicable to me, the apartment in which I was staying was also being used as a film set. An artificial moon had been created, by lighting, above my bed. The setting was Boston in the early sixties; an actor and actress were locked in an embrace. It was like a new 'Ecstasy':

> Our hands were firmely cimented
>> With a fast balme, which thence did spring,
> Our eye-beames twisted, and did thred
>> Our eyes, upon one double string . . .
> . . . And while our soules negotiate there,
>> Wee like sepulchrall statues lay;
> All day, the same our postures were,
>> And wee said nothing, all the day.

The silence was intense; the technicians stared; the moon's heat was like a furnace. And then the director came up to the pair, their lips still firmly sealed each to each, and swivelled them around. They remained locked together as the cameras rolled.

In such a context, to look for any ordinary reality would be as absurd as looking for Martin Buber in Disneyland. From the air, all one can see of Los Angeles are the swimming pools – like some blue jigsaw puzzle with the pieces scattered slightly. As Gertrude Stein said of another place, there is no there there. The city has no observable identity of its own, and so each inhabitant has imported his own style from whatever corner of America he came in search of the dream. Everything is amorphous, irreconcilable. A house in the style of a Chinese pagoda nestles beside a mock-Gothic department store, a Versailles mansion has been jammed up against a pink bungalow. The only feature indigenous to Los Angeles is the pavements: they are all encrusted with stars.

A city with no identity is also, of course, a city without a history; it acquires its character from whoever happens to be most successful at that moment, and so it is appropriate that the oldest artefacts in Los Angeles are the homes of the legendary movie-stars. Here is Shirley Temple's house, and just next door lived Joan Crawford – this is the lawn where her butler used to beat up any children who came to her door on Hallowe'en. And just round the corner is the house where Johnny Weissmuller lives – the garden is full of ropes and foliage. The new stars have also moved here, in an implicit act of homage. Hugh Hefner's palace is surrounded by guards and cameras. The son of the unlucky Shah of Iran has bought a house here, too; unfortunately he shocked his neighbours by painting all the statues green and gracing them with pubic hair. Close by, Getty's house is crumbling over the side of an artificial cliff. The whole area is utterly quiet, deserted except for the occasional security patrol and guard dog. The silence is so intense that the petals fall off the mimosa with an audible crunch. Beverly Hills is one of the most terrifying places in the world.

And, without a history, there can be no sense of a viable culture. Anthony Hopkins was playing Prospero in a local performance of *The Tempest*; the songs had been turned into advertising jingles, Miranda was clearly waiting for her first film part, and Hopkins mumbled and meandered through the lines to rapt applause:

> O brave new world, that has such people in't!
> 'Tis new to thee.

The whole audience laughed out loud, as though they had heard the line for the first time. Most of them had. 'Wasn't that the greatest show?' one rather gaudy American matron asked me. She looked like a Christmas tree on an acid trip; she turned out to be in 'the industry'. The industry, is, of course, the film industry; or, rather, the industry *is* the town. Los Angeles must be the only city in the world where the audience watch the film credits with more attention than they watch the film.

By courtesy of my new friend, the mini-mogul, I was transported to a large party at Paramount Studios. It was a 'wrap-up' party for seven 'major motion pictures', and it was held among the sets of the studio; here, at last, were the real inhabitants of those mock-Western saloons, the nineteenth-century New York street scenes, the façade of an early twentieth-century cinema. The directors, agents, producers, financiers, stars seethed around – looking as if they had just emerged from small nooks and crannies of these cunning replicas, and were still slightly ill at ease in the real air.

'Dustin got all the credit, but he was off the wall on that one.'

'I wanted to put Barbra against Dolly, it would have looked good aesthetically but it was just unreal. Really unreal.'

'What happened to your agent's girl-friend? She was with the wrong group last night.'

'Well she's into a real voyeur trip. She's in a bad space. I don't know where she's coming from.'

Everyone was 'working the party', as the strobe lights flashed, the Paramount extras doubled as nineteenth-century French chefs in order to serve elaborate food on plastic plates, as video-cameras recorded the party live on large screens above the party itself. The dream may change its form, but it never ends. There had been an article the next day in the *Los Angeles Herald Examiner*: 'The lights are the symbol . . . They signify the limitless potential for achievement and creativity in this city. The lights go on for ever, and so do the opportunities.'

It so happened that, that night, I was taken to Terminal Island Prison to watch a play written and acted by the inmates themselves. The energy and enthusiasm here, in an old-fashioned theatrical setting, were powerful and real. At the end, the inmates presented their 'outside' producer with a small wooden box, perfectly crafted and enamelled. The refrain of the production had been an insistent one: 'I am my own man. I am not to be bought and sold.'

Outside, in the city of lights, the cars went zooming past bearing their solitary occupants. All over Los Angeles people were talking to each other on the telephone.

San Francisco, to the north of Los Angeles, is a city that invites platitudes: the cable cars, the gentle people, the possibility of 'liberation'. A young man was talking to me in a bar. He was feeling very 'mellow', he told me, he was 'in his own space'. He had been dealing with his energies, and had decided to relate to their changes. 'I look at it this way: you can either be happy or be miserable.' He was from Idaho. He had a rather vacant smile.

Similar young men and women have come from all over America to this place, in order to discover their 'liberation'. This is still the last frontier: but now the people come to escape from themselves. The easiest way of achieving this, the method which requires the least moral and social effort, is to attach yourself to a group and thereby acquire a new identity: to become a 'feminist', a 'gay' or a 'moonie' – sometimes all three at once. San Francisco is a city of cults and religions, a city of strident white minorities, a city of people who wear their respective uniforms and who wield the impersonal vocabulary of liberation. They have done what they came such a long way to do: they have lost themselves. But what exactly is it that they have found instead?

In the fairy story, the two children have gone astray in the wood; they wander on through the foliage until, finally, they see a hill. This will be their way out, they will be able to see where they are. And so they climb the hill laboriously – only to see more hills stretching towards the horizon, as night begins to fall. It is well known that San Francisco is a city of hills – even here, liberation is not to be readily acquired or easily sustained. The gay community, for example is finding its dream of sexual and social freedom slowly turning sour; after the riots last month, as a result of the virtual acquittal of Harvey Milk's killer (Mr Milk was a homosexual politician, now in the process of being beatified), the slogan on the wall read GAY BULLETS WILL KILL PIGS. A gay bullet is, as yet, an unknown quantity. But the paradox of the language reflects the paradox of the situation itself: a minority is oppressing itself, is dehumanizing itself, with its own rhetoric.

For, again paradoxically, the more people who travel to California lured by the myths of freedom and endless balmy days, the less those myths can be realized. When homosexuals, for example, moved into certain neighbourhoods of San Francisco, they invaded those areas which had been predominantly Mexican and Chicano. They pushed up the rents; they even became the landlords of the previous native inhabitants. It is now common to see young homosexuals and young Mexicans confronting each other on the streets, with equal aggression on both sides. The pursuit of the Californian dream has actually set minority against minority. 'Liberation' is not a human or individual activity; it has to do with sheer weight of numbers and with an external, sometimes aggressive, style. Minorities are not freer here; there are simply more of them.

And what is it, anyway, that such people are being liberated into? As a city, San Francisco exists in a kind of vacuum; it is a pleasant but essentially uninteresting place, a rather more respectable and quainter version of Disneyland. There is a great deal of narcissism in the air – 'How could this happen here, in San Francisco?' one newspaper asked after the riots – but it is the aggressive narcissism of a city which knows itself to be provincial. Boredom has become a habit. I was taken to an elaborate studio where a laser and hologram show was being painstakingly constructed; across the television monitor, a thousand intricate shapes and tones were formed and re-formed. It was beautiful, but it was empty. The shapes were elaborate, but they were quite without resonance.

Nevertheless, there is a quite rare and attractive mysticism in the Californian temperament – it has to do with slowness, with their affinity with this peculiarly exotic land – and in people of great intelligence or even great beauty the effect is astonishing. It is like coming upon some new race of men, some wondrous species who have been able to empty their heads of anything the rest of us have ever learned. At dinner with an eminent academic, I was being rather rude about the work of a certain poet. 'I don't think,' the academic said quite calmly, 'that we need make judgemental values about anything.' After dinner, I drove across the Golden Gate bridge; beyond it, there is nothing but the Pacific. And when you realize that this is all there is left of the land, you realize also that this is the visible, definite limit of the West.

16 June 1979

30

Some Comments upon a Norwegian Joke
Oslo

The university lecturer leant across the table to me: 'We are God's chosen people.' He was 75, as old as Norway itself. 'Sometimes,' he added, 'I feel dizzy when I think of the happiness of my people.' He was a short man; he grinned at me and cocked his head to one side, like a pixie in a magic kingdom. Outside, a young policeman had blond hair down to his shoulders, a prince pretending to be a commoner;

children play in front of the royal palace which sits upon a hill covered with snow; the oil pours into Norway like golden eggs from an enchanted goose.

And here are God's chosen people themselves: on a Sunday morning, outside Oslo, hundreds of them, in bright red and blue anoraks, skiing across the flat, white fields. So many people in so small a space, and yet there is no disorder. The only noise is the flat but soothing sound of the skis, like a thousand floors being scrubbed clean. And then you realize something else: if this is the national sport, it must be the most placid and the least competitive in the world.

I had been invited to dinner by some Norwegians. They talked about their summer cottages, they talked about their boats, they were not wealthy but they talked about taxes; which were, it turned out, extraordinarily high. Did no one, I asked, wish to alter a system that confiscated so much? No, they were all happy with their society; why change something which works; there was room for improvement, but not for change. 'We feel,' I was told, 'responsible for each other.' But didn't they have other aspirations? 'You call it aspiration. That is a good word. We call it competition. That is the bad word.' (A kind of blandness enters the soul.) But were there no disadvantages? A woman, who had lived in England, discovered something. 'There is too much keeping up with the Joneses. We have to keep our houses neat and tidy.' The house I had entered was indeed neat; the books and papers were in perfect order; the windows were so clean that the snow seemed to enter the room; the candles on the table were arranged in elaborate but perfect formation. (A kind of peace settles down.) 'And also,' she said quite abruptly, 'we are frightened of what we do not know. But now I think I am getting a little drunk.'

Oslo itself is an awkward and misshapen city, as though it had been put together by random hands; it is constructed as a place of sojourn, rather than as a centre of activity and power. These are not an urban people, with the habits and instincts of those who live in cities. When the small orchestra stopped playing in one of Oslo's largest restaurants, the air was filled with the barely audible hum of a hundred quiet, level conversations; the sound was that of a refrigerator when the door has suddenly been opened. I was eating alone, but I was just one among many: this was a place of convenience, not of entertainment. In a bar along the street, a score of men and women were ranged on stools, drinking alone, quietly. Their faces were heavy, characteristically round. They are comfortably, but non-descriptly, dressed.

An old socialist parliamentarian was describing to me the nature of Norway's welfare state, a state which reflects the temperament of these people as accurately as their dress. 'It is more congenial to the social and historical traditions of the nation. Here there is no revolt against the state. We have good discipline within the unions, very good collaboration between the parties. The English, individualistic reaction is not needed here. We are country people, used to collaborating very intensely in our daily work.' Around us were the same quiet, flat conversations – as if everyone were talking about money. Outside, the air was as cold as liquid helium.

An interesting combination this, of formality and endurance. A people bound by the complicities of living on a small scale, unconcerned by the larger world outside. There is an intense nationalism implicit in all the conversations I had, a sense of survival sharpened after centuries of colonization. The Norwegians have clung to their land; their familiar weekend return to nature – on boats and skis, in fjords and cottages – is an affirmation of their separateness and their identity.

I am, I suppose, merely adding a few comments to one notorious joke. A group of European children were asked to write an essay on the elephant. The French child described 'The Love-Life of the Elephant', the German child wrote 'A Short Introduction to the Dental System of the Elephant', the English child discussed 'The Hunting of Elephants', and the Norwegian child wrote on 'Norway and the Norwegians.'

And so here we have an intense, almost racist, collaboration of four million people, in an order as carefully arranged as the Sunday skiers. They duck in the cold wind and then stand upright again. If we contemplate this order, we see it in motion everywhere. On an administrative level, it is known as 'consensus politics'. There are barely discernible differences between the parties, and certainly no ideological conflicts. Decisions are made in representative committees, not in adversary debate. Question time in the Norwegian parliament is like an ecumenical service, with a parade of sermons from the rostrum. Unions work closely with the government. Government works closely with the unions. Last year, a voluntary but total wage freeze curbed Norway's rate of inflation. The distant regions of Norway are deliberately over-represented in parliament, so that they won't feel left out of whatever communal decisions are being made. Everyone comes in from the cold. The essential purpose is to preserve the stability and homogeneity of the nation. A Labour MP described to me the process:

'We discuss things without thinking of party differences. I will say to my colleagues in committee, "I regret to say we cannot go so far – we must go a little back."' It is all very soothing: a little forward, a little back, a circle in the middle, like some folk dance of which the central purpose is the order itself.

Meeting Norwegian politicians is like meeting, as in an elaborate dance, the same person over and over again. There are, however, one or two exceptions. Gro Harlem Brundtland is the most popular parliamentarian; a Labour MP, an ex-Minister and now chairman of the most influential parliamentary committee (typically, of this moral-istic nation, on disarmament), she may well become the Margaret Thatcher of Norway. There is something of a resemblance: the same formidable briskness, the erect step, the handbag draped over one arm. She led me, at a rapid pace, through the parliamentary cafeteria, poured me a cup of coffee from a large silver urn, and stopped to chat with the lady behind the till. 'We are a very democratic society here,' she announced – a slight tone of frostiness at my being English and unused to such things.

She had recently read Patrick Cosgrave's biography of Mrs That-cher, and was evidently intrigued. 'She will not succeed, of course. She has certain positive characteristics, I think, but then that book was written to show them, wasn't it?' I agreed. Did she, though, see herself as Norway's first woman prime minister? 'Looking into the eighties, there is no other woman MP who could do it. But I won't fight for it. When I was in America I was sickened by the politicians who fight for themselves. That is not the Norwegian way. We do not compete.'

This was not false modesty; it was an entirely accurate, albeit baffling, description. Erling Nordvick, the leader of the conservative party, could by all accounts take his party to electoral victory in 1981 (not that it matters very much since, he told me, 'on 90 per cent of the issues we agree with the government, only small bits of the items part us'); he is, however, about to resign in order to edit a small conservative newspaper in the far north of the country. 'If I should compete for myself, I would not be objective. I don't think I would be fair in my discussions.' Like everyone else in this giant snowfield, the politicians refuse to proclaim themselves as abler or wiser than anyone else. They will not stand out from the crowd.

There is a mystery here. The Norwegians are not necessarily self-abnegating: one gets used to pious lectures on the decline of England. They are not weak: a kind of hard-nosed acquisitiveness characterizes their dealings. The apparent modesty comes, instead, from a rooted sense of self-certainty. An inner confidence in their own rectitude, as a community, allows them to embrace such causes as the development of the 'Third World' just as easily as it prevents them from questioning the development of their own society. They are as solid as the Viking ships which they preserve like the relics of saints.

To stand out, to question, is unrepresentative; it is, in a sense, to be un-Norwegian. There was only one politician I was warned against meeting: Karl Hagan, the leader of the Progress Party, was an extremist, an outsider. His offices were small and cluttered. Young men were stapling together mimeographed sheets; old newspapers gathered dust; tatty banners were propped up in corners. Mr Hagan, in his blue shirt and blue tie, had that combination of defensiveness and enthusiasm which is a sure sign of the 'fringe' radical. So what was the essence of his programme? A reduction of taxation, a diminution of public spending, and a re-examination of the welfare state.

> We reached our welfare objectives in the sixties, but they have had a momentum of their own. The state is getting into areas where it isn't needed. People now go to public bodies as a first resort. We are creating a society that is asking, not giving. Jobs are now being created to keep the unemployment statistics down, not to produce wealth. We will soon be like the dukes in your country, who suddenly lose the money and do not know what to do.

He was, he told me, sympathetic towards Mrs Thatcher although she was much further to the right than he himself was.

And so this was the extremist. In a society which precludes ideological choice and avoids political conflict, such a man will clearly not succeed. A system that relies upon national 'consensus' will not listen to questions about the nature of the welfare state, about the quality of the citizens who will emerge from it. Is it possible, for example, that this egalitarianism, bred in a people used to a colonizing aristocracy and now enshrined in a modern state, is in danger of undermining those traditional qualities of stubbornness and courage which the Norwegians themselves value so highly? I do not think you will get an answer in Oslo. The young men in Mr Hagan's office had the air of fanatical devotees, as they folded leaflets demanding lower taxes and less government spending. Inside parliament, however, the committees are full of level-headed men and women, taking small steps, not thinking the unthinkable, accommodating everyone. I regret to say we cannot go so far . . .

Consensus, compromise, compassion, egalitarianism, the words are like skis to carry you over the snow. If you are interested in politics, you can read 143 newspapers; all but one of them is subsidized by the state. If you are homosexual, you can go to one central bar and discotheque whose construction was funded by the government. Drink is taxed so heavily that you need a banker's card for each round: this evidently avoids extravagant behaviour.

A general blandness settles down. The state keeps its citizens safe and relatively sober, in the nicest and least intrusive way. And so, as my dinner companions had said, why is it necessary to change? As we talked that night, different drinks were carefully poured in different, sparkling glasses; the windows gleamed with the light of the carefully placed candles. And then I asked about Norwegian writing. There was a silence. I remembered the name of Knut Hamsun. 'Oh, Knut Hamsun was not a typical Norwegian.'

Folk songs introduce the television service; my friends at dinner, having abandoned Hamsun, suggested I try a few sagas and epics. On the outskirts of Oslo, a 'folk museum' has been constructed: wooden huts, churches, smithies and stables have been transplanted to create the illusion of a small and perfect community. I wandered around it, and the snow fell. If you visit the Munch Museum, the Norwegian artist whose fate was to remain estranged from his own people, the first picture you will come across is *The Scream*. One can understand why he painted it. There is a character in one of Ibsen's plays who announces, in lachrymose terms, that there is only one thing upon which the Norwegians all agree: they will turn and throw stones upon anyone greater than themselves.

A small dog pads across a square in Oslo. As you walk through the streets, a kind of gentle weariness descends upon you. The apartment blocks reflect the light from the ice in the street; a few pedestrians walk slowly and heavily along. These people endure city life. There is no excitement here: the city disperses it with its awkward corners and intersections; the hills behind Oslo soak it up; the fjords drown it; the snow cloaks it.

23 February 1980

31

Out of the Wilderness

Reykjavik

The moon was like an arc-light, so close you could brush it with your hand, as though it had been attracted to that land on earth most like itself and had come to guard it. The medical student was walking beside me. 'There are ghosts in every corner of Iceland.' Did he believe in them? 'I will not say "I do not" because then I may see one. We are not really Christians here. We do not believe in the Devil. We do not really believe in God.' He said it in a half-ironic manner, which I was to recognize as characteristic – as if to say, foreigners are not really interested in us, so why should you be?

The editor of the largest newspaper in Iceland stared out of the window, at the small red and blue houses stretching down to a lake. 'I ask myself, what is dream and what is reality? My three best friends are no longer alive, but they are still with me. Who is living and who is dead?' He was a poet; there is a tradition in this country of poets becoming editors.

The President of Iceland, Vigdis Finnbogadöttir, was telling me of the many dreams that had foretold her election.

One woman telephoned me to tell me her dream. She was looking down upon a beautiful green valley – that is a typical site for a dream here – where she saw three men holding a parchment. Suddenly a fair lady appeared and snatched the vellum from them, and then ran very lightly up the hill. There were three male presidents before me and, so you can see, she was right.

Dreams; ghosts; trolls. Iceland is an island of spirits, haunted by its dead and by the primeval powers of the land. It is the central mystery of this place, the first thing to understand. The belief in such matters is not whimsical or merely decorative; it is rooted in the sagas, which are the living literature of Iceland, and plays a powerful role in the life of the race. In the cinema near my hotel, the auditorium had been filled with people; not to watch the latest American film, but to participate in a seance. Mediums were on the stage, trying to invoke the wandering spirits of the Icelandic dead. There were Lutheran ministers among the congregation. These people believe – not in Christianity, not in the pagan gods, but in an amalgam of the two. Their religion represents a sense of continuity, a kind of spiritual lineage, a line with which they are entrusted and which they keep unbroken through even the most perilous circumstances.

The subscribers in the telephone directory are listed under their Christian names (if that is the right phrase) – as if the surnames did not fully belong to them. And, in fact they do not. By law, each Icelander is named 'son of . . .' or 'daughter of . . .'; only first names are used: in parliamentary reports, in newspapers, in conversation. The last name, the social foundation, is unchanging and in a sense anonymous. It is another way of asserting the continuity of these generations, springing directly from the first Viking settlers – generations which foreign conquest, terrible disease and privation, and the no less terrifying forces of this volcanic island, have been unable to change or to destroy. In the cemetery at Reykjavik, the most common image was not of the cross but of hands being shaken in greeting.

In order to explain themselves, the Icelanders continually revert to their history: the Vikings arriving in the ninth and tenth centuries, the epidemics and famines which so devastated the land that there were twice as many Icelanders in 1000 as there were in 1800, the coming of a printing press in the fifteenth century. In conversation, the centuries chime like distant bells. Old legends and ancient myths have accumulated around this history of privation – stories of hardship endured, of the spirits of the mountains. I was being driven over the lava fields towards a dead volcanic range (but what is living and what is dead?), passing small farmsteads where the Icelandic ponies and sheep gazed at nothing in particular; my driver would explain each area we visited, not geologically or socially, but in terms of a story. In the distance, Mount Hekla was still smoking.

These stories, these sagas, are born out of wonder and isolation; out of the need to wrench human significance and human shape from a landscape which seems actively to repel life. Even the language in which these sagas are written is itself seen as a kind of legend, a historical force which has acquired its own identity. It has not changed markedly in the last nine hundred years; the books now written use the same language – syntax, grammar and vocabulary – as those composed in 1300. It is as if we wrote and spoke in the language of *Piers Plowman*, or John Gower; as if our newspapers used similar words and constructions to those of Chaucer. One must not, of course, exaggerate this remarkable fact. New words are continually entering the vocabulary. 'If I was speaking to a thirteenth-century poet,' the newspaper editor suggested, 'it would take us half an hour – no, let us say one hour – to understand one another clearly.' The dead writers of England are precisely that – dead, as distant as sky-writing which we read once before it vanishes. But the Icelandic language, and the culture which shines within it, lives on in its original form. It, too, has survived.

And the tradition continues. There are more books, written and read, here than proportionately in any other nation. Poems are composed by Icelanders as if they were a kind of national sport; they are read out over television and radio. The literature is another register of that identity which must be maintained at all costs. But also, I think, the old language represents a longing to be free – to live in ancient myth as though it were contemporary, to live in a world of high words and high deeds – just as the Icelanders long for the sun; the sun which abandons them, leaving them in perpetual twilight.

'We have an eagerness to read about ourselves,' a young novelist told me. He had just written an account of his own childhood in Reykjavik, which had been immensely popular. 'Being an Icelander is a very curious thing. We try to understand ourselves. But there is something more than that – something difficult to explain. The relationship between land and people is somewhat dramatic; problematical. It breeds stories. This epic thing comes out of the tremendousness of it all.'

I was reading *Little Dorrit* while in Iceland. It is, you might say, one of the great English sagas, in our own powerful and sometimes vulgar language. Here we have a world foreign to the Icelandics, a world of impacted classes and beliefs, shot through with the darkness and closeness of the industrial age, filled with individuals desperately proclaiming their own identity in a maze of alleys, prisons and crowded London thoroughfares. When that book was being written, there was no society of any kind in Iceland. The only buildings were constructed out of mud; there were no wheels. The first permanent buildings, the first roads, the first wagons, were constructed at the close of the nineteenth century. And here we have, on the face of it, an extraordinary fact: the modern state of Iceland has been constructed in just eighty years.

Reykjavik has the features of a modern city, albeit on a small scale. It has the cinemas, the boutiques, the discotheques; the latest American records blare out into the main shopping street, but with the same eerie resonance as signals from some distant planet. Reykjavik does not feel like a city, and it does not have the solid intimacy of a town. It is, rather, a settlement. Families picnic against the walls of the only Catholic church in the country. The houses have the durable look of garrisons, putting a brave face against the dark, the brilliant flowers of Iceland's brief summer like the nosegays of knights about to enter a harsh battle. There is a stillness everywhere. Underneath the paved streets of the city, you can hear the waters rushing from the underground springs. It is the same water which boils up into the kitchens and the bathrooms, with a faint smell of sulphur. It is the water which provides the power of the island. This is a stillness full of motion, replete with energy.

I suppose, at this point, comparisons are in order: the Icelanders are not like the Norwegians, their closest neighbours. They lack the solidity, the stubbornness, the hard-nosed peasant bluntness. They have none of the hysterical moralism, or the authoritarianism, of the Swedes. They most closely resemble the Finns in their good humour, but they lack the Finnish wiliness and occasional surliness. They have, instead, a civilized reserve combined with a natural cordiality. But the relationships they form with each other are not urban ones. They sit together in coffee-bars or restaurants, often in absolute silence, gazing out of the window, reading their newspapers with extraordinary attention.

It is as if the energy which we devote to social relationships were being continually deflected elsewhere; as if it melted with the waters underneath the city, as if it spread out over the lava plains on which they live. There is a poem by Robert Frost, 'Fire and Ice', in which he equates the one with desire and the other with hate. Such concepts would be foreign to the Icelanders. They live with both on equal terms. Natural forces are their dwelling place. They turn their faces towards them; they pay their respects, and wait for the blessings if any should come.

I was wandering around an exhibition of children's paintings. Jon Sigurdsson, aged four, had drawn two mariners apparently drowning in blue waters; above them, he had depicted a spirit hovering, as though it were guarding them. And then, in conversation, metaphors from the natural world kept on appearing: Reykjavik was spreading rapidly, too rapidly, 'like hot lava'; the language must be polished 'like a basalt stone'; the politicians are 'lost in the waters'. Nature is not simply something to be regarded or endured; it is, as it were, the soul of the matter. 'In summer,' the novelist said to me, 'there is a sense of infinite possibility. That one can do anything. When the day lasts for twenty-four hours, I get these illusions. I love the illusions.' The light is, indeed, peculiarly brilliant; it is like crystal reflecting upon itself in a mirror. But then, when winter brings with it the long darkness, the Icelanders sit in their homes; they read and write; they nourish their past. Here are a people living close to the extremity of natural things, who have carved a space within it out of doggedness, a capacity for endurance, an ability to revive themselves with their myths.

But then the question has to be asked: can such a people, numbering only one quarter of a million, settled upon a volcanic island, maintain a modern, industrialized society? Iceland has been an independent republic for a little over thirty years. It is a paradox that a people who have survived the forces of the natural world should now be overwhelmed by a disaster of civilization, inflation. It is now running at approximately 60 per cent a year; my wallet was packed with large notes worth 10p, and my pocket jingled with elaborate coins worth nothing.

The conventional wisdom suggests that no society can easily endure the unrest and the tension which inflation of this magnitude produces. But in a country where even night and day can be reversed, conventional wisdom may have only a small role to play. The affluence here is immediately apparent; there seem to be more cars than people, and the homes of Icelanders are bright and luxurious, like ornate caves. Inflation has simply meant that, in the words of the novelist, 'we get nervous. We work extremely much.' And yet, in the National Museum, the cultural images are all those of work: old agricultural implements, weaving looms, small rough boats. The earliest photographs, taken by travellers, show the men, women and children caught in stiff attitudes at their places of work, drying fish, tilling the stony soil. But had the diseases of civilization, like inflation, changed the spirit of the Icelanders in the time between these sepia prints and the new, 'inflationary' nation? 'When I was a boy,' the novelist said, 'we were together in the family. We were one. Now there are many divorces. Families are split apart.' According to the newspaper editor, 'We are like birds in a rainy forest. We do not sing.' But there is always a saving clause in such discussions, a reminder that the Icelanders are not like the others, the foreigners. 'And yet,' the editor went on, 'we have lived with disaster. We have survived them all. We create stories out of them. We nourish them in order to preserve ourselves.' Inflation, it seems, is a power that they would also learn to control. It might even make a saga.

I went to see President Vigdis, in order to discuss such matters. She began by describing the origin of the Icelandic elves and trolls, as a polite prelude to serious conversation. I asked her about her presidential campaign. 'I was like the ogre of the old legends. I crossed Iceland in three steps.' She was piloted around in a tiny plane to each small community; her hosts would put her up in the children's room. She would make a speech in each place. First, she would begin seriously by quoting the sagas.

I always speak of the sagas. That is what we are, and how we are. And then I spoke of daily life. I was not the candidate, I would say, it is you. There is something in me which is them. We are all the result of this particular past. We live in Iceland, with ancestors who never gave up, who never accepted that life was hopeless. We conquered the land, otherwise clearly we would not have survived.

And now?

In the same way, we will conquer inflation. For me it is a problem to think of a problem. I am an optimistic person; what I experienced in my journeys was great warmth, great understanding among the people. What makes you think we cannot do it?

She brushed cigarette ash off her dress. 'I have quite a lot to say, as you can see.'

The wind was coming up, and whistled around the old house filled with bound volumes of the sagas like a monastic library.

And before, you asked me what is power? My ambition is to be what I am. Perhaps I am now a proper person, a warm person, but that came late in life. So what is this ambition to prove myself? I do not want power. I want inspiration, to inspire people with the thoughts that I have, with the thoughts that have inspired me. That is all. When you get back to England, you must read Njal's saga. You will not believe the complexity of these stories we have.

Then she put on her raincoat, and took me back to Reykjavik. We drove over the plains of lava. Beyond them, only five minutes' drive from the outskirts of the city, one comes upon the wilderness. In the volcanic heartland, the steam rises out of the ground; waterfalls crash down upon large, malformed rocks; the glaciers are covered with black ash from earlier eruptions. It is, in a literal sense, awful to look upon.

And yet these people, these descendants of the Vikings, have survived. They have developed into a nation; they have brought life to the stony ground; they have conquered the wilderness with the human spirit. On the outskirts of the city are the sculptures of Asmundur Sveinsson. There is something peculiarly Icelandic about this medium; it spoke to me more directly than the literature. Here the stones are given form, the rocks are turned into human shape. But there is something else in Sveinsson's work, also. There was a kind of violence yoked within these sculptures. It was not clear if the human shapes were reaching out of the rock, or if they were reverting to it. It was as if the stones, and the stone figures, were screaming – screaming to be freed from their mutual embrace.

It is, it might be said, a simple art – simple in its assumptions, if not in its execution. Like the sagas themselves, and the people, there is a kind of naivety, a clinging to what is known, a willing immersion in the past. But then, think of *Little Dorrit* in comparison with a saga: what it gains in complexity, it loses in aspiration; what it gains in subtlety of language or characterization, it loses in that instinctive affirmation of life which the sagas contain.

On the plane back home, I was sitting next to a twelve-year-old Icelandic boy. As we approached London by night, the clouds parted and one part of the city was lit up to the horizon. The little boy clapped his hands, and sucked in his breath. He turned to me. 'That is beautiful,' he said. 'It is a revelation.' This was the word he used. In a way, it catches the heart. It tells us of what the Icelanders have never had, what history and what possibilities have been denied them. And yet what have they raised in its place – what intensity of longing, what affirmation of themselves, what willing embrace of the land and the spirits of the land. Who could say where the advantage lies?

6 September 1980

32

Glare but not Gloire

Paris

The late *run* to the French capitol may have undeceived my countrymen in very many particulars, on which distance, the illusions of imagination, and the *glare* the French have the address to throw round every object, may have led them to form very erroneous opinions.

A Few Days in Paris, 1802

I found myself in the middle of a great plain; large tower blocks, reflecting the light from each other, would have dazzled Christian and led him astray from his Progress. They receded into the distance like a modernist, more bewildering, version of de Chirico. A painted grotto and a marble hill rose in the middle distance; behind them, placed as the vanishing point in this ever diminishing perspective, was the Arc de Triomphe. The only noises were those of the escalators, running up and down with no people – for this was Sunday morning – to disturb their even motion. Bright electronic messages circulated above my head, one of them announcing a new film, *La Terreur des Zombies*. A sculpture of Miró's, like a great bone painted in bright primary colours, gleamed; it was the presiding deity of the place. It was elegant, perhaps a little chilling. The nineteenth-century traveller had got it right: not *gloire*, but *glare*.

When I retreated underground, into a Metro station as large as a cathedral, I recognized the shining halls. The area is called La Défense, a modern precinct set carefully apart from the old Paris, and it was here that the opening sequences of a recent picture, *Buffet Froid*, had been filmed. In this film Gérard Depardieu had wandered in a Paris so empty of human beings that it resembled a crystal vessel, and had become involved in *crimes de passion* without sequence and without sentiment. The film had been elegant, perhaps a little chilling.

Later that day I found myself sitting in the Café de Flore. Quite without warning a middle-aged man, a few tables in front of me, let out a loud and sinister rattle, like that of a crank being turned too quickly, and fell backwards upon the floor. He may have been having a seizure; he may have been dying. The elegant middle-aged lady in front of me put up a hand to shield her eyes from the sight, looking at me for sympathy in her predicament. Some smart young men and women, immediately behind the now supine man, paused momentarily to take in the spectacle and then resumed their conversation. An elderly man to my right kept on reading his *livre de poche*. Within a few seconds the manager of the café and two of its waiters surrounded the man, as if shielding him from the censorious gaze of their clients, and propped him back in his chair.

He seemed, fortunately, to be recovering when a police van drew up outside the café; three policemen hurried up and, apparently against the man's will and despite his protestations, took him away. Perhaps they were about to take him to hospital – it was, after all, unlikely that he was being arrested for falling ill in public. But it would have been impossible to ask anyone sitting around me since – with the exception of the manager whose dignity seemed in some way to have been impaired – they went on talking and reading, taking not the slightest interest in proceedings. They were all very well dressed, very chic. If the furs around the middle-aged lady's shoulders had come suddenly to life and started eating her face, they would no doubt have remained calm and called for a policeman.

The Pompidou Centre is a miracle of lucidity; it resembles one of those fashionable watches with a transparent back, through which every detail of the mechanism can be seen working in unison. Transparent, tubular passageways hang from it like stalactites. It is so constructed and designed that one knows exactly where one is – both in relation to the building and to the rest of the city – exactly what material it is constructed out of, exactly how it has all been arranged. One gets the same sensation with the Grand Palais which housed the Exhibition of 1900, and with the Eiffel Tower – when the rays of the sun strike the metal girders of the tower, it is like looking into the mind of the engineer. Everything exists in a clear and even light.

And then inside the Pompidou Centre, within a section marked 'La Galerie Rétrospective du Centre de Création Industrielle', the history of technological civilization was marked out as if it were also part of some majestic *son et lumière*. Seven separate screens glowed, severally or together, creating a symphony of information and enlightenment. Reading contemporary French literature affords a similar experience – the screens of the sentences and paragraphs glow and fade and glow again, and the world is transformed into a number of discrete theorems placed in careful relation to each other. You are continually invited to marvel at how it is being done, rather than what is being said. Outside the centre, the travellers are propelled up and down the transparent tubes, like specimens waiting to be anatomized within some future galerie.

It is impossible to overestimate the effect of architecture upon manners. In Paris, it is something to live up to rather than in. The pavement cafés are places where people go to sit and watch, and be watched in turn. It is almost as if the French had invented glass, that medium which imparts brightness but not necessarily heat. The clearness, the unambiguity, the lucidity are everywhere: the relentless clarity of French realism, the lucid structures of French philosophical thought, the sometimes comic obviousness of French fashion. In such a place, the world itself is transformed into spectacle. The main function of Paris is its appearance; the subways look like museums, and the museums like theatres. When certain French radicals, in the early sixties, defined capitalism as 'the society of the spectacle' they were in reality talking about themselves.

The election campaign was noticeable for its posters. There were several images of M. Chirac – to the untrained eye, they might all have looked the same but there were subtle differences. One proclaimed 'Il nous faut un homme de coeur': M. Chirac is wearing a grey suit and a blue shirt. Another, 'Il nous faut un homme de nouveau': M. Chirac is wearing a pullover and an open-necked shirt. Yet another: 'Il nous faut un homme de parole': M. Chirac is wearing a dark suit with a white shirt, the cuffs peeping through. Grey for the heart, black for the truth.

Everything is to be seen to be believed. The waiters of this city look more like waiters than anywhere else in the world, and as a result they have never found any necessity to change their behaviour. The traveller of 1802 had champagne poured in his ear by one of them: 'We were attended by an impudent French waiter. He did everything but attend civilly on us. I never took a greater aversion to a man in my life.' The workmen look more workmanlike than anywhere else, as if they had stepped out of a film starring Jean Gabin. The tramps who lurk in the Metro – relegated, as it were, beneath ground, beneath the level of elegant discourse – more gnarled and twisted than their counterparts elsewhere, as though they had modelled themselves on Charles Laughton's performance in *The Hunchback of Notre Dame*. The elegant young men and women are stridently, ferociously elegant. *Glare*, not *gloire*.

But this attention to, or absorption in, appearance is a great virtue. It leads to a certain vivacity and a genuine freedom of spirit, a wit unattached to questions of 'purpose' or 'meaning'. Only a very clever, or at least quick-witted people understand the virtue and importance of appearance. Walking through the streets of Paris is like being trapped forever in the first fifteen minutes of *Les Enfants du Paradis*. And so it was before, in 1802: 'They are a century behind us in the common conveniences of life, carriages etc; but their great quickness and versatility of talent is visible in everything.' The important word, again, is 'visible'.

Some things, of course, have changed. 'Why Paris?' Ezra Pound wrote in 1921, 'Paris is the center of the world!' And, indeed, so for a while it seemed – Joyce, Picasso, Apollinaire, Ravel, Stravinsky; now all that is left of them, and of those Americans and Englishmen who joined them, are the photographs affixed in the walls of small bookshops. Those Englishmen and Americans I met complain now of the dullness of the place, of the tide of prosperity which has submerged everything else. Prosperity is not conducive to an exciting life; it creates elegance, perhaps, but not value.

Americans still come. I met a young man from California who expatiated on the wonders of Paris. 'It is,' he said, 'just as beautiful as San Francisco.' I suggested that there were more palaces here, more buildings of note, perhaps even more culture. 'But we've got music and movies,' he said. 'Music and movies are universal.' There is still, as in the twenties, a 'lost generation' of Americans – only the present one does not know that it is lost.

Of course there is beauty here. All cities are impressive in their way, because they represent the aspiration of men to lead a common life; those people who wish to live agreeable lives, and in constant intercourse with one another, will build a city as beautiful as Paris. Those whose relations are founded principally upon commerce and upon the ferocious claims of domestic privacy will build a city as ugly and as unwieldy as London. It is the law of life.

The tomb of Oscar Wilde, at the Père Lachaise cemetery, is covered with marks and graffiti – the only sepulchre in that city of the dead which still attracts the living: 'Oscar Nostro', 'Love For Life', 'I Love

You' and then, less plaintively, scratched upon the white stone in large letters 'Sex Pistols' and then, less plaintively still, 'You Old Fruit'. There is no peace for Oscar Wilde even in death. A car zoomed down the path beside his grave (it would be ironic, I thought, to be killed in a cemetery – it would fit the peculiar French sense of propriety). But he would not have minded; at least here – with Bellini and Bernhardt, Piaf and Molière, Proust and Bizet, Balzac and Ingres, Héloïse and Abelard – he would have been in good company. Oscar Wilde, like the French whom he fled to, knew the importance of appearances, the values of the surface.

And it is perhaps the evident truth of this which makes the modernist complex of La Défense, with its Miró and its painted grotto, at once so astounding and so chilling. Everything here is designed to be seen and, once seen, admired. The eye wanders across the buildings as it would wander over the surface of a dead planet thrown into sharp relief by the light of a distant galaxy. The truth is precisely this: there are only appearances. It is foolish to look for any other reality, any other meaning, as the spectacle moves on. The appearance *is* reality. *Glare*, in the end, is *gloire*.

9 May 1981

33
Christopher Isherwood at Eighty

Christopher Isherwood has been proclaiming his fate all his life, but in *Down There on a Visit* it has its classic formulation: 'But now I knew that I didn't belong here, either. Or anywhere.' And his permanent battle against 'the Others' (the sign of the 'Truly Weak Man') seems finally to have been won: estranged from both family and nation, he now belongs to no one culture or tradition. He is neither English nor American, that curiously nasal mid-Atlantic accent suggesting the nature of the ambiguity; he is not a representative of the thirties, although he is perhaps the best chronicler of that period, nor of the seventies or eighties, although he has adopted some of the more egregious fads and fashions of those decades.

Although he is often a very funny writer, he cannot be classified as a 'comic' novelist; but neither can he be described, despite his more solemn moments, as a 'serious' one. He has never fulfilled the role of 'exile' or 'outcast', since he is so obviously at home in his now native California; but he has not become an elder statesman among writers either, principally because he has retained an apparent naivety or boyishness which disclaims such an identification. He is not really even a 'novelist', since his own work combines diary entries, reportage, autobiography and fiction in equal measure. Even the apparent simplicity of his prose (and of his personal manner) is itself ambiguous, since it conceals dramatization, subterfuge and canny obliquity – all of which act as modes both of self-preservation and self-enhancement. He has, in short, remained on the margins – which is perhaps the reason why he and his work are so difficult to describe.

One of the causes of this difficulty, however, lies in the fact that Mr Isherwood has always been busily engaged in the task of reinventing himself; he first made an attempt at autobiography at the age of twenty-six, and has never since dropped the habit, but this urge seems in one sense merely to be another manifestation of his aptitude for fiction: his first real exercise in autobiography, *Lions and Shadows*, was even listed by the Hogarth Press as a novel. His most recent autobiographical work, *Christopher and His Kind*, is, despite its apparent frankness about such matters as his homosexuality, a studiously opaque volume; it is a curious fact that, having read it, one knows less about Mr Isherwood than when one started.

But the public facts of his history are sufficiently well known: his early friendship with Spender, Auden and Edward Upward; the tempestuous relationship with his mother, Kathleen, which seems to have been the major spring of his activity; his time in Berlin, and his European adventures with various boy-friends; his work as a script-writer; his great success with *Mr Norris Changes Trains*, which transformed him overnight from a relatively young and minor novelist into something approaching a literary 'lion'; his collaborations in verse with W. H. Auden; his emigration to the United States, where he has remained ever since; his attachment to Vedanta philosophy; his public espousal of 'gay liberation' (as it was once called). The popular and critical recognition of his work has, throughout this period, been a somewhat haphazard one. He was more or less marked down as a 'thirties novelist' (despite, or perhaps because of, the fact that he wrote three novels in the fifties and early sixties) and it was not until the early seventies, and the success of the film *Cabaret*, that he began to enjoy something of a literary revival.

Isherwood has remained in California for more than forty years, and indeed that State (or state) might have been designed expressly for him: his detachment from others, his credulity, his marginal status and his own self-obsession (mediated through the ventriloquial figure of 'Christopher Isherwood' in some of his novels) find there the right hot-house conditions for their rampant growth: he has always been a writer who needs an 'atmosphere' to live up to. I suspect, in fact, that the true significance of his flight from England to America in January 1939 was not any fear of the approaching war but rather his instinctive sense that he was migrating to the next centre of world power. Part of the charm of his never seeming to have 'grown up' is qualified by the fact that he has never needed to do so; he has always been an inhabitant of empires – and never more so than when he is chronicling their demise or deliquescence.

It is an open question how much this lengthy sojourn has affected his writing. Certainly the fact that he has remained several thousand miles away from this island has meant that, on a public level, he has never attained the exemplary authority of his contemporary, Graham Greene. But he has never been thought of as an important English writer primarily, I suspect, because he has never really attempted to describe English society in his own fiction – only his first two novels, *All the Conspirators* and *The Memorialist*, take English life as their real theme (*Prater Violet*, although set in England, could have been written about anywhere).

But it is possible that the expatriate life has affected Mr Isherwood's writing in more important ways. It has, after all, become something of a cliché that English artists forfeit an essential part of their power when they try to continue their work in America – they become more whimsical, shallower, their marginal status confirmed by circumstances beyond their control. And there is a sense in which this is true of Mr Isherwood. His most respected works are still *Mr Norris Changes Trains* and *Goodbye to Berlin*, both of them written before he moved to America, but the simple fact of transplantation is not the most important one. *Prater Violet* and *Down There on a Visit*, arguably his finest novels, were both written while he was resident in the United States: but these novels are concerned with the past, and it seems to be the case that his writing is at its sharpest and its simplest when he deals with the world of the thirties which he left behind him when he crossed the Atlantic. In novels such as *The World in the Evening* and *A Single Man*, where he is most concerned with describing contemporary America, his writing becomes more verbose and abstract; the dialogue sounds somewhat phoney; the settings are slightly unreal; it is almost as if he were becoming feebly subservient to the 'atmosphere' of his adopted country, and not submitting it to the same relentless scrutiny with which he once anatomized England or Germany.

And yet the finest things in Mr Isherwood's fiction remain very fine indeed.

1 September 1984

Film Reviews

34
Apocalypse Now

Marlon Brando, playing Captain Kurtz and looking uncannily like Aleister Crowley in his last days, tries very hard to appear profound. The light flickers across his face as he rolls his eyes and mutters, 'The horror! the horror!'; flames and shadows engulf him as he walks like a somnambulist through his Cambodian kingdom, where death and desolation are the marks of sanctity; the whole of *Apocalypse Now* is devoted to the increasingly gaudy search for him by Captain Willard (played by Martin Sheen in the American tradition of minimal acting). It all looks very impressive, until one notices Kurtz's reading matter: propped up by his bedside, along with the corpses, are copies of Weston's *From Ritual to Romance* and Frazer's *The Golden Bough*. He is not a victim of the Vietnamese War: he is a victim of pop anthropology. And when he starts reciting, in a broken and desolate voice, from Eliot's *The Hollow Men* it all comes clear: Kurtz is the martial equivalent of a prep-school master, lost in some sentimental view of 'literature' and an equally glassy-eyed notion of 'life'.

No one else in the film seems to understand this elementary point. Coppola, the director, has constructed a spectacular pyramid of sound and colour, which rises higher and higher, only to leave a pea at its apex. Coppola's genius is for visual effects, but he rashly decided that he had to be 'serious' as well. And so *Apocalypse Now* is riddled with allusions to Joseph Conrad, as Captain Willard travels through the rivers and jungles of Vietnam into the 'heart of darkness'. He has been ordered to find Kurtz, now judged insane by the American establishment, and 'terminate his career – with extreme prejudice'. But this potentially interesting theme hardly gets off the ground before it is dragged down in a mire of literary clichés – as deadly in their effect as the bloody mud of the war itself, which enmeshes the combatants in apparently senseless conflicts.

Apocalypse Now, in other words, would have been more entertaining as a silent film. This might sound paradoxical, given the amount of money and the range of technical effects now available to the studios, but it is a measure of how short a distance the cinema has travelled in the last fifty years. D. W. Griffith realized, a long time ago, that huge crowd-scenes and spectacular sets would fill an audience with wonder; Coppola knows all that Griffith knew – but not a great deal more. And so *Apocalypse Now* is filled with images: images of burning, of menacing shadows, of huge trees exploding in clouds of fire, of brilliant and intemperate colours that turn the screen into a panorama of despair and decay.

Images, nothing but images. They are the central element of the film and it is difficult to explain their power – given Coppola's ham-fisted attempts at literary eloquence and metaphysical debate. If the 'heart of darkness' itself becomes a B-minus essay composed by a first-year student of comparative religion, how does one explain the undeniable strength and resourcefulness of the film? These images must come from sources deeper than fashionable books; they have not been, like the dialogue, strained through sub-biblical rhetoric; they are not portentous, like the film score which suffers from an excess of low notes and plaintive strings. They come from Coppola himself, whose intuition is his real genius.

He is a kind of divining rod for the age's madness (his previous film, *The Conversation*, dealt with the ambiguous and menacing effects of small-scale technology) – and, perhaps without realizing it, he transmits that madness through a number of powerful symbols. That is why Kurtz's diabolical settlement in the Cambodian jungle, drenched in cabbalistic signs and invaded by suffering, bears an uncanny resemblance to Jonestown – not to any more glorious, literary predecessor. Jonestown, after all, was in the air; it happened because it fitted that image of reality which many people carry in their heads. It made sense; like Manson, the Reverend Jones was a colourful emblem of a large disorder.

Apocalypse Now is, therefore, a significant film despite itself. It has very little to do with the Vietnamese War (which has, in any event, now become a myth in search of a narrative). It acts, rather, as a medium which transmits the fears and fantasies of the late seventies: the uneasy fascination with the irrational, the obsession with motiveless violence, the interest in cultism. Coppola has presented us with a distorting mirror – we see ourselves, twisted but recognizable.

5 January 1980

35

1941

Mirror

1941 is announced as 'a Steven Spielberg film'. We didn't need to be told. The scenes are as smooth and shiny as lip gloss; image is piled upon image with the relentless impersonality of a comic strip suddenly come to life; the narrative moves with the speed and precision of a Cruise missile. *1941* does for the American entry into the Second World War what Spielberg's earlier films, *Jaws* and *Close Encounters of the Third Kind*, did for sharks and UFOs. It turns it into a spectacle. Each of Spielberg's films has taken a contemporary preoccupation, and transformed it into a vast, visual conceit. It is a kind of magic. In this case, Spielberg seems to have, by instinct, anticipated the current American mood of war hysteria and turned it into the comedy and slapstick of *1941*.

It ought to be empty, crass, slightly tatty. But it isn't. Steven Spielberg is an extraordinary technician; for all the manic energy, which seems to pull the narrative along like an express out of control, each scene is elaborately and carefully composed. War machines crash into each other, fights are staged, houses are demolished, with the precision of a Busby Berkeley chorus. Where Spielberg has always excelled is in the heady realm of special effects. A ferris wheel rolls into the Pacific Ocean; two American jet fighters, one of them ablaze, soar down the boulevards of Los Angeles as flares and cannon fire erupt around them.

It is all very pretty – each frame is platinum-plated, poster-painted. As though everything were made of candy which is just about to dissolve. In this setting, of course, the acting – which is uniformly excellent – and the jokes – some of which are very good – seem almost peripheral, almost an accident. In a sense, the script and plot (such as it is) of *1941* are simply an excuse for Spielberg's manipulation of the audience. Cinema becomes a sheerly visual phenomenon, a panorama of light and colour that entrances the eye without penetrating the cerebellum. This is, in some ways, a peculiarly unsettling experience: one enjoys the spectacle, but without quite knowing why. It is as though we were presented with all the trappings of a superb film and someone had, by accident, forgotten the content.

It seems that socialist realism has lost its charm – even in the Soviet Union. Contemporary Russian fiction has abandoned it (so I read in the literary pages of the *Spectator*) and Andrei Tarkovsky's *Mirror*, on release in London, now performs a similar act of parricide. There are no images here of happy workers or sturdy peasants, but rather of individuals marked by weariness and *ennui*, uncertain of themselves and of their society – a world, it might be thought, similar to our own.

A young man, who suffers from a severe stammer, is being cured by hypnotherapy; at the end of the session he calls out, with the authority of those who have regained possession of themselves, 'I can speak!' This is how *Mirror* begins, and the film itself is a kind of declaration – the visual monologue of a man haunted by himself and by what he loves. *Mirror* records Tarkovsky's personal history; it moves back and forth from his childhood in the Russian countryside – strange, fantastical, isolated – to his displaced and disturbed adulthood in Moscow. His mother and his wife are played by the same actress throughout, an image of the fact that each person's life is marked by a peculiar consistency of tone. This is, in the cliché of critical journalism, a 'poetical' insight and the film is invaded by a consistent literariness. Poems are recited as a commentary upon the action, and there is even a reference to the 'infinite vastness' of the motherland.

But these moments of self-indulgence can be forgiven, just for the way *Mirror* actually looks. Past and present are placed beside each other with uncanny imaginative accuracy; dreams and images of childhood float across the screen – their only logic being that which the observer brings to them. And the whole film is beautifully photographed. The colours look as though they have descended from the ionosphere, and decided to stay.

But *Mirror* is not merely a triumph of aesthetics (though at a time when a meretricious weepie like *Kramer vs Kramer* can win five Oscars, that is enough in itself). It takes passages from old newsreels of battles, of mud, of air raids – in order to modify, and expand, the solipsistic presentation of the narrator. The film, in the process, evinces an intense sense of history – a sense of continuity, as well as struggle and repression, which can be glimpsed in public events no less clearly than in individual ones. *Mirror* holds these disparate spheres together, so that they look as if they are one.

26 April 1980

36

The Shining

This is in many ways a remarkable film; its clarity and resourcefulness far exceed the quality of the original plot material which it uses, and it consistently baffles or defies expectation, as though the general framework of the 'horror film' were being anatomized and then reordered. *The Shining* is Stanley Kubrick's first film for five years, and although we cannot therefore expect profundity, we can at least expect seriousness of intent. The picture, in that respect, is not a disappointment. It does for the 'horror' genre what *2001* did for the science fiction epic; it intensifies it, thereby making it more theatrical but at the same time giving it more depth.

A young couple, the Torrances, have been hired to maintain a hotel during its closed season. But the mansion has its own guardians, who have dwelled there for many years; as the snow and the darkness roll in, the place becomes a bathosphere of shapes and distorted noises. It becomes an appropriate setting, then, for three elaborate and grandiose performances. Jack Nicholson, playing Jack Torrance, an aspiring writer, has the gleam of mania, as though a match has just been struck behind his eyes; his face is stretched and crinkled across his skull like shiny lavatory paper. He is shown a small bedroom in the caretaker's quarters: 'Perfect for a child,' he announces, thin-lipped, eyes swivelling, as though the room in question might easily double as a made-to-measure coffin. He is a study in creeping dementia – he can hardly keep his lip from curling, like stale bread, or his body from reverting to a crouch.

Shelley Duval, playing the wife and mother, is on the verge of dissolving; her hair hangs limply over her eyes, which are the size of cow-pats; she looks like Bugs Bunny carved out of margarine. Their child, who possesses second sight or 'the shining', is driven into a frenzy by his own gifts – as lost and pathetic as a bird reared specifically to be shot. The three of them reverberate through the hotel, aptly named the Overlook. And this is where Kubrick comes into his own: the interiors are brilliantly composed, brightly lit rooms and stairways lead inexorably to one another. It is like watching the interior of some airy, illuminated beast which still lives. There is, and will be, no way out.

And so it is that Kubrick's characteristic device is that of the tracking shot: the three characters are followed relentlessly by the camera, as if all their movements were imprisoned by it. The air seems to freeze around them. The young boy rides his tricycle along the corridors of the Overlook, creating a mood of intolerable suspense; the mother wanders lost through an elaborate maze next to the hotel; the father staggers through the ornate ballrooms and hallways, hardly knowing where he is going, hearing voices, always being led on. And this becomes the pattern of the film itself: Kubrick's characters are caught in the endless maze of the years, full of returns and reversals, from which there is no escape.

To put it as badly as this suggests that it is an imposition upon the narrative. But it is, rather, a pattern which Kubrick orchestrates with great care and subtlety. At the beginning of the film, when Jack Torrance arrives for his interview, the managers and servants of the Overlook seem scarcely alive; they are embalmed in the hotel as if it were some contemporary pyramid. These first fifteen or twenty minutes are, in some ways, the most eerie in the film but Kubrick builds upon this initial tension – pacing it out, as it were, frame by frame – until it reaches an extraordinary climax at the close.

There are, however, one or two melodramatic stretches along the way which lead to some confusion over Kubrick's intentions. Madness and possession are treated convincingly and skilfully, for example, but these human ills are sometimes upstaged by the entry of ghosts, animated corpses, and the other paraphernalia of the conventional horror film. But evil is only credible, and interesting, when it springs from the workings of the human will. And since the evil we create within ourselves is far more terrifying than anything imposed from 'the beyond', Kubrick's occult grotesquerie remains merely picturesque.

When Mrs Torrance comes across her husband's typescripts – in which the same sentence is repeated thousands of times in a multitude of forms – it is a genuinely chilling moment, since it effectively represents the obsessiveness and banality of evil. But then to present evil as spectacle, to confront horror head-on, as Kubrick also does, is to render it lifeless and incredible. As a result, Kubrick damages the skilful and original narrative which he has constructed. And yet *The Shining* lingers in the mind long after most horror films have passed into the vast limbo of the unremembered; despite its evident short-comings, this film bears about as much relation to that debased genre as *Beowulf* does to *Paddington Bear*.

11 October 1980

37

Raiders of the Lost Ark

Dr Indiana Jones is trying to rescue the Lost Ark of the Covenant from a contingent of Nazis. 'I'm going after the truck!' he screams at his dazed accomplice, Marion. 'How?' she calls back. I think at this moment she is being strangled by pythons, or having her wardrobe ripped up in front of her; something like that. 'I don't know,' Jones yells as he races away on an improvised stallion, 'I'm making it up as I go along!' These might have been the words of the director of this film, Steven Spielberg, who has created here an extravagant adventure loosely based upon the characters of boys' magazines, the ethics of Rider Haggard, and the cinematic tricks of two of his earlier films, *Jaws* and *Close Encounters of the Third Kind*. Mr Spielberg is, in other words, an unabashed populist who takes the more violent instincts of the race and transforms them into fantasy. We lose ourselves in his stories as if we were being lulled to sleep. He is the Grimm of his time.

Raiders of the Lost Ark is described in the advertisement as 'the ultimate adventure' – correct in the sense that it is hard to see how anyone could improve upon it. In the opening sequences, Jones is attacked by tarantulas, suspended above an abyss, pursued by a huge rolling stone, shot at by poisoned darts and surrounded by cannibals. Perhaps we might try a little existentialism here: man is not defined by his actions, he is replaced by them. The film is 'set' in 1936, although the time is immaterial: this is everywhere and nowhere, a charmed habitation in which good and evil clash over everything and nothing. The Americans and the Nazis are fighting for the possession of the Lost Ark – hidden for 3,000 years and now recovered, a source of power and divinity, 'levelling mountains and destroying regions', a 'radio to God'. The popular cinema has always required myths in order to give it sustenance, and the theme here is clear enough: man wishes to return to his lost intimacy with God, to recover his inheritance. But, of course, only the innocent can bear the light which will then be revealed; the Ark, in the hands of the Nazis, becomes an infernal machine which destroys those who touch it.

It is easy to discern here the presence of both Spielberg, with his atavistic cravings towards occult power which suffused *Close Encounters*, and also of the producer, George Lucas, who made *Star Wars*, a film in which human destiny was seen in terms of a universal shoot-out. Spielberg himself is an expert in cinematic mayhem; his last film, *1941*, was really only a series of comic disasters and spectacular special effects, turning the world into a fairground which was running at the wrong speed. In similar fashion, *Raiders of the Lost Ark* moves from Peru to America to Nepal to Egypt; there are submarines and snakes and subterranean palaces and ancestral curses. It is intensely watchable, with the relentless accumulation of effects used here for the purposes of eliciting suspense rather than provoking comedy.

Indiana Jones is played by Harrison Ford, whom we last saw in *Star Wars* as the impetuous space crusader; here he takes his particular dead-pan qualities a stage further, and specializes in what might be called characterless acting. Every movement, every facial gesture, is the one you would expect him to make. His comrade, Marion, is played by Karen Allen in the new American tradition of the 'good sport', the heroine who has evolved out of Women's Lib and has now left it behind, who can 'rough it' one minute and wear a diaphanous gown the next. The important thing about such characters is that we know they are not real, and therefore more easily believe in them.

The only danger – and it is one that the film does not wholly avoid – is that of turning such matters into parody. A film which depends upon overstatement should not, I think, too often advert to the fact. Mr Spielberg is now so much the master of cinematic technique that he is inclined to take his own powers of construction less seriously than the film actually requires. His facility leads him to the easy laugh, the self-conscious moments of bravura. In the process, *Raiders of the Lost Ark* becomes too arch, too much a parody of adventure and too little of an adventure itself.

8 August 1981

38

Mommie Dearest

Late one night, I turned on my telephone answering machine, only to hear a demented voice screaming, 'Wire coat-hangers? *Wire* coat-hangers!' The significance of this escaped me – was it a cry from the heart, or was it an irate customer mistaking me for a department of Peter Jones? It was only when I read, several days later, the reviews of *Mommie Dearest* that I understood. This is a film about Joan Crawford's relationship with her adopted children. As a result of it, a strange fever has gripped America: audiences turn up with wire coat-hangers gripped in their hands. In one scene Joan Crawford, in a fit of terrible rage, beats her daughter with just such a hanger. At the same moment, members of the audience hit each other with theirs.

I shall return to this particular scene in a moment, since it must count as one of the most extraordinary in recent film history, but it is the 'cult' status of *Mommie Dearest* which is most remarkable. In America most of its dialogue has been memorized and the audience shout it out as the narrative unfolds. 'Goodnight, good luck and goodbye' is the tearful exit-line of one of Miss Crawford's boy-friends, and the audience roar out the 'goodbye' with him. When Miss Crawford tries to strangle her daughter, in full view of an appalled woman journalist, the audience scream out 'Kill! Kill!'

Let us not mince words: I'm sure Miss Crawford would not want us to. This is a film patronized primarily, though not exclusively, by homosexuals – Joan Crawford being a *monstre sacrée*, a Hollywood Salome to whom large numbers of homosexuals are indebted for their gestures and their conversation and, occasionally, even their clothes. I once wrote a book about the psychology of such matters and it would be otiose to repeat it here: let's just say that the tradition of the masculine goddess is an ancient one. We have simply moved from *The Golden Bough* to the silver screen. Of course many audiences might have preferred to see Stanley Baxter rather than Faye Dunaway in the central role, but they are grateful for what they have. The notion of the 'star' is entrancing, in any guise, because it represents the concept of personality untouched by ordinary human feeling. The camera peers into Joan Crawford's face as if it were moving towards a bright, blank wall.

Miss Dunaway looks approximately right; she wanders through a house which resembles the ground floor of Swan and Edgar's, her shoulders as square as a theodolite, the arched eyebrows and the V-shaped mouth forming a perfect circle across her face. And then the onslaught begins; when Miss Dunaway stares, her eyes are like basilisks. Anything human melts within a thirty-yard range. In this film, her children bear the brunt of it – the beatings, the stranglings, the attempts to lock them away in convents. It is a Twentieth Century-Fox's Book of Martyrs.

But back to the wire hangers. Joan Crawford, her face caked in white moisturizing cream so that she resembles a pantomime clown, is wandering around her young daughter's bedroom; she is smiling, in a rather pained way, at nothing in particular. We have already seen her drinking tumblers of gin, so we suspect the worst. The daughter hides under the covers of her bed. Miss Crawford starts riffling through the infant's wardrobe, perhaps wondering if the clothes might still fit her, when a spasm of rage distorts her already strangely moulded features. 'No wire hangers! No wire hangers!' She brandishes one above her head like an axe. 'What are wire hangers doing in this closet? Answer me!' Pandemonium now breaks out in the cinema, and those with wire hangers tighten their grip upon them: a great tragic scene is being created out of thin air. She is Lady Macbeth who cannot find a missing button, Clytemnestra who has mislaid her bus pass.

Then, oh no!, she finds another wire hanger. 'Why? Why?' she screams, raising her eyes to heaven as if to scorch God. 'Tina! Get out of that bed!' This is the moment. As she beats Tina with the hanger, the audience give wild cries and hit each other with theirs. And then she is forcing Tina on her knees and making her scrub the floor; suddenly she throws cleaning powder all over her daughter (at this point, in America, some members of the audience use talcum powder instead) and makes a sudden, tottering exit. Her adopted son now creeps tearfully out of a nearby bed and says to Christina Crawford, 'I'll help you clear it up.' 'No,' says Christina in terror, 'No. Go back.

Strap yourself in.' It seems that Joan Crawford tied her little son to his bed. It is the culminating moment.

Now here is the paradox: this is a serious film, in no way designed to be deliberately funny; and yet it reduces audiences to hysteria. How could the director, and Faye Dunaway herself, have so miscalculated the mood that, instead of a psychological study of a haunted and bitter woman, we have high comedy of a rare kind? Chekhov was dismayed when his comedies were treated as solemn dramas; how much more disappointing to have created a comic masterpiece by accident.

Certain doubts have been raised about the authenticity of Christina Crawford's biography of her mother, from which this film was made; it has been said that, out of malice or anger, her adopted daughter has embellished the record. But this is, of course, beside the point. If you live the myth of the 'movie star', as Joan Crawford so relentlessly did, then you must expect that same myth to continue and even to grow after your death. There are hints within the film of a real person beneath the make-up – Joan Crawford was clearly terrified of failure, and it was this fear which drove her to the kind of absurd perfectionism and competitiveness which marked her life. An interesting film might well be made out of such an extraordinary personality – apparently devoid of self-doubt and yet filled with fear. But it would have to be of someone working in a different medium – in the cinema such matters are of little account; the legend has to triumph over the reality. And so *Mommie Dearest* becomes a kind of homage to the monster herself – the emotions are so splendid, the scenes so dramatic, the experiences so incandescent. At the end, we see Joan Crawford in death, perfectly made up, the shoulders as square as ever. She is bathed in a faint blue glow, as though the arc lights had been only momentarily dimmed.

5 December 1981

39

The Draughtsman's Contract

Last week I dreamt that I was surrounded by people, all of them congratulating me on my film column. (If you happen to read the correspondence columns of the *Spectator*, you will understand that these could only be creatures of fantasy.) An elderly lady was asking me about a theory of probability which I had concocted in one of these little pieces, when I remembered that I had forgotten to see a film for next week's issue. Contentment at being flattered at once changed to anxiety. And then I woke up. I only record this to demonstrate the efficacy of dreams, which can be almost medieval in their significance: I *had* forgotten to see a film. As is my habit, I turned to the film reviews in the other newspapers to see what I had missed. No new films had been released. Consternation.

Then I recalled that there had been one film, which I had not reviewed but which those who take an interest in such things had mentioned to me. Since the film was being shown only in Belsize Park, my natural laziness had prevailed at the time. But the finger of fate now pointed to the benighted area. The film is *The Draughtsman's Contract*, written and directed by Peter Greenaway. I knew that it was English, and I had heard vaguely that the audience at Cannes stood up and cheered at the end. Since this seems to happen all the time at Cannes, I had not been particularly impressed. But now, as on all the great occasions of life, necessity prevailed over prejudice and I travelled at once in a closed cab to the north of London.

It was a great relief, then, to discover that *The Draughtsman's Contract* is a highly successful film. It is set in 1694, in a post-Revolutionary England which perhaps owes more to Beardsley than to Congreve: wigs like pillars of candy floss, faces patched but still peeling, costumes apparently made out of the scales of silverfish. The plot concerns a Mr Neville, draughtsman, who has been persuaded to sketch twelve views of a country house owned by the Herbert family. Since he is much in demand, he can set his own terms which, in this case, include the ravishing of Mrs Herbert on twelve successive days. Mr Neville is precise, authoritative and somewhat ruthless – a paradigm of the rigour and security which the picture at first seems to celebrate. Elongated figures move across lawns, their high-pitched laughter like the cries of dying peacocks, while social life consists of a number of feints and measured skirmishes.

This is a highly stylized film, devoted to visual display as much as to action or character, and a wonderfully rich surface is created as the camera moves to and fro in a steady rhythm. Everything is seen from a distance – the emotional distance which self-conscious display creates – and as a result the past looks haunting and bizarre. All the meaning has been drained out of it and, instead of the stately vistas of Vanbrugh, we get an odd feeling of emptiness and horror as if we were peering into the vistas of a De Chirico.

The passion for order creates the expectation of, and appetite for, disorder – just as the formal courtesies of speech in this film can accommodate an extraordinary licentiousness or exuberance of expression. 'He doesn't like to see the fish,' Mrs Herbert explains of her husband. 'Carp live too long. They remind him of Catholics.' Certain objects appear in Mr Neville's drawings – a pair of boots, a solitary figure – and, since he is self-confessedly without imagination, he has no explanation for their appearance. He simply draws what he sees. But his employers – and the audience in the cinema, of course – begin to make their own interpretations, and derive from these wayward objects a plot which includes sexual violence and murder.

By degrees the film works on a double level and, with the help of Mr Neville's drawings, two narratives begin to emerge. One of them is formal, deliberate, lucid – an account of twelve days in the country. The other is shadowy, murderous, amorphous. When the formal order is overturned in a series of terrible events the victim is Mr Neville himself, the draughtsman who tried to impose a lucid pattern on the world. Since we are concerned with ways of seeing – the way the cinema audience sees, as well as the protagonists within the story – the cinematic nature of the film is refined and deepened so that we have, by the end, a meditation upon the nature of perception but one achieved with such stylishness and wit that we are a world away from conventional metaphysical speculations upon the subject.

The Draughtsman's Contract is a curious and inventive film, displaying great intelligence – the kind of intelligence which a film-maker needs just as much as any other artist. Here we have an ingenious story which has been sustained in an exuberant and convincing manner – a conceit which lasts two hours, a game of wit in which elaboration is its own reward. A dream world – it was appropriate, perhaps, that a dream should lead me to it.

8 January 1983

40

The Wicked Lady

I admit it, I like trash sometimes – especially when it is not pretending to be anything else. *The Wicked Lady* is the sheer and unadulterated real thing, an eight-tiered wedding cake made of styrofoam, a sport in which the only rules are to make money and to have fun at the same time. It has been suggested that Mr Winner has fashioned his film as part of the 'new romantic' movement, but he is too intelligent a director to pitch himself into a youth fad of that kind. What he has done, instead, is to poke fun at the whole idea of the 'Restoration romp' which this film purports to be. The costumes look like the sort of thing the Princess of Wales will be wearing in a few years' time, and the jewels are as large as fried eggs. Hysterical villagers engage in unadorned copulation, and Tyburn resembles a country fair organized by the village idiot: 'It's changed a bit since then, hasn't it?' said an old lady behind me, in a nostalgic manner. It has, dear, of course, but to add historical authenticity Sir John Gielgud appears on the screen looking as though he is suffering some archaic distemper.

The overblown and over-lush tone of the whole film is in fact characteristic: I have not seen so many nipples since the heyday of the Blackpool postcard. It is cheap, but it is wonderfully cheap; we know that the bridges are made of plaster and the elaborate Restoration interiors of plywood, but Mr Winner knows that we know and makes it part of the joke. It is an illusion, and no one need bother his head looking for something else. Self-consciousness on such a grand scale would be intolerable in a more mannered film-maker, but Mr Winner has never been accused of seriousness on any level. And the cinema devoid of serious purpose is often a marvellous thing – *The Wicked Lady* is, if nothing else, intensely watchable.

It also has a rather good story. Lady Skelton (Faye Dunaway) is bored by her rich but fastidious husband, and assumes a new career as a highway robber. She joins forces (as well as everything else) with another bandit (Alan Bates), betrays him when he jilts her and is then herself shot. She dies in a picturesque manner, with blood only on the outside of her nightgown. The only thing you can do with such a plot is to play it for all it's worth, and Miss Dunaway has had a great deal of practice in going 'over the top'. She looks very good in black, although her face is alarmingly flat, like that of a Maori goddess; she rolls her eyes and opens her legs with great gusto – and who says she cannot do both at the same time? Sir John Gielgud, playing the part of her pious butler, wanders in as if by accident (perhaps it was); no film is complete without him these days, and after many years of practice he has perfected the art of the withering look so that everyone around him turns to stone. This used to be called scene-stealing, although occasionally he meets his match in Miss Dunaway. If looks could kill, they could between them wipe out a small city.

Having recovered from the shock of seeing Alan Bates naked, the audience wait with bated breath for the famous whipping sequence. This, you may remember, caused a small fuss when Mr Winner objected to its deletion by the censor; a number of great and good people declared that whipping was just what they wanted to see, and the cuts were restored. In fact it is anodyne stuff, and would not arouse a cat, although it gave Miss Dunaway the chance to re-enact her part as Joan Crawford in *Mommie Dearest* and suffer some kind of nuclear melt-down.

The film is an elaborate joke, but often a very funny one and there are few directors who could carry it off with the verve of Mr Winner. He can parody the whole idea of such a film, caricaturing both the kind of direction and writing associated with it, while at the same time extracting the last ounce of filmability (if there is such a word) from such ingredients. His strengths as a director are, of course, best seen in 'action films' of this nature because he is adept at conveying excited movement, flourishes, fluid activity upon the screen. His skill lies not in portraying human emotion – any number of directors can do that, and it is in any case such a cheap commodity in the cinema – but rather in depicting human busyness: intrigue, commotion and confusion are his tools.

But he is also impatient with his own skills, as many clever men are, and has now reached a level of sardonic self-consciousness where he is able to make jokes at his own expense, just as he is scornful of the more po-faced attitude of many film directors to their medium. He knows his primary purpose is to entertain (there are, after all, much worse activities) – even if he does have the last laugh, I suspect, by implicitly mocking those who giggle at his well-placed jokes and well-constructed scenes. There are so many putatively 'serious' films which are wholly incompetent or inadequate that a film-maker who knows his limitations – as well as his strengths – has an immediate advantage. Yes, it is trash but it is unashamed trash.

30 April 1983

41

Octopussy

Towards the end of this film, Commander Bond and 'M', the delightfully quirky English scientist, descend upon an Indian palace in a hot-air balloon; a large Union Jack is emblazoned on the side of the balloon itself, and inside the wicker receptacle there are cameras, pocket televisions and computers: yet again, Victorian Values have been brought bang up to date as our most famous secret agent cuts a swathe through various brown people. Although *Octopussy* is the thirteenth of the Bond films, which stretch well back before the Conservative victory of 1979, the whole enterprise has finally found its spiritual home in Mrs Thatcher's Britain.

All those gadgets which are a characteristic part of the Bond legend might have been designed by Clive Sinclair; Mrs Thatcher might have visited the laboratory where they make the fountain pens which turn into parachutes at one minute and spurt acid the next. It would be an 'exercise in futility' for James Bond to attempt to negotiate with his enemies – they understand only the quick chop to the throat, and the knee in the groin. And how nice that all this violence can be happening elsewhere, in India or South America, while at home we have Miss Moneypenny arranging the flowers in her Whitehall office. Perhaps only the sex would seem out of place, but since Commander Bond has a habit of killing or otherwise revenging himself upon the wicked women he sleeps with, we can put all those antics down to the ordinary male spirit of fun.

It would be absurd to suggest, of course, that *Octopussy* is altogether a vehicle for contemporary English fantasies and values but it displays a certain coldness or hardness which, when compounded with a high degree of irony, suggests at least the presence of similar preoccupations. The association of advanced technology with a certain kind of superiority is one aspect of this but, more importantly, it is the way in which patriotism, and the spirit of Englishness in general, are depicted in a glossy and shallow manner which makes the connection. They are the marketing techniques which will help to sell the film and, if we are moving into the era of rule by the lower middle class, in these films we have a bright image of the fantasies of that class.

Octopussy itself makes the same point; in one scene, an ambitious Russian General – who is Bond's sworn enemy – notes with satisfaction that 'The West is decadent and divided . . . throughout the West there are demonstrations for unilateral disarmament.' Stand up, Commander Bond, and speak for us.

Roger Moore has grown old in our service (perhaps the film should have been called *Octogenarian*). Marshmallow has entered his soul, and he has now reached the stage where he lets the twinkle in his eye do all the work for him. His foil here is Louis Jourdain, actually rather an accomplished actor, who, beside the other members of the cast, seems to be Sarah Bernhardt and Charles Laughton in one. There is nothing much for either of them to do except look disgusted with each other – the real physical stuff, the leaping off trains and the falling out of aeroplanes, is of course accomplished by the stunt men. In fact the 'stunts' are the most important part of the film, the Bond formula having now become so stereotyped that it hardly needs a narrative to support it. In *Octopussy* some diamonds are being smuggled out of Russia, and an atomic bomb is about to explode in an American army camp – the only connection between these two events being the inordinate amount of violence expended in order to get from one plot to another.

A *Tom and Jerry* cartoon was being played before the film, in the cinema which I visited, and indeed the violence of *Octopussy* is very close to the comic violence of that cat-and-mouse animation: all the manic squashing and battering, as the victims rise up and start all over again. If there is a difference, it lies in the fact that the violence of the Bond film is not characterized by ordinary comedy but by irony and parody – the killing is done with a smile, the rape and carnage are not meant to be 'taken seriously'. This seems to be a peculiarly English characteristic: in the general absence of real values, even the most brutal events are drained of significance or meaning.

I am perhaps becoming portentous about a conventional example of trashy cinema, but I am convinced that films such as this are far more corrupting than the usual targets of puritanical censure. You know where you are with ordinary pornography and 'video nasties': they are so straightforward in their preoccupations and so recognizable in their methods that they are not insidious in their effects. The kind of subliminal emptiness of the Bond sagas is much more difficult to detect and therefore to reject.

In the credits at the beginning of the picture, naked women are merged with pictures of guns cocked and ready to shoot (with obvious implications). Sex and death are associated, just as technology is seen in the picture as only another instrument of death. The general fascination with that subject suggests to me something approaching a cult of death – underneath the bright images and the brash music, that is what we are really dealing with. I am not sure that the 'parental guidance' certificate is really enough.

18 June 1983

42

The Company of Wolves

This is a film which at once creates an atmosphere of mystery, as a respectable middle-class family is seen to possess its own secret passages and desires. The young daughter of the house, Rosaleen, is asleep and in her dreams we move from the conventional English countryside to a place where the world itself becomes a dark wood populated by carnivorous teddies, by trees which grow cobwebs, by storks that preen themselves in graveyards, and by wolves that lurk beyond the paths. And as Rosaleen, now on the edge of puberty, wanders in this dream state, all the characters and events of her comfortable middle-class life are quite transformed: she faces a world in which her charming storybook characters take on a symbolic and threatening life, and where the natural world is as malevolent as it is beneficent. For her dreams concern a small human community surrounded by a forest – a perilous community invaded by tales of men that turn into wolves, and of devils that creep up from the underworld to entice and torment the living.

If this is not the landscape of childhood, which tends to be altogether a more prosaic affair, it is at least that landscape of simplified morals and messages which adults impose upon children; this makes it rather disturbing, yet *The Company of Wolves* employs neither conventional horror nor conventional fantasy and it is precisely this elusive quality which makes it interesting. Certainly a British film (it is directed by Neil Jordan) which has escaped the claws of pallid realism is to be applauded at first sight, but one's pleasure in seeing it is more than simply a reaction against the ever-increasing restrictiveness of conventional social drama. This is, in fact, an alternative form of cinema.

For the film uses the material of fairy story with astonishing results: the plot itself, which concerns the nature and origin of the werewolf, is at once established within some timeless world where symbol and fantasy can cohabit, and where the conventions of the fairy story can be married with more arcane matters. Angela Carter, who has adapted one of her own stories for use here, evokes sexual images throughout the narrative so that the dangerous enchanted wood becomes a metaphor for Rosaleen's own pubescent state. If that sounds portentous, the richness and elaboration of the narrative make it much less so: the great advantage of using the format of a fairy story, after all, is that the old imperative of 'Once upon a time' remains and carries the audience from story to story.

The Company of Wolves is also a pleasing spectacle, as the glowing interiors are set against the more threatening life of the forest itself. Some of the 'special effects' are very effective indeed, and the transformation of man into wolf is done with a faithfulness which makes parts of the process difficult to watch; why on earth this film was given an '18' certificate, by the way, is impossible to understand – unless it was on the grounds that fairy tales are really only suitable for adults.

Certainly the adults within the film performed with an appropriate amount of conviction: Angela Lansbury, as the wise grandmother, was both as reassuring and as frightening as grandmothers often are; she mingled well with the other archetypes in the film as she muttered through pursed lips the age-old warning, 'Never stray from the path, never eat a windfall apple, and never trust a man whose eyebrows meet.' For the windfall apple will contain a worm, and adjacent eyebrows is a mark of lycanthropy, both of them neatly suggesting one of the film's major themes: that of the violence which lurks beneath the shiny and beneficent world, and how that violence is often mediated in the relationships between men and women.

This was a mysterious, rather horrifying but consistently fascinating film which acquired an inner coherence and purpose – and, in the process, the cinema itself became a simile for dream and a vehicle for myth. 'Seeing is believing' was one of the repeated phrases, and in a sense that became true as a number of evocative images helped to reawaken the capacity for wonder in an audience. If I have one complaint, it is only that the symbolic intentions which Carter and Jordan wished to incorporate became too intrusive towards the close, when Rosaleen herself dreams that she has become a wolf and wakes to find the relics of her childhood shattered around her. The point here may have been that the 'animal' element exists in the woman as well as the generally more bestial man, but this fact may already be quite evident to the general public. Nevertheless it gave a suitably climactic ending to a film which never failed to please and which often managed to astonish.

There has been in recent years a return in fiction to what has been labelled as 'magical realism'; I am not sure what that phrase means, except that it is meant to unite the work of such disparate talents as those of Michael Moorcock and Angela Carter herself: certainly it is one of the strongest elements in the contemporary English novel. There seems no reason why Neil Jordan, and other British directors of similar intelligence, might not therefore find in modern fiction material much more persuasive than 'social realism', since it is material which, as *The Company of Wolves* suggested, can be rendered on the screen with great inventiveness and grace. And that, in the end, may be this film's most important lesson.

29 September 1984

43

A Private Function

This is a film about the English – certainly not celebrating them, and yet not exactly burying them, either; somewhere in between, proving yet again how macabre and also how daft they can seem. The script-writer, Alan Bennett, has established a reputation for writing dialogue of a devastating flatness; there is nothing to beat the dour distinction of a Leeds vowel sound, especially when it is employed in the kind of conversation which can go from the Royal Family to an unhappy state of the bowels without showing any signs of strain. And by fortunate coincidence both elements are present in *A Private Function*, a film set in 'austerity Britain' two years after the end of the war. The public occasion which sets this private function in motion is the wedding of Princess Elizabeth and her consort; but this Britain, although it pays lip service to royalty and 'all that we fought the war for', is a place of quite extraordinary hypocrisy and squalor, where the most that can be expected is a seedy gentility barely concealing the greed and meanness of small-town life.

It is, in other words, a comedy – we know it to be a comedy, in any case, because it is centred around Betty, a pig which is being reared illegally in order to provide meat for the loyal wedding dinner. The local chiropodist (Michael Palin), urged on by his wife (Maggie Smith), then steals the animal from under the noses of certain local worthies who proceed to lose all their local dignity in trying to retrieve it. Plots such as this do not exactly grow on trees, so both director and cast can be expected to squeeze every last drop of peculiarity out of it. There are some horrible scenes in the chiropodist's household, for example, as Maggie Smith takes on the role of Lady Macbeth and follows the pig with a knife exclaiming:

'Kill it!'

'But she's my friend!'

'Kill your friend!'

Or words to that effect – the effect in question being 'farce' or 'surrealism', according to the cultural aspirations of the film reviewer who describes it.

But if there is any substantial English comic tradition, it is that of the grotesque in which the eccentrics (or worse) get all the best lines. This is certainly true of *A Private Function*, since there is practically no one in the film who is not larger and more horrible than life. When this is combined with the severe literalness of Alan Bennett's script, the nature of the comedy becomes clear: terrible people are given very sharp outlines so that they cut all the more deeply. It becomes in the process a cautionary tale, a film about human appetite in which food is always being eaten and animals are always to be chopped up – a great chain of being which, in Bennett's comedy, is generally to be found hanging in the lavatory where all this eating comes to an end. 'We're only human, after all' is one of the clichés on the lips of a lustful and blousy widow – a remark which, as someone in the film explains, is generally made by those who have behaved in a more than usually bestial manner. This is perhaps why half the cast seem to have been chosen for their porcine or bovine features, and why it becomes clear that the only thing which distinguishes humans from animals is their capacity for self-deception. Certainly this is not an environment in which the finer things of life can be said to flourish – unless the occasional shout of 'andante' from Maggie Smith to her piano pupils can be taken for culture.

The purpose of thus reducing human beings to the sum of their appetites is that it provides the raw (sometimes very raw) material for the most bitter comedy – it is when people are in the grip of purely animal needs that they can be at their most ridiculous or pathetic. The problem for an audience, however, is that such a tone can be rather lowering to the spirits when it is not alleviated or interrupted by something in a more light-hearted vein. But this is a quality which Bennett's script alone cannot provide – his parody of domestic clichés is glacial enough, but in any case the nuances of his dialogue are much more suited to the more intimate tones of the television screen. There were moments here when he was swamped by a medium which relies upon broader effects than he generally cares to produce.

And so, in the end, the ebullience was left to the cast – and, in this sense, *A Private Function* could not have been a more triumphally British film. Maggie Smith, as the housewife with dreams of glory, has a suburban imperiousness which has to be seen to be believed. Michael Palin is excellent, also, as the chiropodist: the part might have been created for him (perhaps it was). Denholm Elliott, as a 'bent' doctor, once again brings to bear upon the English accent that terrible moment of ambiguity when he hovers, as it were, between classes. Richard Griffiths is excellently stoic, and Liz Smith proves yet again that no one can beat her in playing a really unattractive woman. Despite the fact that this film is perhaps rather less than the sum of its parts, as a screen comedy it still comes in before most of the rest.

8 December 1984

44
Body Double

Brian De Palma is both one of the most fascinating and most vulgar of American directors – and in that paradox we may see why he poses such problems for critics, if not necessarily for audiences. He is slick, he is cheap, but of his filmic skills there can be no doubt; and the fact that he manages to be both so tawdry and so interesting might suggest that the cinema itself is a medium which encourages or even welcomes the meretricious imagination.

Let us take this particular film: *Body Double* is concerned with salacious sexuality and brutal murder (the latter with an electric drill); it has elements of soft-core pornography, of the 'horror film' and of any cheap detective series. And yet at the same time it is beautifully and on occasions astonishingly directed. An unemployed actor becomes obsessed with a young woman who lives in the apartment opposite his own; he follows her, convinced that she is in danger, and then later witnesses her murder. The rest may be left to the imagination of anyone who has not seen *Rear Window*. Those with beady little eyes may even be able to anticipate the denouement but that does not lessen its interest, since *Body Double* is in some ways a triumph of manner over matter.

Like other directors of his generation De Palma has grown up with cinematic imagery, and he is now so familiar with its resources that he can deploy it in any number of ways. It is natural, then, that *Body Double* should open in a film studio where a conventional 'horror film' is being made and that its credits should roll across scenery which is seen to be only a *piece* of scenery when it is removed. It is suitable, also, that the story should be set in Hollywood, where the extraordinary theatricality of the urban environment matches that peculiar over-brightness which De Palma always brings to the screen. He has often been compared to Hitchcock, and it is certainly true that he borrows certain effects (and even, on this occasion, a plot) from him; but their true similarity lies in the fact that both men have entirely cinematic imaginations. De Palma's is not a literary or theatrical talent put to work in a different medium: he thinks in images, he feels in images, and as a result one of the most noticeable aspects of this film is the studied absence of dialogue in the more important scenes. He resembles Hitchcock, too, in the way that he manages to orchestrate imagery in order to create an atmosphere of quite unbearable suspense even when, in fact, there seems to be nothing in particular to be suspenseful about.

He always has his eye on the audience, in other words, and he is just as busy manipulating the response in the stalls as he is manipulating the actors in front of the camera – incidentally, De Palma is well served by his performers here, who are not in themselves 'stars' (everyone is subjugated to De Palma's vision) but who attain a very high standard of professionalism. I do not know how De Palma prepares his films, but I suspect that – again, like Hitchcock – he has very clear ideas about what he wants and very firm means of attaining it. It is in fact not easy to describe the precise nature of his direction; there are no literary or theatrical allusions which would help to elucidate the particular tone of his films and perhaps the fullest explanation would be a technical one. It is largely through his remarkable and fluid use of the camera, for example, that he is on occasions able to sustain the momentum of a scene so that we have the illusion that it was all taken in one shot. It seems effortless, almost, but it is a triumph (if nothing else) of editing. One of his favourite tricks – so familiar that it has now become almost the hallmark of his style – is that of the camera circling around a character or group of characters so that they become the only recognizable objects in a shifting landscape. In this film he even re-employs the technique as a self-conscious joke which, in a film always veering close to a parody of itself, is not out of place.

And, in addition, all of De Palma's usual themes are here – perverse sex, violence, horror and, most importantly, the nature of voyeurism. In this case the actor who watches the murder is aligned with the murderer himself – 'your blood brother', as the investigating detective put it. De Palma is always half-entertaining and half-abusing his audience with reminders of its own voyeuristic status, and in *Body*

Double he makes the explicit connection between visual pornography and sex crimes, between the re-enactment of death and the responsibility of those who are content to watch it. Whether in fact he has anything very profound to say about these matters must remain in doubt (I think his is the position of the waiter who is quite proud to point to the fly in the soup which he is serving you), but there is no doubt that his power over the audience is very strong. It may not go very deep but it stretches very far – although it has to be said that those who have not grasped the fact that De Palma works in images rather than realities may have some problems with an ending which pays no obeisances to 'real life' at all.

28 September 1985

45

Young Sherlock Holmes and the Pyramid of Fear

It was clever of Steven Spielberg to choose Sherlock Holmes for his latest cinematic fantasy, since the famous detective fits with his own sense both of juvenile theatre and of nostalgic mystery. Certainly the devotees of Holmesiana and the fans of Spielberg share a certain interest in the baroque and the sensational: that is why, at the beginning of the film, a mid-Victorian setting is transformed by hallucinatory effects (some of them quite terrifying) which do not seem particularly out of place. Conan Doyle is a more 'literary taste', sanctified by time and a predominantly middle-class readership, but he appeals to exactly the same perfervid imagination which sends young children into *Star Wars* or *Gremlins*.

And how clever of Spielberg to make this the 'young' Sherlock Holmes – he is seen here as a boy (played excellently by Nicholas Rowe) whose burgeoning powers of deduction are wasted on his 'set' at Brompton School. Everyone understands the mature Holmes too well, and by thrusting him back into early adolescence Spielberg can continue his resourceful exploitation of an essentially childlike imagi-nation. I have talked about Spielberg here even though he is only the 'executive producer', but the fact is that anything connected with him seems to bear his imaginative and technical stamp.

It has to be admitted, of course, that as a result this is an American version of mid-Victorian England – I suspect that it is largely derived from other films and television series, although the script-writer (with the charming name of Chris Columbus) clearly has made an effort to master some of the technicalities of the English language. There are even one or two complete sentences, even though their provenance seems to be more David Niven than Conan Doyle. But none of this matters since the characters and setting are really only an excuse for what, since the success of Spielberg, can only be described as international fantasy – underground caves, a world of threatening adults, children flying through the air, and so on.

On this occasion a hooded stranger walks through the streets of London and blows poisoned darts at various respectable personages. The young Holmes immediately suspects 'foul play' and, in the face of opposition from Detective-Sergeant Lestrade, decides to investigate. He is led to a public house managed by an Egyptian, where a belly-dancer performs among the low life: it is as if *Oliver Twist* has been mixed up with *King Solomon's Mines*, thus providing a lethal concoction of popular entertainment. There are also scenes, at another vivid turn of the plot, which were strongly reminiscent of those films I watched as a child at Saturday matinées: here, once again, was a gorgeous subterranean world of power and perfidy where slaves writhed in ecstasy or dragged monstrous objects with bits of rope.

There is a wonderful climax at an Egyptian temple cunningly concealed somewhere in Wapping, where a large pyramid has also been erected. Curiously enough Wapping itself is dominated by the church of St George-in-the-East, in the grounds of which there is also a pyramid. Of course this must be put down to coincidence, since neither Steven Spielberg nor Chris Columbus could have known about this early eighteenth-century anticipation of their plot. But, on another level, there is no such thing as coincidence; it is certainly the case that this area of London has been associated with particularly odd rites, and the fact that they also appear in a late twentieth-century American film suggests, if nothing else, the divining power of the popular imagination.

But to return to *Young Sherlock Holmes*: its plot is of course preposterous but what would be unacceptable in print (although some of Conan Doyle's stories are rather similar in conception) is perfectly feasible in the cinema where spectacle, animation and a certain rhythmic momentum are enough to maintain interest and, therefore, conviction. Certainly the closing scenes are extremely exciting, and I defy anyone not to be impressed by the technical artistry of their climactic battle. The acting is excellent, also.

29 March 1986

46

Caravaggio

Long, long ago, in the early twenties, Caravaggio was described by Roger Fry as 'the first Hollywood painter', or words to that effect – no doubt in oblique recognition of that painter's notorious *chiaroscuro*. Hollywood got its revenge, of course; the cinema is now the recognized mistress of the art of shadows, and *film noir* might almost be described as a seventeenth-century form. But Derek Jarman goes one step further and, in the opening sequence of this picture devoted to Caravaggio's pictures, he employs the screen as if it were a canvas. Everything is directed towards painterly ends, and as a result *Caravaggio* is a small masterpiece of composition.

The painter is dying in a bare room, the customary setting for a lengthy 'biopic' which then promptly ensues; various unseemly episodes in Caravaggio's life are introduced, and are used as a counterpoint to Jarman's glowing evocation of his actual paintings. These scenes are intermittently interesting, although, by the strange alchemy of film, each 'great artist' commemorated in the cinema becomes indistinguishable from any other. He tends to be penniless, misunderstood, sullen and drunken. Caravaggio is no exception on this occasion and, although Derek Jarman has a reputation for being an 'experimental' film-maker (which means only that he has never been employed by Goldcrest), his conception of the artist is a conventionally Romantic one. His is a view of Caravaggio as an 'outsider', with some of the known facts of the painter's life being employed to serve this interpretation.

The conditions under which the film was made (with the possible exception of the BFI grant) were far from conventional, however. Apparently *Caravaggio* was constructed on a small budget in the furthest reaches of the East End – some of the cast are apparently inhabitants of that area. But poverty can be the mother of invention, and some of the most striking aspects of this film are managed with a minimum of fussy and expensive cinematic 'business': I was particularly struck, for example, by the way in which Jarman managed to turn Caravaggio's paintings into a series of tableaux. On occasions this brought back terrible memories of those *poses plastiques* which were once the theatrical equivalent of pornography, but at their best they show remarkable bravura. They do tend to impede the progress of the action, however, and their impact upon the narrative was such that the film resolves itself into a number of episodes or images which can only fitfully acquire any kind of coherence. They are not much help to the actors, either; given the slightly erratic pace of the proceedings, they are generally working in a vacuum giving isolated performances which contribute very little to the actual texture of the film.

This is one of the problems which accompany too great an emphasis upon painterly composition: such an interest tends to usurp all the other functions of the film. Certainly more attention ought to have been given to the script, which suffers from a fetid romanticism that has not been seen since the days of Ouida: 'silent as an echo . . . a ripple spread out beyond the furthest horizon . . . I love you more than my eyes', and so forth. Pondering on the occasion when you last heard a silent echo, you may miss the fact that the words in this film veer wildly between such grandiose nonsense and a clipped demotic (replete with expletives). This reveals a peculiar uncertainty or ambiguity of tone, as if Caravaggio were at the same time to be seen both as a 'modern' – speaking 'for our time' – and as an artist whose violence has been sanctified by time.

The same uncertainty marks Jarman's insistent use of anachronistic detail, as the torrid airs of the early seventeenth century are interrupted by the sound of a lorry or the bleep of a personal calculator. This can be effective (it provides a nice frame for the general theatricality of the proceedings), but there were also occasions when it seemed really a technical trick designed to camouflage the essential orthodoxy of the film's conception – the cinematic equivalent of real toads in old-fashioned, imaginary gardens.

Whether any of this bears the smallest relation to the 'real' Caravaggio is neither here nor there; the 'real' Caravaggio has been dead for some time, and he will live only by being reinterpreted in just such a manner. The important thing, therefore, is that this *Caravaggio* should be convincing as a cinematic interpretation. In large measure it is, thanks to the excellent performance of Nigel Terry in the principal role. But there were problems: I suspect that the painter's homosexuality, for example, has been grossly over-emphasized for reasons not a million miles removed from Jarman's own sensibility. There are some rather precious 'gay' scenes starring various dignitaries of the Holy Roman Church, and the camera lingers over the muscular bodies of half-naked male models with the inane lustfulness previously only seen in those photographs of Sicilian boys taken by pederasts at the turn of the century. There is something passé about this – the interest in a specifically homosexual sensibility or culture was really part of the seventies climacteric, and the general effect is only to turn Caravaggio into the seventeenth-century equivalent of an old queen looking for a piece of 'rough trade' (I think that is the expression).

So Mr Jarman has been rather naughty. Still, it is his best film to date and it contains some very pretty pictures. He may not be out of the 'art house' syndrome yet, but he is getting there.

10 May 1986

47

When the Viewing had to Stop

There comes a time when Mr Pickwick, bewildered by the horrors of the Fleet Prison, announces that 'I have seen enough . . . My head aches with these scenes, and my heart too. Henceforth I will be a prisoner in my own room.' These are very much the sentiments of your film critic on abandoning his generally undistinguished and no doubt ineffective career; enough is enough. No more films set in what journalists call 'Thatcher's England'; no more tearful tributes to the elderly starring

Katharine Hepburn; no more masterpieces with the subtitles in Americanese. And no more questions from the only mildly curious, on the lines of 'What film is worth seeing?' I never really knew. I never remembered. Yesterday I turned back to the pages of the *Spectator* in 1979 when I began to write film criticism, and I could recall nothing of the films I then either praised or damned. They had gone, vanished, disappeared. I usually find it difficult to recall even the film I saw in the previous week, so effortlessly do the images slip or slide away.

Of course there were some good pictures and, funnily enough, the most memorable are generally the ones which were also the most popular – the films of George Lucas, of Steven Spielberg, of Brian De Palma have lingered in the mind where the work of some of the more apparently 'serious' directors has completely disappeared. Of course there are many cinema critics who, nervous about the status of their chosen field, tend wildly to overpraise any film which has even the remotest chance of seeming 'important': hence the enormous solemnity with which the last film by Tarkovsky was received, when in reality it was nothing more than turgid melodrama. And so it was often with heavy heart that I made my way towards the latest celebrated offering from Eastern Europe, or Japan, or the American 'avant-garde'. There were times when I was agreeably surprised, but there were also times when I was not. In any case I was not a professional or even a well-informed film critic. It was always an interest rather than a passion, and on Sunday mornings – before writing my review (since Sunday is a day of rest, I always reserve it for journalism) – I would have to scrabble through the newspapers, looking for the names of the director or actors involved in that particular week's offering. As the readers of this journal have probably realized by now, I only ever saw one film a week rather than the statutory three or four; I have to admit, also, that there were times when I walked out of a film before its end. Flesh can only stand so much.

Perhaps more memorable than the films have been the cinemas themselves. There were ghastly places in north London, where health food was sold over the counter; there were dank crypts off the Tottenham Court Road which people used as refuges rather than as places of entertainment. But there were also some agreeable little spots, somehow removed from this world: the Minema is generally billed as the smallest cinema in London but it is also one of the most comfortable, and those who have a taste for macabre interiors should visit one of the auditoria of the Cannon Haymarket. And I regret the passing of the Academy, Oxford Street, which curiously resembled a toy theatre blown up out of all proportion.

And of course the cinema itself was always as important as any of the films being shown in it. The queuing, the buying of undrinkable coffee, the harridans bearing trays of ice-cream, the advertisements for Levi's jeans and the Electricity Board, the warnings about one's handbag, all furnished the slow and cosy passage into the filmic world. And yet even as I enjoyed these simple pleasures I was aware of the fact that they were essentially of an old-fashioned and even anachronistic sort – not ones, perhaps, which will survive the end of the century in their present form. I seemed to be participating in a social activity that was already past; I was still part of the audience that first went to the silent cinema in the twenties and I was certainly not part of that unimaginable future populace to whom the cinema will mean no more than the penny gaff or the diorama do to us.

So perhaps I am not the right person to answer the usual boring questions. If asked to summarize the state of the British film industry over the last eight years, for example, I would be hard pressed to do so. Certainly I have not noticed any particular improvement in British productions, despite their much heralded 'rebirth', and in fact films which were generally praised – films such as *The Mission* or *Chariots of Fire* – struck me at the time as being more than usually repellent. In a similar way contemporary English film actors seem to have been ludicrously overpraised – ranging from the ubiquitous Bob Hoskins to the even more ubiquitous Jeremy Irons. I suspect that they were in large part lionized because they handily represent, for Hollywood consumption, certain English stereotypes. For what it's worth, after my long spell in front of the silver screen, I would suggest that the two greatest film actors in the world (including men and women) are Robert de Niro and Gérard Depardieu.

When the British film industry is not in question, the argument generally turns on the nature of censorship. There is no doubt that prolonged attendance in the cinema can blunt the sensibility (I am living evidence of this fact), but this is only because film is necessarily a narrow and limited medium which must generally purport to represent 'reality'. Hence the confusion in certain minds, when they mistake film for life. On the other hand, I would not dream of censoring cinematic material, and this because it is equally difficult to know where to start and where to stop. Of course there are rapists or murderers who will blame the latest Channel 4 co-production for their crimes, just as in the last century criminals used to blame their reading of the novels of Harrison Ainsworth, but such death-bed confessions should not be taken too seriously. And, if they are, the consequences might be unfortunate – there was the recent case of the murderer who ascribed his behaviour to an inordinate admiration for the screen persona of Clint Eastwood. Should his films, therefore, be banned? I would be quite happy never to see him on the screen again, but not for those reasons.

I used to be more appalled by violence than by sex; the latter was never particularly interesting, while there were times when the former did genuinely leave me feeling diminished in spirit as well as in imagination. I am also a rather squeamish little person and, despite many years of effort, I found it impossible to sit unbowed through the latest 'horror' epic; I suspect that at least ten per cent of my time in the auditorium was spent with one hand across my eyes – although this was often at the sight of Meryl Streep or Woody Allen, rather than any more ostensible horror.

So I shall miss nothing in particular after leaving this column – nothing, that is, except an association with the *Spectator* which has remained unbroken since 1973. And what am I most proud of having achieved in these eight years? I am proud never to have used the word 'movie', and of never having had a quotation from one of my reviews used to adorn a cinema advertisement. Goodbye.

7 March 1987

II
Writings for the *Sunday Times* and *The Times*

1981–2001

Sunday Times *Book Reviews*

48

If on a Winter's Night a Traveller
Italo Calvino

Italo Calvino has decided to write a novel about the ambiguous status of fiction, as both a measure of the world and a denial of it. In this book he addresses the reader familiarly as 'you', he describes himself in the third person, invents the first chapters of some ten novels, and introduces as his main characters 'the Reader' and 'the Other Reader'. The tone is often arch, with the coyness of an 'I know you know I know you know' approach, and the form is rather like that of a pantomime horse, where artifice is deliberately used to create laughter. We may be amused by it – Calvino is a very stylish writer – but we know the trick.

Many great novelists have, after all, worked on that boundary where life and art are so powerfully felt that it would be vicious or self-defeating to confuse them – Victor Hugo continually introduces himself as '*l'auteur de ce livre*' and Charles Reade turned the inherited conventions of the three-volume novel into a comic motif in *The Cloister and The Hearth*. But Mr Calvino, springing from a culture which has made a purblind virtue out of specialism and which insists that the 'medium' is in fact the 'message', takes this one feature of the novel – its inherent artificiality – and devotes 260 pages to it.

The central character of this novel, 'you' or 'the Reader', has bought a book which he imagines to be by Italo Calvino; it turns out, however, to have been written by a Polish novelist. Through a series of misadventures and false trails, 'the Reader' begins a number of novels, moving from one to another like a desert traveller between mirages. The point is a metaphysical one: 'reading is going towards something that is about to be, and no one yet knows what it is.' Different kinds of reader are introduced into the narrative – a publisher, a semiologist, a censor, a translator – to complement the different kinds of text which

Calvino transcribes. And so we get a novel about the experience of reading itself – its majestic passivity combined with its willed determination to wreathe the world with the meaning which only sequential narrative provides, its serenity combined with its obsessive need to find out 'what happens next'.

If on a Winter's Night a Traveller is entertaining in the sense that it deals with familiar subjects in an elegant way: the trickiness, the 'world-within-a-world' in which meanings are in infinite regress, the parody of novelistic styles, the Nabokovian fussiness (well captured here by the translator, William Weaver) have, in fact, formed the staple of 'advanced' fiction for many years. What gives the book its quality of bravura, however, is the fact that it derives from, and is supported by, the glittering phalanx of contemporary critical theory – in 'S/Z', to pick one obvious example, Roland Barthes did to Balzac's *Sarrasine* what Italo Calvino does to himself.

What we have here, in other words, is the domestication of modernism. In the early part of the century it constituted a literary revolution; then it became a critical orthodoxy, tidying up what had been left before in fruitful chaos; and now, finally, it has been transformed into a pleasant literary parlour game, an acquired skill – the literary equivalent of those 'abstract' paintings which are sold along the railings of Hyde Park.

This is the real interest of the novel: it is modernism made accessible, flattened out into two dimensions, buoyed up by the sentimentality which attracts the popular imagination: 'And here you are,' Calvino tells us, 'in pursuit of all these shadows together, those of the imagination and those of life.' Romanticism has returned in modern dress.

Mr Calvino is in fact a perfectly straightforward writer – 'middle-brow', if you like – who has an instinct for what is most timely, for what has the most 'buzz', as the Americans put it. He can please the more knowing critics with his parade of smart techniques at the same time as he preserves the more conventional virtues which make for readability. It may well be, of course, that the contemporary novel has indeed lost its sacred and social functions – certainly Mr Calvino thinks so and, with tongue in cheek and eyes fixed upon Paris, he has turned modern fiction into a marketable game.

2 August 1981

49

The Outline of Sanity: A Biography of G. K. Chesterton

Alzina Stone Dale

It is difficult, at this late date, to do justice to Gilbert Keith Chesterton; the corpulent and bewhiskered figure has faded into an outline merely, like a large balloon which its owner has abandoned. He is remembered, if at all, for the diminutive Father Brown, saying the most disconcerting things with an odd little giggle, and for the lines about 'the rolling English road'.

His most recent biographer, Alzina Dale, is an American and there are, it seems, branches of the Chesterton Society throughout America – like London Bridge, our apparently 'quaint' institutions are rebuilt there. We might expect, then, the biography of an Edwardian eccentric conducted along conventional lines: public bar epigrams and merry profundities, Chesterton as Charles Laughton.

In fact she has done nothing of the kind: she has written a sober and most convincing study of Chesterton as a child – or, rather, orphan – of his age whose arguments in favour of familial responsibility and private liberty were intended as a challenge to the collectivist tendencies of the time and whose hard-won faith (he was an agnostic who first became an Anglican and then entered the Roman Church) was based upon the intellectual merits of Christianity and opposed to the socialism or bogus humanitarianism of his contemporaries. The heartiness concealed a most hard-headed man but, precisely because he did not underwrite fashionable opinions, he was called a 'romantic' or a 'reactionary', the taunts which the world throws at those who do not follow the conventional wisdom.

But he was not taken seriously principally because he did not take himself seriously. He described his own work as 'bosh' and became embarrassed if anyone read it in his presence. He was too good a writer to want to pose as one also. More 'serious' artists can bore their contemporaries into a silence which posterity mistakes for awe but, as Chesterton said of Chaucer, the great artist can seem, in a 'dissolving civilization', to be a buffoon. The appropriate response to confusion is laughter, just as the only remedy for earnest but empty-headed orthodoxy is paradox (at which he excelled). Certainly there is an air of buffoonery about Chesterton, but it disguised great strength of intellect and a man who stood in fear of his God. As such he was, and remains, a puzzle to those who confuse frivolity with triviality, simplicity with banality.

According to a friend, he was 'by nature the happiest boy and man I have ever known'. He was a 'messy, absent-minded child with a high voice and a loud laugh' – the infant who became the 'metaphysical jester'. In late adolescence, however, he suffered a profound mental and spiritual crisis which brought him close to insanity and suicide. His wife, Frances, converted him to Anglicanism which he approached, not through an emotional act of obeisance, but by a series of rational steps. He examined the alternatives to Christianity and found them untenable. He started work with an occult publisher but, as soon as he began contributing to the *Speaker* and the *Daily News*, his reputation as a journalist solved the problem of earning a living. He started writing books, also, and thus set the tone of his whole life.

He called himself a journalist, and he was a journalist of genius. But he was so prodigal of his genius that he scattered it in all directions – a master, someone said, who never wrote a masterpiece. Kafka admired his allegorical novels; both Eliot and Auden praised him; he wrote a book on Thomas Aquinas, after only the most modest research, which the Thomist theologian Etienne Gilson, said was so good that it made him despair. He had a large popular following also, established upon the fact that he said the most extraordinary things in an ordinary way.

And so we have a figure as paradoxical as any of his own epigrams or insights. A jolly, sensible Englishman who found sanctuary in the Roman communion; a good-humoured and equable man who, in his Father Brown stories, was obsessed by the nature of guilt and of sin; a man who could do nothing else but write and who damned his own writing with no praise at all. Now that his assaults upon 'collectivism' and the bureaucratic state seem to have some contemporary relevance, however, perhaps he will enjoy a revival. Alzina Dale has written a biography in which the imaginative and intellectual stature of the man is seen in full measure. Despite his own best efforts, he runs the risk of being taken seriously.

8 May 1983

50

Under the Sign of Saturn

Susan Sontag

The Benefactor

Susan Sontag

At the end of her essay on Antonin Artaud, in *Under the Sign of Saturn*, Susan Sontag suggests that

> ... Artaud is relevant and understandable, a cultural monument, as long as one mainly refers to his ideas without reading much of his work.

A 'cultural monument', especially a 'relevant' one, is most likely to be situated in a grove of academe, of course, and certainly the notion of Artaud's 'ideas' as opposed to his 'work' smacks of a certain kind of lecture-hall professionalism. In fact Susan Sontag is very much a product of the conventional academic establishment in the United States, having spent much of her time either teaching in universities or in receiving grants from American foundations.

But she is also a fashionable essayist: *Against Interpretation* was the collection of occasional pieces which established her reputation (specifically her essay on what was then called 'Camp'). *Under the Sign of Saturn* is the third such collection and although age may have induced a certain plangency in her writing it has not significantly widened the range of her concerns. There was an essay on Artaud in *Against Interpretation*: there is one here also; there were numerous references to Roland Barthes in the earlier volume: an essay on him here.

Although there are other pieces in this book (most notably on Walter Benjamin and Leni Riefenstahl), her attachment to European culture has always been essentially that of a Francophile – covering the waterfront, or at least the Seine, from Robbe-Grillet to Godard. She is part of that 'special relationship' between American and French intellectuals which, although it has borne strange fruit recently in the work of the Yale critics, has lasted for almost a century.

That relationship is based upon certain resemblances which Sontag's own writing exemplifies. There is, for example, a native tendency in both languages towards abstraction (Sontag writes, 'In the established conception under chronic challenge . . .', which sounds like a bad translation from the French) and towards rhetorical formulations. This is combined with a capacity for somewhat broad historical generalizations: in two pages, Sontag invokes the work of Hegel, Valéry, Descartes and Rimbaud; Nietzsche, Savonarola and Godard soon follow. This is the 'painting by numbers' school of cultural investigation, in which the academic bent for constructing 'traditions' or 'schools' is subtly fused with a belle-lettrist insouciance and abbreviation. The notion behind it is the essentially French one of making literary history as lucid and as functional as possible, so that it resembles a large Pompidou Centre in which all the pipes and ventilation ducts are exposed to public view.

In this spirit, Sontag refers on occasions to 'strategies of discourse', by which she means 'the way people write'. Her own characteristic 'strategy' is to locate the theoretical or aesthetic concerns which animate a particular writer or artist – 'Mind as Passion' is the title of her piece here on Elias Canetti. Her domain is that of 'ideas'; she links them obsessively, sometimes to illuminate (there is a brilliantly destructive essay on Leni Riefenstahl) and sometimes only for the pleasure of seeing them thus intertwined.

The trouble with those who barter in ideas, however, is that their ordinary intelligence tends to become deracinated in the process. Academics who are also observers of contemporary culture, like Sontag, are often extraordinarily gullible, swallowing whole what is currently fashionable or 'avant garde'. She is able to decipher the theoretical assumptions or context of Barthes and Artaud (as she did once of 'happenings': 'an asymmetrical network of surprises' she called them) without attempting to discover or explain whether the work itself is valuable or even interesting. I suspect that she would find the question too conventionally bourgeois to admit a proper answer.

Her defence of 'more than a century of literary modernism', however, is itself suffused with some very familiar concepts. What we will generally find under the surface of Sontag's vocabulary, like so many juicy bugs, which remain healthy only so long as they are concealed, are some quintessentially romantic notions. She lays a great deal of emphasis on the idea of literary 'revolution' just as she does upon the idea of the 'suffering author'; she is fascinated by the 'melancholy temperament' of Walter Benjamin and the 'outrageous, essentially forbidding' Artaud. We are back with De Quincey, Charles Maturin and the early nineteenth century – an academic version of *Melmoth the Wanderer*. I suspect that if we were to do a Sontag, and interpret her ideas, we would find them to be very close in spirit to those in Burke's essay on 'The Sublime and Beautiful'.

This is evident in her novel, *The Benefactor*, which has just been reissued after sixteen years. Hippolyte, the narrator, has an appetite for thinking which is fuelled by the desire for certitude. An inhabitant of Paris in the thirties and forties, Hippolyte decides to allow his life to interpret for him his increasingly bizarre dreams.

His ambiguous persona, and the absence of a conventionally realistic narrative, may have been meant to echo the tone of the *nouveau roman* (*nouveau* then, at least) but its elegant prose and languorous hero bring it much closer to the texture of the novels of Pater and Huysmans. The affiliations are as clear in Sontag's fiction as they are in her criticism: her sensibility finds values only within art and the things of art. At this late date such a sensibility may perhaps be regarded as derivative or, not to put too fine a point on it, academic.

3 July 1983

51

The Diary of Virginia Woolf
Volume V: 1936–1941
Edited by Anne Olivier Bell

This last volume of Virginia Woolf's diaries continues until 24 March 1941, just four days before she went down to the water and to her death, and it completes the publication of her writings. Few writers of our century have left so exhaustive an account of their 'life and times', but at last the work of transcription is finished – even as we admire the author we must congratulate and thank the editor since, if these volumes are a testimony to Virginia Woolf's genius, they are also a monument to Anne Olivier Bell's ingenuity and scholarship. She has transformed thousands of pages of rapid and sometimes troubled handwriting (often illegible to the lay reader) into the volumes which must now rank as one of the most important cultural documents of our time.

Just before her death, Virginia Woolf told one acquaintance, 'I've lost the art', and this last volume documents her precarious hold upon the fine but durable stuff which she wove out of her nerves. The remark was made after she had completed *Between the Acts*, a novel she considered a failure, but in the last four years of her life she also wrote *Roger Fry* as well as *Three Guineas*, and she laboured over the revision of *The Years*. The diaries record her obsession with her work, an obsession which sometimes paralysed her and sometimes galvanized her into frantic life: as an account of a writer's fears, this volume might well become a classic of morbid psychology.

The nervous prostration which accompanied the completion of her books often brought her close to madness, and was in the end responsible for her suicide, but she suffered also from a more generalized sense of horror and insufficiency when she contemplated what she had written – feelings which were expressed in her hysterical dread of what the critics would choose to say about her; 'a doomed mouse nibbling at my daily page' was the way she described herself. Generally her fearful anticipations were quite misplaced but the enthusiastic reviews of *The Years*, for example, afforded her only momentary exhilaration before she climbed once more into the treadmill of fear, self-distrust and despair.

It is one of the unique qualities of her diaries, however, that this brooding disquiet is matched by her ability to lose herself in the quotidian detail of the ordinary world; she could not stop the impressions and images rushing in upon her, and there were times when she was overwhelmed by them, 'leaving my mind in a torn state'. Her mind was like a thin wire which curls and then melts in the very heat it generates. And yet those who expect her usual anecdotal and often scandalous accounts of the literary and intellectual 'worlds' with which she was associated may well find this volume the least satisfactory.

There were fewer parties, fewer intrigues, fewer occasions to prompt her into the wit and exuberant gossip at which she excelled. Everyone was getting older now; certain contemporaries such as Eliot and

Forster were part of the settled furniture, while others were dying around her – among them Ottoline Morrell (whose peculiarly bleak 'burial service' she describes), Mark Gertler and her nephew Julian Bell. But the difference in mood was inevitable in any case, since these last diaries are dominated by the prospect and then the reality of war. Both the Woolfs planned to commit suicide if the Germans mounted a successful invasion, and their house in London was bombed. But, despite all this, her comments on the atmosphere and events of that time are curiously dispassionate, perhaps because they are the comments of one for whom the world has already become somewhat unreal:

> One glass door in the next door house hanging. I cd. just see a piece of my studio wall hanging: otherwise rubble where I wrote so many books.

This difference in content does not change the nature of Virginia Woolf's diaries, however, which remain remarkably consistent throughout – abrupt, discontinuous, impressionistic, employing a prose that can sometimes lash out and take hold of a person like a whip. Of Kingsley Martin, the editor of the *New Statesman*, she writes,

> A sensationalist – his mind rotted with coterie talk – all pitted and soft as a hot dishcloth – steaming, unwholesome, unreal.

Hers was not simply a power of description, since she also possessed an almost clairvoyant ability to enter another person's consciousness, and then look around to see what it contained; but it was a dangerous gift, since she had so weak a grasp on her own personality that it could on occasions slip its leash entirely.

At one point she declares that she will avoid introspection (just as she disliked being photographed), and I suspect that this is because she did not know what, if anything, she would find in the process. As a result it sometimes seems that there is no real centre to these diary entries – Virginia Woolf being the recipient of a number of random impressions which never quite cohere into that larger statement which would be about the writer herself.

That is in the nature of a diary, of course, and yet Virginia Woolf's solitary attempt to set everything down (she could not work on it when anyone else was in the room with her) was more than a simple amusement or daily record: the nature of time and its passing is one of the major themes of her fiction, and her diaries were one way of alleviating the meaninglessness of simple chronology. It was difficult for her to keep a 'hold' on things, as she said, unless it were in the act of inscribing them – words were a literal lifeline, as if the world did not properly exist for her until it was written down, described, defined, captured.

As in her fiction also, the diaries contain passages of conversation, fragments of monologue, quotations from literature, words or phrases remembered from childhood, all of them rising like sparks above a fire which is in danger of going out. The effect can sometimes be monotonous – if a single drawn-out note of hysteria qualifies as a monotone – or, rather, the effect of image succeeding image, of impression piled upon impression, is so startling that the mind draws back from it (or else the reader, too, might grow mad at the sheer unmanageability of the world and its parts).

'And I know,' she wrote, 'that I must go on doing this dance on hot bricks till I die.' But she ended that dance voluntarily, and this record of her final months is one of a mind going to pieces – if there is a narrowness or thinness about the writing in this period, it is the thinness of the knife's edge. Her world becomes shallower and brighter; her sentences become shorter; during the London bombings she imagines her own death, 'the crushing of my bone shade in on my very active eye and brain'; the phrases acquire an odd ring: 'I had a gaping raw wound too . . . I cannot fix my mind to detail . . . I have the double vision . . . Many deep thoughts have visited me.' And it was the 'deep thoughts' she most feared, for they would be thoughts about herself.

Her last diary entry reads, 'L. is doing the rhododendrons . . .', an apt image of the secure world which she saw slipping away from her, before her madness took her out and led her into a dark room. Her last written words, in a note to her husband on the morning of her suicide are, 'Will you destroy all my papers' – a measure of her inward anxiety and doubt. As an account of the intellectual and cultural life of our century, Virginia Woolf's diaries are invaluable; as the record of one bruised and unquiet mind they are unique.

24 June 1984

52

The Collected Letters of Thomas Hardy
Volume III: 1902–1908 &
Volume IV: 1909–1913
Edited by Richard Little Purdy & Michael Millgate

The Complete Poetical Works of Thomas Hardy
Edited by Samuel Hynes

Those who made the pilgrimage to Max Gate were sometimes disappointed by the apparent ordinariness of Thomas Hardy, who would rather talk about his cats than his novels. The reader of his letters may suffer a similar disappointment; it is not simply that, once again, the household pets figure more largely than that work for which he will be remembered for ever but, more importantly, Hardy's reticent and defensive temperament did not encourage a dashing epistolary style. The mail was for him a convenient way of transmitting necessary facts, not a stage for self-dramatization. In fact so cautious was he in his dealings with the world that he destroyed many of his own letters: the first volume of this excellently edited and annotated series covered the first fifty-two years of his life in less than 300 pages.

These third and fourth volumes move at a perceptibly slower pace, however, as Hardy entered his sixty-second year and the burden of his correspondence with editors, admirers and other writers became ever greater. He was by now a famous if not yet quite grand old man: as he walked one day to the cottage in which he was born, 'I was unknown to myself Kodaked by some young men who were on the watch'. The years of his novel writing are over and, as this third volume opens, he is about to begin work on that strange epic assemblage *The Dynasts*. It was to occupy him for five long years, and so the letters of this period are from one who was somewhat removed from life – allowing it, as it were, only to swirl around his feet. As a local JP he attended Sessions and Assizes, he took up bicycling and refreshed himself in the countryside he knew so well (and which, as far as the rest of the world was concerned, he had practically invented); he characteristically described Max Gate as a 'dull' place, and his own life there as that of a hermit, but in the late spring and early summer he and his unhappy wife, Emma, came up to London and suffered the inflictions of his popularity.

The fourth volume ought to contain more material of intrinsic interest since it covers some of the most difficult years of Hardy's life: he and his wife had grown increasingly estranged, and he had met a young woman, Florence Emily Dugdale, of whom he had become increasingly fond. And then in 1912 his wife died in great agony: in letter after letter he described it as 'quite unexpected', when in fact she had been suffering from a lingering illness which Hardy did his best to ignore. But at once Florence was sent for, only to discover that she had attached herself to a man so obsessed by his dead wife and his own guilt that he could only wander distraught through his memories. Such an account must be derived from his biographers, however, rather than from this correspondence. And this is the central problem with all such letters: they are either written to those who know so much that they need not be told any more, or to those who must be told nothing.

And so the editor must become a detective, seeking beneath the bland messages the events or feelings which the letters themselves are designed to conceal. When Hardy writes to his wife on 9 July 1909, gently suggesting that she should not come to London to attend an operatic version of *Tess*, we need to go elsewhere to discover that he wished to take Florence instead. And when he writes to a friend to arrange a visit with Florence, his editor notes that he used Dorset County Museum stationery to do so; it seems that he furtively used the reading room there so that his wife would not discover his plans. And then, two months after the death of his wife, he is writing to Florence, 'If I once get you here again won't I clutch you tight' – and one senses the sudden blind animal movement of the old.

But such passages are rare. The general tone of this correspondence is of a settled and rather formal truthfulness – a flatness of emphasis characteristic of one who tried in his art to achieve that which he sometimes failed to do in his life, to see the world steadily and as it is. He wrote to his friend Lady St Helier on the death of her husband, 'But you must remember that people have borne such things before and will have to bear them as long as human nature lasts.' 'Nature is *unmoral*,' he writes on another occasion; but this cheerless vision is not necessarily a gloomy or even pessimistic one. It can, in quite opposite fashion, induce a form of cheerfulness – and just as some visitors noticed the geniality of Hardy's manner, so there are in these letters instances of a knowing and ironic humour which balance the seriousness of some of his more 'important' statements.

About his own writing he tended to be either melancholy or flippant – he called his fiction 'ephemeral' – and he could on occasions adopt the role of a self-confessed 'journeyman' writer; one of the baldest, and best, statements on the writer's agonies must surely be, 'Literary composition, I think, interferes largely with digestion: I don't think it affects one much in any other way.' But I suspect that this was just another aspect of his self-defensiveness, to hide from others his true and genuine feelings about his art. In that sense, these letters are, like the letters of many other writers, masks of a most complex character who could combine *ad hoc* generalizations and private confessions, pride and nervous uncertainty, in equal measure.

We cannot expect such a man to reveal himself to others. And although he was cannily practical in his dealings with the world (many of the letters collected here have to do with the minutiae of royalty and copyright matters), he was not a great admirer of its ways. He refused a knighthood and, in one revealing letter, he declined an invitation to attend the coronation of King George V because of 'unavoidable circumstances' when in fact (as his editors point out in their admirably thorough manner) he was simply taking a holiday in the Lake District. But part of this lack of interest in, or dislike of, the world derives from the fact that he had been long embittered by it – its conventional morality had, in particular, often been used as a stick with which to beat him. He was in any case sensitive to the point of morbidity, and was peculiarly susceptible to criticism – in one letter he remembers the exact date of a bad review some forty years before, and the furore over *Jude the Obscure* was, as he admits here to another correspondent, directly responsible for his decision to abandon the writing of novels and to take up poetry again.

Quite how important that decision was is embodied in Samuel Hynes's admirable edition of Hardy's *Complete Poetical Works* (although, for obvious reasons, *The Dynasts* is not included). For no modern poet (with the exception of Yeats) has so transformed his old age with the beauty of his vision: it ought to be remembered that the first volume of Hardy's verse was not published until he was in his fifty-eighth year, and his most remarkable poems are those lyrics which he composed after the death of his wife.

What we sense in this poetry is a peculiar directness of feeling expressed with such traditional simplicity that the specific emotion seems to approach the anonymity of ballad: it is almost as if the man who remained so secretive throughout his life was trying to reach a further anonymity – an almost unthinkable anonymity for in the lyrics of his last years he reaches, like Blake, something very close to general or impersonal emotion. Here is the sense of time irrecoverable and blank, of those moments of memory rendered brilliant by the sense of their own imminent loss, of time's passage and its resistless force; all these things he explored, as he bent over his own past like an old man exploring a patch of bare soil where once he had planted something. If the correspondence is measured and unrevealing, the poetry which he wrote in the same period displays the strength of those feelings which he laboured so hard to conceal from the ordinary world.

19 August 1984

53

The Laughter of Carthage
Michael Moorcock

This is the second in what will be a tetralogy of novels, a four-volume sweep of modern history which in this book moves from Constantinople in 1920 to America in 1924. The first of the sequence, *Byzantium Endures*, received high and general praise when it was published three years ago for its ambition no less than for its technical skill. The protagonist is Colonel Pyat, a refugee from the Russian civil war who (as we come to understand) is now a half-crazed memoirist living in the seedy purlieus of Westbourne Grove: this is his narration of the past, and it is one as perplexed and ambiguous as the narrator. Pyat is a hero to himself but to few others – he is a great inventor and a great braggart, a romantic and a hypocrite, a prophet and also a liar. And this is Moorcock's achievement: he has rewritten modern history by seeing it in the distorting mirror of one man's perceptions, so that the novel has the imaginative grasp of fantasy while remaining solidly based upon recognizable facts.

These facts are indeed central to the novel's design, since Moorcock has chosen to chronicle the contemporary development of cities. Pyat is a wanderer, half renegade and half outcast, whose itinerary includes extended visits to Rome, Paris, Constantinople and New York. In these places he is assaulted, traduced, fêted and despised – as a picaresque adventure alone, *The Laughter of Carthage* is great fun – but as he suffers the consequences of his various exploits he still dreams of a new urban age: 'A future of skyscrapers and undersea tunnels, of television, the matter transmitter and greatest of all, the flying city.' All these things are represented by the symbol of Byzantium, just as Carthage is for him the repository of all that is earthbound and enslaved.

But there is no doubt that his vision is fundamentally misconceived, just as his fantasies are established upon hatred and repression. Pyat is a notorious racist and anti-Semite and, even as he recounts the glorious adventures of his past, we are offered an inglorious present in which he is pumped full of Largactyl and left to rot alongside the Portobello Road.

He may, as he suggests, be watching 'the last years of a senile civilization' but his own last years are those of a horrible and horrifying character. And the art of the novel is to make both cohere, so that he himself becomes an image of the culture he despises – both of them rabid, hypocritical and violent. Moorcock may even be playing a further game with fantasy and reality, for it is quite possible that the whole of the historical past recounted here is the fantasy of a crazed old man. Pyat, like Eliot's Gerontion, may simply be contemplating the vision of his own emptiness.

So the ambition of this novel, and the sequence in which it takes its place, is large but it is matched by Moorcock's resourcefulness as a writer. He has often been accused of writing too much or too quickly, but long and assiduous practice has given his prose a vitality, as well as a simplicity, which few other English novelists possess.

Moorcock's other gift is that of the historical imagination, by which I mean he can invent or recreate a past quite instinctively and without resorting to the subfusc devices of most historical novels. And the reason that he can see the past so clearly is because he sees the present equally clearly: when he is writing about the one he is at the same time writing about the other, and it is this which gives his narrative such clarity and force. *The Laughter of Carthage* and its companion volumes will be seen, then, as an imaginative record of our own time rather than as a simple reconstruction of that which has gone. There are few English novelists who have tackled the larger themes of Western civilization, in its rise and its fall, but equally, there have been few novelists who have risen above the orthodox categories of fiction – 'realism' and 'fantasy' being the most egregious – to produce something as expansive and as elaborate as this.

2 December 1984

54

The English Novel in the Twentieth Century
Martin Green

Martin Green's theme is the 'doom of empire' – a plangent phrase but one of uncertain meaning, since it is used both to describe writers as different as Evelyn Waugh and James Joyce and to cover the general plight of all those novelists who seem to echo Britain's melancholy, long, withdrawing roar. In his most recent books Dr Green has examined the aftermath of empire. A wonderfully acute study of British decadence, *Children of the Sun* (1977), suggested that the 'dandies' of the 1920s and '30s represented a high culture which challenged the more ferocious Englishness of the generation before them – a 'high culture' which was in turn displaced by the serious young writers and novelists of the 1950s.

In *Dreams of Adventure, Deeds of Empire* (1980) he widened his analysis to examine the imperialist ethic as it emerged in the hitherto despised 'adventure tale'. Now in this book he has gone one step further, since he discusses the relationship of literature with those who hold power – the 'master class', as he calls them.

Rudyard Kipling is, naturally enough, his major example – a *jongleur* who celebrated the triumphs of the men who fought or ruled, a storyteller who tried to break with the middle-class tradition of domestic fiction only to be scorned by the 'men of letters' and reduced to the status of an entertainer. And yet Dr Green's account is of a Kipling *redivivus*, a writer who may have been the paramount literary influence in this century.

To support this thesis, he examines the work of six novelists for traces of that influence. Kipling's spirit is said to pervade the work of an 'entertainer of the master class' such as Evelyn Waugh or Kingsley Amis, and it is not even properly exorcized from the novels of D. H. Lawrence, Doris Lessing or James Joyce, even though they try to destroy or curtail it. It seems that all of these writers are examining the values and assumptions of imperialism even as they are being affected by them.

As a theory this has the advantage of simplicity. Since empire is one of the larger facts of this century, and since Kipling is one of the larger writers, the shadows of both can always be found in English fiction: but then so can the shadows of a great many other matters, and it is only an arbitrary principle of organization that selects empire as opposed to, for example, feminism or commerce.

Dr Green sees fiction in a largely political rather than narrowly aesthetic context, and his principal concern is with a 'cultural dialectic' in which individual authors are part of a large historical process. Kingsley Amis first rebelled against Evelyn Waugh, only to end up by imitating him – or so the theory goes. Of course, the advantage of dialectic, from Dr Green's point of view, is that he can have it both ways: writers are continuing the imperialist ethic even when they think they are defying it, novelists are really imitating Kipling in the act of cursing him, and so on.

But behind Dr Green's thesis there lies an even larger assumption that Britain's fall as an imperial power has also been responsible for a decline in British fiction, that the modern novel is somehow a weak and impoverished thing compared with the achievements of the nineteenth century. This is one of those propositions which is generally accepted without protest, but in fact it deserves to be challenged: the fiction of the last two decades seems to be in at least as healthy a state as fiction in the 1880s and 1890s, when Britain was at the height of its power. And certainly the contemporary English novel rivals anything which is being produced in the United States, which can still properly be considered as an imperial culture. It would take an act of purblind pessimism to suppose that novelists such as Angus Wilson, William Golding and Iris Murdoch are necessarily inferior to George Gissing or

Robert Louis Stevenson on the one hand and Saul Bellow and Joseph Heller on the other.

So when Dr Green writes of a 'certain blighting of literary hope and ambition all through the twentieth century', we are entitled to ask what precisely he means. The same combative but rather pointless assertiveness can be seen in his remark that '. . . writers are called upon, by their vocation, to disentangle themselves from the ruling class'. This is arguable, to say the least, but he only touches upon such issues before launching into a series of *ad hoc* comments on specific novels and biographical summaries which never quite match the apparent seriousness of his theme.

The English Novel in the Twentieth Century in fact displays the weakness implicit in trying to use literary criticism as a basis for intellectual history: it cannot support the burden placed upon it, and tends to crack or slide under the strain. It is impossible to insert a variety of authors into a theoretical scheme without resorting to careless shorthand (Joyce here is described as a 'public artist' and is linked with H. G. Wells 'because both were fond of characters like Leopold Bloom': not even Bloom is 'like' Bloom!), just as it is difficult to elicit large cultural generalizations from specific texts. The ambition and originality of Dr Green's earlier works directed attention from such problems, but this volume is both sketchy and etiolated, and is a contribution only to the shadowy world of academic 'lit. crit.'.

16 December 1984

55

Auden in Love

Dorothy J. Farnan

The first words which W. H. Auden addressed to the author of this biographical study, who may now be classed as the Mme de Sévigné, or at least Daisy Ashford of the 'gay' world, were 'You must read *The Allegory of Love* by C. S. Lewis . . . Romantic love was never heard of, you know, in the days of the early Church Fathers.' Dorothy Farnan was a young student at the University of Michigan where Auden was then teaching and there is a hint of uncanny prescience in his remarks, now that she has become the less than romantic chronicler of Auden's love for Chester Kallman.

This is still a sensitive area: although the wives of great writers can become almost as famous as their husbands (one thinks of Nora Joyce, Frieda Lawrence and, most notably of all, Vivien Eliot), the partners of homosexual writers tend to disappear from sight or are mentioned by biographers only with a certain embarrassment and reticence. This is grossly unfair since, in many cases, the homosexual writer only survives by virtue of the companionship or support of the shadowy 'friend'; and, as Dorothy Farnan suggests here, Auden 'became dependent on Chester'.

Kallman was in Auden's description 'a Jewish boy from Brooklyn', of precocious talent in more than one direction. They met in 1939, at a poetry reading, soon after Auden had arrived in America with Christopher Isherwood: Kallman was eighteen, and the already famous poet was thirty-two. It was love at first or perhaps second sight, since Kallman came round to interview Auden two days later.

In subsequent years Auden was to compare this meeting with that between Siegmund and Sieglinde, and the Wagnerian analogy suggests one aspect of a relationship which was always tinged by 'camp', a parodic theatricality which allowed both men to banish ordinary reality from the messy but cosy apartments in which they lived. Auden liked to be known as 'Mother', at least by those who admired him, but Kallman perversely preferred to call him 'Miss Master'; and there were occasions when Auden used to berate Kallman for, in more than usually impulsive moments, 'behaving like a shopgirl'. If Auden's correspondence is ever published, it may seem to the uninitiated reader that he was surrounded exclusively by female friends.

They had begun to live together, after these first meetings, rather like the Phoenix and the Turtle (the latter of which Auden came to resemble), but Dorothy Farnan suggests that the sexual side of their 'marriage' lasted only two years. She professes some astonishment at this but in fact it is not at all unusual in homosexual partnerships where camaraderie is often more important than passion.

Kallman had a succession (even a parade) of lovers and although Dorothy Farnan deduces from this that Auden 'had a second-hand position in Chester's love life', this would only be true if 'love life' were synonymous with 'sex life'. But it rarely is and in the first area, at least,

Auden's pre-eminent position was secure. In the best sense theirs was a marriage of convenience: Auden sought comfort and domestic habit in love while Kallman found, in their relationship, consolation from an otherwise distracted life.

Yet this book does for the first time provide evidence that, despite Auden's genius and fame, Kallman was characteristically the dominant partner: Auden understood poetry, but Kallman was equally a craftsman in the melodrama of the emotional life. I suspect this was particularly because of Auden's 'need to love', as Dorothy Farnan puts it, since this vulnerability put him at a great disadvantage when confronted with someone of Kallman's manipulative skills. But the hold which a weaker nature can exert over a stronger is more complicated than this; Kallman often behaved in the impulsive manner of the *divas* whom he so much admired (it was he who introduced Auden to the delights of opera) and, since Auden was in many ways a reticent and defensive man, Kallman's histrionic temperament liberated and invigorated his own. Humphrey Carpenter, in his biography of the poet, records him saying, 'He is a far cleverer person than I am . . .'

And so from the beginning Kallman determined the nature of a relationship which, after the first heady days, assumed a routine as reassuring as it was predictable. For some time they commuted with the seasons between America and Italy, but when the going got too rough (in every sense) Italy was exchanged for Austria; spring and summer were spent in Kirchstetten (by a street renamed Audenstrasse), autumn and winter in New York.

It could be said that they were only really happy in each other's company for, on the many occasions when they were apart, the world of age and loneliness almost overwhelmed both of them. Auden kept it at bay with the 'chemical life' (booze and pills), Kallman with the promiscuous life (booze and boys), but in the end it proved too much for both of them. Auden died quite suddenly in the autumn of 1973 and Kallman, certain of nothing in his life except Auden's love, descended into a maelstrom of self-indulgence and self-pity. He survived only another fifteen months.

Despite the biographical information which Dorothy Farnan provides here for the first time, this is not the most appropriate memorial of such a friendship. *Auden in Love* is on occasions acidly written – she has a sharp pen and a certain talent for writing comic scenes (of which there are inevitably a great many), but one does not in the end leave this narrative with any great admiration for its author's perceptions or even her manners. Her attitude towards Kallman is patronizing (all the more puzzling since she married his father), and her ostensibly high opinion of Auden is marred by an obvious but inexplicable resentment. And since Auden's sexuality is not the most important, and is certainly the least interesting, aspect of his poetry, this book will fascinate only those who do not share Auden's own queasiness at the spectacle of '. . . public faces in private places'.

17 March 1985

56

Frost: A Literary Life Reconsidered
William H. Pritchard

The conventional picture of Robert Frost is of a 'monster' and 'mean-spirited megalomaniac', to quote two of his more recent critics, a man who posed as an American sage while possessing the familial virtues of Caligula, a poet who professed himself to be a *naif* of farming stock when in fact his promotional skills would have done credit to Saatchi and Saatchi. William Pritchard, with a charity matched only by his scholarship (he is a Professor of English at Amherst College), attempts to redress the balance in this short study.

The facts of Frost's life remain the same in his account: as a young man he was so possessed by 'the astonishing magnitude of my ambition' that he became quickly dissatisfied with the teaching and farming jobs which he took, and in his thirty-eighth year he travelled to England in order to be recognized as a poet. So he was, both by Ezra Pound and by the Georgians, and after his return to America his burgeoning fame meant that he could attach himself to various colleges as a 'symbolic teacher'. Then there came the veritable cataract of Pulitzers and other honours, from which he emerged as an American institution. He was the poet who read at John Kennedy's inaugural, and who later visited Khrushchev in order to give the Soviet leader the benefit of his cracker-barrel philosophy. This was the public career, at least, but it has also been suggested that the private man was so poisoned by vainglory and envy that he rejoiced in the discomfiture of his contemporaries, betrayed those closest to him, and propelled the members of his family to mental illness or suicide.

The source from which these facts are drawn is Lawrance Thompson's three-volume biography, an elephantine work of scholarship which by dint of repetition suggests that Frost was a self-obsessed, paranoid, manipulative and positively sinister human being. But Professor Pritchard states here that this account is based upon a humourless and over-literal reading of Frost's life – that in fact the writer's behaviour was conceived 'poetically', as 'poetical enjoyment', and was essentially related to the kind of verse he was composing. This new biographer's motto might be summarized: to read all, is to forgive all. For his central proposition is that Frost conceived both his life and his art in terms of 'playfulness', manifesting a spirited combination of irony and wit, and that the significant moments in his existence can be associated with the themes of his poetry – particularly in the importance of 'reckless choice' and 'wildness'.

Of course Pritchard is also aware that a writer – at least one who believes himself so eminent that he may one day merit a biography – will reinvent his life in order to give it a purpose or pattern. In Frost's case, this became a life-long habit which in lesser men would be described as lying. But this is the essential point, since the duplicity is related to the apparent 'simplicity' of his poetry. To rephrase the cliché, the simplest poetry is the most scheming, and we must look to deliberate rhetoric rather than to direct feeling, to theatrical monologue rather than to self-expression, in order to understand Frost's work. Of that most famous of his poems, 'The Road Not Taken', Pritchard suggests (quite convincingly) that it is by no means the piece of sagacity and sincerity which it is taken to be, but rather a specimen of high-spirited 'fun' close to parody.

So the biographical method which Pritchard employs is a useful one, and he deals seriously with that joint configuration of life and work which the writer presents to the world; it does not have quite the improving effect which he intends, however. To say, as he does, that Frost was as 'guarded' as his poetry is only to confirm his self-obsession, just as Frost's often-mentioned 'playfulness' seems only to be another aspect of that vanity which allowed him wilfully to disregard the feelings of others.

But the fact that Pritchard has even made the attempt to salvage Frost's reputation is significant in itself, since it suggests that he still places some credence in the touching but dubious notion that great or even good poetry sanctifies the person who has written it. This is not the case: many great poets have possessed personalities which would empty a crowded room, and their understanding of language does not necessarily imply the kind of emotional or intellectual proficiency which Pritchard seems ready to ascribe to Frost. Indeed it may have quite the opposite effect: it is often poets' inability to 'grow up' (so that they remain infantile or narcissistic) which makes them such masterly manipulators of the words the rest of us tend to use in a conventionally 'adult' fashion.

But Pritchard's biography is nevertheless valuable: the virtue of his more benevolent stance is that he refuses to moralize about his subject, just as he declines to speculate in a romantic manner about Frost's unspoken thoughts or feelings. This is admirable, and should serve as an example to those biographers who are all too ready to assume the role of lay magistrate or of novelist. So, too, should Pritchard's warning that the biographer should 'refuse to settle on any single explanation which explains everything and doesn't explain enough'. As a result, he himself manages to capture the sheer facticity and momentum of Frost's life, that unanticipated and reflective course upon which he, like any other human being, is bound.

And that, paradoxically, may be the best way to rehabilitate Frost's reputation: he, too, was constantly 'guessing at himself' (as he once put it) and, because he did not fully know himself, his wilful behaviour might most charitably be seen as a constant but baffled effort to define himself in relation to others. Certainly the truth lies somewhere in this now hidden ground, and Pritchard's short biography is valuable precisely because it suggests the complicated and ambiguous nature of the man – and, in the process, evokes the troubled and ambivalent nature of the poetry itself.

31 March 1985

57

Footsteps: Adventures of a Romantic Biographer

Richard Holmes

Towards the end of this Baedeker of the historical imagination, Richard Holmes describes the 'magical properties' of twentieth-century biography; it seems a strange phrase to apply to so secular and even prosaic an activity, and yet it is an appropriate one since the biographer's purpose can be similar to that of the shaman: to raise the spirits of the dead and to hold intercourse with them. It is significant, therefore, that this book opens with Holmes, at the age of eighteen 'dreaming of the dead coming back to life again'. He was then following the track of R. L. Stevenson through the Cévennes, as recorded in *Travels with a Donkey*, and the first chapter here describes Holmes's experiences on what the French villagers called the '*vieux chemin*' of 'Monsieur Steamson'.

But this was only the start of a much longer journey: Holmes is best known for his *Shelley: The Pursuit*, and in *Footsteps* he charts the history of his biographical investigations into William Wordsworth, Mary Wollstonecraft, Shelley himself and the doomed poet Gérard de Nerval. The title of the book suggests its inspiration, since for Holmes biographical research is primarily attached to journeys and to places: in that divagatory life away from home, he seems to lose himself in order to understand the identities of his subjects and, when following the track of Shelley through Italy, he explains how 'my outward life took on a curious thinness and unreality'.

Yet, paradoxically, the prestige of contemporary biography is such that biographers themselves can become significant literary figures, and the single most enduring impression in this volume is that of Holmes himself. This is not to say that he is either solipsistic or vainglorious, since in fact his wanderings through the landscape of imaginative history have a curiously childlike quality. He is revealed here as solitary, disarmingly enthusiastic, attaching himself so fervently to the lives and personalities of the long dead, that it is as if he were in some way dispossessed. Just as he sketches here the progress of Romanticism through Wordsworth to Nerval, so in his own wanderings we find traces of the same restless and haunted spirit.

But the analogy can be extended further than that, for when Holmes describes biography as offering 'the vague excitements and cloudy enthusiasms focused down to an intense burning point of a single life', he might be echoing Mary Wollstonecraft's own description of the imaginative faculty itself:

> Imagination is the true fire, stolen from heaven, to animate the cold creature of clay.

There are other parallels as well, and in this book the biographical imagination is granted a kind of spiritual legitimacy by being compared with the Romantic 'Imagination'.

That is perhaps why Holmes is at such pains to uncover the emotional life, the 'feelings', of Shelley or Wollstonecraft; his purpose is to locate 'the personal life that is hidden in, and below, the printed page' and then to understand that life by an act of identification. And so it is that he describes biography as a form of sympathetic initiation in 'the creation of a fictional or imaginary relationship between the biographer and his subject'.

It is, however, a narrow path which he is treading here. Just as the interest in imagined sentiments can become novelistic or coarsely misplaced, so in the same way the romance of identification can be taken too far: it is one thing to follow Stevenson's actual mountain track, quite another to stand in the streets of modern Paris in order to evoke Mary Wollstonecraft's presence there at the time of the French Revolution.

Footsteps itself offers a variety of themes; it is part travelogue and part biography, part memoir and part literary criticism. But, most importantly, it is a disquisition on the nature of biography itself. There are some very astute passages here on the problems of the biographer who must combine the roles of scholar, private detective and literary artist (Holmes is very good, also, on that vague sense of prurience and guilt which biographers suffer); and there is nothing more eloquent in this book than Holmes's account of the biographer's obsession with the past – that feeling of being 'haunted' which renders the most trivial of memorabilia exciting and which animates the arduous and often frustrating search amongst old letters and faded manuscripts.

But he also seeks to make a larger point: 'biography', he says, 'is based upon the profoundly hopeful assumption that people really are responsible for their actions, and that there is a moral continuity between the inner and outer man.'

The shadows of Shelley and Wordsworth are just visible here, but Holmes's attachment to the Romantic 'imagination' has affected his perception of biographical writing. His hopeful assumption may or may not be justified, but there is no reason why a good biography should not be written on a quite different understanding of human nature. People need not be 'responsible' in this way, and there may be no 'moral continuity' of the kind he describes.

As a result, there is no reason why the principle of indeterminacy should not be introduced into biography, lending fresh strength to the idea of 'multiple personality' and to the concept of unknowability in the interpretation of character or behaviour. It is, at least, open to debate and even to technical experiment – the problem with Holmes's otherwise admirable study is that his humanistic and engagingly moralistic approach avoids the central problems of form and of narrative method. After all, the wanderings have to stop somewhere; the 'identification' can only go so far, the 'feelings' are in the end putative. The biographer is still left with the central problem of constructing a narrative: the real 'adventures' begin only when the research has ended, with the rolling of the blank page into the typewriter and the composition of the first word.

7 July 1985

58

More Letters of Oscar Wilde
Edited by Rupert Hart-Davis

Oscar Wilde was a natural letter-writer; he had a genius for rapid improvisation (he wrote his plays very quickly) but, more important, his aesthetic life was established upon the theory that the expression of personality should itself become an art.

So he bestowed at least as much attention on his letters as he did upon his prose, or his drama; sometimes, in fact, it is difficult to distinguish them from his 'creative' writing and perhaps his most famous imaginative work is still *De Profundis*, a lachrymose epistle addressed to Lord Alfred Douglas from a prison cell. As a result this volume of newly discovered letters, the first since the collected edition of 1962, is of literary as well as of biographical interest.

There is nothing quite as important as *De Profundis* here, but there are letters from every period of Wilde's life and it is possible to trace through them the juggernaut of his ambition ('I want fame,' he says in one of the earliest) as it careered through the streets of London before running over Wilde himself. But if no particular letter is marked by genius, most are irradiated with that wit which is his single most important contribution to the nineteenth century. There is one characteristic description of an early Ibsen production:

. . . the pit full of sad vegetarians, and the stalls occupied by men in mackintoshes and women in knitted shawls of red wool. So at least it seemed to me.

Even the smallest letter of apology is unmistakable:

I cannot sufficiently regret that I have been deprived of the privilege of lecturing before a Bournemouth audience.

The humour is generally a matter of cadence combined with the skilful deployment of rather plummy vowel sounds – part of Wilde's Irish inheritance, of course, but one coloured by a classical education and modified by a hedonistic temperament. There are times when he can go almost too far – '. . . your prose is worthy of that sinless master whom mortals call Flaubert' – but the joke is directed principally against himself; he knows that he has gone too far and asks his correspondent to laugh with him as he cavorts in the airy distance.

That is of course why we cannot expect from this volume anything 'new' about the practical details of Wilde's career: he never let anything so vulgar as real life affect the contents of his letters, and his epistolary style is one which generally employs the grand gesture without pointing towards anything in particular. The only exception lies in those letters here in which he deals directly with the thing that most mattered to him, his art. In his instructions to George Alexander, the actor-manager who was preparing *Lady Windermere's Fan* at the

St James's Theatre, we see the painstaking care with which Wilde approached matters of staging and of production.

His was an instinctive genius but his inspiration was complemented both by sound financial sense and by an exacting attention to the smallest points: 'Details in life are of no importance,' he tells Alexander, 'but in art details are vital.'

The world is less interested in Wilde the practical artist, however, than in Wilde the emblematic figure whose burly frame has been used to represent either the saint or the outcast. He was not averse to adopting either position himself, and he proceeded along his chosen course to infamy with all the relish of a penitent hurrying from the Joyful to the Sorrowful Mysteries. Within a year of his marriage to Constance, for example, he was writing impassioned letters to young men – there is a lyrical message here to Henry E. Dixey, an American actor who played the title role of Adonis at the Gaiety Theatre. He sounds almost too good to be true but perhaps, for Wilde, he was neither.

Such people were in the end to destroy him, and even in this necessarily small volume we may trace the thread of his fate which he generally described as 'purple' or 'violet'. 'Blue' might have been a more appropriate colour. There is a letter from him in Algiers as he and Alfred Douglas spent their last happy days together – 'We are followed by lovely brown things from forest to forest,' he writes, and he was not describing the camels.

The solicitors then tell Wilde that his own colleagues at the St James's Theatre will not assist him in his prosecution of the Marquis of Queensberry; in a later letter he explains that the idea for *The Ballad of Reading Gaol* came to him as he stood in the dock of the Old Bailey before being sentenced. And then, quite suddenly, there are some previously unseen letters from that prison;

an address which, however admirable from an ethical point of view will not, I trust, be permanent in character.

It is this extraordinary spirit, as wit finds its proper expression in serenity, which marks Wilde's letters both from prison and from his later exilic wanderings in France. When he said that he had turned his personality into a work of art it is almost literally true since he seemed able effortlessly to rise above the most unhappy accidents of fortune. The letters in the last three years of his life – when he was poor and almost friendless – are in the circumstances miracles of good humour and calm observation. 'I am now neurasthenic,' he writes a few months before his death in a ghastly little room in the Hôtel d'Alsace.

> My doctor says I have all the symptoms. It is comforting to have them *all*, it makes one a perfect type.

And indeed he was – apart from anything else (and there was much else) he remained until the end a perfect letter-writer who, like a literary version of those Greek deities whom he so envied and admired, scattered burnished images of himself whenever he raised his pen.

17 November 1985

59

Gertrude Bell
Susan Goodman

Madame de Staël
Renee Winegarten

Emily Dickinson
Donna Dickenson

This series presents short lives of famous women, as if returning to the moral belle-lettrism of those Victorian 'Collections' of biographies which offered instruction rather than scholarship; and these first three books, in fact, are essentially long essays which emphasize the practical values or the laudatory ambitions of the women in question. Of course both values and ambitions have changed since the nineteenth century, as has the nature of biography itself, and a new series such as this ought to provide a useful benchmark for changes in social or literary taste.

The nature of the enterprise – in which women will recount the lives of other women – suggests a fashionable or at least contemporary feminist attitude towards the great female dead. But, in practice, very few concessions have been made to the vocabulary of ideology or polemic. Susan Goodman's life of Gertrude Bell, for example, is almost anti-feminist in its tone: despite the vicissitudes of Gertrude Bell's career in the years around the turn of the century, both as a traveller and then as a political agent in the Middle East, Susan Goodman refers to her quite warmly as a paradigm of the Victorian 'lady'.

Her aptitude as a mountaineer no less than her courage as a traveller through the Syrian desert might conceivably be seen as a rejection of domestic servitude and patriarchal society but, instead, Susan Goodman ascribes to her only the 'spirit for adventure and romance'. And although Gertrude Bell eventually settled in Baghdad her biographer goes on to suggest that, '. . . there was nothing she longed for more than domestic bliss'.

This sounds perfectly fair, but there are a number of reasons why this orthodox interpretative style is not wholly satisfactory, the most important being the simple fact that it is now so orthodox. Of course the vocabulary of feminism can itself become the verbal equivalent of an Iron Maiden, but at least it offers a coherent framework in which any life can be located: the difficulty with this biography is that, although it avoids a merely fashionable interpretation of Gertrude Bell's assertive temperament, it has very little to offer in its place except a recital of conventional pieties. The book becomes a succession of facts: not random facts but unassimilated, and therefore unmemorable, ones.

There is a similar problem with Renee Winegarten's life of Mme de Staël. Of course Winegarten has the advantage of an even more extraordinary subject: Mme de Staël's career as a literary theorist, political propagandist and creative writer is one of the miracles of the late eighteenth century. But the facts of that exemplary life are presented here as part of a simple narrative: Renee Winegarten writes well, and shows psychological acuity, but she seems to have no central theme or principle which would lend her book anything other than chronological coherence. Mme de Staël herself was aware of her special status as a female active in the predominantly male worlds of literature and politics, and a feminist approach by her biographer might actually have imparted significance to a life which is otherwise only important.

Mme de Staël was an astonishing woman, but even the astonishing dead cannot be expected to speak for themselves: they have to be reinterpreted by biographers in each generation if their work is to survive, and any interpretation requires a theory or ideology to support it.

Donna Dickenson's biography of Emily Dickinson is, for that reason, the best of these three books since she adopts a definite theoretical stance towards her subject which allows her to understand, as well as simply to record, her life. She concentrates upon the 'professional' rather than the 'private' Emily Dickinson, for example, in order to dispel what she describes as the 'sexist' myth which conceives of the poet as a genteel or even browbeaten little spinster. As a result, this is a convincing account which presents her as an assiduous and ambitious writer who found her lack of contemporary recognition very hard to bear. When a biographer adopts a theory of this kind it animates the entire narrative and, by the strange alchemy of the biographer's art, the theoretical or 'abstract' insights also generate a much more coherent presentation of personal relationships or private temperament. So it is that Emily Dickinson is portrayed here as playful, exuberant, sometimes wilful – a woman who enjoyed her own company (rather than simply existing in some lachrymose domestic exile) and whose poetry is meant 'to recapture the transient moments of ecstasy or grief'.

But Donna Dickenson never loses hold of the larger points which she wishes to make – she rightly criticizes, for example, the absurd belief that 'satisfied "normal" women are unlikely to become great poets'. In other words, only a judicious interpretation – springing from a definite point of view, feminist or otherwise – can bring life to the illustrious dead, just as some theoretical or general strategy is needed in order to understand the significance of their achievements. A reading of these three biographies, in fact, leads one to suggest that the most important thing about any biography is the biographer.

5 January 1986

The Times *TV Reviews*

60

The Evolution of Darwin

Watching *The Evolution of Darwin* (Thames) was rather like entering a church and hearing a lecture on the Married Women's Property Act, or something equally remote. A photograph of Darwin himself was shown upon the screen; he looked bearded and benign, almost indistinguishable from other Victorian patriarchs like Carlyle, Ruskin or Mill. Curiously enough Darwin is still the only figure from that pantheon who is treated with reverential awe, although his perceptions are as much a part of their period as anything in *Sartor Resartus* or *Fors Clavigera*.

But such is the power of his reputation that four television lectures have been instituted for his centenary; they are being held at the Linnean Society in front of an invited and respectful audience, with the viewer as the uninvited guest, as it were, stunned into silence by the conventionality of the format. In the first of these, last night, Sir Andrew Huxley discoursed in a learned manner on Darwin's achievement.

His story is indeed remarkable, although perhaps not in the manner which Sir Andrew expected. As a young biologist Darwin journeyed on the *Beagle*, after what Sir Andrew described as a 'semi-professional training'. He established his extraordinary theory solely upon 'observation', but his observations were directed and fired by the obsessions of his period. And although it is not surprising that *The Origin of Species* attracted controversy – after all, 'natural selection' and 'descent by modification' subverted the authority of the Bible which had until then been read with the same literalness and ferocity which we devote to manuals of slimming – what is more remarkable still is the speed with which these heretical opinions were safely established. Within ten years, Darwinism became orthodox.

And why, in fact, should it not have been accepted? It confirmed in an apparently verifiable and scientific manner all the preconceptions of the time – natural selection, the survival of the fittest, that elaborate hierarchy of order, 'the grand fact in natural history of the subordination of group under group'. It must have been comforting to look at the world and see one's political and social assumptions in ready-made form. But it was a stroke of genius on Darwin's part to design that famous tree, as a natural image for an unnatural theory. It looked bizarre upon the television screen, as grotesque as anything in a Bruegel engraving, but Sir Andrew suggested that it still conveyed the essential truth of the matter.

And indeed the lecture ended on a note of firm certainty. What astonishes me is the purblind stance of scientists, quite aware of how other scientific theories have been usurped or disproven, who still cling obstinately to a theory fashionable some hundred years before. I am willing to bet that no one 'believes in' the theory of evolution, at least in the manner in which it was once believed. It is no longer an appropriate myth and, like all myths, it will give way to another. Perhaps the next three lectures will be devoted to starting that process.

24 September 1982

61

The Invisible World

Last night *Q.E.D.* disclosed *The Invisible World* (BBC 1). As one might have guessed, this was 'a film about what your eyes cannot see' – which is as it should be. It was once said that, if we could hear the grass grow, it would sound like thunder; if we could glimpse a fraction of what was displayed here, we would be blinded by the light.

Using film which has been speeded up or slowed down, using micro-photography or radio telescopes which are nineteen storeys high, the universe is transformed into an area of inexplicable beauty. Heat-sensitive film reveals that the human body emits streamers of white and yellow light, flaring out as if from the sides of a volcano. In one extraordinary sequence a blue field of light is seen to emerge from animate objects: a yogi's fingers looked like branches full of blossoms.

Ultra-violet film, in its turn, displays the strange markings on flowers and leaves – graffiti for the bees.

There are more things in heaven and earth, etcetera . . . but, despite the cliché, the visionaries are proved to be right. When William Blake suggested that the universe might be seen in a grain of sand, he could hardly have known that he would be proved right by an electron microscope. A piece of moon rock, magnified some 100,000 times, is rocky and cratered, uncannily resembling the lunar landscape itself.

The bad sight of the programme was a close-up of the dust mites which live off pieces of dead human skin: two creatures out of a nightmare lumbered towards something which looked like a giant pizza. To make matters worse, it turns out that every hair upon the skin harbours 'alien life' – fungi cover us like a carpet. But the good sight was that of a newborn child: billows of heat and energy rose from the body and as they curled upwards they resembled the clouds which, in fast motion, stream across the sky.

Everything connects, just as the microscopic picture of a raindrop falling upon the ground shows it to form the same elaborate spirals as a galaxy spinning 600 light years away in deep space. The world presents a complex and formidable pattern which we can marvel at, but which we seem hardly to understand. Clearly, the use of accelerated photography has many advantages: it might, for example, have been used to great effect on *Smiley's People*.

28 October 1982

62

The Pantomime Dame

'I'm dirty Gertie, and I live at number thirty.' There is, thank God, nothing like *The Pantomime Dame* (Channel 4). The lines never change, and neither does she: somewhere near the centre of English humour there lurks this stout, sex-starved party who will always give a man a second chance. You only have to mention knickers, and she blushes; then she shows them to you. Give her an inch, and she wants a mile.

The point is, of course, that there is a man hiding within her all the time. The history of male actors *en travesti* is as old and as respectable as that of the theatre itself, but only in pantomime have they survived unscathed. In last night's documentary, certain middle-aged performers tottered into their dressing rooms; as they applied mascara to their bags, and powder to their sagging chins, they became noticeably more frivolous. By the time they wriggled into their dresses, they were positively sparkling.

For some it was the opportunity of a lifetime: 'I'm still an old scrubber,' said Mr Billy Dainty. 'I show me knickers.' Mr Terry Scott dressed up in memory of the aunts he had known as a child. Mr Douglas Byng just enjoyed being a duchess. If any of them did it in the street, they would be arrested. On stage, they become familiar and somewhat laughable.

Why this should be so remains a mystery. The reasons, apparently, range from male fears of women to male empathy with them – although neither would explain the fact that dames provoke as much laughter in women themselves. Perhaps every Englishman wants to look like his aunt or his mother: that would, at least, explain the chequered history of situation comedy in this country. Explanations, however, are not needed in pantomime and, despite the best efforts of Victoria Wood, the presenter, to inject a note of seriousness into the proceedings, she was overwhelmed by all the winks and nudges. Certainly she looked out of place in tie and shirt.

This was a relentlessly jolly programme, and as a result it became a little repetitive. I would have liked to have seen some of the more outrageous or bizarre performers in drag: Edna Everage or Mrs Shufflewick would have placed the dame in a less comforting perspective. Perhaps the dames, legs akimbo, would have been outclassed, but they would have put up a game show. They will try anything once.

17 December 1982

63

Claire Rayner's Casebook

Reports have reached London of a Necrophiliac Action Group in Yeovil; elsewhere, a small but caring community of bisexual grand-mothers has started an information 'hot line'. At once Claire Rayner, casebook in hand, rushes to the scene – only to discover Mavis Nicholson (*Predicaments*) interviewing everyone in sight. They agree to split the difference: Mavis can be nice but 'down-to-earth', and Claire can be concerned.

Last night *Claire Rayner's Casebook* (BBC 1) was examining the 'plight' or 'problems' of homosexuals – one of the major problems being, I suspect, the amount of time they have to spend being interviewed on television. Miss Rayner herself fills the screen, pullulat-ing with goodwill and sporting so many rings and bracelets that she looks like a nanny who has won the pools. 'So many homosexuals,' she was saying, 'are made desperately unhappy because of the unjust and cruel attitudes of the people they meet.' I doubt that outside the Army and the school system, this is in fact the case; but I am open to correction: I must wait for one of her famous 'information sheets'.

The two people Claire Rayner interviewed were not, however, typical. Tom Robinson is a pop singer who has 'come out' so many times on television that he might pull off a major feat of public relations by going back inside again. And the other was a female homosexual called 'Femi' who, despite her name, seemed to be a most intolerant and aggressive person – although it was not clear against what or whom her aggression was aimed.

The categories of 'gay' and 'straight' are, in any case, so narrow and exclusive that their relevance is strictly limited to the bedroom. Mr Robinson may be homosexual but that does not make him a more skilful, or more serious, musician. And who cares, anyway? Half the acts on *Top of the Pops* are composed of young men and women whose sexuality is so casually defined that they might as well be going to bed with coffee percolators.

The preoccupation with sexual stereotyping which the programme displayed is, in that sense, a conventional and somewhat old-fashioned one. The over-emphasis on sexual orientation, and the elaborate structure (organizations and so on) which has been established upon it, are some of the least attractive legacies of the 1960s and 1970s. Programmes of this kind do not, in the end, help anyone.

11 March 1983

64

Comic Roots
(Kenneth Williams)

Kenneth Williams is the chameleon of speech; his voice hits a high note and then plummets to the earth, a duchess one minute and a dustman the next. The low nasal sound of Cockney can be discerned in even the most regal circumstances, however, which is no doubt why his *Comic Roots* (BBC 1) are in St Pancras, London. Mr Williams is an unmistakable part of that breezy, vulgar tradition of London humour, all bloomers and Army medical examinations, which died in music hall only to be revived on television. How else can you rise above the size, dirt and anonymity of the great city except by being outrageous – a London 'type' but, like the great music hall performers, so intensely so that it becomes a form of art?

The programme was a presentation of little Kenneth in London before the war – the piano in the pub, the dilapidated school where he learnt to recite Browning, and any number of aunts and grandmothers who could only now be separated from Mr Williams by an act of exorcism. This was the only television autobiography in which the hero played all the parts.

Mr Williams is a natural comedian, although the flaring of the nostrils and the narrowing of the eyes have come from long practice. As a child he played Princess Angelica in *The Rose and the Ring* and the local paper described 'his mincing step and comic demeanour'; he has never looked back since, although on occasions he must have been followed. But he is a most engaging man – he lives in a world of comic fantasy, in which he is the only inhabitant. Who can blame him for leaving St Pancras?

3 September 1983

65

An Evening with Quentin Crisp

'Think of this,' Quentin Crisp told his Los Angeles audience, 'as a consultation in which the psychiatrist is madder than you are.' He is nothing of the kind of course; he is almost too sensible as *An Evening with Quentin Crisp* (Channel 4) demonstrated. His has been a remarkable transformation: once almost as notorious, although not quite so fabulous, as the Antichrist, he has now become a benevolent guru for the dispossessed and the unhappy. They come to him with the rubble of their lives, and he constructs for them a shapely edifice in which they can hide themselves.

He arrives on the stage with his felt hat, his make-up, his dyed hair and a cravat like a whirlpool around his neck – half priest and half actor, with that touch of Edwardian gentility to disguise the stridency of his message as he announces the 'profession of being'.

Certainly he comes as a shock to those who expect only a few epigrams in the manner of Wilde. But it is often forgotten that wits tend to be moralists also – that is why their remarks are so memorable – and there is a sense in which Mr Crisp sees himself as a prophet in the wilderness: 'If we all got what we deserved,' he remarked with his eyes raised towards a heaven which he knows does not exist, 'we would starve.'

This was a brilliant performance in which he managed to retain the enthusiasm and affection of an audience by repeating what is essentially a simple message: turn your personality into a form of art, have the courage to impress upon others what you feel yourself to be. 'It wasn't her acting which made Miss Bernhardt divine, it was her nerve.'

Only the most profound people understand the importance of style, and Mr Crisp is a living exemplar of the power which it can confer; here he is without a home, without even a past now, an entirely self-invented creature who had last night's American audience rising to their feet to applaud him.

As he said of Joan Crawford, he is 'incandescent with belief' in himself – a 'televisionary' who once said 'Never keep up with the Joneses, drag them down to your level' but who has triumphantly raised other people to his.

29 September 1983

66

Meantime

(Mike Leigh)

The setting of Mike Leigh's latest play, *Meantime* (Channel 4), was a familiar one – a world of high-rise flats where most of the occupants are unemployed, of bingo and skinheads, of 'video nasties' in the living room and fish-fingers in the kitchen. One might be forgiven for thinking that two hours of unrelieved despondency was enough, however, and watching it was rather like being left bound and gagged in a launderette (Mike Leigh likes launderettes as well).

His vision is a grotesque one and last night's drama, despite its apparent improvisatory tone, was about as close to realism as Racinian tragedy – a genre which in some ways it resembles, since the women are all monsters and the men pathetic victims of circumstance. The mournful music which succeeded each burst of inconclusive dialogue suggested, in fact, that we were being asked to watch 'art' rather than 'life'.

Mike Leigh's plays have become bleaker over the years, and where once he presented eccentrics he now concentrates on the maimed and the oppressed: those who spend their lives in futile rebellion or in terrified compliance. *Meantime*, about a semi-retarded adolescent, is no exception. It offered a detailed picture of a mean time, down to the last missing button on a cheap denim jacket, but the general effect was one of detachment which on occasions came close to being patronizing – an effect compounded by certain actorish mannerisms from the cast.

These stunned and thwarted characters could have come out of Dickens – Magwitch and Smike growing up in Tower Hamlets – but they were not treated with a similar sympathy or affection (an instructive contrast might be made with *Coronation Street* which, although sometimes sentimental, is never patronizing). Mike Leigh's is a genuine vision, in the sense that it is coherent and sustained, but it excludes too much to be a forceful one. That is why the general tone is one of caricature (the skinheads and the ageing hippy are now stock types and were again on show last night) – as a result, he is convincing when he produces comic plays, rather less so when he tries to create drama.

2 December 1983

67

Earth Year 2050

Broadside

Earth Year 2050 (Channel 4) continued on its futurological course with an examination of the computer, an object which has now become the juggernaut in front of which we are supposed to throw ourselves. Hence the extraordinary prognostications in last night's programme – computers with 'super intelligences', computer systems which will replace large corporate organizations, robotic intelligence which will represent 'another species' on the planet.

Only scientists would be credulous enough to advance such nonsense – 'computers are addictive,' as one of the experts put it, and it would be most unwise to trust the addicts' advice on the efficacy of their drug. Certainly one of its effects is to impair the use of language: 'information' was employed as if it were synonymous with 'knowledge', and a computer was said to 'imagine' visual patterns when it was simply reproducing them in a mechanical and banal manner.

I suspect that the scientists become so over-excited about the putative ascendancy of the computer because, in the unlikely event of such a future, it would represent the triumph of the rational or mechanical world view. And to describe those who cannot operate the devices as 'the new disadvantaged' was to take the scientific fallacy to hubristic lengths. My own prediction is that computers will only manage to bore us to death.

It was salutary, then, that *Broadside* (Channel 4) should document some of the less agreeable aspects of scientific 'progress' – in this case the damage inflicted on human beings as a result of nuclear testing in the Australian area of Maralinga (its aboriginal meaning being, curiously enough, Field of Thunder). The experts considered these explosions to be a great adventure, as the contemporary newsreels testified, but the physical effects on others were much less satisfactory. It seems that the scientific establishment is only now admitting its error; perhaps they have been too busy with their micro-chips.

18 April 1984

68

EastEnders

The first character to appear in *EastEnders* (BBC 1) seemed to be dead on arrival, although he might just have been playing possum in order to escape the predatory attentions of his neighbours. In the first two episodes, they have spent their time either abusing each other, fighting in the local pub or, if they are lucky, suffering the last stages of alcoholism. It may well result in a Cockney version of the Jonestown Massacre, and it is hardly a good advertisement for the lovable London spirit: by comparison, *Coronation Street* looks more like *Vegetarian Kitchen*.

But old habits die hard, and there is still room for a reminder of the music hall in the two ghastly old dears, Lou and Ethel, who never miss an opportunity of talking about the 'good old days' and abusing the Asian shopkeepers. Despite the fact that Lou talks scathingly about 'that cow in Downing Street', I would not be surprised to find that she was a member of the National Front – a lot of these glorious old Cockneys are.

You would imagine from this series that east London has the status of Troy or Mafeking, since all the inhabitants behave as if they were living behind a stockade: there are too many strangers, it seems, and the fictional borough of Walford is continually being threatened by the world outside. 'The community spirit went out when the Tories came in,' one character (I think it was the bluff fruiterer) suggested – which would imply that the original spirit was about as strong as watered-down beer.

The only thing that keeps them going now is gossip: Albert Square is awash with it, and one incident is enough to send eddies of whispers right round the launderette, where Pauline keeps constant guard, through the grimy café and into the public house so nostalgically named the Queen Victoria. Perhaps Lou or Ethel will 'pop off' in an episode soon, and afford us all some light relief. And one further piece of advice to the script-writers: a little rhyming slang can go a very long way indeed.

22 February 1985

69

Ours to Keep

A Pocketful of Rye

Ours to Keep (BBC 2) is concerned with those who have made the effort to reacquire our history – in last night's example, the new inhabitants of Spitalfields who have restored the early eighteenth-century houses of that area. One resident described his role as that of 'living the past': it may seem an odd position to assume but it is a most important one since, if London loses its memory, it also loses its identity.

And these living historians could not have chosen a more significant area: Spitalfields, in the shadow of the great Hawksmoor church, in the vicinity of the Ripper murders, the area which has housed successive waves of immigrants, represents all the horror, the magnificence and the heterogeneity of London itself. And that is why it is so necessary for these houses to survive; they embody something which is not to be found elsewhere and, as one resident suggested, 'there is some sort of emotional response to these buildings'. This was an evocative documentary, even if the slightly superficial nature of its presentation suggested that television is a less suitable vehicle for cultural understanding than the very people it described.

What television can do, instead, is to provide a more nostalgic or at least stereotypical version of the past – the moving-picture equivalent of Madame Tussaud's, as the current sequence of Miss Marple dramas (BBC 1) has demonstrated. Last night's first episode of *A Pocketful of Rye* was in the usual vein, as the well-known nursery rhyme was succeeded by images of the baffled policeman, the tearful chambermaid and the other paraphernalia of television drama. Joan Hickson is probably the best Miss Marple of recent years since she manages to keep the element of caricature to a minimum.

The period detail of this series has been accurate to the point of becoming elaborate, but it lends everything a museum-like quality which does not help to accelerate the action. Last night's episode was diverting enough, however, even if the 'excitement' would make a cat laugh. Its end will no doubt be impossible to anticipate and equally difficult to credit.

8 March 1985

70

Arena
(Old Kent Road)

Arena (BBC 2) illustrated the opening words of *The Canterbury Tales* with some images of modern life along the Old Kent Road: this was where that famous pilgrimage started, although the only remaining religious site appears to be the Thomas à Beckett public house, where boxers engage in their devotions. But, even if there are few reminders of the past in the immediate surroundings, there may at least be some continuity in the English character which adds significance to Chaucer's words: that was the theme of this programme, *Old Kent Road*, and that was why a number of colourful locals were asked about their memories of an older London.

If television has wrought any permanent change in our perceptions, it is in our understanding of time. This was apparent in last night's documentary which, through old newsreels and photographs, so constantly and evocatively recalled the past that it seemed to overwhelm a thin and wayward present. The old fire station has now become an arts 'co-operative', the ancient cinema is now being demolished, and the Victorian hatmakers has been transformed into a shop which sells tyres. The tyre-seller himself suggested that the spirit of the hat manufacturer still haunts his old premises, but there are so many ghosts in this area that it would be invidious to mention one in particular.

And yet some things have not changed: Bert's pie shop is still very much in evidence, fishing tackle is still being sold in an eighteenth-century dwelling, and some of the older parties (to be seen having their hair 'done') have triumphantly survived the passage of the years. And, in pubs called the Rising Sun or the Green Man, they still sing certain of the old songs. The generations pass over this small area of London, themselves like pilgrims. This was an ingenious and agreeable programme but somehow it managed to become more than the sum of its parts: by hinting at much larger themes of time and permanence, it was often very moving.

26 March 1985

The Times *Book Reviews*

71

An Insular Possession
Timothy Mo

Timothy Mo is the most important living chronicler of his birthplace, Hong Kong; it is perhaps an invidious position, a Virgil singing of arms and plastic, but in the circumstances of that colony's imminent demise a necessary one. His accomplished first novel, *The Monkey King*, depicted Hong Kong as wicked, greedy, and intensely comic; now, in *An Insular Possession*, he has traced the origins of that interesting condition to the Opium Wars of the early nineteenth century – in the turbulent wake of which the colony was established.

The novel itself is set in the 1830s, at the time of this little local difficulty; yet it is an aspect of the curious but agreeable obliquity of Mo's narrative that the principal combatants, the English and the Chinese, are consigned to subordinate roles. His two central characters are young Americans, traders so disgusted with the traffic in opium that they set themselves up as the crusading editors of the *Lin Tan Bulletin and River Bee*. Gideon Chase is an incipient sinologist, while Walter Eastman is no more than a daring entrepreneur; and it is through their respective fortunes that Mo faithfully restores the old life of South China.

So *An Insular Possession* is a historical fiction. There was a time when this classification would have amounted to a term of abuse, since the historical novel was considered (together with romantic fiction and science fantasy) as the last haven of a tired imagination.

It was the era of 'Prithees!' and strange objects known as dirks or poniards. But in recent years the importance of the form has been recognized. If 'post-modernism' means anything, it is in its disavowal both of conventional realism and self-conscious experimentalism; and this is precisely the area where historical fiction has come into its own.

In simple terms, it increases the novelist's options: he can choose his style, and thereby choose his world.

And so it is that in *An Insular Possession* Timothy Mo has constructed a polyphonic narrative. He has created a rich and elaborate narrative voice while at the same time he has managed beautifully to reproduce the idioms and cadences of early nineteenth-century prose, whether in the form of newspaper reports or private letters, diary entries or intimate conversations. There are occasional false notes, but the delight he takes in creating these heterogeneous styles is successfully communicated and therefore shared.

He is a great impersonator, in other words, but it is not a question merely of pastiche. It has been said that a novelist should not undertake a work which does not educate either himself or his readers, and *An Insular Possession* is as much an act of creative scholarship as it is of imagination. Timothy Mo has laboured over the past (the research must have been extensive), and he has so lovingly recreated it that it surrounds him with its own mysteries: it is like an echo-chamber, in which his own voice is magnified.

Clearly he decided to write a 'big' book at the same time; but if it displays a Victorian scale it also acquires a contemporary significance: *An Insular Possession* has a largeness borrowed from recent fictional epics set in Australia and in India. This is the literary version of Montezuma's revenge, as those born in quondam colonial territories are seized with the desire to explain their own past (and therefore, of course, themselves) in novels which are more exuberant, more extravagant, and often more interesting than the native English products. Timothy Mo is in the same tradition as Carey or Rushdie.

His is a complex imagination, as well, of which mockery and obliquity are the two most important elements. The tone of the narrator is one of humorous irony, but this effect of distance is displayed by the characters themselves who are seen variously drawing or photographing the local territory.

Everyone is sketching or capturing their own especial scene, just as each character is a prisoner of his or her own particular verbal style – whether it is the romantic bravura of colonial conversation, the polysyllabic absurdities of the local newspapers, or the demotic lingo of the native Chinese. They are all attempting to arrest or at least to define a world which persists in changing – and from this springs the comedy as well as the pathos of the book.

This sense of change is in fact evoked by the novel's consistent use of the present tense – apparently very much like Chinese fiction, which is described here as 'occurring in an immediate present' so that there is 'no sense of recession or distance from the past, or superiority to it'. This in turn confirms the speculation of one of the principal characters: 'But what is good and what is bad? Can it be just a matter of perspective, with one seeing it quite differently from another?' *An Insular Possession* suggests that this is indeed so, and Timothy Mo has written a novel in which various interpretations of the past can be suggested with equal lucidity. This is a 'historical novel' in a deeper sense, then, since it is concerned primarily with the nature of history itself.

8 May 1986

72

The Faber Book of Political Verse
Edited by Tom Paulin

If politics is the art of the possible, then political verse is an almost impossible art: whoever heard of a lyric on the nature of compromise, or an elegy to pragmatism? But in fact there is a tradition of just such poetry (sometimes suitably disguised by allegory, or worse), and it is a merit of Tom Paulin's new anthology that it emphasizes the neglected aspects of poets who are generally regarded as 'immortal' and therefore above the routine business of life. But if man is a political animal, there is no reason why the songs of Apollo should not sometimes issue from the lips of partisans.

And so, in his interesting introduction, Paulin rightly discounts the theory that 'art' and 'politics' are mutually exclusive occupations, and that a poem is a free-floating agent which by some miracle has been cut loose from social, historical or biographical realities. This was a modern heresy inaugurated by T. S. Eliot, endorsed by I. A. Richards, and subsequently institutionalized by a variety of mulish academic critics. But there are no electrified fences between the world and the poem: as Paulin says memorably here, '. . . politics is like a rain-storm that catches us all in its wet noise'.

This of course poses peculiar problems for an anthologist since it means, or implies, that all kinds of poetry can be interpreted as expressing political awareness – any poem without an overt ideological stance might be described as *conservative*, for example, and even the most hermetic lyricist, concerned with Love and Death, could be diagnosed as a purblind supporter of the status quo.

Given this difficulty, a diffident editor would probably only have included those poems that are directly and overtly engaged with political realities – certainly they comprise a long list, stretching from anonymous thirteenth-century lyrics through Dryden and on to Pound. Tom Paulin has adopted a broader attitude, however, which in practice has meant that he is happy to include poems that appeal to him for a variety of reasons; thus we have twelve pages of John Clare, whose 'To the Snipe' could be described as 'political' only in the vaguest sense. Perhaps as a protest against blood-sports?

But Paulin does have a theoretical perspective to lend a certain coherence to this heterogeneous selection, and in his introduction he distinguishes between a broadly 'conservative' or 'monarchical' tradition and a 'puritan' or 'republican' one – thus Dryden and Milton, Johnson and Blake, Eliot and Lawrence, can be seen as resisting each other in endless battle rather than resting together in the quietus of a putative 'great tradition'. As a theory it has the merit of simplicity, but unfortunately it avoids what might be described as the problem of belief, aptly summarized in the expression that the truest poetry is the most feigning.

The problem is best stated by the poets themselves. It was Thomas Chatterton who once said that he held in contempt any man who could not write on both sides of a controversy – a fluency emphasized by the American poet, Karl Shapiro, who maintained that he wrote as a Christian on one day and as a Jew on the next. It is in this context, of course, that 'politics' is best seen as an extension of aesthetics – since the overriding aim of the poet is to create significant form, he or she will entertain almost any belief in order to reach that happy state. Eliot was not really a 'monarchist', despite the enormous cultural weight he is forced to carry in Paulin's introduction as an emblem of conservative pessimism. He was not really a monarchist because he was never really anything. In any case, if the history of modernism teaches us anything it is that the greatest 'conservatives' are also the greatest poetic revolutionaries. What is the politics of that situation?

But if Paulin's theory has the virtue of simplicity it also has the further merit, for an anthologist, of wide applicability. This book begins with Dante and ends with Miroslav Holub, including Ecclesiastes and 'Please to remember the Fifth of November' en route. In fact the choice is eclectic to the point of oddness. There are 36 pages of Marvell, for example, and only two pages of Shelley; and, if there was room for 27 pages of Dryden's *Absalom and Achitophel* (readily available elsewhere), surely a small space could have been found for Rochester's famous

> God bless our good and gracious King,
> Whose promise none relies on . . .

It is easy to play the game of omissions, but it is a necessary task with an anthology that at least aspires to being authoritative. Why, for example, is Thomas Hood omitted? His 'The Song of the Shirt' was arguably the most important, and certainly the most popular, political verse of the last century; Elizabeth Barrett Browning's 'The Cry of the Children' might share the palm with it but she, too, is not to be found here. Nor is Crabbe. But surely the most significant absence is that of Ezra Pound? There is not one word by or about him here, although he is without doubt the most important political poet of the twentieth century.

Some omissions are necessary and even instructive as an index of fashionable taste. It is easy to understand why Paulin has avoided all the 'beat' and 'bomb culture' poetry of the sixties and early seventies; unfortunately, however, he has included some equally dubious material of a later date; and one has only to look at recent Irish verse, overgenerously represented here, to realize that the pressure of political events is no guarantee of poetic merit – or even of poetic interest. As a result this anthology, to paraphrase the words of a former 'monarchist' Faber editor, begins with a bang and ends with a whimper – or, rather, a yawn. The notes are random and cryptic; the textual apparatus (why have the spellings been variously modernized, half-modernized or left intact?) notable for its absence.

26 May 1986

73

Writing Against: A Biography of Sartre
Ronald Hayman

Jean-Paul Sartre was both polemicist and playwright, novelist and journalist, biographer and philosopher – each book he wrote is little more than part of the ever-flowing material that is Sartre himself and, as Ronald Hayman says in this excellent biography, 'the whole of his work can be read as an inconsequential series of instalments in one enormous unfinishable book'. He was always in a hurry – intellectually speaking, that is. He began gargantuan projects only to abandon them; he consistently revised or ignored his past in order to embrace an imagined future; he was happy to contradict himself and even to denounce his earlier opinions. He had the theoretician's appetite for total certainty, which was consistently at odds with any understanding of human experience itself: he wanted to create a synthesis that contained no less than everything, but the project necessarily failed. There is always something that evades his grasp, something which he sees but which he cannot completely understand – and that something is his own self, that unstable mass of impulses that comprise Jean-Paul Sartre.

Like many great writers, he was also something of a charlatan; from his schooldays he possessed the ability 'to write fluently on ideas he had only partially digested'; 'each of his theories,' Hayman goes on to say at another point, 'was an act of appropriation.' And when this facility is combined with his 'strong streak of exhibitionism' – at university he acted in reviews and 'cherished the idea of becoming a jazz singer' – there are the makings of a most erratic, if theatrical, intellectual. And yet he had genius, if one can ascribe that nebulous term to someone who lives in a symbolic relationship with his own age. For he was able to impart to his experience 'the quality of myth'.

How did he get that way? Like many creatures of myth he believed in auto-genesis; he wanted 'to think of himself as self-created, indebted to no one'. As a young man, moving up the various rungs of the French educational system, he 'counted on liberating himself by becoming totally independent of other people'. Which is why the title of this biography is so apt – Sartre was always writing *against* his family, his childhood, his teachers, and his own past.

He always attacks those philosophers to whom he was once indebted; but, on a more private level, this supporter of the working class was also never at ease with individual members of that fraternity. As Hayman says here: 'His liking for the people was generalized and theoretical.'

This intellectual's insensitivity (for such it is) partly emerges in *La Nausée*, the first in a series of books that was to bring him great fame. The novel was published just before the war, but it was really after this conflict that he first achieved celebrity as the proponent of 'existentialism'. A shell-shocked Paris was probably the best place for a philosophy that 'mingled optimism and responsibility'; and it was appropriate that a man who had spent half his life disregarding or reformulating his past should become the philosophical leader of a country that wished to do the same.

Existentialism is not a particularly rigorous philosophical discipline – like much of Sartre's work, it represents a popularization and even a vulgarization of other writers who are more accustomed to speak *de haut en bas* – but it was a philosophy for putative intellectuals, and so it was effective in a country that tends to be run by them. In the years after the war his novels and dramas increased his fame, just as his editorship of *Les Temps modernes* lent him great political influence. In England a man with so relentless a theoretical perspective would long ago have been immured in a university – the thought of a philosopher writing novels, biographies, and even journalism is anathema to the English soul, which is as departmentalized as it is sceptical – but in France Sartre was able to flourish. And so there is a sense in which he never needed to grow up – in the country of *clarté* he could remain a somewhat naive theoretician because his theories were taken seriously.

But this is where his problems started: as soon as he thought of himself as a public figure, his predilection for melodrama and his propensity for revolt sent him straight through *la littérature engagée* to the wilder fringes of Western political life, a position in which he remained – stuck – for the rest of his life.

One of the weaknesses of many writers is to believe that a 'writer' by virtue of his skill becomes an immediate expert on social or economic matters; in fact, a writer's opinion on nuclear disarmament, for example, is no more interesting than that of a butcher or a traffic warden. Sartre was one of those who overestimated his capacity as a political thinker; and as a result, he got himself into a terrible muddle.

Politically, he was an easy lay: he was involved with Maoists, Stalinists, Leninists, Situationists – almost anyone, in fact, provided that they were sufficiently young and sufficiently hostile to the political establishment. And it was all such a waste: in the last years of his life he could have been writing plays or novels that would have survived for many generations, and instead he was passing the time of day with the Baader-Meinhof gang.

One can understand why he did it: he was a genuinely international figure, and one with an equally genuine disruptive consciousness. He saw beneath the conventional world, in other words, and it was his settled belief that all organized government was a conspiracy against the people. Like Blake or Shelley, he was a free spirit who saw others being crushed. But his motives are one thing and his practice quite another – time and again he became the accomplice or dupe of the corrupt and the stupid. And yet, as Hayman says, at the end of his formidable biography, 'there is something heroic in Sartre's indomitable persistence, in his boundless willingness to be wrong'. And, as a result, Sartre is somehow larger than any of his books. In *Writing Against* Ronald Hayman has been able to create a life that relates the man to his work in quite new ways, and so manages to take a proper measure of both.

16 October 1986

74

The Orton Diaries

Edited by John Lahr

The shade of Oscar Wilde is from time to time invoked in these pages; and no doubt Joe Orton understood Gwendolen's remark that she kept her diary in order to have 'something sensational to read in the train'. Certainly Orton's own diary is sensational, but possibly not in the manner he intended, since it led directly to his death. When Kenneth Halliwell, his male lover of some sixteen years, beat him to death with a hammer and then committed suicide, he left a note for the police which was in the nature of a clue: 'If you read his diary all will be explained.'

This is not strictly true, however, since this book hardly suggests the possibility of such an abrupt ending. If Orton's plays read as if Oscar Wilde had been brought up on a council house estate, and had become very bitter as a result, the actual world that Orton describes here seems to luxuriate in the same vainglorious and slightly seedy comedy. The diary opens in December 1966 (just after the success of *Loot*) and one of the first treats is the death of his mother. She had popped off on Boxing Day, meriting only the briefest of mentions; then Orton has casual sex with a labourer in Leicester before returning to the familial dwelling where, he is told, the corpse of his mother will be waiting for him in the living room. As Orton said of a friend's startled surprise at this episode, 'He suddenly caught a glimpse of the fact that I write the truth.'

But of course diaries are a kind of fabrication, too, and in *The Orton Diaries* sixties London becomes yet another theatre of the absurd: it may have been 'swinging', but here it is practically in orbit as old ladies, old queens, theatrical impresarios, actors, and male prostitutes make their entrances or exits. If some of the more amusing episodes seem to have the benefit of the prompt-book, that is only to be expected in so skilful a dramatist: this is social history rewritten by an epigrammatist and it can be very, very funny.

Of course there is a sense in which it is really laughter in the dark, since over it all hangs the long shadow of Kenneth Halliwell and the hammer he took to Orton's skull. Halliwell had originally been the partner with creative ambitions, but he was failing miserably just at the time when Orton was enjoying his greatest success. It is a cautionary tale worthy of one of Belloc's verses, but it is unusual only for its somewhat grisly ending. Halliwell was the archetypal companion or lover who is crushed by the juggernaut of the other partner's fame. The history of literature is crowded with such people – in his very interesting introduction, John Lahr quotes the words of Thomas Hardy's wife, 'If he belongs to the public, years of devotion count for nothing.' And indeed as Lahr goes on to say, Orton 'edited Halliwell out'. He is here in the diaries, but only just. Sometimes Orton refers to him quite formally as 'Kenneth Halliwell', as if he were a character he had invented; and his presence in the book brings with it a general atmosphere of sickness, argument and moral disapproval. The busier and more successful Orton becomes, the more Halliwell withdraws into himself – as if he is going into a cupboard and locking the door, so that he cannot see the light outside.

The point about doom and gloom, however, is that Orton often found them irresistibly funny, and there are times when even his ghastly relationship with Halliwell blossoms into comedy. Certain scenes in Tangier, for example, are of a tackiness almost beyond compare (in the holiday snaps, Orton resembles some hybrid of Mishima and a pub landlady), but Orton sees the tackiness and revels in it: he manages to turn the entire escapade into grotesque farce, with enough physical detail to fill several filing cabinets of the nearest VD clinic. Quotations are not to be attempted in a respectable newspaper.

Editing, too, must have presented problems. Lahr seems wisely to have left most of the journal intact, although he is perhaps over-zealous in his scholarship. Practically every reference to anyone living or dead, is explained: surely, for example, we do not need a footnote on Dante in the middle of some more than usually exotic episode in Tangier? On second thoughts, perhaps we do.

And yet despite these escapades it is extraordinary how Orton's *normality* shines through everything – at one moment he may be playing the Rimbaud, or at least the Verlaine, of Noel Road, Islington, but at the next he is discussing budgerigars with the old lady who lives beneath him. And that of course was the secret of his charm: his ordinariness had a menacing quality, while at the same time his oddness was somehow cosy and unthreatening. Lahr says that 'Orton had willed himself into the role of a rebel outcast: beyond guilt or shame.'

The last days of his life are, in that respect, typical. In July 1967 he sees *The Desert Song*; he picks up stray men; he spends a damp weekend in Brighton. Halliwell himself was slowly breaking down, but Orton shows no real sign of noticing it. A friend saw them a little later, when Halliwell was clearly on the edge of the disaster that killed them both. Orton was, as usual, being 'hilarious': 'And I thought, my God, he can't see. He hasn't noticed.' It is a terrible irony that Orton could invent the grotesque or the macabre without recognizing it when it was in front of his nose; on the stage he created murderous and defeated lives, but he did not know when life itself was beginning to take the same form. It is the kind of blindness that makes an artist, but it may also kill him.

6 November 1986

75

The Royal Beasts and Other Works
William Empson
Edited by John Haffenden

There is no reason why academics should not also be what is popularly known as 'creative' writers. American universities are stuffed with them (although they tend to adopt the unscholastic title of writer-in-residence) and there are some notable examples of the double life in this country, David Lodge and Malcolm Bradbury being two of the most eminent. But it is rare here; and it was rarer still when William Empson was both a Professor of English Literature and a celebrated poet.

He was best known as a critic, however, which must have been a particularly galling fate for him – a disappointment all the greater because, as John Haffenden explains in his introduction to this collection of Empson's previously unpublished work, he began with high hopes as a playwright and poet. In fact when he was an undergraduate at Cambridge, in the twenties, he and his writing became something of a cult. This is generally disastrous for everyone concerned, of course, and English life is littered with the burnt-out relics of young men and women who were once hailed as 'promising' or acclaimed as 'geniuses'.

By all accounts Empson was a clever, spirited and quick-witted young man; such people flourish in university conditions (and by the strange alchemy of fate then tend to produce work which university audiences particularly admire), but they are also the ones who seem most easily to go astray in the outer world. There is an old phrase about being so sharp that one cuts oneself; and that seems to have been Empson's especial destiny. How else is it that a writer once as promising as he should now be remembered only for two or three critical studies – chief among them being *Seven Types of Ambiguity* and *Some Versions of Pastoral*? They may be what are called 'seminal' books, but they are not literature.

The famous organ of hindsight might also discern danger in the fact that Empson achieved a clear-cut literary success at a very early age; *Seven Types of Ambiguity* itself was published when he was twenty-four, and his best poetry was being written and praised in the same period. In fact much of the material collected here is drawn from those years – his poetry and drama were then as tense as a wire but often as thin, with the ratiocinative complexity of the born critic manifesting itself. As a result much of his early work now seems jejune and somewhat flat, displaying an intellectual precocity that is fatally aligned with something very close to emotional naivety. Empson was a smart manipulator of language, with a talent for cultural allusion matched only by his instinct for parody and pastiche. This is what one would expect in a clever and highly educated young writer, but these are abilities that have to be transcended or enlarged before any serious work can be done. Empson was a water-diviner of language who stayed upon the surface, finding only a fine spray rather than the hidden springs.

And was it also malign fate which sent him to the Far East? Certainly it is yet another graveyard for the incipient English writer, who often ends up in a kind of cultural no man's land, half estranged from the West, and only half understanding the East. Empson began the longest item in this collection, 'The Royal Beasts', during the early part of the Sino-Japanese war when he was lecturing in China. It is an unfinished 'fable' concerning a new species of creature, neither human nor animal, and within its mainly didactic and dialectical form one sees again how firmly Empson's writing is dominated by intellectual concerns. It is a book pervaded by purely mental excitement, exhilarating or wearying according to taste; but the example of Aldous Huxley ought to be enough to suggest that such excitement is not in itself enough to animate or direct fiction. You run the risk of giving the reader a terrible headache.

The same problem besets the last piece here, 'The Elephant and the Birds', which is essentially a scenario for a ballet designed to combine Buddhist and Western attitudes in some zoological spectacle. Again Empson is trying decently to clothe intellectual points or themes, but, in the absence of properly dramatic garments, they seem more like scarecrows. The Buddhist elements are not a success; they rarely are in the West where, to put it crudely, Buddhism is generally regarded as a great bore.

But Empson himself was never boring: he was clever, provocative, a writer distinguished both by the subtlety and by the rigour of his intelligence.

But he was not an artist. He was moved or excited primarily by ideas, where his more creative contemporaries merely exploited them when it was necessary to do so. Empson *believed* in ideas; someone like Eliot, one of his literary heroes, picked them up for a particular poem or play only to put them down again when they were no longer convenient. Empson seems also to have suffered from the kind of analytical obsessiveness that precludes genuine creative achievement; he seized upon a central perception or interest (he had an especial affection for images of the Buddha, for example) and never let it rest. But this is the enthusiasm of the analyst, or the collector, rather than of the artist.

Of course it could be said that he was cleverer than most creative writers. And yet the melancholy fact remains that it is possible to be too clever to be a properly imaginative artist – to be too self-conscious, too academically parsimonious with language, too aware of the various cultural and historical contexts in which one works, and so on. Empson seems to fall into that special category. It is interesting to examine his previously unseen work; but the most intriguing and significant aspects of this volume are really those of the cautionary tale.

13 November 1986

76

The History of England from the Accession of James II

Thomas Babington Macaulay

He had thought, Macaulay wrote, 'that the book would have a permanent place in our literature'. And so it has proved, even on the most literal test: this *History* has never been out of print. But his ambition is not one that most contemporary historians would share –

few of them seem to know enough about 'literature' to want to attach themselves to it; but even the more enlightened would prefer to claim some connection with 'knowledge' instead. As for the idea of 'duty' or of 'mission', two words which Peter Rowland uses in his excellent introduction to this new edition, they would be laughed right out of court. Perhaps that is why modern history is now generally read only by other historians.

Macaulay's audience was rather larger, and when he finished the first two volumes of his work in 1848, the street outside his publisher's office was jammed with the carriages of booksellers waiting to purchase them. One contemporary critic said that he and Dickens were the two most popular authors of the age, and, just to prove that literature can also pay, he has been described as 'the first literary millionaire'. That success is the more remarkable when you consider that of all generations the mid-Victorian is the one which could most justifiably have dispensed with any national past. Theirs was so prosperous and mighty a civilization that they could have treated the Elizabethans or the Stuarts with the same irony that led Charles Dickens to label one of the false books in his library *The Wisdom of Our Ancestors* (among the subtitles of this compendious volume were 'Ignorance' and 'Superstition').

But even if they did not choose to applaud their ancestors, they wished to understand them, no doubt on the unstated principle that a nation without a historical sense is a nation without identity. So in our own time historical research has become specialized only at a great cost: most schoolchildren seem to think that anything before Harold Wilson is lost in the mists of time.

Of course it might be said that Macaulay is great precisely because he lived before the age of 'professional' historical research, that he was untouched by various statistical, textual or demographic inquiries. But this is to miss the point. He knew quite enough about statistics in what was, in any case, a great age of commissions and reports – after all, he helped to draft legal and educational legislation for India.

But he understood that history required another kind of understanding, and could be written successfully only on quite different principles. He realized that facts alone do not persuade, and that evidence by itself cannot enlighten; only good prose can achieve both those ends. He was not providing some chimera of 'objectivity' or 'scientific explanation'; he set himself the task of interpreting the past in a certain definite way, and he did so with all the rich and eloquent resources of his literary art.

One of the differences between his age and our own is that the Victorians had a belief in, and appetite for, certain kinds of permanent or inviolable truth. So it is that Macaulay constructed a Whig interpretation of English history in which the steady consolidation of parliamentary government is also seen as a slow progress towards the light. But, more importantly, he suggested an organic view of history in which past and present were part of a general movement forward – a movement towards power, stability, social harmony and national benevolence, in which fertile soil grew certain 'moral virtues' that protected the weak and tempered the aggression of the strong. This was his vision, and he offered it to his contemporaries in a language which, with its rich syntactical insistence and its clausal progress, offered a simulacrum of the very order he was in the process of celebrating.

This is not to suggest that Macaulay was an incompetent amateur when it came to the more pedestrian aspects of the historian's work. He studied most of the available sources. As Thackeray said of him, 'He reads twenty books to write a sentence; he travels a hundred miles to make a line of description.' But the 'facts' and the 'evidence' became part of a larger pattern, and had no real meaning outside it. Of course this is also true of even the most apparently dispassionate histories: I have never read a historical work which did not tell me more about the historian than about the period he purported to describe.

But the success of Macaulay's *History* was not established simply upon its ability to confirm certain Victorian habits of thought. For in another sense he was a great innovator, and this principally in the realm of the historical imagination. He *saw* the past; and his great gift was to evoke that past so that his readers could see it too. The chapter of this work in which he describes 'The State of England in 1685' is unrivalled as a sustained act of imaginative re-creation; it is written in the same spirit as, but is in some ways superior to, the historical fictions of Charles Dickens or Bulwer Lytton.

The point is that Macaulay belongs in the same company. His concern was to give 'to truth those attractions which have been usurped by fiction', and he was delighted when his friends remarked that his *History* was 'as entertaining as a novel'. The modern professional historian might not wish to claim a similar success: but so much the worse for him. It is only by reanimating the past that it can properly be understood; and for that reason, if for no other, historical writing at its best is a form of literary inquiry. Surely every historian wishes to carry conviction? Macaulay understood that simple point, which is why his *History* has survived where a thousand superficially more 'accurate' works have been forgotten.

18 December 1986

77

The Oxford Illustrated History of English Literature
Edited by Pat Rogers

Perhaps the most significant aspect of this collective attempt at literary history lies in the fact that each chapter is written by an academic. There was a time when English literature was discussed by English writers; but that was a barbaric period when the proper worth of literary criticism and literary research was not fully appreciated. Now we have professors and lecturers instead. Of course this is safer, and, if more predictable, also more reassuring: a book of this kind, with its glossy pages and its agreeable illustrations, is as cosy as an old-fashioned tram-ride down a busy street. All stops from *Beowulf* to W. H. Auden, and no spitting out of the window. But even though the journey is a photogenic one, it is not clear what other purpose it might have.

The difficulty pre-dates this particular volume, however, since over the last few decades academic criticism itself seems to have lost any real sense of purpose or direction. It has veered between pseudo-moralism (F. R. Leavis *et al.*) and pseudo-scientism (I. A. Richards *et al.*), with the whole discipline of 'English Literature' clutching at various respectable straws in order to justify its increasingly tenuous existence. But no member of that vast army of students currently reading paperbacks of D. H. Lawrence or Geoffrey Chaucer is going to become a 'better' or more 'sensitive' person by doing so; and at a time when indeterminacy or unknowability has entered the realm of proper scientific research, it seems a little odd to be constructing known 'traditions' or elucidating determined 'themes' by which various poems and novels are to be explained.

It was not always so. In the middle decades of this century there was in fact almost an academic hegemony in literary matters; and as a result there were even writers who deliberately pitched their work to appeal to a university audience because they knew that it was with just such an audience that their reputations were to be made. T. S. Eliot is the prime example of this phenomenon, and it is significant that in this latest Oxford History he is mentioned more often than any other writer, except for Shakespeare and Pope.

The academics needed 'complex' and 'ambiguous' work to justify the time spent in its study, so Eliot gave it to them; they wanted 'symbols' and 'allegories' so that they might have something to teach, and Eliot handed them over on a platter. And of course it was Eliot, also, who most ably expounded the theory of literary 'tradition' which lies behind this particular volume. But we need not look to him only. We can revert to an even more eminent Victorian for this ideology, and remember Carlyle's dictum that the two essential laws of human activity are 'Habit and Imitation'. So it is that the history of English literature can profitably be seen as a history of thefts and plagiarisms, of formal borrowings and melodic echoes.

Of course, if you look hard enough you can find other more solid connections; and certain of the contributors here emphasize that one great English literary tradition which lasted for most of the period under review (700 to 1970) but which has now vanished – the tradition of religious prose. For almost eighteen centuries it was the most significant aspect of English cultural life; but now I suspect that, if we are to find it at all, it is only to be discovered lurking in textbooks of quantum physics.

So there are good and judicious essays in this collection – Andrew Sanders on 'High Victorian Literature' and Bernard Bergonzi on 'Late Victorian and Modernist' are particularly good at conveying the appropriate information without becoming overtly schematic. Martin Dodsworth's essay on mid-twentieth-century literature also has a refreshing sharpness of tone, all the more invigorating at a time when academic judgements about contemporary work tend to lean either towards the fashionable (I remember one Cambridge don in ecstasies over the somewhat barren lyrics of Bob Dylan) or towards the safe.

But to what particular destination is this book travelling? The editor, Pat Rogers, suggests that all his essayists maintain 'a vital concern with the critical ideas of the present'. It is not clear what those ideas might be, unless they are connected with a general veneration for such codewords as 'ambiguity', 'complexity' and something referred to as 'experience'. Academic critics often profess to believe that literature is somehow about the pressure or illumination of 'experience'; but this is a most unhealthy doctrine, and is really no more than a recondite version of that ridiculous demand made of schoolchildren: 'Write About Something You Know'.

The whole point, of course, is to write about something you don't know. Experience has nothing to do with it; and I suspect that the academic emphasis upon this strange injunction masks a puritanism which insists that literature is something to be studied rather than enjoyed. Literature must have a didactic or at the very least a clarifying power, so the argument runs, or how could it be taught? The realization that literature might not possess these no doubt excellent qualities – that it might, after all, be simply an object of pleasure – would be enough to deprive several university departments of their government funding. But all is not lost: of the making of books about books there will be no end.

23 April 1987

78

Charles Laughton: A Difficult Actor
Simon Callow

Charles Laughton did not really look like an actor, let alone a star. He had a face which, as he said, resembled 'an elephant's behind'. But if his physiognomy might have come from the more *louche* elements of the animal kingdom, he was still able to startle audiences with his sudden graceful movements, with his scuttles across the stage, and with a voice that in *The Hunchback of Notre Dame* sounded like a moonbeam caught in a bottle.

Like any good actor, therefore, he was not what he seemed. In one of the many perceptive passages in this wonderfully percipient biography, Simon Callow describes the stark apartment that Laughton shared with Elsa Lanchester: most people would have expected Laughton's rich and somewhat cheesy personality to overflow into an expanse of ornament; but of course the bareness and the indiscipline of his living quarters were exactly right. He was a formalist, as Callow tells us, a rigorous artist whose acting was 'made up of strong clear strokes'.

He was the son of Scarborough hoteliers, and a homosexual – not a unique combination but unusual, and one with which he never quite came to terms; there was always a touch of the hotel manager about him, even if it was only to put at ease the various personalities who lodged within his own breast. Then in the twenties he seemed to emerge fully armed upon the stage: it is hard to realize from the strangely contorted and somehow slightly vicious plumpness of the young Laughton that he never had to struggle to succeed. He went in easy stages from the West End to Hollywood; and it was the film camera that first pierced the face of Caliban to find the soul of Prospero.

Yet there *was* a struggle, but it was one against himself. He wanted to be a great actor, but he was never really at home in the theatre; even in his early days he acquired a reputation for eccentricity, and was notoriously difficult and taciturn at rehearsals. Callow suggests that he could never have become a classical actor in the Olivier mould, because that would have meant imposing external standards upon himself when the real imperatives and restrictions came from within – he was an actor who had to create each part out of his own often desperate imagination. The agony he suffered was that of rebirth.

Just as the biographer of a poet or novelist will analyse his subject's writings, so in a similar manner Callow here analyses Laughton's performances; and it is part of the strange alchemy of the actor's art that this book should be an account of Laughton's *personae* as much as of Laughton himself. Thus he emerges as himself and yet not himself – a creature who is part Nero, part Quasimodo, part Bligh. And although there are times when Callow perhaps over-emphasizes that element in Laughton that he describes as 'existential anxiety', there is no doubt that in each role he felt himself to be purified; he was releasing a little part of himself into the upper atmosphere, where it might create its own strange shapes. He was liberating his 'obsessed, repressed, fanatical, conscience-ridden' psyche by objectifying it.

Quasimodo was the role in which he finally found his quietus and, after that, his creative energies were turned elsewhere. He kept appearing in films, but only to serve up thin slices of ham. He even collaborated with Brecht, which must surely be one of the strangest partnerships in the history of the theatre. But although he directed one wonderful film, *Night of the Hunter*, and made a brave attempt at Lear in his last years, his major activities became those of teaching and public reading. He no longer needed to dive into the depths of the sea, to use his biographer's metaphor; instead, he began swimming towards other people.

Callow continually questions the status of acting as an art; but, on the evidence of this biography alone, it is clear that the actor is just as much an artist as the novelist or the painter – perhaps no one more so than Laughton himself since, as one early critic noted, he seemed determined to seize the essence of the character. The techniques of this magical transference are in fact very interesting and, in one of those perceptions that make this biography as much a study of acting as the study of an actor, Callow remarks that 'if you imitate the outer life of someone with sufficient connection, you sometimes get an inner life for nothing.' This is a mystery which other artists have also come to understand – it is in the visible surface that the 'soul' is generally to be discovered. Or, as Edith Head put it more pithily, 'Charles had an amazing ability to adjust his body to his clothes.' Actors ought to read *Sartor Resartus* just as often as *The Stage*.

Simon Callow himself is an actor and, although his publishers have tried too hard to draw a resemblance between him and his subject through the unhappy medium of a dust jacket, there is no doubt that he brings to Laughton a potent mixture of sympathy and objectivity – he understands the springs of acting while at the same time he retains that cold eye that actors always bring to each other's performances. And the magic of re-creation works here just as it does upon the stage: out of the narrative emerges Laughton himself, stumbling, blinking, and yet somehow always remarkable. Dickens once said that 'The more real the man, the more genuine the actor'; and it is the achievement of this biography to confirm that point. Those who want a little shop talk about Laughton's homosexuality will be disappointed – this is not a spit and tell biography – but those who are interested in the nature of performance, and indeed in the nature of art, will not be.

3 September 1987

79

A Various Art

Edited by Andrew Crozier and Tim Longville

If it is true that each generation discovers its own appropriate medium, then surely this is an age of prose: fiction is flourishing while poetry has become something of a sideshow, conveniently used as a signal for 'deep' feeling by certain Irish poets, but otherwise seen as a piece of candyfloss to fill spaces in the columns of the weeklies, or as a publicity stunt, or as a springboard for some other kind of literary career. It takes an anthology such as this, therefore, to remind us of what ought not to be forgotten – prose may be a more difficult art, but poetry is the higher, the only discipline that can really save language from corruption and misuse. Poets are indeed the unacknowledged legislators of mankind, since poetry offers the only language that can in the end reshape the world.

This is not a polemical anthology on the old model, however, since, as its title suggests, the poets collected in this volume represent a group only in a chronological sense – most of them began writing in the sixties, and the vast bulk of the poetry here was composed within the last fifteen years. If it represents any kind of reaction it is not against the fashionable poets of the moment (who will in any case die of inanition sooner rather than later) but rather against the whole context of English poetry which prevailed when these particular writers began to publish their work – a reaction, in other words, against the orthodoxy of the fifties and sixties when this 'right little, tight little island', to borrow a Victorian phrase, produced right little, tight little poems. It was a time of insularity and of an almost wilful philistinism, when English poets, believing that they had nothing to learn from the great modernists of a previous generation, fashioned a style that was at once parochial and outmoded – characteristically dealing with what were considered to be the more 'ordinary' emotions, as if that were some kind of riposte to the pioneering work of Pound, Eliot and even Auden. It represented an aesthetic of narrow forms, narrow cadences, and an even narrower idea of poetry, which reached its apotheosis in the work of Philip Larkin. This is not to say that such verse was necessarily barren or inconsequential; at its best it had the virtue of good prose chopped up into conveniently smaller lines. But it did mark a time when English poetry entered a kind of self-imposed retreat.

So what does this anthology offer instead? The context in which these poets operate may itself be of some significance. They have all been distributed in what would once have been called 'small magazines' and by small publishers; but if they have been ignored by the metropolitan publishing houses, they have been equally overlooked by the national press (with the honourable exception of the *London Review of Books*, which has included long articles on at least three of the poets represented in this volume). This is no doubt in part because some of these poets are not readily comprehensible to the casual reader, but it should be pointed out that those writers who never go beyond the inherited dispensation of language are unlikely to make progress of any other kind. And that, after all, is the main point: as Andrew Crozier says in his introduction, all these poets share a 'commitment to the discovery of meaning and form in language itself'.

In fact, some of them ought already to be well known – J. H. Prynne, for example, is without doubt the most formidable and accomplished poet in England today, a writer who has single-handedly changed the vocabulary of expression, and who, through his teaching at Cambridge, has re-educuated the sensibility of an entire generation of students. Then there are younger poets here, too, such as Iain Sinclair and Nick Totton, who have in very different ways redefined the possibilities of political or 'public' poetry at a time when it has fallen into disrepute.

Some of the writers in this anthology have been connected with Cambridge University – in a way they represent the fastidious distaste for metropolitan fashion which characterizes that place – but it would be wrong to label the collection as in any way academic. There are poets here, like John James or Tim Longville, who manage to bring into the cadences of their verse a quite new range of urban imagery and popular metaphor – and they often do so through the medium of a direct, speaking voice. It is appropriate, too, that a number of long poems have been included – Douglas Oliver's 'In the Cave of Suicession' (*sic*) and Iain Sinclair's 'Lud Heat', for example, are two works that really create new forms of narrative poetry.

What is most significant about this collection, then, is the enlargement of the possibilities of poetry that it represents; to read it is to experience a rare sensation of freedom since within the space of something fewer than 400 pages a range of wholly new concerns can be seen to enter the sphere of poetic language. As a result, there are poets here whose work could redefine the world of any reader interested enough to pick up this anthology in the first place. Of course, there are dissimilarities of tone and of meaning – in many ways this is as disparate a collection as anyone is likely to find – but what all these poets share is an attention to language so profound that the words themselves draw them forward into new areas of meaning and connotation. And that, after all, is the truest definition of poetry: it is a language that recreates itself, becoming both familiar and unrecognizable, and which in the process recreates the world.

There are two or three other writers who ought to have been included – Lee Harwood and Kevin Stratford among them – but nevertheless this is the finest collection of contemporary English poetry to be published for many years.

3 December 1987

80

The Letters of T. S. Eliot
Volume One: 1898–1922
Edited by Valerie Eliot

On 7 April 1921 T. S. Eliot wrote an extremely interesting and significant letter to Richard Aldington which, among other things, expressed his 'profound hatred for democracy'. You will not find it in this volume. For reasons at which one can only guess, it has been omitted by Eliot's editor and widow. It can hardly be for want of space, since she has decided to include letters from other people as well as those from her husband – an inconsequential letter *from* Aldington *to* Eliot, which takes up a whole page here, could easily have been replaced. It can hardly be for lack of interest, since there is plenty of material here which – to put it mildly – is of no great import. Is it a fake? No, it is in what might be described as Eliot's house style. Has it been wrongly dated? All the internal evidence points to April 1921. And surely its omission can have nothing to do with Eliot's statement of his 'profound hatred for democracy' – by now it ought to be common knowledge that he was as authoritarian in political affairs as he was in literary matters.

Whatever the reason, the fact remains that this highly significant letter does not appear in a collection that is supposed to be definitive. Similarly, the editor has passed over some of Eliot's letters to Wyndham Lewis while including others, and those who seek in this volume for a complete picture of Eliot may have cause to wonder on what principle of selection she worked. There is no mention of the subject in her very brief introduction. For the scholar, in other words, the book will be of necessarily limited value. To any general reader who chances upon it, it may also be something of a disappointment.

This is largely because of the nature of the man. He was not a great or even a good letter-writer, and for much of the period covered by this first volume he used the Royal Mail as a vehicle for his complaints and for the airing of his various minor illnesses. The thin mosquito whine of self-indulgent misery is to be heard on almost any occasion – almost but not quite, since in early years he displayed more bravado.

V. S. Pritchett once described him as 'a company of actors inside one suit' and here are examples of the youthful Eliot as the comic singer, the parodist, the dirty-minded lyricist and the sharp-tongued sophist. And, since he was something of a literary ventriloquist, he tends to address his correspondents in borrowed tones – the letters to Pound might have been composed by Pound himself, the letters to academics could not be more academic, and so on. Anyone who wants to understand the striated personality of the man who wrote *The Waste Land* will find ample evidence here. He was also a keen observer of other people's follies, and there are some characteristically waspish asides on his contemporaries. He describes Katherine Mansfield, for example, as 'one of the most persistent and thickskinned toadies and one of the vulgarest women'. No wonder his contemporary at Harvard, Conrad Aiken, gave him the nickname of 'Tsetse'.

But the acidulous high spirits were only intermittent; and this volume charts the progress of a poet who never seemed able to enjoy his fame, and for whom, from the age of maturity, life became one long ordeal by fire. After a cosseted childhood in St Louis and a period at Harvard, he could not resist the blandishments of the Old World – or what, in a vague manner, he called 'Europe'. He took up graduate studies at Oxford, but within a relatively short time made his way to London. It was here, under the auspices of Ezra Pound and the

Bloomsberries, that he began a career in which public success was matched only by private unhappiness.

He was a schoolmaster, and then a banker; but it was in these apparently routine years that he made a reputation both as a critic and as a poet. By the time this volume ends, he has written *The Waste Land* and has published that wonderful collection of essays, *The Sacred Wood*. Of course he has also married Vivien Haigh-Wood, and the results of that hasty and unfortunate union are to be found in Eliot's increasingly shrill complaints. He was the strangest combination of intellectual seriousness and emotional immaturity, and that great divide within his life is easily recognizable in his correspondence: in his thirties he is writing to his mother as if he were still an adolescent, while at the same time lecturing his contemporaries on modern taste.

These are not astonishing revelations, however, and any fresh information in this volume tends to be of a negative kind – it will come as a disappointment to erstwhile gossips, for example, that the letters to him from Jean Verdenal are of the highest probity. Certain silly writers have tried to suggest that Eliot had a 'homosexual' passion for this gentleman when they were both young students in Paris, but this is quite clearly not the case. The only thing they got excited about was philosophy.

It is hard to believe, then, that anyone without a prior interest in Eliot will derive much instruction or amusement from this volume. And it has to be said that it is unlikely to do much to enhance his reputation, either as a writer or as a man. It is a matter of opinion whether Eliot, who forbade any biography, was right to sanction (as his wife reports) the publication of private letters which show him in so distinctly unflattering a light. It is unquestionable, however, that the publishers ought to have made it much clearer that these are *selected* letters only – even if the criteria for that selection are not apparent.

29 September 1988

81

Flaubert

Herbert Lottman

Oscar Wilde described him as 'That sinless master whom mortals call Flaubert' – a purple phrase for a novelist whose own words glide from the bleached whiteness of *Madame Bovary* to the scarlet sonorities of *Salammbô*. But of course Gustave Flaubert was not sinless: he was selfish, even egotistical, and on occasion compulsively promiscuous. Yet even in his lechery is Flaubert's greatness apparent for, as he said in a letter to one of his many conquests, 'I write a love letter, to write, and not because I love' – a remark amplified by his confession that in starting such a passionate correspondence he was only concerned 'to practise style'. This attitude has helped foster the belief that Flaubert's writing is somehow 'cold'. If so, it embodies the coldness that burns – like the embrace of the devil which, in books of medieval magic, is so intensely cold that it is described as fiery. That is the origin of the passion in so thoroughly objective a book as *Madame Bovary*.

From his earliest years Flaubert possessed what at the age of twenty he described as '. . . the same *idée fixe*, writing!' It is well known that he bellowed as he wrote, and these cries were for the only real passion he ever felt – the passion for literature. Nothing else mattered to him. And what does it mean, then, to be a 'writer'? It does not necessarily mean to be honest or truthful, and certainly not to be good. It represents simply a majestic command of the language, an instinctive and decisive skill which pre-empts anything one might care to 'say'. A writer *qua* writer is necessarily amoral. *Qua* human being he can be practically anything.

Flaubert himself was not easy. His conversation was said to be exuberant, loud and obsessive – George Sand called him 'over-whelming'. With his blotched Norman features and straggling mous-tache, he looked like a pork butcher. But a pork butcher of genius. He also suffered from epilepsy, in whose grip he felt covered with tongues of fire. Throughout his life, in fact, he suffered with depressing regularity from illness, as though his body understood that he was not really at home in the world – that his real health lay in words and words only. In his early twenties he declared that perpetual illness meant '. . . I have said an irrevocable goodbye to practical life'. That is why, as a young man, he was attracted to the lives of hermits and martyrs; he was preparing for his own troubled vocation.

Of course there were events in a life which Henry James described as 'anchoretic', and his life of literary piety was from time to time interrupted by acts of secular lust. But, in a sense, nothing ever happened to him. He visited Egypt. He lived through the Prussian occupation of France. But that is, more or less, that. He settled with his mother in their small estate at Croisset, and remained there for the rest of his life – looking from his study at the Seine beneath his window, shouting out as he wrote laboriously. He sometimes spent five days on a single page of manuscript and he declared that '. . . when I displace a word, I sometimes have to change several pages.' This was his existence – this endless revision, this perpetual struggle for the appropriate word.

The assiduous research on his second novel, *Salammbô*, demonstrates precisely what kind of dedication his was – he became an expert upon ancient Carthaginian civilization, he made sketches of its houses and floor plans of its temples. As his latest biographer explains here, he was concerned even to know the times of the tides and the names of the fishes. In other words, he was creating his own world, and only the blood of his painful labour could give it life. 'Books are made, not like children,' he once said, 'but like pyramids, with a well thought-out plan.' Every true writer understands this, and there is no true writer who does not revere Flaubert in the same spirit as Oscar Wilde. Almost every remark he made about his work still rings clearly, this author who wanted to write 'a book about nothing, a book without exterior attachments, which would hold together by the internal strength of its style'.

This is a competent, instructive and often amusing biography, but Herbert Lottman suffers from having to deal with a man who lives in his books rather than in the world. One could say, in that sense, that the book is spiritless; Flaubert's real spirit is nowhere within it for the very important reason that Lottman must discuss and detail all those accidents of Flaubert's life which were for the novelist purely incidental and secondary. In the same way even the most tentative biography must necessarily obscure that work which was for Flaubert of overwhelming importance; '. . . One must live as a bourgeois and think as a demi-god,' he once said, but here we have only the diminished life, not the semi-divine art.

Better, perhaps, to have Sartre's huge and incomplete life of Flaubert

– for in that ridiculous and yet moving enterprise there is an earnestness analogous to Flaubert's own. He needs absurdity, grandeur, even prolixity, to capture that wonderful extravagant, isolated spirit.

6 April 1989

82

Baudelaire

Claude Pichois

To be damned at an early age may be considered premature, but only in the annals of religion and not in those of literature. Certainly it was Charles Baudelaire's especial fate, since his life as dandy, as *poète maudit*, as Imp of the Perverse, was thoroughly grounded in a childhood when, according to his mother, he was 'so frivolous, so light-headed and loves playing so much!' This is almost the definition of a poet, and nothing in Baudelaire's life so became him as the beginning of it. His father was a defrocked priest, his mother a monstrous specimen of maternal devotion, and he himself found refuge from his family in the study of classics – at the same time as he thoroughly understood the terrible mysteries of the religious life, therefore, he was also introduced to the sorrowful consolations of both life and literature. Of course the latter had the most powerful effect upon him, and it was through his reading of the ancient poets that he learned how to combine form with plaintiveness, the most disordered passions with the most ordered cadence. Reading Baudelaire is like reading Racine through violet-coloured spectacles.

He was a young man of inconstant ambitions and conflicting impulses, as indolent as he was profligate, and it is no surprise that he should quickly become the sport of syphilis, laudanum, drunkenness and indigence. And yet surely it is unwise to suggest, as did an earlier biographer, that by the age of twenty-five he had 'already led a full life'? He had never really lived at all, and both his promiscuity and his laziness are only slightly more elevated instances of a pervasive infantilism. He remained what he had always been – a spoiled mother's boy who, even at the time he was writing some of the poems that make up *Les Fleurs du Mal*, was economically dependent upon her.

This biographer notes that 'Baudelaire's road to freedom lay through extravagance', but what a strange freedom it was – constrained and administered by a *conseil judiciaire* appointed by his family, and subsidized by his mother. But this only meant that his moral life had acquired judicial status – he had in every sense embraced the position of 'legal infancy'. And is this state not unlike the 'freedom' of his poetry, constrained as it is by its syntactical discipline and subsidized by the harmony he derived from his childhood experience of language? In another culture he might have been just another 'beat' poet celebrating his emptiness with the cant and rant of 'free verse' (the poetic equivalent of that other modern chimera, 'free speech'), but Baudelaire was saved by his language and by his tradition.

It is hard to believe on the evidence of this latest biography that he was anything but happy with his unhappy life – people tend to get what they want (even when they do not really deserve it), and Baudelaire could not have held his existence on any other terms. Not so much *nostalgie de la boue* as a positive wallow in it, a kind of juvenile revenge against the world that did not treat him as he believed he ought to be treated: to despise or mock the world is one way to dominate it, after all. And yet one might say that his very bohemianism was the result of a comfortable middle-class childhood – Baudelaire had no deep-seated fear of poverty, no incubus within him crying dereliction, and so he was able to float in a sea of debt and indigence and corruption without ever really being in fear of drowning.

It was a gift from heaven, therefore, that *Les Fleurs du Mal* should be prosecuted for immorality and blasphemy – he considered the scandal to be 'the start of my fame and fortune'. And, as M. Pichois says here, 'The Courts of the Second Empire are to be congratulated for having made Baudelaire fully aware of his own originality' – one of the insights in a biography which, although somewhat disjointed, has all the fearsome lucidity of one Frenchman writing about another.

But did Baudelaire really know what he was doing? There are some writers so arrogant or splenetic that they do not understand the real source of their talent, and believe that it lies in the troubled surface features of their work. After his trial Baudelaire's own definition of modernity was 'the transitory fleeting beauty of present-day life', thus at least implicitly consenting to the contemporary fallacy that he was himself a kind of 'realist' when in fact his own work had nothing whatever to do with its immediate ambience, except as an aspect of the past and of the literary tradition. It is the poetry of a thorough Catholic who gained from his religion a hatred of banality as well as a taste for theatrical dress.

He collapsed in 1866 at the age of forty-five, the victim of what looks like the tertiary stage of syphilis which destroyed part of his cerebellum – he lingered for seventeen months in what his biographer calls a state of 'living death'. His mother stayed with him, asserting that 'I shall keep him *like a little child'*. Since he was suffering from paralysing aphasia, Baudelaire's own thoughts on that subject have not been recorded. All we have left is the evidence of a desperately miserable end – 'Whenever you looked his way, you found his eyes intelligent and attentive, though darkened by an expression of infinite sadness, which those who glimpsed it will never forget.'

And yet there was euphony even here – his condition of helplessness was precisely the kind of infantilism to which all his behaviour seems to have been related, and, although he would no doubt have despised the easy symbolism, at the end of his life he did truly return to his beginning.

29 June 1989

83

An Appetite for Poetry: Essays in Literary Appreciation
Frank Kermode

Madness: The Price of Poetry
Jeremy Reed

It is not often that books of literary criticism contain the power to shock, but there is a statement in Frank Kermode's book of essays that sends a definite jar through the system: 'The number of people now teaching literature is probably greater than the total of critics who formerly existed throughout history.' Leaving aside the fact that most of these new-found eminences probably have little idea of *what* literature is, discounting the additional fact that they are unlikely to know *how* it should be taught, and entirely ignoring the strong possibility that they do not know *why* they are teaching it at all, the sheer mass of verbiage is enough to induce a kind of nausea. These endless cycles of commentary and interpretation and response and practical criticism, this endless recital of mindless clichés about the need for 'relevance' or for 'deconstruction', produce students who are probably no wiser and certainly no better than they were before.

Kermode lays much of the blame for this odd state of affairs on the teachers and critics themselves. 'Criticism,' he states in his prologue, 'seems to be in rapid decline', and he goes on to suggest that much academic theory 'seems to entail an indifference to, and even a hostility towards, "literature"' – although the difficulty with modern pronouncements on the subject is noticeable in his own use of inverted commas here. Of course traditional academic criticism – from the twenties, let us say, to the sixties – in no sense represents some golden age of the inquiring spirit. There were either half-baked attempts to relate literary criticism to the methodologies of genuine scientific disciplines, or there were equally half-baked attempts to extract 'values' and 'meanings' from selected texts, on the quasi-puritanical presumption that you should only read what is in some sense 'good' for you. Lit. crit. as science, or lit. crit. as spiritual improvement.

Nevertheless, Kermode has a point – the new breed of academic critics is worse, if only because there are a lot more of them. But they are less sympathetic, also, because they tend to think of themselves as a new avant-garde which has quite supplanted the old breed of 'creative' or 'imaginative' writers. As a result they take themselves very seriously indeed; they write almost exclusively about each other, and they have created a criticism that is self-referential, self-perpetuating and self-everything-else. But essentially they are simply a new breed of university careerists, establishing and perpetuating their position with their own linguistic version of bureaucratic red tape.

Kermode has rightly set his face against all that. His own essays here are concerned with those writers who remain genuinely great, however frequently the critical fashions in describing them may change – among them Milton, Eliot, Freud and (perhaps more dubiously) Wallace Stevens. But it is noteworthy that he provides very few specimens of orthodox literary criticism as such – his essay on Milton is rooted in the social and political ambience of the time, and his account of Eliot pays particular attention to the poet's metaphysical yearning towards exile. Which in turn suggests how difficult it has become to elucidate or evaluate literature *per se* now that the simplest questions seem unanswerable. What do we mean by 'great' literature? How does it differ from the not so great? What criteria do we employ to determine what is 'good' or 'bad' or even both at once? All we can really do, if we so wish, is to talk *about* and *around* these problematic subjects. Kermode's essays, therefore, tend to veer off at a tangent – that is perhaps why he writes most cogently on such less contentious subjects as the nature of editorial 'divination' (by which is meant the sudden lighting upon the real meaning of a corrupt text).

He is particularly interesting on the nature of biblical scholarship and the standards of biblical criticism. Here, if anywhere, some real sense of value, and some awareness of canonical authority, are to be found. At least the pitfalls and pratfalls involved in the pursuit of contemporary literature can, in these circumstances, be avoided.

Jeremy Reed is not an academic, post-structuralist or otherwise, and it shows. His are enthusiastic essays on several poets, Rilke and Baudelaire among them, who in his account live within the shadow of the wings of madness. It is an entertaining and often illuminating book, but it cannot be said that its separate essays prove the force of Reed's contention that madness is indeed truly the 'price' of poetry. Certain of his subjects, such as Hopkins and Crane, were surely 'mad' in only the most nebulous sense; and in many of his other examples – such as those of Hölderlin and Robert Lowell – it could be argued that far from madness being the 'price' of poetry, it was poetry itself that acted as a compensation for madness. If it is true that lyric poets, in particular, dwell within the infantilist regions of language, then it is possible that they will fall an unresisting prey to narcissism and the associated delusions of paranoia. Further than this, however, it is not necessary to go.

But in any case Reed has a larger point – his is, in a sense, a last-ditch effort both in defence of the romantic theory of poetry, and in defiance of what he considers to be the neglect of contemporary poets as somehow marginal and unnecessary figures. These are not so much essays in criticism, therefore, as a series of lyrical or polemical meditations, shot through with Reed's own poetry and his poetic reconstructions of the great dead. Kermode's study will probably be to the taste of more severe or classical spirits. In any event, there clearly will be no end to books about poetry, books about books, books about critics and critics about critics. Somehow, however, the real thing still manages to flourish beneath the rubble.

16 November 1989

84

The State of the Language
Edited by Christopher Ricks and Leonard Michaels

A few years ago it was fashionable to declare the Death of Language. As some adjunct to the McLuhanite fantasy that the printed word was rapidly becoming obsolete, certain academics and cultural journalists flirted with the entertaining notion that discursive or complex language was being replaced by pervasive visual imagery or, more romantically, by Silence. It was nonsense then, and it is nonsense now – nowhere more clearly revealed than in this volume, the contributors to which display a far more sophisticated awareness of language than the cultural mentors of the recent and not so recent past.

Here are essays on the language of the law, the language of advertising, the language of Wall Street, the language of computers, the language of rock music, the language of graffiti, the language of bad language. The contributors address language, attack or celebrate its various forms, plead with it, denounce it, and analyse it. There is an interesting discussion, for example, on the nature of censorship and 'free speech', although of course speech is never free for those who know how to use it properly. In the context of the book itself it is important to note that there are variations of syntactical constraint (let alone overtly social or political restraints) which determine the nature of what is said or what is written. And, if this makes language resemble some deity to be propitiated, or some life-force of which the manifestations are uncertain, then no clearer evidence is needed than the three essays in this volume which examine the way in which words can tyrannize the victims of Aids, the very term 'victim' in this sentence being a case in point. In fact these essays cogently demonstrate how the adoption of a certain vocabulary, the use of certain key terms, even the choice of transitive or intransitive verbs, can actively shape the public awareness of the condition – can indeed shape the experience of the sufferer and the understanding of his own body. Language ceases to be that abstract context in which somehow we all float harmlessly, but instead takes its place at the frontier of sensibility and response; it becomes the pressure which pushes us forwards through the world.

That is why a volume of this kind is of vital importance in registering the movements and changes in the language itself. But if there is one useful generalization to be elicited from these essays, it is perhaps the one most to be expected. A study by Keith Thomas of the way people salute each other at the beginning and end of correspondence, for example, comes to much the same conclusion as an analysis of swearing by Roy Harris: that there has been a steady rise in the use of the demotic in formal contexts as well as an increase in general informality of address. This does not imply imprecision or any necessary deterioration of standards, but rather a general movement towards what Thomas describes as the trust in 'unpretentiousness, ease of access, consideration, amiability'. This may in turn be connected with another conclusion here, that the interest in the etymological roots of meaning is declining.

But these changing ideas of the nature and status of grammar, the rise of what one contributor calls 'the ideology of pluralism', and the evident fact that 'Language that would once have been debarred for its grammatical sloppiness or incoherence is permitted in any newspaper or broadcast news bulletin', all relate to the one central phenomenon: there is no longer one common culture, one accepted set of values, one 'core' of stable meanings, from which English can be said to derive.

Nevertheless it really does no good to complain about changes in the vocabulary and structure of our language, and those who over-emphasize the niceties of grammatical structure run the risk of ignoring the capacious and forceful life of proper English. Language is dynamic and comprehensive; as soon as it becomes defensive or exclusive it loses half of its real strength. If language is indeed the very proof and test of identity, as so many of the essayists here suggest, then surely it is wrong to encase it in a historical plaster cast? It must always, naturally, grow and change.

It is undoubtedly true, for example, that there is something close to the 'internationalization' of English and that 'to write it no longer seems an Anglo-Saxon prerogative'. It is not now seen as the domain of a superior race or culture, and in any case, as Randolph Quirk observes, 'we are witnessing a significant relative decline (perhaps even an absolute decline) in the currency of English worldwide'. Chinese, Hindi and Spanish are spoken by more.

But there is a further point to be made here about Australian writing (and by extension that of other English-speaking cultures), even if the contributor on Australian English does not make it for himself: the evident fact that many Australian novelists now use English with an almost magical fluency suggests how closely they resemble Irish poets and prose-writers of the earlier decades of the century. They have learned how to subvert a colonial language from within, and thus to render it capable of more subtle and more surprising effects than those who are still, as it were, imprisoned within their inheritance. It might be interesting to note in this context that, of the 62 contributors to this volume, 30 are academics and 33 are American or Canadian. To use a dead and now apparently forgotten tongue, *quis custodiet ipsos custodes*?

11 January 1990

85

Reinventing Shakespeare: A Cultural History from the Restoration to the Present
Gary Taylor

It has always seemed absurd that at the end of *Desert Island Discs* each week's Crusoe is summarily dispatched into oblivion with editions of Shakespeare and the Bible. What if the putative castaway did not want Shakespeare at all? There could have been room beside his hammock for the collected works of Henry James or Sir Thomas Browne instead. And why in any case should the writings of a sixteenth-century dramatist be associated with the truths of Christian revelation? Gary Taylor, in this suggestive study, provides a variety of answers. He is concerned with the cultural transmission of Shakespeare, with what he calls the 'mechanisms of cultural renown' – in other words, with 'Shakespeare' as we have come to know him, complete with the vague penumbra of cadences and quotations and characters and scenes that comprise his contemporary reputation.

Reinventing Shakespeare is a fascinating account of culture as market, a place of business as well as entertainment, the engine of those processes through which name or reputation are secured and manipulated. Taylor sees Shakespeare in particular as the emblem of a primarily conservative and hierarchical culture, a talisman borne aloft in the face of threatening social or civic chaos, a form of 'nostalgic assurance' and, in our own time, a defence against threatened national identity as well as a potent weapon in the commercial quest of publishers or theatrical companies for markets and audiences. The book will no doubt therefore offend those who are engaged in just such activities while pretending to altruism of the more egregious sort, and it will no doubt also disturb those who picture Genius, like some angel on a Gothic panel, soaring into another sphere quite apart from all earthly considerations. But those who want to know how great writing enters the commercial and theatrical circumstances of the day will derive great profit from Taylor's study.

Shakespeare was restored at the Restoration, and was used as a weapon by William Davenant in his fight against the rival company of Thomas Killigrew: the dramatist's reputation was then guided by the bookseller Jacob Tonson, and by a succession of combative editors who were more concerned with the proper notation of their own glories. In the eighteenth century Shakespeare became celebrated once more at a time of burgeoning nationalism and conservatism. In all cases Shakespeare's fame depended as much upon the political conditions and cultural imperatives of the time as upon his genuine worth as a writer.

But it was not until the later stages of the twentieth century, when the academic industry came into its own, that the angel really fell to earth and Shakespeare was entombed beneath the Mountain of Dullness. In recent decades interpretation has followed interpretation, just as edition once succeeded edition. And if one of the salient facts of the twentieth-century university has been the specialization of literary studies in order to provide more and more jobs for the expanding number of academic labourers, so in this same period Shakespeare has been praised for his difficulty, his ambiguity, his complexity – characteristics which could then only be deciphered by the expert critic. Of course Taylor himself is an associate professor somewhere in America, and his account of the contemporary academic exploitation of Shakespeare reveals the very shop-fronts and gutters of the modern Grub Street, which has moved from the much-abused metropolis to suburban seats of learning in Sussex or Iowa.

There are times, however, when Taylor seems almost to berate Shakespeare for his ready availability to different criteria of taste and to different varieties of exegesis. But the fact that he is so adaptable, so malleable, is an important aspect of his genius. This is not to repeat the usual clichés about his 'protean' nature, but rather to suggest that his very openness to meaning mirrors that purest state of human creativity which dwells in the cadence and sound of words only. What is described here is the endless process of interpretation which is in fact all we ever know of art and of the artist; the meaning of the plays changes continually as Shakespeare is rewritten by one generation after another.

And rewritten, sometimes, in a literal sense. For what are we left with at the end of this intriguing survey? A Shakespeare whose spelling and punctuation are to a large extent the invention of compositors; whose texts and scenes have been radically altered or reconstructed by the plethora of editors who used him for their own cultural purposes; whose characters and dialogue have been transformed by the vainglorious expedients of generations of actors. This should be added to the portrait of a dramatist who did not hesitate to steal the lines and plots of others; who rewrote lost plays of forgotten playwrights when the opportunity presented itself. Truly a Shakespeare who, at the end of the twentieth century, is as appropriate to the whole new science of chaos as ever he was to Renaissance cosmology.

In fact the whole history of cultural accommodation and transmission, as described in this book, suggests that we really no longer know what real value to ascribe to Shakespeare's plays. He has become so much a national, cultural and academic icon that there is no critical vocabulary with which to describe him or by which he can be judged. There is a further conclusion to be drawn from *Reinventing Shakespeare*: by convincingly demonstrating the instability and relativity of even the most ferociously espoused critical values, Gary Taylor presents a dramatist who has become not valueless, but value-free. Will this be the Shakespeare of the next century?

8 February 1990

86

A Dictionary of the English Language

Samuel Johnson

Coleridge described it as 'a most instructive and entertaining book', but had scant praise for it as a 'dictionary': there may be a difference, after all, between a work of literature and a work of lexicography. Johnson himself referred to it as 'my Book', and when, in the course of his lengthy perambulation around the language, he suddenly confesses that 'I know not the meaning', it is clear that we are in the presence of a work which claims no spurious objectivity or suspect universality.

It all began in 1746, when the impoverished and melancholy writer signed an agreement with Robert Dodsley; it gave Johnson a certain security of employment after a period in which he achieved little but hack-work and ghost-writing but, more importantly, it afforded him the dignity of a fulfilled ambition. For although he defines the lexicographer here as a 'harmless drudge', his own notion of his role was somewhat more capacious. His was no less than a dream of universal learning, for he understood well enough that in the course of his researches he would be creating a history of the language, as well as a compendium of English literature. Umberto Eco once described a dictionary as a 'disguised encyclopedia', and, indeed, such a work as this represents a testament to the past, a whole taxonomy of knowledge.

Johnson was the man, if any, to achieve such a feat. He had enormous intellectual ambition, but he also possessed the wonderful ability to lose himself in the past, to lose himself in books, to forget all the pain and blankness of his daily life, to slough off the burden of his large and stumbling frame, in the endless refining of the words circulating around him. There are some 40,000 in all in the completed work, and it is as if he were creating a cave of purity in which he might hide himself.

His working methods were acquired by chance and formulated by habit; he would work with his amanuenses in the garret of his house in Gough Square, surrounded by books and papers, sitting on an old three-legged stool which was propped against one of the decaying walls, reading the texts of Burton and Dryden, Hooker and Swift, noting the passages which he wished to use as illustration, underlining the words of particular interest. He had expected to complete the entire work within three years, but in fact the first volume did not appear until seven years later.

There had been distractions: he was at the same time working on the *Rambler* and the *Adventurer*, and the death of his wife sent him spinning into an agony of grief. We must imagine him, this large, lumbering, pock-faced man, walking the streets at night, melancholy and alone. And then, next day, the work would begin again.

He completed his task in 1755, and so great was the eventual achievement that this dictionary was not really challenged until the great philological labours of the nineteenth century; it was only with Webster in the United States, and *The Oxford English Dictionary* in this country, that Johnson's work was overtaken. Overtaken but not superseded – as Dr Fleeman says in an introduction here, his was 'a lasting statement by his age of its confidence in its own language and literature'.

Philological exactitude did not, after all, preclude a moral and even on occasions a spiritual purpose. Johnson frequently cited Locke, for example, while rigorously excluding the more impious Hobbes. His major sources are Shakespeare, Dryden, Pope, Spenser, Addison, Bacon, Milton, Locke and Swift; indeed, most of his quotations are taken from seventeenth-century texts (the boundary line was Sidney), and it is possible to see at once the kind of humane culture that the Dictionary was supposed to represent.

To read through two volumes (well reproduced here by Longman) is to be reacquainted with the wonders of the language, and the glories of the English inheritance. To move from Bacon to Crashaw, to Swift and Dryden, to Milton, Philips, Sidney and Addison all in the space of defining 'Brim' and 'Brimful' is to work through a network of affiliations and relationships by means of which a whole culture can be restored. This Dictionary is a valuable concordance to a vanished age, therefore, and a way of bringing forth its inner identity and form. For it is only in words that the past can truly be said to live again – words we still employ, and whose buried histories are still part of the meaning which we ascribe to them.

There are other aspects of Johnson's achievement which have less to do with words than with the world. It is clear, for example, that he saw his task as one not of magisterial prescription but of aesthetic refinement. This was the time when his great contemporary Hogarth (a man with a robust native spirit very similar to that of Johnson) was trying to re-create the diurnal world with something he called the serpentine 'line of beauty'; in a similar spirit, within his preface to the Dictionary, Johnson describes the pressing need to correct 'wild exuberance', as well as to extirpate the 'corruptions of ignorance' and chasten 'caprices and innovation'. All around him were 'perplexity to be disentangled, and confusion to be regulated', yet out of this chaos he would bring forth order.

He became known as 'Dictionary Johnson', and Thomas Carlyle remarked that 'Had Johnson left nothing but his Dictionary, one might have traced there a great intellect, a genuine man.' For it is indeed one man's vision of his culture, and one man's sense of his English inheritance. Fortunate was he, also, to have been able to give his vision such definitive form and so noble a purpose.

22 September 1990

87

A *View from the Diners Club*
Gore Vidal

Fates *Worse than Death*
Kurt Vonnegut

Unlike many American novelists and critics, who spend their waking lives going from universities to conferences and back again, Gore Vidal runs alone. Of course he lives abroad, but in any case he writes as if he were in perpetual internal exile, more than a mere ocean away from the prizes, committees, literary festivals and other nonsense perpetrated by people who have nothing better to do with their time. He also seems to have freed himself from the altogether disappointing company of other writers, and has never in living memory been associated with a group, or a cabal, or even a movement.

Perhaps that is why the reprinting of his essays is almost as interesting as the publication of one of his novels, since in both cases he exhibits the same clear-eyed contempt for the status quo. This latest volume contains a number of Vidal's reviews and essays which have appeared over the last four years; although a few of them are routine affairs conducted from a great height and with only a modicum of sympathy, his disdain for the values of *bien pensants* and his interest in literature as an art rather than as fodder for glossy magazines or gossip columns make him never less than interesting. In literary as well as in political matters he is at his best when defending an apparently lost cause or lambasting favourite sons; when he rescues a writer from unmerited oblivion, or mocks the pieties of New York literary life ('that happy island where it has never been possible to be too phoney'), the true character of his writing becomes apparent. He is a polemicist as much as a wit, a prophet perhaps without honour but not without effect.

As a result he prefers artists who like himself have remained on the edge of things – self-exiles, misfits voluntary or involuntary, who from their unique vantage have been able to cast a curious light upon the values of a dominant and generally imperial culture. That is why Vidal writes here about Oscar Wilde, Somerset Maugham, Ford Madox Ford and Orson Welles. None of them ever quite fitted; none of them became part of that literary consensus which generally determines a writer's immediate reputation, if not his eternal fate. In the last resort none of them actually cared what run-of-the-mill commentators or critics thought of them: and that is because, with the possible exception of Ford Madox Ford, they all possessed a highly developed sense of humour.

This is where Vidal comes into his own. He may not exactly be Wilde (the wit sometimes slides into irony or even archness) but at his best he can express in a phrase what a more solemn essayist would be hard pressed to put in a paragraph. He is funny about literary theorists; about novelists who treat themselves as seriously as latter-day saints; about the whole spurious business of literary reputation.

There are two sections here, subtitled 'Book Chat' and 'Political', although in practice it is hard to know where one ends and the other begins. He is better at writing about people than anything else, and so his central essay on Mencken does not differ essentially from that on Maugham: the only good political journalist is one who does not take politics seriously at all, and so Mencken joins Vidal's pantheon of writers who have adopted much the same position towards the literary establishment.

In every respect Vidal makes an informative contrast with Kurt

Vonnegut, whose own collection of essays, *Fates Worse than Death*, is too often marred by the sort of folksy philosophizing which should have gone out with the cracker-barrel. His heart is all too visibly in the right place (he attacks what Vidal himself contemptuously describes as the National Security State) but his prose is vitiated by self-indulgent whimsicality. Vidal came to Europe and discovered America; Vonnegut stayed in America and seems to have found himself with increasingly little to write about.

One could put the point differently by noting that Vidal, unlike Vonnegut, seems to have some interest in, and knowledge of, the world before the United States of America could be said to exist. He is not a cultural imperialist, in other words, and it is hard to imagine him describing the Latin language, as Vonnegut does, as a 'hocus-pocus laundromat'. Such an attitude is only possible in a country with a profound ignorance of the past. There is in fact one essay here in which Vidal examines the nature of his own task as a writer, 'How I Do What I Do If Not Why', and it is quite clear that he is intent on imparting some sense of history to his own culture.

It would be inappropriate for an English audience to feel in any way superior about this; the same ignorance is rampant on what Vidal tends to consider our tight little island, where the majority of novelists and critics seem to think that human history began in or around 1930. It is possible to come across apparently well-educated people who can say all the right things about Saul Bellow without knowing one word of John Milton, or who can discourse knowledgeably about the world of Norman Mailer without having once ventured into the world of Edmund Spenser. What kind of culture is that? It is ghetto culture. It is precisely what Vidal is attacking here in the ignorance of the littérateurs, the ignorance of hack reviewers, the ignorance of much contemporary writing.

There are some minor problems with this book – in particular Vidal, who is so good about the vanity of writers, is a little over-sensitive about his own reputation – but it is in large part an astringent and necessary corrective to the rubbish which is always being written about rubbish.

16 November 1991

88

The Complete Essays
V. S. Pritchett

V. S. Pritchett is perhaps the last representative of what was once a true literary culture. In our time, when the only thing that seems to matter is the latest overpublicized American novel or the most recent and meanest 'profile' of a writer, such a concern might seem faintly absurd. Who wants to read an essay on Meredith or Lewis when we have the 'Christmas Books of the Year' to tell us what to buy? What does it matter about Scott or Butler as long as we can chatter about something from *The Late Show*? This book is evidence of a time when there was some sense of, and belief in, the living force of a national literature.

The work of a good writer is all of a piece; that is why the first essay here, written in the early years of the Second World War, is recognizably by the same hand as the last, composed no more than two or three years ago. They are described as essays but in fact they are occasional articles, many of them reviews which have no pretensions to any grand design. They do not need one. They are knowledgeable, enthusiastic, even inspired, but they seem to have come into the world with no greater desire than to entertain and instruct. Pritchett is, among other things, a professional.

But what else is he? He is a very English writer, concerned not only to describe a range of English authors but also to celebrate the nature of Englishness itself. This does not mean that he is in any sense chauvinistic (there are as many accounts here of Russian and French novelists as there are of the home-grown variety) but, rather, that he is inescapably imbued with the English spirit; he eschews theoretical or philosophical analysis in favour of what he once described as 'the portrayal of character for its own sake'. That is why he is particularly good on English comedy, with an especial fondness for such late Victorian or Edwardian purveyors of 'light humour' as Saki and Jerome K. Jerome. In fact it is one of the secrets of Pritchett's own inimitable style – he has the same lightness of touch, the same modestly epigrammatic bent and, most importantly, the same refusal to be overawed by the ostensibly grand or browbeaten by the apparently fashionable; he was only ever mildly interested in Koestler and Beckett, and is quite rightly more enthusiastic about Firbank and Wodehouse. Yet at the same time he maintains an extraordinary alertness to the terrors of the soul: I cannot think of any other writer who could justly interpret the work of both Surtees and Dostoevsky.

It has become a matter of course among the younger breed of reviewers to mock or belittle anything in sight, but Pritchett has always possessed a larger spirit. He has the great gift of entering the scenery of the book which he is reviewing (not to be separated from his gifts as a writer of novels and short stories) and, as it were, to observe it from the inside. He seems for the moment to become the writer and to report on the world from that unique and temporary vantage; as a result he is good on writers as diverse as Gide and Bennett, Synge and Dickens, Scott and Lawrence, Tolstoy and Gissing. He is interesting on the tradition of the Puritan autobiography, excellent on the eighteenth-century English novelists and practically indispensable on the great Victorians.

His reviews from the forties are quite naturally attuned to the perils of war, and in these earliest pieces he is most concerned with those writers who have tried successfully or unsuccessfully to interpret contemporary reality. What he most criticizes, in this context, is 'our lack of moral and political perceptiveness' – note the 'our' here, as an indication of his engagement with what was still a distinct and distinctive culture. In an essay on Henry Fielding, for example, he suggests that 'from the beginning, the English novel set out to protest and to teach'. But in the same essay (one of the best in the collection) he also emphasizes the fact that the novel did not derive from the reportorial tradition of Defoe but from the theatrical world of melodrama and pantomime. It is an important point, and crucial to the understanding of the English genius.

There is some relaxation of astringency in the fifties, but even then one feels the close attention of the critic who is discovering the lineaments of his culture (and thus of his own gift) in the act of understanding. Yet through the length of more than 200 reviews, Pritchett himself rarely emerges. We learn that he was brought up in a late Victorian world, that he lived in Dulwich, that he was a journalist for a while; but not much more. The truth is that as a reviewer he does not consider himself interesting beyond his reaction to this or that particular author; in that respect he is a great relief from those literary journalists who manage to smuggle the first personal pronoun into even the most remote disquisition. There are no false notes here because he has a directness of response and expression that have their root in the actual practice of art and not in the manufacturing of disposable opinions. He is not interested in scoring points off the dead or living, but in listening to what they have to say; envy is not the spur, but curiosity. And it is curiosity that keeps his prose alive.

There was once a character known as the 'bookman'. Now it sounds absurdly wooden, evoking images of carpet-slippers, pipes and gentlemen's clubs. But there is a living sense to the word, and it is one that Pritchett exemplifies: he loves books, he understands them, he savours them, he devours them, he dwells within them. He is sometimes enraged by them, but nevertheless they offer an inexhaustible well of consolation. The excitement and interest he conveys are surely worth preserving, especially in a world where a book as comprehensive and as informed as this will soon become extinct.

12 December 1991

89

Stephen Hawking: A Life in Science
Michael White and John Gribbin

If indeed there is no living scientist 'as famous as Stephen Hawking', as the authors of this biography assert, that fame has as much to do with his bestseller as with his scientific research. He has become something of a celebrity, a 'master of the universe' confined to a wheelchair by motor neurone disease, and it is somehow appropriate that this book should open with an account of his meeting with Shirley MacLaine. A film made out of *A Brief History of Time* is soon to be released. It is not that science itself is particularly popular or generally understood, but rather that it has become associated in the public mind with the special effects of Hollywood. 'Black holes' have a perfectly legitimate scientific status, but for most people they are connected with the Gothic enchantments of *Star Wars* or the vivid melodrama of *Star Trek*. In the public imagination, science is simply material for the most exciting new fiction.

Of course this is not the message of a biography which, despite its somewhat chatty tone, takes great pains to depict Stephen Hawking as the archetypal scientist. Even when he attended St Albans School he never allowed 'his emotions to compromise his intellect'; he was a 'rationalist' who, according to one contemporary, seemed to be 'watching me as though from a great height'. Certainly he was bored by the routine scholarship of Oxford, although he became 'definitely raffish' when he took up rowing. It was only after he moved on to Cambridge to study cosmology, however, that everything changed. In 1967 he developed motor neurone disease and was given two years to live: it was then that the essential struggle of his life began. Somehow he survived the darkness by changing the whole course of his being, and it was during this period of gradually increasing physical incapacity that his serious intellectual work began. Although the authors suggest that his disease is 'simply not that important to him', they quote the testimony of others to the effect that 'the turning point in the application of his abilities was the onset of his condition'. And how could it not be so? Even Hawking himself seems ruefully to acknowledge the significance of his incapacity. 'Before the illness set in,' he said to one interviewer, 'I was very bored with life . . . It was really rather a pointless existence.'

So the point of his life was, somehow, made by his involuntary withdrawal from it. As he progressively became more disabled, his internal vision grew more intense; as his own physical existence became more and more complicated, he looked to numbers and equations for an essential purity and simplicity. Even now he is searching for a Grand Unified Theory, a set of equations which, combining general relativity and quantum theory, will account for the very nature and destiny of the universe. It is the same dream which possessed Paracelsus or John Dee; the authors themselves describe this total explanation as the 'Holy Grail' of modern research, and this term itself suggests that the quest may have roots deeper than those of contemporary science.

Professor Hawking's own work on black hole physics is of great complexity and, although it is explained here in a perfectly lucid way, it is an area which the non-scientist need not necessarily enter. It is a self-contained system of signs and numbers – no doubt one of great intricacy and beauty, but one which can perhaps best be described as a language trying to come to terms with itself. The real point seems to be that nothing, not even the existence of black holes, can be 'proved' in an orthodox sense. On many occasions, as the authors suggest, a theory arrives long before any evidence can be adduced for it. And in one of the most intriguing passages in this generally intriguing book, it is made clear that Professor Hawking, a man who has spent his life struggling to understand the laws of the cosmos, 'has looked through a telescope no more than a handful of times'.

There are larger questions here than the life even of this singular man. Is it possible that the scientist somehow creates the reality he is supposed to be investigating or describing? Is he a mythologist, rather than an observer or interpreter, whose true role is to construct a narrative which the rest of us can believe, just as human beings once saw horses and fish among the stars and were told that these forms were there? The authors describe here, for example, how neutron stars were entities 'predicted by theory' which then suddenly, and almost magically, appeared. Are black holes, or white dwarfs, our own version of horses and fishes in the sky – a wonderful dream through which we try to make sense of unending space? Perhaps modern cosmological theory bears no more and no less relationship to 'reality' than *Ulysses* does to Dublin or *Bleak House* to the nineteenth-century legal system.

Other questions remain. Surely the greatest scientists – Newton of course pre-eminent among them – have been deeply imbued with mystical or religious teaching. Even mathematics has its roots in cabbalistic learning. Are not all scientific disciplines, at their 'cutting edge' (to use a phrase employed here), marked ineradicably with the traces of their origin? This is not to say that science is simply another version of magic, or of fantasy, but rather that it contains these elements and needs them as an indispensable aspect of its power. So it is that Professor Hawking once said of black holes, 'I feel in a sense that I'm their master.' These might have been the words of a sixteenth-century magus, and we are on the brink here of a mystery as great as that of an extraordinary man whose mind and imagination have soared beyond the disabling confines of the flesh.

19 December 1991

90

Minotaur: Poetry and the Nation State
Tom Paulin

The subtitle of this book sets out its theme: what do poetry and the 'nation-state' have to do with each other? On the face of it a great deal; it is the steady belief in the English as a chosen race that underpins the authority of Spenser and Milton, while poets as diverse as Tennyson and Whitman staked their own claim to significance by espousing something very close to a national consciousness or conscience.

In his introduction to this interesting collection of essays and reviews, Paulin puts that theme in a slightly different context. He defines the Protestant aesthetic in terms of its denial of history and its attention to oral rather than written language, to the immediate presence of speech rather than the mediated traditions of language.

But this is essentially a fashionable and academic spin upon what is for him a more fundamental position. He situates himself within the Protestant community of Ulster, within a tribe rather than a nation, and so he remains peculiarly sensitive to the claims and sentiments of nationhood; as a result he brings to his reading of poetry a finely honed sense of political and historical reality. Not for him the formality of what was once called the New Criticism or the tedious hermeneutics of the various post-structuralist and deconstructionist schools. He looks for the 'power relations' that exist within the most apparently innocent or vatic language, and quotes Milton on 'the mists and intricacies of state'.

So it is that he expands upon the virtues of that poet's prose, arguing that the author of *The Tenure of Kings and Magistrates* was pre-eminently a political writer. Those who know Christopher Hill's work will already have recognized the truth of this but, more interestingly, Paulin identifies some of the rhythms and images of Milton's elaborately topical prose within the movement of his poetry. Paulin is a very close reader of verse, a talent he demonstrates in his sensitive analysis of Robert Frost and his 'secret, cold, calculating, Yankee vision'.

But his more general political preoccupations always bring out the best in him. An account of Southey's response to the execution of

Robert Emmet leads into a consideration of the 'reactionary nature' of much English criticism, since the 'minotaur' to be glimpsed within the bewildering labyrinth of discourse is the naked power of the state. John Clare is no longer the private lyricist, but a man acutely aware both of the political forces undermining 'rural England' and of the pressures for linguistic uniformity which curbed his 'oral writing'. Christina Rossetti and Emily Dickinson subvert, in different ways, the authoritarian masculine tradition of syntax and oratory.

There may be times when he exaggerates the political allusiveness of a poet or a poem – it is hard to follow him all the way, for example, in his reappraisal of Gerard Manley Hopkins – yet even this oversensitivity means that he is always open and live to the possibilities of language. You do not necessarily have to be radical, or Irish, to realize that Yeats is more than a formal obelisk of stately words, a poet plucked out of history and reduced to timelessness; but, in a closely argued essay, Paulin returns him to a living world of hunger-strikes and political prisoners. There is also a fine piece here on Dickens, which reaffirms that imaginative violence with which he was always threatening to tear down the very edifice of the state. When you give writers back their context, as Paulin does, you give them back their vitality.

Perhaps that is why he risks most, and says most, about certain contemporary poets. In a brilliant essay on Philip Larkin, for example, he describes him as a poet representing and describing 'national decline', whose version of cultural loss and social disgust is not so subtly disguised as private threnody. He characterizes Larkin as someone possessing false consciousness, trapped by an 'Englishness' he despises but cannot escape, which is perhaps the same thing as saying that he is a mediocre poet. But if a true national culture cannot be created out of second-rate work, that is not to say that a national culture itself is necessarily retrogressive.

For, to paraphrase another political poet, it is possible to read white where Paulin reads black. There are occasions when he suggests that it is wrong for a writer to espouse the values of a nation-state although his great avatar, Milton himself, has been described by Christopher Hill as one who conceived his role as that of 'the English national poet'. If there is a distinction between a nation-state and a nation, then Paulin will have to draw it more carefully. At one point he seems to endorse Yeats's belief in '. . . our central fire, all our nationality', while also implicitly criticizing Ted Hughes for representing these aspirations within his own more English poetry.

If a poet embraces historical consciousness and the written tradition, he may well lose that romanticized identity and power which comes under the rubric of 'self-expression', but surely there is much to be gained in return? What of poets who have so great a love of their country's history, and so strong a sense of its traditions, that they can make a literature out of the things Paulin abhors?

Nevertheless it is a tribute to this book that it raises such questions, without always answering them. Paulin is in favour of orality, immediacy and vernacular liberty. This is fundamentally an evangelical Protestant strategy but, whether one agrees or not, at least it is a strategy. *Minotaur* provides a coherent and tenable argument, a serious literary position at a time when such seriousness is rare.

23 January 1992

91

The Literary Companion to Sex
Edited by Fiona Pitt-Kethley

Fiona Pitt-Kethley's full and detailed companion to sex 'contains no censorship', at least according to its publishers; in fact, it contains more than that, if such a thing is possible, since Pitt-Kethley has decided to put back all the once-deleted rude words. Some particularly lubricious passages, written in Latin for the eyes of the select, are here paraded in stark vernacular, and the editor has translated some of the juicier passages from the great authors.

She has other credentials besides those of an excellent translator, however, and in her notes she reveals that she once placed a priapic image in her mother's garden and named her cat Merkin after the eighteenth-century term for a pubic wig. Such devotion must surely be rewarded.

In this erotic equivalent of *Hymns Ancient and Modern*, she begins with the Bible and ends with a short contemporary poem. Some of the choices between these two poles are obvious enough – Burton, Rabelais and Boccaccio among them – but the editor has also managed to rescue from the oblivion of the Private Case collection in the British Library some less familiar examples.

Sodom, a drama by an unknown hand, contains such characters as Buggeranthus, Bolloxinion and Clitoris, while Thomas Flatman lets it all hang out in 'An Appeal to Cats in the Business of Love'. Robert Gould's poem 'To My Lord Chamberlain at Bath' proves yet again that half the fun of sex lies in talking about it afterwards, while John Oldham, in a set of verses which is discreetly entitled 'Upon a Lady, who by overturning of a Coach, had her Coats behind flung up, and what was under shewn to the View of the Company', is gallantry itself with:

> In pity gentle Phillis hide
> The dazling Beams of your Back-side.

The great tradition will never be the same again.

But the actual practice of sex is here only an excuse for more vivid descriptions of human relations both before and after the 'act of darkness' – the temptation followed by the despair, the coquettishness succeeded by complaint. Just as the description of food in fiction is far more interesting than that of mastication or ingestion, so the accoutrements of sex are more colourful than anything which actually happens between or on top of the sheets. The problem with the literature of sex is that sex itself, like death, is a great leveller: the instincts are simple, the variations few, the effects more or less predictable.

Sex is a little death in miniature, also, because it represents for that moment the extinction of personality; that is why some of the modern writers in this collection, educated on a belief in the personality, are reduced to torpid complaint and even despair. In fact, our own century, according to Pitt-Kethley's introduction, runs the gamut of 'everything from bestiality to vibrators', although the emphasis does tend to be upon the former. (It was a stroke of genius on her part to include J. R. Ackerley's account of his relationship with Tulip, his dog.) The existence of the latter does suggest, however, one of the salient features of this volume: the large number of female writers she has chosen. In the modern selection alone, almost a third of the contributors are women.

There is a theory that sexuality changes with the language employed to describe it, so that it becomes part of the larger vocabulary of human and social need. But if the manner of our speech determines our sexual behaviour, then the continuing presence of a large number of slang terms stable over the centuries would suggest that attitudes towards the act itself have remained much the same. Both 'swyve' and 'pintle' may be out of fashion, but other terms of endearment have survived.

There are variations between the ages, however, which Pitt-Kethley's chronological survey does much to elucidate. There is something faintly marmoreal about the sex of classical poetry, for example, even in the editor's own energetic translations: at this late date, Ovid and Juvenal are no more than stone carvings in the Temple of Love. Or perhaps it is simply that poetry and sex do not mingle naturally: can the act be measured out in dactyls or iambic hexameters without losing much of its formless delight? Perhaps that is why verse is best at depicting fetishistic activities, where the amount of ritual involved helps to animate the necessary ritual of the poem.

The centuries bring in other changes, too, and, from the examples in this literary cornucopia, sex in the Middle Ages seems to have been intimately related to sin and to the fear of death. Yet lechery was probably less strongly condemned than either usury or blasphemy; life then was so short and uncertain that sex must have been a constant and necessary palliative. Indeed everything Pitt-Kethley includes here suggests the same thing: despite the protestations of our own latter-day moralists, men and women of the late twentieth century seem signally more restrained and less lascivious than any of their predecessors.

Life was rather more sprightly at the Restoration, and it might be said to represent the high point of literary sexuality – far from the closeted horrors of the nineteenth century, or the banal revelations of the twentieth; there is in the verse of Etherege or Sackville an ability to handle licentiousness without licence. In the nineteenth century, sex was not important enough, and in the twentieth it became too important; perhaps it takes an Age of Reason to put it in its proper position.

The most disgusting details occur in Swift, the most amusing in Butler, but the palm must surely go to Rochester, who is rivalled only by de Sade for the sheer relentless frenzy of his pornography. Yet the true prize must go to Pitt-Kethley, who proves herself an erudite if somewhat wayward companion in this Baedeker to the wilder shores of love.

8 February 1992

92

The Oxford Book of Gothic Tales

Edited by Chris Baldick

To be truly Gothic is, in a sense, to be English. The term has a history almost as devious and mysterious as the stories it represents. Armed with this anthology and such necessary reading as Kliger's *The Goths in England*, the faint-hearted connoisseur can make his way down the gloomy halls and secret passageways of the genre. The Gothic is English (and was seen to be so in the eighteenth century), precisely because it is not part of the classical European tradition. It came, in some writers, to represent the vigorous national life of a country that rejected the languor of fallen Rome or the effeminacy of Greece. That is why it also became associated with Arthurian legends and druidic lore, and anything else that emphasized a specifically English mythology or folklore.

Of course, as Chris Baldick points out in his admirable, if brief, introduction, Gothic literature cannot be directly compared with neo-Gothic architecture, or even with the vogue for such literary curiosities as the work of Ossian. Nevertheless, there is a deep connection which this anthology itself reveals. The meaning of Gothic has changed over the past two centuries. What was once applied to Stonehenge can now be affixed to the latest horror film, and what was once seen as one of the chief glories of our national heritage (Percy's *Reliques of Ancient English Poetry* being one example) can now be invoked to describe the cheapest piece of pulp fiction. Nevertheless, certain associations and sentiments remain buried, appropriately enough, beneath the new structures of Gothic fiction: from Charlotte Brontë to Angela Carter, from Horace Walpole to Thomas Hardy, there is the same suggestive use of the past and the same propensity for the irrational and the inexplicable. That is why the genre has flourished over the past 200 years, during a period when the scientific model of reality has been apparently the pre-eminent one. There can be no Gothic in periods when ghosts, miracles and spirits are considered to be a true part of the world; this literature flourishes on repression, marginalized beliefs and panic fear.

So it was only when the spirits were banished, and numbers took their place, that the fascination for the unexplained and the mysterious could take on the powerful but indistinct form which is revealed in these stories. In Charlotte Perkins Stetson's 'The Yellow Wallpaper', the heroine sees 'a strange, provoking formless sort of figure'. In Clark Ashton Smith's 'A Rendezvous in Averoigne', a scene of vampires evokes a sensation of 'insuperable constraint, of smothering horror and hideous oppression'. Baldick includes both of these stories in his collection. When, in his introduction, he describes a characteristic Gothic fear that 'the despotisms buried by the modern age may prove to be yet undead', one of those despotic powers must surely be that of the magical or spiritual world which has been banished from our equations but which still prowls around the charmed circle of scientific belief. The use of the past is also significant here, since in Gothic fiction it is considered to be somehow still present and to be associated with malevolence. Here, also, we see the traces of an old world with which the scientific era is not wholly comfortable. In H. P. Lovecraft's 'The Outsider', the narrator himself is a living embodiment of just such a past, 'a compound of all that is unclean, uncanny, unwelcome, abnormal and detestable'.

Baldick suggests that the Gothic form turns on itself to condemn the settings and the characters which it so lavishly embellishes, and to reveal its superstitious past as truly barbaric. But this assumption is open to question, at least on the grounds that the authors included in this volume manifestly love the form. Again, this seems to be primarily, if not wholly, a national characteristic: English writers tend to mix moods and genres, and with Gothic they are able to depict horror with a certain theatricality, and garnish evil with a touch of humorous relish. That is why it is present in Charles Dickens as much as Ann Radcliffe, and why it has survived to the present day. It represents a very English sense of art which, in the late twentieth century, has been maintained by writers as diverse as Michael Moorcock and Carter (whose recent death robbed English fiction of one of its most vigorous exponents).

Baldick also makes the interesting point that the eighteenth-century Gothic tale was at least theoretically anti-Catholic, with its emphasis upon the horrors of the Inquisition and the madness of the monks, yet even here there is a certain ambivalence: there is a Catholic streak in English culture, and the theatricality, the explicit colour and the typology of evil within the Gothic tale may well be indications of its continuing presence. Of course, it has in the process hit on genuine dreads and real, if unacknowledged, beliefs. There is, for example, the fear that old buildings are in some sense alive, or at least contain evil presences. In 1979 Carter created a castle in which a female vampire sits and waits, while in 1773 Anna Laetitia Aikin conjured up a ruined mansion in which their lurks 'a lady in a shrowd and black veil'. For the English writer, part of an old culture, there is also the fatal attraction of decadence and of that slow decay of a noble family into horror and darkness which is so much a part of the Gothic sensibility. But there is also a Celtic sense of mystery, in part aligned with Catholicism, which accounts for the extraordinary success of Irish writers – Oscar Wilde, Charles Maturin and Sheridan Le Fanu among them – in this form.

There is no end to Gothic. There can be no end because it is part of the English imagination. So it is that one of the last stories here is also one of the best. Patrick McGrath's 'Blood Disease' perfectly combines comedy with horror, a sense of death with a taste for gaiety, and thus illustrates the formidable appeal of the genre. Gothic literature, after 200 years, still stalks the Earth . . .

14 March 1992

93

The Reckoning: The Murder of Christopher Marlowe

Charles Nicholl

This book has as its frontispiece a portrait of a young Elizabethan, discovered by chance in builders' rubble. Like most such portraits, it is both austerely unfamiliar and yet strangely recognizable – the expression of the young man, both direct and unfathomable, reaches out to us beyond the confines of his doublet and the Latin motto along the border. It seems probable that this is a portrait of Christopher Marlowe, found by chance and now restored to face the living once again. It is an appropriate emblem for a narrative which, with astonishing scholarship and brilliant ingenuity, revives a lost episode of sixteenth-century history.

For a long time the facts were thought to be simple: that on 30 May 1593, Marlowe was killed by Ingram Friser in a Deptford brawl, over a 'reckoning' (a bill) or perhaps over a homosexual lover. Thus did the roaring boy, the atheist, the sensationalist, meet a fitting end. But nothing really did fit. In the explanation of the event, even the weighty deliberations of the inquest omit the most important evidence of all. Who were his three companions on that fatal evening? And why were they all ensconced in a respectable lodging house (not a tavern, as legend suggests) for most of that day? In order to answer these questions, Charles Nicholl has made a strange pilgrimage into what he describes as 'the underside of Elizabethan politics' and found 'history in the raw'.

But this is not simply history: it has the force of life within it. To read *The Reckoning* is to enter one of Robert Greene's pamphlets and find oneself bewildered, surrounded at every turn by spies and conny-catchers (confidence tricksters) and hanged men. For the truth is, as Nicholl convincingly demonstrates, that Marlowe was not only a great and successful dramatist; he was also, from his time at Cambridge University, a government spy. The men who murdered him were part of the same network of paid informers and agents as himself. He had become an embarrassment, nothing more, and had to be removed with a dagger in his brain.

At the age of twenty-one, Marlowe was first employed as an *agent provocateur*, posing as a Catholic in order to spy on other Catholics, and acting as a renegade in order to trap other such disaffected people. It is possible that he had real Catholic sympathies, but he was 'turned' by the authorities to act on their behalf. And for what reason? For money, of course.

Nicholl goes on to suggest that Marlowe then insinuated himself into the household of the Earl of Northumberland in order to spy on him, and later practised a similar deceit upon Lord Strange. But he was not simply an informer on putative Catholic conspiracies; he was also a 'projector' who actively fostered treason in the employ of Sir Francis Walsingham and later of William Cecil Burghley. But the weaver of snares was caught in a net not of his own making. He was set up as a conspirator by the Earl of Essex, as a way of striking at Sir Walter

Raleigh. Although nominally under the protection of Burghley, he could not be saved. So came the great reckoning in the little room.

As a portrait of the age, *The Reckoning* is remarkable for its consistency and strength. Nicholl combines historical scholarship with a literary imagination in order to recreate a world of shadows and double-dealing, of turned men and marked men, all involved in (to use one of the author's most consistent metaphors) the theatre of conspiracy and intrigue. It was, in every sense, a theatrical period and Nicholl has, as it were, taken us down through the trap door beneath the ostensible stage. And what a dark place it then becomes, this Elizabethan civilization, which was not much more than a police state, where no man was safe from the reach of the torturer or the smell of the dungeon.

But this book is also extraordinary for its portrait of Marlowe. We can no longer see him simply as the extravagant and boisterous dramatist, the unconventional poet *in extremis*. He was, rather, a spy who betrayed the people to whom he was closest and in whose nature were the 'elements of falsehood and coldness'.

At the same time, Nicholl gives an excellent description of the world of Elizabethan minor writers, pamphleteers, dramatists and hacks who also found service in Walsingham's employ – men such as Anthony Munday, a 'government thug and gallows-haunter', who wrote prose romances and volumes of poetry with such titles as *A Banquet of Dainty Conceits*. He would have been a more interesting case if he had been a better writer (like Marlowe); but the connection between literature and treachery, poetry and falsehood, is an intriguing one. Was Marlowe able to espouse values and opinions according to taste, precisely because he had none of his own? And did that also help to make him a good dramatist?

The Reckoning restores a lost time in more than one sense. Such a close acquaintance with the past brings its own changes and, like some normally occluded field of force, the tone and cadence of the sixteenth century rise up within Nicholl's prose. Here is his description of one of Marlowe's feline colleagues: 'He is your bounden friend until the ink is dry, and then the countenance changes.'

By such means can the past be revived, and yet there are times when it needs no prompting. When Nicholl was in pursuit of Marlowe, and conducting some research in Flushing, he came across a café where a group in a corner were 'to a pair of archive-weary eyes unused to the darkness – like young men *wearing doublets*'. In this book he comes just as close to Marlowe's dark world, and for the first time reveals the true mystery of his death.

6 *June 1992*

94

The Intellectuals and the Masses: Pride and Prejudice among the Literary Intelligentsia 1880–1939
John Carey

For most of this century, the English have dismissed 'intellectuals' as irrelevant bores, foreigners or worse. Now John Carey brings that attack up to date with an account of the antagonism between certain intellectuals and 'mass culture', an often malevolent battle, depicted here as a literary foreshadowing of the Third Reich. In this spirit the Holocaust is to be seen 'as the ultimate indictment of the idea of the mass and its acceptance by twentieth-century intellectuals'.

It is in many respects a cogent and persuasive analysis. Carey notes how the rise of the popular newspaper, with its own particular 'stories', provided a palatable alternative to the stuffier fiction of the early twentieth century (in this book intellectuals, writers and artists tend to be herded together in the pen of high culture). He documents, also, the interest of certain twentieth-century intellectuals in eugenics and the extermination of the masses as an apt preface to the deliberate exclusivity of modernist literature. Yet the 'mass' against which these purblind artists reacted was always an illusion; it was an invention, a metaphor that could be revised to fit the most appropriate set of anxieties, from the pseudo-scientific investigations of Mass Observation, which treated the working class as particularly interesting bacteria, to Freud's atavistic notion of the 'primal horde'.

Carey is always good with detail, and here he advances the claims of tinned food and the camera as specimens of the 'mass' activity which intellectuals hated; but who ate all the tinned salmon? Carey goes on to investigate the role of the suburb and its typical inhabitant, the clerk, as a larger index of intellectual disgust. The suburban sprawl was seen as the end of England, and in the triumph of cheap housing was located some destitution of the spirit. This was a particular problem for left-wing middle-class intellectuals, whose loyalties were fatally divided, but it posed less of a challenge to conservative intellectuals. In opposition to the values of suburban man, they hoisted the pennant of the 'natural aristocrat' who disdained 'grey' logic as much as the imperatives of sentimental humanism. Carey goes on to associate that aristocratic spirit with the fetid Catholicism of Greene or Waugh. It is one of many incisive touches.

So Carey makes a persuasive case against these writers, largely on the ground that they actually invented the 'mass' which they professed to despise. The only problem is that with this criterion he seems to be damning most of the important writers of the past hundred years, among them Yeats, Hardy, Woolf, D. H. Lawrence, Forster, Waugh, Joyce, Ibsen, Eliot and Huxley. Only Arthur Conan Doyle and Arnold Bennett emerge relatively unscathed. And of course these are all literary artists. It would have been interesting to see Carey enlarge his argument to take in, for example, painters like those associated with the Euston Road School or the Camden Town Group, who were certainly just as 'intellectual' as the novelists of their periods.

There is also the danger of foreshortened perspective. The disdain of artists for the 'mass' is not a recent development, however hard Carey presses the point about a new 'mass culture'. He quotes Lawrence and Huxley, but he might just as well have employed Spenser's taunt against 'Th' amazed vulgar' or Milton's animus towards 'the people but a herd confused / A miscellaneous rabble . . .' The truth is that most writers have always despised the 'herd', and Carey could have mounted a similar attack upon Carlyle and Johnson, Sidney and Pope.

In the second part of this volume he concentrates upon more recent writers. He plots the divided mind of H. G. Wells, who sympathized with the weak even as he itched to destroy them. He scolds George Gissing and scorns Wyndham Lewis, while adding an intriguing postscript on the literary career of Adolf Hitler, who emerges as an orthodox European intellectual. (It is a little unfair to suggest that all supporters of 'high' culture are therefore crypto-Fascists.)

But then, in the best chapter of this section, he recommends Arnold Bennett both for his imaginative interest in the 'intricacy and fecundity of each human life' and for his ability to see the extraordinary within the apparently mundane; his novels are a great plea for the ordinary rhythms of life, for the poor, the failures, the housewives and of course the clerks. In that sense they represent Carey's alternative to the intellectual world of the same period, except that they are no alternative at all. Arnold Bennett is Arnold Bennett, and no other writer could have been expected to imitate him.

And so what, precisely, is Carey suggesting? He cannot be saying that somehow Woolf or Hardy would have been better writers if they had freed themselves from their prejudices, since it may have been their prejudices which made them writers in the first place. He seems to believe that the intellectuals would have been wiser or nobler if they had embraced 'mass culture', but at no point does he list the constituents of that culture. He mentions Jerome K. Jerome, *Tit-Bits* and the *Daily Mail*, as well as tinned salmon, but interesting though these phenomena may be, they do not constitute a serious challenge to the literature of the period. He may only be suggesting that the elements of popular culture are of equal value, or that 'value' cannot be determined – in which case he is occupying the same ground as much modern academic theorizing. Or his may be the simple *nostalgie de la boue* of an English critic who has an empiricist's disdain for theorizing itself.

It is enjoyable to see him using the T. S. Eliot Memorial Lectures to demonstrate that Eliot was an inhuman prig, and there are many insights along the way, but in other respects *The Intellectuals and the Masses* remains inconclusive.

2 July 1992

95

The Maker of the Omnibus: The Lives of English Writers Compared

Jack Hodges

This is an unusual and refreshingly old-fashioned production. In part a collection of anecdotes very like an eighteenth-century anthology, and in part an amalgam of fact like a modern encyclopedia or 'companion', it is the work of a bibliophile who has managed to survive the treacherous terrain of English literature. Apparently Jack Hodges has been making notes in the catalogue of his private library for the past fifteen years and here, born out of his fascination for books and their authors, is an exhaustive survey of the English writer.

It begins, as all good books should, with the finances of the trade. As Archbishop Temple told one aspiring writer: 'You must never forget that Shakespeare wrote for money.' He might have mentioned Charles Dickens as well, and it is an apt preparation for this history of literary achievement to realize that the greatest geniuses of English verse and prose were also skilful businessmen.

But what else keeps these strange creatures at their desks? In his chapter on 'motivation', Hodges mentions the appetite for fame as well as for money, while noting in passing the number of writers who have preferred to shelter underneath pseudonyms. Of course other instincts come into play: one of them might be called a sense of vocation if it did not have such Jesuitical implications. But there is no doubt that true writers have a sense of their destiny at some point in childhood. Whether they have anything of pressing significance to impart to the world is not in the least important: most poets and novelists have 'nothing to say', only a way of saying it.

Hodges does suggest that writers can be inspired by 'gatherings' of their kind, although, from general observation, it is hard to resist the conclusion that writers who congregate together – or who consider themselves to be part of a 'generation' – are of only passing interest. If it is permissible to use a mixed metaphor in such an elevated context, they tend to clutch at each other like last straws. The argument about 'motivation by their Time', as Hodges puts it, is more complicated – it is characteristic of this book that, almost by chance, it seems to raise the most profound issues of creativity.

If there is one 'time' of the greatest importance, however, it is that of childhood; Hodges lists almost ninety great writers who were orphans, and documents the cruelty or neglect which inspired men as diverse as Kipling and Swift. Of course some writers were happy in infancy, and there are even 'accounts that he [Shelley] laughed as a child – which he is not supposed to have done as a man . . .' Some endured dominant mothers, and others suffered from autocratic fathers; some were coddled, while others remained unloved.

All of which suggests, if nothing else, that the genesis of a writer is a mysterious and unpredictable process. So although there are several chapters here on education, the real feature of any writer's early life seems to be a form of instinctive and even obsessional self-education. 'Reading as if for life' was Dickens's description of the process and, after that first revelation of the power of words, it is simply a question of finding the shining path which will lead you to your own. Of course a particularly sympathetic teacher can help to save an aspiring writer (there are examples quoted here) but perhaps the most important lesson to be learnt from any school or university is the habit of sustained reading and disciplined attention. Energy and self-confidence can create the conditions for the growth of genius, but organization and method are necessary for its proper development.

That is why the working habits of writers are always of absorbing interest. It seems that 'if Wordsworth sat with a pen, it made him perspire and brought on a pain in his chest' – this may explain his Ecclesiastical Sonnets – whereas Maugham 'bricked up the wall of his writing-room to shut out the Côte d'Azur'. Carlyle needed absolute quiet, while Thackeray preferred to work in a tavern and Trollope was quite happy in a railway carriage. This did not prevent the author of *The Eustace Diamonds* from writing at a steady rate of 1,000 words an hour – no doubt on the admirable theory that, if he had to wait for 'inspiration', he might never write at all. As William Morris said of his own work '. . . it is a mere matter of craftsmanship'. It is well known that Shakespeare 'never blotted out a line', at least according to one authority, but a surprising number of other authors have also written rapidly and without revision – Smollett and Johnson among them.

The entrance of Dr Johnson suggests the physical and mental defects which may be the price of genius. He was susceptible to a variety of nervous afflictions; Swinburne 'was not quite like a human being', according to Gosse, and the incidence of malformed bodies and nervous peculiarities would seem to consign the literary world to a travelling freak show. Gibbon was 'almost grotesque', George Eliot 'magnificently ugly', and Walter Pater resembled a frog. It is remarkable how many writers have been short of stature: James Barrie was 'almost a dwarf', and Maria Edgeworth used to practise hanging herself by the neck in order to elongate her diminutive body.

There are also chapters here on TB and on cancer, on piles and on insanity, on speech impediments and suicide. It is a fascinating compendium; a Baedeker of oddities and a threnody to wounded spirits, a voyage around a world which seems part funfair and part asylum. Welcome to the history of English literature.

30 January 1993

96

Philip Larkin: A Writer's Life
Andrew Motion

It was no doubt predictable that the childhood of Philip Larkin should be spent in an atmosphere of nervous gloom; it was middle-class middle England with a vengeance, except that his respectable suburban house in Coventry was dominated by a father who kept a statue of Hitler on his mantelpiece. In an unfinished passage of autobiography Larkin wrote that his family was 'dull, pot-bound and slightly mad' and, from Andrew Motion's own account, there is no doubt that the elder Larkin was a bitter and frustrated man who poured all his thwarted energy and repressed mania upon his son – the son who began unpromisingly enough with his worship of D. H. Lawrence and eventually descended into a maelstrom of bigotry. There is something dark, and sour, about such an upbringing; it smacks of the concealment and angry frustration which haunted the poet for the rest of his life.

By the time he arrived at Oxford, he had begun to develop that carapace of wilful ordinariness which he was to carry with him everywhere. Originally it seems to have been a facetious way of pricking literary pretentiousness, in an era when poetic rhetoric was at a premium, but in the end it became a rancid and insidious philistinism which was to do him enormous damage. He did once possess enthusiasm, and even forcefulness, but they were soon lost beneath his suburban cynicism: they were the treasures he once owned but, in later life, he could not remember where he had buried them. The only thing that saved him, at Oxford and elsewhere, was his sense of humour. While still a student he wrote lesbian novels under the name of Brunette Coleman, and Motion suggests that in this period he began tentatively to act upon homosexual impulses. In the preface to a booklet of poems, *Sugar and Spice*, Larkin noted that 'I dedicate this slim volume to all my sister-writers', but Motion is good at seizing on the psychological truth behind such jokes.

253

Nothing ever came of his diffident homosexuality, and in fact nothing really ever came of anything. Already, in his early twenties, he was measuring himself for a life he was obliged, by temperament and circumstance, to lead – 'blocked and inert', as Motion puts it, 'a life of compromise'. When he attended his first job interview, for the post of librarian somewhere in Shropshire, he carried with him through the rain a copy of *The Public Library System of Great Britain*. In small gestures like that, one's fate is sealed. From this time forward, in fact, he began to rehearse that drab monologue of misery and self-pity which was to fill his letters and poems. Even Motion's intelligent commentary cannot rescue Larkin from the taint of an insipid and self-imposed greyness: 'the instinct for misery' may have become 'the authority of sadness', as he puts it, but the effect is the same upon the reader.

He took up a post as librarian at Hull University in 1955 (the Brynmor Jones Library there may well turn out to be his most significant and certainly most enduring achievement), and in the same year he attained his first success with the publication of *The Less Deceived*. But his literary reputation served only to make him more self-indulgent; he began to parade his more unfortunate prejudices as if his fame, modest though it was, gave him a licence to do so. In later life he pretended to dislike his public position, but Motion's account makes it clear that he loved every minute of it; it allowed him to be as mean and as boorish as he wished, and in the process he created an artistic 'personality' as grotesque as anything conjured up by Edith Sitwell. He became secretive, self-obsessed and always plaintive, while his 'love-life' (if it can be so described) was a paradigm of indecision and deceit. If there is a mistake of emphasis in this otherwise well-balanced biography, in fact, it is the extent to which Motion dwells upon affairs which are really only of concern to the people involved. It might be said in extenuation, however, that for much of Larkin's life there is very little else to write about.

This is an exemplary biography of its kind – detailed, meticulous and sympathetic. In certain respects it might even be seen as too sympathetic, since in his introduction Motion claims that Larkin is 'one of the great poets of the century'. In adolescence Larkin proclaimed himself a 'genius', too, but produced very little subsequent evidence to justify the title. Far from being a natural genius confined and cramped by circumstance, as some people might assume, he made a small talent go a very long way indeed. He is in the same mould as

Martin Tupper and Robert Service – essentially a minor poet who, for purely local and temporary reasons, acquired a large reputation.

Perhaps, in the end, he realized as much himself. He had adopted the manner of an old man while he was still in his fifties and it seems that, as far as he was concerned, his life was over before it had begun. Of course he had picked up honours and doctorates along the way, and could on occasions still exhibit that icy humour which is the revenge of the mild-mannered man against the world, but he continually complained about his 'aimless life' and often lapsed into what Motion calls 'a drink-sodden depression'. His was a minor talent which exhausted itself too soon, leaving only a few slim volumes as a memento. There was a brief controversy last year about Larkin's more unfortunate obsessions, but they hardly matter. Of course you do not have to be a master of political correctness to realize that, by the end of his life, he had become a foul-mouthed bigot: that does not necessarily prevent anyone from being a great poet as well, but in Larkin's case no such consolation was ever available.

1 April 1993

97

The Lives of Michel Foucault
David Macey

The Passion of Michel Foucault
James Miller

There is a plausible case for taking Michel Foucault to be a characteristically French phenomenon; for someone so concerned with the taxonomy of knowledge into which human beings are (as it were) inserted, there would be a pleasing irony in relegating him to type – as an example of the *savant* who, like Rousseau or Sartre, develops a fine literary persona while at the same time engaged in contemporaneous political debate. In the present climate of philosophical studies it is inevitable that his own style is as perplexing as it is ingenious, but it still might be assumed that he was a traditional *philosophe*. But neither

Macey nor Miller chooses that easy course; these biographies explore a more equivocal and, in certain respects, more unhappy figure. If Foucault is a *philosophe* he is, to mix the idioms of the eighteenth and nineteenth centuries, also a *philosophe maudit*.

He is not an easy man to find, as the title of Macey's study suggests. He tried consistently to deny or to eschew his personality with a variety of teasing narcissistic escape routes, although Miller reveals that, towards the end of his life, he confessed that his theoretical work was based upon 'elements from my experience'. The simple facts of the case are available in both biographies: he was an industrious and ambitious child, but even then his scholarship was tinged with a somewhat caustic humour. As soon as he was enrolled in the Ecole Normale Supérieure, of course, he entered the particularly bracing climate of French intellectual life in which the paramount aim is *briller* – to shine – the verb itself suggesting the clarity and lucidity of the French intellectual tradition.

The trajectory of Foucault's enthusiasms, from Hegel to Nietzsche, is charted by both biographers; it is not a necessary or even a predictable development, and testifies to Foucault's mental acrobatics as well as to his more orthodox devotion to philosophical texts. 'Libraries,' as Macey suggests, 'were to become Foucault's natural habitat'; it could be argued that part of his comprehensiveness and range lay simply in his ability to regurgitate other books. Perhaps that is why he remained, for most of his life, an academic attached to one institution or another. With his shaved skull, white roll-neck sweater and rimless glasses he might resemble Nosferatu but, in temperament and attitude, he was closer to the spirit of a medieval monk.

His first book (which, typically, he later disowned) was *Maladie mentale*, which can be best viewed as the seed of his more renowned *Histoire de la folie* in which madness is discussed as a cultural representation and production. It was published in 1961, and from that time Foucault became a member of what can legitimately be called the French intellectual establishment. There is something to be said for such a hierarchy; it is often claimed that in England there are really no intellectuals, but this is simply because the tradition of intellectual inquiry has never been given the public sanction and authority which it enjoys in France. In this country we pay too much attention to fiction, and not enough to writing.

Not all French intellectuals are impressive, of course, but there is something unnervingly brilliant about Foucault's intellectual man-oeuvres. His ambition was, in Macey's words, to provide 'a general corpus or encyclopedia of all the techniques of interpretation that have ever been used in Western cultures', an aspiration which he pursued in *Les Mots et les choses* as well as in *L'Archéologie du savoir*. His style is more difficult to describe, but in its languorous precision it is as if Heidegger had been translated by Walter Pater; he probably would not have appreciated the comparison with the English writer, but there is no doubt that the aesthetic appeal of Foucault's writing is an intrinsic element of its popularity.

But Foucault was a man of various selves, and in these accounts we come across a man who had an affair with a transvestite in Hamburg, who was blackmailed by a Polish boy-friend and who, most signifi-cantly of all, was attracted to various sado-masochistic rituals. No doubt it is a tribute to his protean nature that both biographies have various but complementary strengths. Miller is better on his last days, Macey upon his early years; Miller is more interesting about Foucault's time in America, where Macey concentrates upon his life in Europe. Macey is more illuminating about Foucault's philosophical conscious-ness, where Miller is the best exponent of Foucault's sexuality. Macey describes how Foucault extended the philosophical tradition with his extensive taxonomy of formal power relationships, whereas, character-istically, Miller is intent upon examining the nature of Foucault's attraction to power in the first place.

His is in that sense a more troubling narrative because it tends to emphasize Foucault's absorption in pain. There must be some connection between the man who wrote *Surveiller et punir* and the writer who engaged in sado-masochistic activities; there must also be at least a loose association between the man obsessed with prisons and the writer who indulged in homoerotic fantasies. It is also interesting that the philosopher who so ferociously 'deconstructed' medicine and the culture of hospitals had a surgeon for a father. And could it not be suggested that Foucault's need to master and to control the language of an entire culture was part of his need for dominance on a more private level? Both of these biographies, and all the other lives of Foucault, extend the parameters of sexual debate as much as they refine our sense of contemporary French culture.

3 June 1993

98

Modern Painters: Reflections on British Art
Peter Fuller
Edited by John McDonald

Although it is perhaps unhelpful of Peter Fuller's editor to compare him with Ruskin (the disparity is too glaring), this volume of posthumous essays and lectures does suggest his craving for belief and certainty. His intellectual biography is in one sense predictable: he abandoned his Baptist upbringing, embraced communism, and then converted to psychoanalytic theory. It is the trajectory of an enthusiast or a missionary, but rarely has so severe a temperament been applied to art criticism and art history.

That is why Fuller is primarily concerned with the problem of evaluation and in particular with the spiritual dimension of great art; from his early allegiance to a wholly Marxist aesthetic, he developed a taste for the Gothic and Romantic art which aspired higher than any materialistic dynamic. His is in that sense a peculiarly English vision, which has its roots as much in the 'babooneries' of illustrated manuscripts as in the spiritual intensity of Turner or of Palmer. It is in this context, also, that he traces a national tradition through Constable and Cotman to the Pre-Raphaelites until it emerges unimpeded in the neo-Romantics of the thirties and forties; the importance of this lineage lies not so much in its constituent parts but, rather, in its positive assertion that there is a native English tradition which has nothing to do with modernism or with Americanism.

Fuller cites Nash, Bomberg, Spencer, Moore, Sutherland and Piper as the great artists of the century who were united in their determination, or ability, to 'depict the spiritual essence of things'. At the same time he condemns the 'cultural anaesthesia' of those artists and reviewers who simply parroted the fashionable doctrines of the last thirty or forty years, saving his most vitriolic asides for those who have exhibited a slavish obeisance to American taste and who have, as a consequence, been prepared to find evidence of art in the most trivial activities.

All this is very helpful, and just, but there are occasions when Fuller overstates his theme. His concept of secular spirituality, for example, is not wholly convincing and seems to owe more to his evangelical childhood than any considered attitude. He is also too inclined to follow Ruskin and to conflate religion with the experience of nature and the practice of landscape painting. When he repeats St Hilary's question, 'Who can look on Nature and not see God?' he should have reminded himself of the fact that many great artists and visionaries have paid no attention to Nature at all. William Blake, one of the great exemplars of any national spiritual tradition, considered it to be a delusion and denounced Wordsworth as an atheist for his pietistic attitude towards it. Fuller quotes with some scorn the words of the first director of the Museum of Modern Art in New York, Alfred Barr: 'Since resemblance to nature is at best superfluous and at worst distracting, it might as well be eliminated'; but it is at least conceivable that Blake would have agreed with him. It is not so far, after all, from the sentiment of Fuseli with whom Blake did agree: 'Nature puts me out.'

But enough of Nature. Fuller is certainly right in his central emphasis: the importance of *theoria* (which was the title of his last published work), or vision, in the creation and understanding of art. It is most noticeably lacking in contemporary literature, for example, where fiction has tended to become a highly stylized form of journalism or satire; certain novelists, like many of the artists whom Fuller condemns, simply do not understand their limitations and are thus incapable of transcending them. And from that essential proposition spring many of Fuller's most interesting judgements: that is why, for example, he is able to locate and to celebrate the tradition of painting in this country and to discount American art as 'already dead'. (The same analysis might apply to the American novel which, although not moribund, is certainly in need of intensive care.)

The resources of the national tradition are, however, perhaps even more substantial than Fuller calculates, and his attack upon post-modernism misfires precisely because he does not realize that its essential constituents (theatricality and an awareness of the relativity of style) have always been an essential component of English taste. The Elizabethan vogue for medieval funereal monuments, the rise of neoclassical architecture, and the revival of Gothic in the nineteenth century all suggest that stylistic borrowings and a certain theatrical historicism are essential aspects of the native genius. Post-modernism is simply a belated academic recognition of what is a very old tradition.

But Fuller's criticism does suggest the strength which comes from having a *theoria* of his own, and his artistic judgements are on most occasions sound and convincing. There is a very interesting essay here on English drawing, for example, in which he examines Bomberg's description of 'the spirit in the mass' (the implied religious terminology cannot have escaped him). But it is the mark of a good critic that he is as astute about contemporary art as he is about the old masters, and Fuller passes the test admirably: his essays on Frank Auerbach and David Hockney demonstrate his ability to recognize the essential qualities of two very different artists. He also has a strong historical sense (without which no critic can ever be competent), and makes some interesting analogies between Francis Bacon and Joshua Reynolds, Lucian Freud and Frans Hals, Maggi Hambling and George Frederick Watts. In an essay on Adrian Berg he illustrates a point which might even be the summary of his theme. 'Parochialism,' he writes, can be 'a great source of strength.' That is why he is able to attack that shallow internationalism which was once so much part of fashionable critical discourse.

He is often an astringent critic – at one point he calls himself 'an absolutist and a dogmatist' – but he is a necessary corrective in a culture which has for too long suffered under a self-imposed sense of inferiority. In this context, too, it is important for artists to understand what he means when he calls for a return to 'imaginative vision or revelation'. Here, after all, is the voice of the authentic critic.

15 July 1993

99

A World Elsewhere
Bernard Levin

It is the description, rather than the making, of Utopia that has enthralled the human spirit. That is why, in this Baedeker of mortal yearnings, Bernard Levin reserves much praise for *The Dictionary of Imaginary Places*. Of course they are better than the real thing, and such books as More's original *Utopia* and Italo Calvino's *Imaginary Cities* testify to the universal affection for that which has never been and cannot be. In Levin's study it is 'the serpent', rather than the Covering Cherub, which prevents us from entering Eden. *A World Elsewhere* sets out to narrate the incomparable drama of the Fall, in which innocence and lack of self-consciousness must eventually be destroyed by the knowledge of reality.

He begins with Homer and with the story of Atlantis, which is surely the most appropriate introduction to his theme. It is one of the great mythic beliefs, since the legend of the submerged continent can act both as an emblem of some lost golden age and as a metaphor for that lost part of ourselves to which we long to return. The central aspect of the Utopian vision is that it can unite otherwise disparate bands of perception: in the seventeenth century it was possible to believe in a 'giant race before the Flood' as well as to entertain millenarian or apocalyptic fantasies.

Levin's is a relatively brief survey and he has deployed various versions of the myth in order to convey his own argument. He moves from Fourier to post-war reconstruction, from Proudhon to the Socialist Workers' Party, from the Webbs to Shirley Temple, from Rabelais to P. G. Wodehouse, from Tolkien to Leibniz, from Joanna Southcott to the Bloomsbury Group. The inclusion of Southcott (who was not, by the way, a 'prophetess in England in the late nineteenth century' but a hundred years earlier) suggests that the Utopian dispensation can be a form of displaced religiosity, on some occasions close to madness; but the central preoccupation of these visionaries is to liberate humankind from its weaknesses.

But since those weaknesses make up half the sum of human activity, and more than half of human happiness, the places of aspiring bliss are bound to seem sterile or denuded. Utopias are also generally based upon the assumption that human beings are reasonable creatures who will make rational choices, once they are offered; yet much of the personality still lives in the dark, with its dreams of magic and infancy, and there is no power on earth that can withstand the force of that darkness.

At least some Utopian schemes have the merit of being quite beautiful. As Levin tells us, 'Vitruvius proposed to carve Mount Olympus – the entire mountain – into a figure on one knee, with an outstretched hand through which a river would run, and in which there would be a city of 10,000 souls.' Casanova, of all people, contrived one of the most ingenious Utopias of androgynous creatures:

They go naked except for shoes, and live on milk, which is red. They are rarely more than 18 inches high, and their horror of drunkenness is such that a sleeping drunk may be robbed with impunity. They have a vocabulary of 30,000 words, they venerate serpents, and there are penalties for lying, yawning and immoderate laughter.

The merit of Levin's writing is that he is not a philosopher but a journalist, which allows him to see the world in a fuller perspective than might otherwise be the case. He is particularly good on the Utopianism of contemporary science – a set of disciplines which can truly be said to have created an idealized and enclosed world which works according to its own self-imposed laws. The Utopia of the scientist is the same Utopia as that of the alchemist, and it might be interesting to analyse the intimate connection between the two. In fact, a psychological study might profitably be made of Utopians in general who, incandescent with self-belief, have on occasions struck the world like lightning. Some, like Fourier, spent a long life in elaborating upon their delusions; others, like Hans Böhm, have been burned at the stake for heresy and sorcery.

Levin also suggests that the pursuit of Utopia is in one sense a search for 'the new', and the great flaw in Utopian visions is that they tend to become intellectual schemes with very little regard for history or precedent. There is always some novel 'big idea', like 'post-modernism' or 'the death of history', which turns out to be only a familiar little idea dressed up for the sake of the foolish. Most Utopias are aspects of that same ahistorical, and therefore false, consciousness. Yet this desire to destroy or forget the past is also part of the obsessive desire to manipulate and to control the present which is so characteristic of Utopians; the need is for some final completeness or immutable order, as communities of model citizens are woven out of thin air.

But the problem then becomes one of belief. Levin lists many examples, from Jim Jones and David Koresh to the rulers of the Soviet Union or Cambodia, in order to ask one overwhelming question. How is it possible for human beings to believe what, at first or even second glance, seems folly and madness? Unfortunately, you can never overestimate the loneliness and misery of many people, lost in the world but constantly seeking to be 'found' and made safe once more. If Utopians are infantilist schemers of a self-created world, then there are many other infantilists willing to join them. Such people will also tend to be prone to accept that notion of 'equality' which is so potent an aspect of Utopian myth. Levin quotes B. F. Skinner from *Walden Two* declaring: 'A society which functions for the good of all cannot tolerate the emergence of individual figures . . .'

Levin is sometimes better at polemic than historical analysis: he is good on the Utopianism of Hayek and Friedman, while his potted biographies of Bentham or Leibniz are not quite so successful. There are occasions when he shows a propensity for the facile phrase. Despite these minor problems of style, this is a well-informed and stimulating survey. The author has been working on it for twenty years but he has hit upon one of the oldest explanations of all. 'Have our Utopians never heard of original sin?' he asks. And that is the point: Utopias always begin in Eden, but they must also always end there.

2 June 1994

IOO

Lytton Strachey: The New Biography
Michael Holroyd

Who now recalls the virtues of nineteenth-century biography? In works such as Forster's life of Charles Dickens or Carlyle's life of Frederick the Great, the intimate details of private lives were altogether ignored in favour of heroic or romantic narrative. As Michael Holroyd says in his introduction to his own exemplary study, Lytton Strachey helped to change all that. In his anatomies of certain great Victorians he took the wax out of the fruit and lifted the antimacassar from the armchair. In the process such luminaries as Queen Victoria and General Gordon were lowered to earth with a resounding thud.

With the first publication of this biography in 1967, Mr Holroyd performed a similar act of recovery or revival. It may seem paradoxical that the writer of such short lives was afforded so ample a life, but the truth was that Holroyd had a great deal to say. In particular he explored, with certain discreet changes of name, the nature of Strachey's homosexual amours; the names have finally been disclosed in this revised edition, but the damage – as some of the more censorious critics saw it at the time – had already been done. It was possible in the forties and fifties of the present century to read lives which seemed to revert to mid-Victorian standards of gentility; they concentrated upon the exemplary lives of their subjects to the exclusion of anything approaching gossip or sexual disclosure. After the publication of *Lytton Strachey*, however, such squeamishness became almost impossible to maintain. In recent biographies of Auden or Picasso or Wilde, for example, the most candid erotic detail is included.

But such an approach is not guaranteed to be successful. In his introduction Mr Holroyd seems to assume that the virtues of (predominantly sexual) revelation outweigh any possible damage to the general reputation of the subject; in that sense he might be said to be the true heir of Strachey himself. Reviewers who use the first person singular are not usually to be trusted (they tend to use 'I' relentlessly, although it is not at all clear that they have a personality in the first place) but perhaps I can be allowed to introduce a personal note in this context. In my own biographies of T. S. Eliot and Charles Dickens, I did not feel it necessary to repeat items of sexual gossip or innuendo which I had read or heard; nor did I speculate about what went on behind the closed door of the bedroom. This reticence will no doubt seem absurd to many people, if only on the grounds that sex is not of much significance in any case. A man can be another De Sade, a woman another Messalina, without provoking the slightest criticism these days. So if Strachey made love to young men, for example, what of it?

But what of this? The biographer is drawn to a subject because of that person's achievements; unless it is to be a pure exercise in debunking, the worth of the biographical subject is the primary reason for the writing of any life. That is why the great literary biographies have all the elements of a good story, in which the curve of a writer's reputation and career becomes the central movement around which everything else is arranged. To include the multifarious details of sexual adventures may, in such a context, be a formal or technical mistake; it may distract attention from the central narrative, and on occasions unbalance it altogether. And why are sexual details considered to be of such significance in the first place? Do we have lists of food eaten in restaurants, of clothes worn on each occasion; do we compile the details of household chores or culinary skills? When Mr Holroyd quotes with apparent approval a critic's remark that his biography was 'post-Wolfenden', he may also be categorizing his own work as part of that climate of liberalism and relativism which marked only a specific period in twentieth-century history.

This is in no way to criticize the book itself, which is a splendid example of literary biography well worth its present revision and republication. It can be said that, almost single-handedly, Mr Holroyd revived the reputation of 'Bloomsbury' as a result; for that reason alone he has contributed as much to English literary culture as Strachey himself. By treating his subject's homosexuality in a sympathetic manner, also, he encouraged a broader acceptance of that condition among what might be called a public library readership. The fact that he also started something of a fashion for very long biographical works is perhaps not quite so signal an honour, although this reviewer is hardly in a position to condemn him out of hand.

There may be something to be said for Strachey's form of biography, however; following Johnson and Aubrey, he devised shorter lives in which the tone of the essayist is more important than that of the researcher or academic and where the formal skills of the narrator are considered to be as significant as the technical resources of the archivist. Holroyd's great achievement was to maintain that tone and style throughout a much longer narrative. The whole purpose of biography, after all, is to create a work of art which can be as convincing as fiction while remaining as substantial as history. There is only one difference; in fiction one is obliged to tell the truth, whereas in biography you are permitted – indeed often compelled – to make things up.

The work of reconstruction for this revised version of *Lytton Strachey* has been thorough and remarkable; Mr Holroyd has deleted whole passages of narrative and criticism while at the same time interpolating passages which have not added to the length of the book. Of course, largely owing to the efforts of Mr Holroyd himself, 'Bloomsbury' has become something of an industry in recent years – so he has had to trawl through all published autobiographies, memoirs, biographies, diaries and letters to find fresh information about his subject. In the process Strachey emerges as a more complex and ultimately more convincing figure. He looked like a stick-insect and laughed like a hyena; yet beneath his perplexing and sometimes disagreeable demeanour, there was a true man and artist.

Holroyd's prose, in this second version, is as elegant as ever. He is also one of the few biographers who has retained a pronounced sense of humour, which he manages to combine with an instinctive gift for story and for the description of character. But his general and original achievement is still the most remarkable. In his introduction he recounts the wealth of material put at his disposal by the Strachey family, and others, but he is too unassuming to mention the sheer intellectual rigour and architectonic skill necessary to create order out of that chaos. It requires the abilities of a novelist as well as the patience of a scholar; the fact that Holroyd has combined the two has also meant that he is in large part responsible for the revival of biography as a literary form in the late twentieth century. It has also led the way to a filmic treatment of literary figures – among them *Carrington*, which is to be based upon this particular book. We have entered a very different culture from that which Strachey and his friends represented, but it is the great virtue of Holroyd's biography that it returns them convincingly and memorably to life.

15 August 1994

IOI

An Intimate History of Humanity
Theodore Zeldin

As the century, and the millennium, come to an end, new forms of writing are beginning to emerge. Consider, for example, some of the chapter headings in Theodore Zeldin's remarkable study of humankind – 'Why it has become increasingly difficult to destroy one's enemies', 'How people have freed themselves from fear by finding new fears', 'How humans have repeatedly lost hope, and how new encounters, and a new pair of spectacles, revive them', 'How even astrologers resist their destiny'. This is a work of scholarship, but it is more than that; it is a narrative of private lives, but it extends much further; it is a universal history, but it has an extraordinary intimacy of tone.

The first chapter, for example, opens with the personal narrative of a French domestic servant; but then it expands into a discourse on slavery and an analysis of the problems of freedom. It is a book about patterns of desire and behaviour which persist through that continuum we choose to call history, and which we carry with us everywhere without any knowledge of doing so. Theodore Zeldin is senior fellow of St Anthony's College, Oxford, but his subject is still so little understood that his book can hardly fall into any orthodox academic category. It is a study in which time is broken open to reveal the real world which lies beneath it (in one marvellous aside, he describes the medieval concept of time as that of a cloud which will one day clear), that real world of memory and inheritance which is all the more powerful for being obscured from sight.

The book shifts rapidly and continually from personal history to conceptual analysis, in a manner which unlocks those influences of the past. To follow the history of conversation, as Zeldin does, through Socrates, Renaissance court officials and Samuel Johnson into the present time is to uncover one of the more enduring aspects of human history which is ordinarily taken for granted and therefore very clumsily defined. 'Everybody's style of speaking,' as he declares, 'is a mixture of echoes dating from different epochs of the past . . .' There are other, equally convincing, themes – the history of loneliness, the aetiology of failure, the universal quest for origins, and a disquisition on the fact that 'nobody foresaw the world shortage of respect'.

In a sense this is a book made out of other books – there is a bibliography of suggested reading at the end of each chapter – but, then, what good book is not? Zeldin has read very widely within various disciplines, and has therefore managed to provide an intellectual *tour d'horizon* on a grand scale. In some ways it reflects the type of discourse characteristic of French intellectuals such as Foucault or Merleau-Ponty, but Zeldin is too much an observer and naturalist to be excessively influenced by their brand of fluent generalization. He stays closer to the ground of the world, and, in trying to understand the inflections of human behaviour, he is able to uncover the secret springs which lie within it.

But *An Intimate History of Humanity* is also in tune with other speculations of our period. In an early chapter Zeldin remarks that 'One may feel isolated in one's own town, but one has forebears all over the world' and then goes on to suggest that 'You belong with those people with whom you sympathize, in whatever century they lived, in no matter what civilization.' This is very close to Rupert

Sheldrake's speculations on the nature of 'morphic resonance', and also has affinities with that element in contemporary English fiction which has redefined the nature of time. All of these works seem to be speaking the language of a new millennium.

Zeldin's is an interdisciplinary study in a quite new sense, therefore, since he is able to connect what are normally disparate phenomena to reveal something unfamiliar and surprising. In the chapter on loneliness, for example, he brings together monasticism and immunology, Hindu mythology and the fifth Duke of Portland. As a result he begins to see new shapes emerging through the processes of time. One of his chapters is entitled 'How new forms of love have been invented', where that elusive emotion, or sensation, or quality, is seen to change its meaning in a variety of cultures. It is followed by a chapter entitled 'Why there has been more progress in cooking than in sex' which provides a suggestive culinary drama, in which we learn that eroticism can be seen as a form of cookery and that a peasant in the Andes 'can distinguish without difficulty between three hundred varieties of potato'.

One of the keys to Zeldin's writing, in fact, is his rediscovery of forgotten objects or passions; in the course of this book, he manages to retrieve that which was once considered unworthy of notice or study. That is why he is intrigued by the various social movements of the last twenty years, such as feminism and environmentalism, which have begun to exploit new forms of knowledge or information. But he goes further than the causes of the moment; he sees a politics based upon 'wider imagination' as well as the evident failure of techniques of aggression or dominance. He is interested, also, in the new role of 'catalysts' or 'intermediaries' who are replacing the conventional hierarchies of ordered power – 'There is a new way of looking at the world, as a series of minute interactions in the presence of others.' The central point, however, is that 'Imaginations are beginning to work in a new way.'

All the contexts are changing, then, and the recent disparagement or questioning of scientific 'truth' is only one example of the transformation which is taking place. Is it possible, for example, that in the next millennium orthodox concepts of time and space will be radically revised? That the universe, as it is supposed to exist, will turn out to have been the myth or dream of blinkered scientists? As Zeldin puts it himself, 'it is becoming clear that the limits which science places on curiosity have increased in recent times.' Of course it is as yet impossible to discern the elements of this great alteration, and perhaps the least satisfactory part of the book lies in Zeldin's sometimes bland prognostications – 'Exploring the mystery of other people's thoughts and feelings is the new spiritual quest', to be seen in the growth of compassion and the increasing equality of the sexes. It could be that the world will go another way, however; human beings may turn towards regionalism and tribalism when they discover how much they owe to the earth or territory in which they were nurtured.

But this is a fine book about 'new affinities', as Zeldin completes his circumnavigation of the known and unknown worlds. It is also an optimistic work, based upon the assumption that 'a new era in human relations' has now become possible and that 'The age of discovery has barely begun'. So it seems, then, that the best is yet to come.

12 September 1994

102

The Western Canon
Harold Bloom

It is a pity, perhaps, that a book such as this has to be written; but Harold Bloom is Professor of English at New York University, and is therefore a member of an endangered species which must protect itself. A fellow academic tells him that Hemingway has been dropped from a fiction course in favour of 'a rather inadequate Chicano short-story writer' on the grounds that 'her students would thus be better prepared to live in the United States'. Another colleague declares that 'we are all feminist critics' – to which Bloom adds, with a dark humour in evidence throughout this book, 'That is the rhetoric suitable for an occupied country, one that expects no liberation from liberation.' But if this is a necessary book, it is also one that, within its own sonorousness, carries the trumpet note of doom – you cannot divert the lemmings once they have reached the clifftop, and Bloom can only helplessly note the mad flight towards 'feminism, African-American culturalism, and all the other politically correct enterprises of our moment'.

So what does he suggest in their place? He suggests that we might look again at Dante or Milton; Goethe and Cervantes might make an acceptable substitute for Alice Walker or Maya Angelou, while Johnson or Shakespeare offer a diversion from 'dirty realism'. His list of twenty-six 'canonical' authors, put forward in an assertive spirit to those students who (apparently) find *Julius Caesar* too long for their attention span, also includes Austen, Chaucer, Whitman and Tolstoy.

Bloom is in fact engaged in a very American enterprise in order to fight a very American problem. It is difficult to think of an English or European critic who would consider drawing up a 'canon' (a word to which we will presently return) made up from so many dissimilar works from so many diverse cultures. F. R. Leavis tried his own home-grown version with disastrous results: it was a mistake, on his part, to turn the reading of literature into some secular substitute for religious experience and the notion of a 'great tradition' corrupted more readers than a thousand television book programmes. When literature becomes a duty, then it ceases to be a pleasure. Yet, in the present climate of disaffection and ignorance, *The Western Canon* has become a necessary book. And only an American could have written it.

Of course Bloom bears the marks of his own particular culture. He refers constantly to the literary inheritance as a form of challenge, or '*agon*', in which living writers are struggling against the dead. Like such American contemporaries as Norman Mailer, he seems to view works of poetry or prose as part of some strenuous competitive process. Mailer directs the competition against the novelists around him, but Bloom sees it happening through the centuries. There is more of New York than Mount Helicon, for example, in the comment that '. . . the Canon not only results from a contest but is itself an ongoing contest.' Which means, for example, that 'Dante in a way is a stronger Milton, and his overcoming of rivals, ancient and contemporary, is even more convincing than Milton's triumph . . .' There are occasions when he might be a sports reporter rather than a literary critic.

It is also important that Bloom creates a level field for the writers involved in this hypothetical struggle. He is not particularly interested in the cultural and historical contexts of the works, perhaps for the very good reason that they may then become blanched by the cultural determinism of neo-Marxist critics. But the no doubt unanticipated consequence is that all these writers, taken out of their native lands, become in a sense Americanized; they become part of some vast competitive drive in an alien field.

Bloom is very interested in the powerful 'characters' which are thrown up in the process. He celebrates Goethe's 'unique and overwhelming personality', Montaigne's 'highly original personality' and various critics' 'vehement and colourful personalities'. In this he takes his cue from Johnson, who reinvented the art of biographical criticism. But Bloom lacks Johnson's restraint; instead he is imbued with a strain of neo-Romantic fervour which allows him to speak continually of the 'sublime' and to invoke the principles of 'strangeness' and 'originality' as the canonical qualities of great writing. He is also preoccupied by the actual characters within various fictions and imagines, for example, Falstaff and the Wife of Bath in some titanic confrontation. He is not very far here from Hazlitt or Lamb, but he is a Romantic essayist who has also been touched by Pater's aestheticism. It is hard, however, to think of a better tradition for any literary critic.

The Western Canon is not a book of criticism or of scholarship; it is an act of celebration and of self-affirmation. It is hard to argue with it, therefore; it would be like taking an exalted man to one side, and reciting the reasons why he should calm down. There is no reason why Professor Bloom should not extol the virtues of Chaucer or Browning at the top of his voice – everyone in the English Departments of the universities ought to be doing so – but the newspaper reviewer can only feebly murmur 'I agree, but . . .'

There are in fact problems with the idea of a 'canon', since there is some danger in presenting literature as a form of sacred scripture. Shakespeare is not, and should not become, what Bloom calls him here – a 'mortal god'. In that direction lies the debasement of the religious spirit, and an approach to literature which will in the end destroy its true efficacy and power. Certain readers would rather be amused by Firbank or Waugh than uplifted by George Eliot – a criticism which discounts such reactions is incomplete.

Yet it is hard to argue long or hard with a critic who writes so acutely on artists as diverse as Whitman and Ibsen, Pablo Neruda and Emily Dickinson. One can only applaud, for example, when he describes the feminist 'readings' of Virginia Woolf:

Woolf, the lover of the prose of Sir Thomas Browne, would have suffered acutely confronting the manifestos of those who assert that they write and teach in her name. Herself the last of the high aesthetes, she has been swallowed up by remorseless Puritans, for whom the beautiful in literature is only another version of the cosmetics industry.

And to say of Freud that he is 'prosified Shakespeare' is little short of genius. That is why Bloom's enthusiasm is always more important than his occasional stridency and, although there may be a few doubtful passages in the narrative, *The Western Canon* remains a wonderful and, indeed, invaluable reaffirmation of the central literary tradition.

26 January 1995

103

Cyril Connolly: A Nostalgic Life
Clive Fisher

Cyril Connolly was, in certain respects, a disappointed man. He aspired to the writing of fiction and serious criticism, but believed that he would only be remembered as a newspaper reviewer. There is nothing wrong with that, of course. It is a fine profession, as they said of Mrs Warren, and, being both erudite and generous, he was perhaps the last of his race. Yet he had wanted to be more, much more, than that. He had wanted to be an artist, not a journalist. But the truth is that he had neither the temperament nor the talent for the former role. He had the gift of creating an immaculate phrase, and then stringing it upon another one, but he lacked what might be called weight. He had no vision of the world: he was only a talented observer of it.

He seems to have arrived ready-made. At school he was described as a 'peacock among fowls', and by the time he arrived at Oxford he already carried what Kenneth Clark described as 'the millstone of promise' around his neck. He wore it in a very striking fashion, however; it glittered even in the scintillating company of Brian Howard, Harold Acton and Evelyn Waugh.

Connolly once said that Oxford was 'the cloakroom where I left my youth', and with youthfulness he lost any real hope that great things might be achieved. When he entered the world for the first time, he drifted. He abandoned any sense of purpose or direction, although it cannot be said that he had a very firm one in the first place. He was at last rescued by an elderly American littérateur, Logan Pearsall Smith, who is perhaps best remembered for his aphorism, 'An improper mind is a perpetual feast.' Connolly became his secretary, always an interesting position for a young man, and was soon introduced to the assorted semi-nonentities who then, as now, comprise 'literary London'. He never guessed that the real work was being done elsewhere. As Virginia Woolf said of another eminent reviewer, Desmond MacCarthy, 'Desmond was the most gifted of us all. But why did he never do anything?'

That might have been Connolly's own epitaph. He followed the now well-beaten path of cultured young men; he took up novel reviewing for a weekly periodical, he wrote an occasional essay on a subject of no importance, and made an unsuccessful attempt at a book. Then he married a rich young woman, not a moment too soon, and decided to travel instead. On occasions Clive Fisher describes Connolly as a 'romantic' but in fact his own subtitle – 'A Nostalgic Life' – is closer to the truth. If there was romance, it was of the cheaper kind that entails pity for oneself and one's own shortcomings. He was simply too indolent and wayward to do anything about it.

So reviewing became his natural element. He went back to the newspapers, but at some point made the cardinal mistake of using the first person singular; there is nothing more depressing than a reviewer who takes himself, or herself, too seriously. Yet he was a clever and sensitive man, so his natural intelligence could not help breaking through – 'Reviewing is a whole-time job with a half-time salary,' he wrote, '. . . where nothing is secure or certain except the certainty of turning into a hack.'

In fact he did try to be more than a hack, and managed to write a novel to which Mr Fisher wisely allows only four pages. *The Rock Pool* resembles a work by George Orwell which has been heavily rewritten by Walter Pater. *Enemies of Promise* is a much more successful and interesting volume. Here with almost fatal prescience Connolly suggests that drink, journalism and domesticity can ruin any aspiration towards literary achievement; more revealing still is the final part of the book, in which he discusses his days at Eton with a certain charming morbidity. In that respect he was typical of his time: it is hard to think of another generation of English writers who have come so exclusively from the upper middle class and who have been so obsessed with their education. The result was, of course, that many of them remained perpetually immured in their adolescence.

Certainly this was true of Connolly himself and, in Clive Fisher's account of his amours and alarms, there is no doubt that we find the footprints of a perpetual and often petulant youth. There is a full record here of his philandering, which led to various absurd scenes or confrontations: it seems that people insist upon leading difficult lives when they have very little else to do. He was a man of great intelligence which was consumed in conversation; he was a writer of immense discrimination and judgement, but he consigned those qualities to the obscurity of forgotten reviews.

Perhaps his most enduring claim to attention arises from his editorship of *Horizon* during the Second World War. There are some people who seem ideally suited to the editing of literary magazines – it requires a mixture of low cunning and immense charm – and under his direction that magazine became the single most important vessel of English letters since the days of the great nineteenth-century periodicals. Connolly published Orwell and Auden and Waugh (the magazine first printed *The Loved One*); he discovered Angus Wilson and Denton Welch.

Yet in the end he tired, as always, of his responsibilities. He drifted away once again. He signed various contracts for the writing of books, few of which were ever fulfilled. He married several times. He lay in the bath, and groaned. He joined the *Sunday Times* as their chief literary reviewer. He was always close to bankruptcy. He drank too much. In fact prolonged exposure to Connolly's general sloth can prove wearisome; this is a relatively long book, and there may be a case for saying that Clive Fisher takes his subject a little more seriously – and at greater length – than he properly deserves.

But it is the only disadvantage in what is otherwise a splendid biography with a distinctive, sparkling and, most important of all, well-written narrative. Clive Fisher's prose is redolent of the period which it describes and, despite the occasional majestic longueur, it maintains a broad and persuasive momentum. Cyril Connolly could not have been better served. Possibly he would have liked to have written it himself. But of course he would never have had the energy.

30 March 1995

104

Auden
Richard Davenport-Hines

Wystan and Chester
Thekla Clark

As I Walked Out One Evening: Songs . . . and other light verse
W. H. Auden
Edited by Edward Mendelson

He called himself 'Mother' and gave homage only to 'Miss God' and 'Miss History', the two female deities with whom he felt most at home. He was a homosexual who firmly disapproved of homosexuality, and a lyric poet who once told a frustrated admirer that 'If you want romance, fuck a journalist.' He was dishevelled to the point of being almost dirty, a heavy drinker and a chain smoker. He was, in the language of his period, absolute bliss.

Certainly it was bliss to be born in the first decade of the twentieth century, when anything and everything seemed about to happen. If Richard Davenport-Hines's latest biography is as much a history of ideas as of people, that is because it remains true to those decades of hope and despair which Auden commemorated in his occasionally didactic verse. In his introduction Mr Davenport-Hines denounces the usual biographical mélange of gossip, scandal and 'sexual tale-telling'. He is not one of those writers who rushes into the bedroom, and the closet, at every available opportunity; as a result his portrayal of Auden is sometimes a trifle dry, but always alert and convincing.

Auden believed himself to have been an autistic child, immured in visions of ice and limestone, and he really first came to life at Oxford. He was hardly an undergraduate at all but, rather, a force of nature and/or culture. He had an extraordinary exuberance, described by Cecil Day-Lewis as 'vitality' and by Stephen Spender as 'overwhelming cleverness'. When you combine these qualities with ambition, and a fair helping of luck, you have the makings of a great writer. It is often said that he looked old, even in middle age, because he had burnt himself out; he had been fuelled for too long by red wine and benzedrine. But there was, at the beginning, an energy which was so bright that it eclipsed all of his contemporaries.

His contemporaries did not always enjoy the experience, of course, and there were occasions when his self-confidence lapsed into dogmatism and an almost wilful lack of interest in other people. When 'Mother' pronounced (his own mother, by the way, was a singularly tough and snobbish old party), the children were obliged to listen. He never stopped entertaining opinions of assorted kinds; they were generally absurd and contradictory, but that did not matter. As Thekla Clark explains in one of the many astute observations within her charming memoir, he often said things because he liked the sound of them. He enjoyed creating sentences which, like poetry, admitted no response; he relished the air of authority, even when he had nothing whatever to say.

But they have a larger context. It has been said that a genius is one who lives in symbolic relation to the age, and there is no doubt that, in Auden's successive espousals of Communism, Freudianism and Christian existentialism he gave voice to the most significant concerns of his century. His famous, and for a while notorious, removal to the United States could also be seen as an emblem of what he once called 'the following wind of history'.

Chester Kallman was, perhaps, the tiniest puff of it. They met soon after Auden's arrival in America, and Kallman rapidly became both muse and monster. If he had not existed, the combined resources of Ronald Firbank and Tennessee Williams could not have invented him. He first encountered Auden at a poetry reading in New York, and from the front row hissed 'Miss *Mess*'. Those were the days when it was a pleasure, rather than a painful duty, to be homosexual. Auden in turn opened the door upon Kallman on a subsequent visit, and announced that 'It's the wrong blond.' Eventually their relationship turned into an *opéra bouffe* of the most debilitating, if diverting, kind. 'Auden at moments of stress had used book reviewing as a public commentary on their relationship,' Davenport-Hines writes at one point, 'and Kallman used his position in 1945–6 as operatic columnist of *Commonweal* to retaliate.' The liberty of the press had not been abused so much since the days of William Randolph Hearst.

Auden could, indeed, be very playful. He often said that he always felt the youngest person in the room, even when he was in the company of teenagers, and indeed he often behaved as if he was. This is in part related to the infantilism which seems necessarily an aspect of the greatest poets who do, at moments of crisis or high spirits, act like big but not always beautiful babies. But that condition (if one may use a medical word) is also an aspect of Auden's use of language. In some of his most wonderful poetry the syllables seem to issue from him without any private or self-conscious control – on those occasions the English tradition, with all the formality of its inheritance, speaks through him. That is why Edward Mendelson's collection of Auden's 'light verse' is filled with the ballads, nursery songs and lullabies which could have been sung in eighteenth-century theatres or pleasure gardens.

There is a passage in 'The Poet and the City', quoted by Thekla Clark, where Auden writes of 'the right to play' and 'the right to frivolity'. In fact it is possible that his playfulness, and his sense of humour, were his most important gifts. He never took himself too seriously – he was far too great a writer to do that – and, as a result, his work can be very serious indeed. That is why it is no good lamenting the outward conditions of his life. However depressing or disordered they might seem, they were the necessary conditions for the expression of his genius. In this context it is worth noting Davenport-Hines's remark that 'The private life of a poet is ... the lesser part of his existence.' Auden knew as much, too, and during one particularly uncomfortable and messy period a friend recalls him intoning 'an utterly idiosyncratic, absurdly eccentric version of "count your blessings".' He *had* counted them. They were his collected works.

19 October 1995

105

The Life of Samuel Taylor Coleridge
Rosemary Ashton

'Never saw his likeness,' Charles Lamb wrote of Samuel Taylor Coleridge, 'nor probably the world can see again.' They had met at Christ's Hospital. No doubt Coleridge wore the blue coat with a difference, since his ebullient and elusive character had been largely formed. He was already a great talker and a voracious reader, with the gift of enthralling all those whom he encountered. It is not necessary to expatiate on the delights and difficulties of his childhood, therefore, since they remain present throughout the rest of his life. It is best to encounter him in full flood.

His career at Cambridge, and his brief role as an enlisted soldier under the name of Silas Tomkyn Comberbache, are well enough known. He was discharged as 'insane', and in that sense he was already the perfect young man. He was so in love with his feelings that he was able effortlessly to parody them, perpetually tumbling between laughter and despair as if he were not at all sure of his own destiny. Much more than Byron or Shelley, in fact, he is the poet of adolescence; despite what might be called his pantheistic Unitarianism, he saw nothing in the wide universe except the trembling of his own sensitivity. Only Wordsworth was more self-obsessed. And then, at twenty-two, as Rosemary Ashton writes in this detailed biography, 'Coleridge comes of age as a poet.'

He came of age as a talker, too, and it is not surprising that some of his best poetry takes the form of heightened conversation. But talk can also be a kind of oral fixation. What Coleridge himself once described as the 'sucking child', and the bibulousness of infantilism is present in his achievements as well as in his addictions. On one side are the Conversation Pieces, and on the other the intense and insistent verse of 'Kubla Khan' or 'The Ancient Mariner'. It is also the difference between the drink and the opium which he imbibed constantly.

He was so busy becoming addicted to literature and life, in fact, that he could never settle to anything. He veered between Jacobinism and Unitarianism, Pantisocratic enterprises and provincial lecturing. He took up poetry, criticism, philosophy and journalism only to abandon them. It is very surprising that he actually managed to marry, but the omens were not good when he named his first child Hartley, after the philosopher of sensationalism. His poor family were forced to follow the caravan of his own divagatory and desultory nature until, that is, he decided that he ought to travel alone. He was in Germany, and then in Malta; he was always the searcher, although it is never clear what precisely he was searching for.

He was not meant to be a husband or a father. He was too vague and too undependable for anything but brief and ecstatic friendships. The fervid cycle of rapture and eventual disenchantment is seen to its strongest effect, of course, in his relationship with Wordsworth.

Wordsworth was for a while infatuated by Coleridge's loquacity and knowledge, while Coleridge was mightily impressed by the other poet's understanding. It could have been a fine match if Coleridge had remained in London, where the rapid beat of the city matched his own tumultuous sensitivity, but to be alone with Wordsworth in the country was a mistake. He was so oppressed by the other poet's genius that he quite forgot about his own. He came to think of himself as a 'metaphysician' rather than as a poet. He never possessed that solid, self-sustaining vision upon which Wordsworth could draw. Coleridge was too quick, and he knew too much. He was too clever to be a poet, and too imaginative to be a metaphysician. So, like Muhammad's tomb, he was suspended between two worlds. And what, then, was the result? Thirty years of apprenticeship, as Rosemary Ashton sees it, with the next thirty as 'his years of wandering'.

This is in many respects a detached and restrained biography; it does not have the imaginative fervour, for example, of Richard Holmes's wonderful *Coleridge: Early Visions*. But it is described as a critical biography and, since Rosemary Ashton has written previously on Lewes and on Eliot, she is thoroughly conversant with those pulses of German idealism which animated Coleridge and which briefly stirred the English critical spirit. But she is a very astute observer of Coleridge's life. She is also, on occasions, objective to the point of being censorious. Of course it is not hard to be unsympathetic about various aspects of his behaviour, not least in his treatment of those closest to him, and yet perhaps it is necessary to be half in love with him in order properly to understand him.

Certain people seem born to be the object of other people's gossip and pity, and it could be said that Coleridge was created by the needs of others as well as by his own. He was always there, for contemporaries of lesser genius, to criticize, to direct and attempt to control. With his inordinate desire to please and to entertain, he pretended to capitulate. In the end he always managed to escape, while making an almost pantomimic show of self-doubt and self-criticism. Yet perhaps the expectations of others were quite wrong. His letters and notebooks are wonderful, and there is a sense in which his unfinished works form a greater achievement than that of any of his contemporaries. We must think of a writer who is perhaps at his best when he remains incomplete; his genius and imagination are so restless that they can only be brought into play momentarily. Richard Holmes put it well when he described one of Coleridge's most haunting images as 'a protean form or a force-field, lacking fixed structure or outline'.

This is also the shape of Coleridge's genius. He had too fine and sensitive an imagination to dwell on any perception for too long. He adapted brilliantly to whomever he accompanied. He spoke without limits or distinctions. He followed the glow-worm of an idea until it burst into flames above his head. Just as his poems thwart any real attempt at narrative, so his life and career seem plangent, incantatory, insistent but without any formal resolution. Yet it is the mark of his greatness that the reader does not want Rosemary Ashton's book to end. He was a Socrates in the wrong civilization, a Hamlet in the right one, a man whose universal genius made him prodigal of his own.

25 January 1996

106

Bernard Shaw: The Ascent of the Superman
Sally Peters

In this intriguing study, part biography and part sexual case history, Sally Peters has the courage to take Bernard Shaw seriously. In one of those 'Maxims for Revolutionists' which preface *Man and Superman*, Shaw declared that 'The unconscious self is the true genius.' In this spirit Sally Peters tries to isolate and to examine those emotions or situations of which Shaw himself might not have been aware. It is as if she were trying to bring into clear focus the invisible man who accompanied him on his great journey, but whom the artist himself refused to recognize. She also goes on to suggest that this invisible man may even have been homosexual but the point is, perhaps, debatable. Hers is in any case a dangerous and speculative venture, as any textual scholar will tell you (if he has time to life his nose from the page), but it is not without its rewards. It is possible that some writers are great precisely because they cannot, or will not, understand where the sources of their greatness lie.

The curious arrangements of Shaw's family and household during his childhood, for example, seem to have left him with the fantasy or desire of being 'a foundling'; indeed, like many great artists who manage to project some impression of their personality to the public, he was largely if not wholly self-created. In flight from his own family, he established an intimate if imaginary alternative household which included Shakespeare, Goethe and Mozart. He bartered the security of mundane and familial ties, according to this account, for the more precarious but permanent bonds of cultural inheritance.

Sally Peters is very good on the symbolic detail of that life which he preferred to forget. At the age of sixteen he became a Dublin clerk, for example, and intermittently dreamed of the office for much of his life. Even the most tatty business premises can be the arena for tyranny and cowardice, and Shaw's continuing horror at his temporary confinement is a sure sign that the carapace of the successful artist in his case concealed a more frightened and awkward creature. He was so afraid of life, in fact, that he decided to dominate it. He controlled the chaos of the world by simply treating it as the material for his art; if he moved fast or far enough, no one would ever catch him. On looking back at this 'destiny', he claimed that 'like Goethe, I knew all along'; but he could not have been so certain at the time.

Eventually he moved from Dublin to London, so that he might be able to recreate himself in every sense. The process of self-dramatization began when he started to write musical criticism under an assumed name; when not scribbling down articles in the Reading Room of the British Museum he spent his time, like any late Romantic, in studying Marx and Wagner. He also began to read books of etiquette, but the drawing room was not his natural habitat. He was so aware of his own talent, and so frightened of its being overlooked or rebuffed, that he shunned social life. He preferred to lecture in under-heated halls, or make speeches on street corners.

He wasted a great deal of time as a journalist as well (he even descended to book reviewing) but the years under the dome of the Reading Room were helpful in one sense. He was biding his time, waiting for the right instinctive moment to strike, sharpening his imagination so that it would effortlessly impale the public. A sense of occasion is necessary for genius, of course, but Shaw also possessed those two other attributes which are essential for its proper growth; he named them himself, accurately, as 'irrepressible gaiety' and 'a prodigious fund of vital energy'. No writer should attempt to take on the world without them.

There are times when Sally Peters's fondness for psychological jargon affects her prose, but she is generally very good at describing the energetic vagaries of Shaw's ambition. His was an energy of the mind, however, and not of the body. Shaw's attitudes towards vegetarianism and alcohol, let alone his health in general, are in that sense highly significant – rooted, as they were, in his deep sense of personal threat and his disgust at the physicality of his own body. So he learned to conquer life by etherealizing it and turning it into play while at the same time he conducted all of his affairs, both social and romantic, as a form of drama.

In fact, like other artists who live in fear or distrust of physical being, he lived off words. In his various, and always theoretical, love affairs he sighed words and he cried them. In the ordinary world he was a very lean man dressed in a yellow Jaeger suit; in his letters he was a demon, a god, and a Casanova. The amorous correspondence between Shaw and Ellen Terry must constitute the longest epistolary novel since *Pamela*. He managed the same trick with his drama since, by writing essays and 'maxims' around it, he was able to fashion the very climate of opinion by which he wished to be judged. He did not only create plays, he created his critics. 'Art,' as Sally Peters puts it, 'was a way to live on the earth while transcending it.'

So he remained in all respects manipulative and apart. Was it Oscar Wilde who said that Shaw had not an enemy in the world but that none of his friends liked him? He was delicate and fastidious, shying away from any touch of flesh and hiding his fear or guilt in that mist of words which followed him everywhere. Sally Peters detects within him not so much a fear of the feminine as a fear of femininity, especially his own. In fact one of the central arguments of this study is that Shaw was a latent or at least non-practising homosexual; certainly, in the Jaeger suit, he would have made an impractical one. He might possibly be placed somewhere upon what is already a very long list, but the importance of such a position is a matter for debate. Not everyone is wholly convinced by what Sally Peters calls 'current gay theorists'.

Her book is in fact most interesting on Shaw's early career and, since it is concerned with his 'ascent', it is not particularly surprising that she should devote less than thirty pages to his last fifty years. Yet there may be a larger point to be made. Shaw ceased to be wholly interesting when he had successfully created the persona which was to guide him through the rest of his life. His struggle was more significant than his victory, because in the process he found a vision of the world. Or perhaps it found him. 'This is the true joy in life,' as he said, 'the being used for a purpose recognized by yourself as a mighty one.'

25 April 1996

107

Eden Renewed: The Public and Private Life of John Milton

Peter Levi

Milton was already learned as a child; he pored over his books late into the night, in the very heart of London, inaugurating what would become a life of labour and of discipline. At Cambridge he was known as 'The Lady' because of his delicate features and refined manners. But his contemporaries missed the hardness within him. He was as ambitious as he was resolute, and had determined from an early age that he would be a great poet. He wrote Latin verses because he wished to acquire a European reputation; he wrote English poetry because he wanted to be a British Virgil.

His first years in Cambridge and in London were spent in the quiet pursuit of learning. He read history and philosophy and seems to have indulged in that antiquarian passion which is inseparable from the English genius. That is why Peter Levi properly reminds us that he wished to write an epic upon King Arthur before he ever thought of *Paradise Lost*. He managed to escape taking holy orders and, although he thought of entering an Inn of Court (the most respectable path for an educated Londoner), he still retained only one true ambition. 'What am I thinking about?' he wrote to one friend. 'Immortality, so help me God.'

The origins of Milton's political affiliations are not easy to grasp, but Peter Levi believes that he succumbed to a fit of 'creeping Puritanism' in the 1630s. He might seem an unlikely representative of that cause steeped as he was in classical learning and classical literature, the writer of masque and the lover of music. It may have been self-belief that turned him into a dissenter, however; he sensed

283

that the Spirit worked within him, both as poet and theologian, and he needed no other assistance to interpret Scripture. The rest of his private creed derives from this. Yet the richness of his buried nature – one might almost say, his Catholic nature – emerges in the powerful cadences of his prose no less than in the melodic harmonies of his poetry.

Peter Levi is a voluble and confiding, even a chatty, biographer; he is not elegant, but he is enthusiastic. He has, of course, been Professor of Poetry at Oxford, and so devotes much space to a critical reading of Milton's verse. He is particularly sensitive to its music, a quality which was largely forgotten by those critics such as Eliot and Leavis who believed that *Paradise Lost* formed some great wall in English poetry through which no one could break. It was not Milton who contorted the language into strange shapes – there is a very good case for saying that the King James Bible performed that particular feat. But Levi is also erudite enough to follow the poet's classical allusions to their source; he is one of the few modern biographers who can make his own translations from the Latin and the Greek.

There is always a place for criticism in any literary biography – not because in any vulgar or simplistic sense an author's work 'reflects' the events and passions of their life but, rather, because the form and cadence of the work represent their very bearing and tenor in the world. That is wholly true of Milton himself. In his late twenties he journeyed to Italy as 'a citizen of the world', in Levi's words; he travelled as a gentleman, with one servant, and was greeted as a poet and scholar. He claimed later that he returned to England after hearing news of civil unrest, yet at first he simply reverted to his old concern for the epic and for fame. He did begin writing pamphlets against episcopacy, but his prose is always that of a poet; it is bedecked with imagery, striated with metaphor, and generally controlled by a powerful cadence.

Milton also had a wonderful talent for abuse and, in his tirades against his opponents, can join the rank of those other London visionaries, William Blake and Thomas More, who also combined a strong religious consciousness with the language of a Billingsgate fishwife. Levi suggests that he wasted his time writing religious tracts, but it would not have seemed so to Milton at the time. Religious controversy was taken very seriously indeed, and books of that nature sold far better than anything of a secular cast.

Yet it is difficult to understand why Milton postponed his career as a poet and took up polemical prose; it may simply be that he wanted to acquire influence and recognition before it was too late. Certainly he was rewarded for his efforts by becoming Secretary for Foreign Tongues to Cromwell and his Council, although Levi goes too far when he describes Milton's position as 'something lower than a hack'. He believed that the republican cause represented 'piety to my country', and it is quite likely that his antiquarian passion helped to elevate his role as propagandist for the republican cause. Antiquarians were once, characteristically, radicals.

On the return of Charles II Milton's books were burned by the public hangman but he, miraculously, escaped death. No one is quite sure how he avoided the penalty which was inflicted upon many less culpable than himself – he had, after all, been an enthusiastic apologist for the regicides and had mocked the dead king – but Levi suggests that it might have been at the behest of the newly restored monarch. But even though he escaped death, he could not avoid suffering. He had already gone blind, and his condition was generally interpreted as God's salutary lesson. He was cordially detested by his daughters, who considered him to be a tyrant and possibly also a bore.

So he retired to a quiet part of the city with his third wife, among sympathetic dissenters, and undertook the real work of his life. Levi has a good image of Milton 'entering a state of trance' before writing *Paradise Lost*. This biography also gives a fitting description of the poem itself as the work of a blind man, employing 'the original oral technique of epic poetry' and thus rediscovering 'some of the freshness of ancient epic'. Yet how much it also resembles the poet's permanent nature in its wilfulness, its energy, its persistence through difficulties and its elaborately controlled interior music.

At the end of his life he was visited by the learned, and scorned by the partisan as a 'dead dog' and a 'canker worm'. He himself told his wife that 'my aim is to live and die an honest man'. It is likely that he succeeded in that ambition, although the years of pamphleteering between the composition of poetry have often been considered ill-judged and self-defeating. Samuel Johnson once wrote of Milton's last great work, *Samson Agonistes*, that 'the intermediate parts have neither cause nor consequence'. Perhaps the same might be said of Milton's own variegated, unhappy, but ultimately triumphant, career.

18 July 1996

108

Lights Out for the Territory
Iain Sinclair

Recent work in cosmology and quantum physics seems to suggest that the 'flow' of time and causation do not really exist – that it is possible, for example, for events of the 'future' to determine the 'past'. Those of an imaginative disposition have known this for some years, of course, and Iain Sinclair is one of the leading exponents of what might be called the quantum novel. *Lights Out for the Territory* is not a work of fiction, however, but an act of imagination.

It is a book about London; it is, in other words, a book about everything. The London essay has a long history, encompassing Washington Irving and Charles Lamb, but in the hands of Sinclair it also becomes a form of urban necromancy. There are times when he resembles a revenant walking the streets of an ancient city, looking for runes or grimoires, but there are occasions when he also seems to exist in some unimaginable future when strange territorial configurations or patterns of energy shape the character and destiny of the city dwellers.

There are essays here on the clouds above the capital and on Rachel Whiteread's *House*, on London cinematography and London Gothic, on dogs and graffiti, on graveyards such as Bunhill Fields and the extraordinary Abney Park Cemetery off Stoke Newington Church Street which seem to harbour all the mystery and bleakness of the city. Both of the latter are resting places for dissenters, and London has always had a history of spiritual radicalism; the heady atmosphere around the graves, therefore, is all the city's own.

Sinclair sets out to walk the bounds, as it were, and in the process to trace the sacred paths of a city which has for many hundreds of years been suspected of containing 'occult lines of geometry'. His first journey is down the fateful Kingsland Road, a voyage worthy of the pen of Conrad himself; Sinclair walks along this avenue of boarded shops and 'squats' and cheap cafés, yet from it he derives such energy that his prose rises up in celebration.

These are all essays in praise of walking, and in praise of that mood of aimlessness and excitement which the streets of London seem to create – 'drifting purposefully' as Sinclair puts it, at those moments when the alignment of buildings or the pattern of courtyards and alleys leads the walker ineluctably forward. The pedestrian then mimics the movement of time in the city itself. There are parts of London, in Sinclair's book, where time even may be said to have come to an end. There is a wonderful study here of Charlton House, for example, which is set beside the holy place of Horn Fair Field; it has forms of obelisks and demons on its staircase and, in the White Room upstairs, there is an allegorical study of *The Triumph of Death*. This ancient house should surely become a site of pilgrimage.

That is why Sinclair's prose is that of a poet, each phrase charged like an incantation, but it is also the prose of a Londoner finding his inheritance. It is, after all, a city of books. Each chapter of this survey has its own bibliography, as if he were walking through pages as well as streets. The great aim of his prose is not to discover or to describe, but to recollect; it is a dialogue with the dead in which only one can speak. His understanding of place is a refraction of all the memories associated with it and there are times when, like Huysmans, he sees the capital primarily as the invention of other writers.

He comes across the London Psychogeographical Association, which advertises its 'Thirty-Five Years of Non-Existence'; he roams the streets for evidence of the marvellous Mr Blake and sometimes treats London as some second Atlantis only recently recovered from the water which provides its own 'theatre of obelisks and pyramids, signs, symbols, prompts, whispers. The lovely lies that take you out into the light. That bless each and every pilgrimage.' As a stylist he is incomparable; he is the De Quincey of contemporary English letters, scathing and sometimes savage, fierce and even contemptuous, but always with an exultant humour that might belong to some classical masked actor.

Some of his themes are familiar. The interest in gangland 'villains' goes further back than Colin MacInnes to Defoe and Ned Ward's *London Spy*, but Sinclair's account of Ronald Kray's funeral invokes primeval fears only to mingle them with the farce of that dead man's Easter parade. It is a wonderful performance by Sinclair, deliberately histrionic and yet desperately plausible like some frantic tale shouted out by a crazed pedestrian. Who else would place Frankie Fraser's autobiography, *Mad Frank*, beside Robert Graves's *The White Goddess*?

Londoners have always admired, or been fascinated by, criminals because they represent an alternative source of power – power other than that of the commercial and political 'establishment' that has turned London into such a dark city. The luminaries of London are always trying to find a way of confronting that darkness on their own terms; hence the perennial interest in occultism or antiquarianism which, in the capital, have generally been connected. The names of Dee, of Tradescant, of Ashmole, and of Fludd resound throughout this Baedeker of London's haunted past.

There are occasions, however, when Sinclair's own interest in such matters threatens to overburden his narrative journeys with too much significance. He is like some golden dustman sifting the heaps of St Pancras for ever more relics or ruins, and thereby he runs the danger of being caught in the ashes; his essays then become so fraught with coincidences and correspondences and connections that the reader may find it difficult to follow the author's thread into the centre of the London labyrinth.

He also has an unnerving habit of turning his friends or acquaintances into fictional creatures, but then all great fabulists will wish to extend their range to the living as well as to the dead. And that is indeed Sinclair's project, creating out of the world of time a city that has a manifold and perpetual presence. The mysterious photographs of Marc Atkins complete the process.

9 January 1997

109

The Origins of English Nonsense
Noel Malcolm

There are forgotten areas, and secret histories, within the literature of this country. The music hall songs of the late nineteenth century are as interesting as the poetry of Lionel Johnson or Ernest Dowson, for example, but they are not to be found in any critical survey of the period. Now Noel Malcolm has discovered another unfortunate omission; in this most scholarly and original study, he has discovered the first stirrings of English nonsense. Everyone knows about Lear's 'Jumblies' and Carroll's 'Jabberwocky' but who now remembers the inspired persiflage of the 'water-poet', John Taylor, who in the early seventeenth century could out-Shakespeare Shakespeare with such inspiring lines as 'From out the heels of squeamish magnitude' and 'Then smooth thy brow with milk-white discontent'?

It is magnificent, but is it poetry? Mr Malcolm makes a persuasive case on its behalf and in fact reveals its place within a formidable and highly respectable literary tradition. But although its origin may lie in German macaronics or Rabelaisian neologisms, English nonsense has a life and spirit all its own. It was one aspect of that great exuberance or explosion of language which marked the late sixteenth and early seventeenth centuries; it gilded Lilly and undid Donne with conceits both quizzical and metaphysical. The latter half of Malcolm's book provides an anthology of the best, with lines such as 'Oh that my Lungs could bleat like butter'd pease' or 'Mount meekly low, on blew presumptuous wings'.

A case could in fact be made for nonsense as an intrinsic part of the English genius. It is related to that heterogeneity within a literature where matters oratorical, poetical and farcical can all be fastened together. Dickens called it the 'streaky-bacon' effect, and Noel Malcolm a 'category mistake', but it is the same thing.

It is the humour found in the mock disputations of the sixteenth-century Inns of Court, as Malcolm sugests, and it is also the humour to be found in More's *Utopia*. But it is also the mainspring of theatrical farce, and represents the spirit of the London streets when even in recent memory children could be heard chanting 'Sam Sam, dirty old man, washed his face in a frying pan'. It is the comedy of medley and drollery, which has no proper written history.

That is why the writers covered in this meticulous volume are now quite unknown to name and fame. All that does not aspire to 'high' art tends to disappear from view, even though the more popular or 'low' material may contain the most vital forces within the culture. Indeed Malcolm tentatively suggests that the more serious, or at least established, poets of the seventeenth century learnt something from the 'water-poet' and his colleagues. This movement from 'low' to 'high' is another very interesting feature of English culture but, again, it has yet to be thoroughly investigated.

Yet nonsense can also be plain fun, and the verses which Malcolm celebrates were part of a culture already replete with mock love-songs, mock-recipes, mock-heroics and mock-encomia. In a formalized and ritualized society, such parodic inversions or diversions can be a source of endless pleasure. But why should nonsense not be pursued for its own sake? It is a form of liberation from orthodoxy, of course; and although it is indeed part of a tradition, it still encouraged inventiveness of the most private kind. That is why its most vigorous exponent was a 'water-man', member of a 'low' trade renowned for bad manners and filthy language while rowing their unfortunate passengers across the Thames. His success as a nonsense-poet may well be related to the wealth of dirty slang or sexual demotic all around him, but fundamentally it was just another way of being heard. In a later century he might have been seen upon the boards, engaged in what was called 'energetic vocalizing'.

Is it also possible that the crudity of the Thames somehow infiltrates apparently harmless and sexless nonsense? It would certainly be easy to create a lubricious subtext from such phrases as 'a Glister to the Torrid Zones' or 'Reach my fierce flye-flap', and Freud might have been surprisingly right in claiming that 'comic nonsense' was related to infantile sexuality. But Malcolm's impeccable scholarship does not allow him to explore such speculations; he dismisses the notion of dreams, or folk-festivity, or madness, as a fertile source of nonsense. Instead he makes the very interesting point that these writers were engaged 'in a highly self-conscious stylistic game'. This is certainly the context in which we might place such later works of nonsense as James Joyce's *Finnegans Wake*.

It cannot be said that all nonsense verse is of a uniformly high standard. The lines of Taylor or 'Anon' should be read sparingly and at short intervals. Otherwise the reader becomes dazed by inconsequence and smothered in trifles. But, at its best, it is delightful. The parodies of Marlowe's bombast and the 'inkhorn' terms of seventeenth-century academics, for example, are very delicious.

The *Origins of English Nonsense* is a work of some wit, and itself tends towards parody of the more solemn critical studies. Malcolm's book has all the elaborate paraphernalia of scholarship, complete with learned footnotes and a lengthy bibliography designed to promote the cause of nonsense. This book is as rare, then, as hedgehog's feathers or baskets of water.

24 April 1997

IIO

Hogarth
Jenny Uglow

Hogarth and His Times
David Bindman

William Hogarth was forged in the very crucible of London. His infant world comprised a great hospital and an even greater prison, the roar of Bartholomew Fair as well as the bellows of the shambles. When Jenny Uglow writes of this 'brash artist from Smithfield' who became 'the votary of an ideal' she is charting the progress of a true Cockney genius.

The sorrows of the city were never far from him, even in childhood. His father was arrested for debt and imprisoned in the Fleet, and it seems likely that this early catastrophe sent Hogarth raging into the world. At the age of sixteen he moved to Leicester Fields as an engraver's apprentice, but he had already found the landscape of his imagination.

Almost at once he began to characterize and caricature the life in the streets around him, and his first commercial engravings testify to his urban spirit as well as his own particular vision; they are pugnacious, opportunistic and caustic but they are also satires upon the forms of modish fashion and facile cosmopolitanism which ignore genius closer to home.

So he was trying to assert his own worth; he was an artist who combined energy with ambition, and who promoted himself with as much skill as he caricatured others. He always seized the main chance, and the cash which came with it; he was truly inspired.

It was perhaps inevitable that his work as a painter began with the theatre – he depicted *The Beggar's Opera* six times and in the process conceived a style both dramatic and graceful, expressive in detail and dynamic in general movement. In fact very soon his reputation as a painter (and particularly as a portraitist) equalled his fame as a caricaturist; but no one form could hold him for very long.

David Bindman, in his essay, emphasizes the energetic and varie-gated career which Hogarth enjoyed, making the just and significant point that in his lifetime there was no institutional structure within which art or the artist might be confined; Hogarth's 'different and sometimes contradictory *personae*' were therefore reflected in work that itself embodies all the contradictions of a city where the extremes of the human condition meet, solemn and farcical, tender and pantomimic. Of course he was derided by the more obtuse critics, but Charles Lamb saw the point when he associated Hogarth with Shakespeare and Chaucer; we in turn may mention Dickens and Defoe.

At the age of thirty-four he had, as Jenny Uglow puts it, 'become news'. Good art is news that stays news, to paraphrase Ezra Pound, and Uglow's voluminous and colourful account emphasizes the extent to which Hogarth combined the most detailed realism with moral and even spiritual intent; the events and the people of the day can be immediately recognized, in streets which were hauntingly familiar to his contemporaries, and yet they are also the emblems of a self-conscious and strikingly elaborate art. Hogarth was created by the city, but in turn he brought it back to life. *A Rake's Progress* and *A Harlot's Progress* are the prime materials for any mythology of London.

That is why Uglow's biography is suffused with local and historical detail; she depicts the city at close hand, almost as if she herself has been wandering through Hogarth's engravings. The real life of the period – drunken, violent, riotous – is thereby revealed in scenes which show the world both as carnival and as prison. On the print *Cruelty in Perfection*, Uglow notes that the affair takes place in Thavies Inn, and she describes the posters for cock-fighting and wrestling plastered upon the decaying walls. She also mentions the fact that one of the fighters thus advertised had in fact been hanged two weeks before the print was published. That is the kind of detail needed in any account of Hogarth.

There is also a certain nervous fever, or delirium, which seems to follow in the wake of the artist's own progress. He was short, energetic, impatient, and always brightly dressed. In some respects he was the quintessential Londoner – irreverent, pugnacious, opportunistic and publicity mad. He was assertive but easily wounded, irritable and insecure. He was also, as Uglow puts it, 'quick off the mark, taking set-backs as a spur'.

This was nowhere more evident than in his financial dealings and, as a contemporary somewhat caustically put it, he managed 'to be well paid beyond most others of the same profession'. He decided to distribute his own prints, for example, thus neatly cutting out the 'middle man' with as much skill as he caught hold of the fashions and fascinations of the moment.

Yet all the time he had ambitions grander than that of obtaining public favour. He became the champion of a specifically national art, and saw himself as an artist who could create work greater than that of the Italian masters. He was, fortunately, also very practical. He was instrumental in passing a copyright act, and he established an academy supposed to foster an 'English school' of history painting.

But he, of all people, could never have followed any academic line. He would never be 'told' what to do, as Uglow emphasizes, and he remained defiantly unorthodox until the end. All his life he moved between disorder and order, in every sense contrasting English 'freedom' with Continental formality; it is a preoccupation found in his wonderful theoretical essay, *Analysis of Beauty*, which celebrates the Englishness of English art two centuries before Pevsner.

Yet perhaps it is instructive to turn back to his birthplace. The tradespeople and shopkeepers of Smithfield are, even to this day, more acerbic and assertive than their counterparts elsewhere in London – principally because they are surrounded by the meat of slaughtered animals. It is this very local flavour, with its universal implications, which Hogarth himself understood and represented. This 'gross, uncultivated man', as one contemporary put it, was also a great visionary.

4 September 1997

III

Isaac Newton: The Last Sorcerer
Michael White

The apple did not fall. Isaac Newton invented that happy story in order to conceal the fact that his theory of gravitation was the direct result of alchemical experiment; he was the 'last sorcerer' who believed that the secret knowledge of the ancients could be recovered by reading occult texts and, according to his latest biographer, by practising the blacker arts of magic.

He came from a family of Lincolnshire yeomen, born without a father (who had died a few weeks before) on Christmas Day. Newton himself often emphasized the miraculous aspect of his origin; if in later life he was treated by his contemporaries as a 'demigod', in the words of Michael White, he was receiving the only appropriate compliment. His family seems to have been practically illiterate, but the young Newton was enrolled at the King's School in Grantham. He lived above an apothecary's shop, devoured religious pamphlets, and constructed elaborate models of windmills and sundials; it is perhaps suggestive that he never studied mathematics before he arrived at Cambridge, but White suggests that at this juncture he discovered 'the principles of hard work and dedication to learning'. He was also something of a prig, with misanthropic tendencies; he first distinguished himself at university by becoming a part-time moneylender.

But his self-imposed isolation encouraged the kind of mental solitude which can manage great leaps of speculation. He almost blinded himself by staring at the sun, and conducted optical experiments by inserting a knife or bodkin behind his eyeball. The laws of analytical geometry lay hid in night, until Newton said 'Let calculus be' and all was light. At the age of twenty-six he was appointed as Professor of Mathematics but, even as he began his great career, he was immersed in less orthodox experiments; as White puts it, the Cambridge professor had also become 'the last wonder-child of the Magi'. He believed alchemy to be the grand unifying principle of creation or, in other words, that 'theory of everything' still pursued by contemporary physicists and cosmologists. He set up a furnace in his rooms at Cambridge, and entered what was known as the 'Invisible College' of adepts which was eventually transmuted into the Royal Society.

Thus did alchemy enter the modern world and Michael White suggests that earlier triumphs of magical experiment, the telescope and gunpowder, were quite outmatched by Newton's achievements in the sphere of the occult. He credits him with creating the conditions for the Industrial Revolution, and suggests that his lunar calculations were 'at the heart of the computer programs employed by Nasa scientists'. So the great magician set people to work and then sent them into space.

This is an informative and genuinely interesting biography, despite Michael White's propensity for journalese and his occasional obeisance to the wonderful modern mind – as if somehow we know more than those who came before us. We do not know more; we simply know different things. What is more striking, however, is the portrait of Newton which emerges in the course of this narrative. He was secretive and hypochondriacal; he was afflicted by paranoia and what White calls 'almost demented self-motivation'; he was obsessed by the colour of crimson and believed that the Universe was, in a real sense, the body of Jesus Christ.

He was, in other words, possessed by a powerful genius. He worked in silence and isolation, broken only by ferocious arguments with scientific colleagues. Then came the great triumph. In an intriguing passage, White recounts the nights when Newton watched with wonder as a comet traversed the heavens; as he observed this bright form, he meditated upon the still occult notion of secret attraction or repulsion at a distance. Alchemy blended with the night sky to produce the great theory of gravitation. Gravity became his 'Universal Spirit', and he expounded its majesty in *Principia Mathematica*. He worked upon the project continually, scarcely bothering to eat or sleep. It is perhaps not surprising that he suffered a temporary spell of madness before re-entering the world.

White describes Newton as one of the twin pillars of the 'Age of Reason', together with his friend Locke, and it was perhaps inevitable that he felt drawn to a setting larger than that of his laboratory. The moneylender became a money-maker. He was appointed Warden of the Royal Mint and, in that capacity, brought to the manufacture of coin all the precision and thoroughness of his experimental work; the sorcerer triumphed again, by creating the 'scientific economy' which still exists. In turn he became the prosecutor of anyone who defied his inexorable laws, dispatching to the gallows all those who clipped or counterfeited the currency. He became, as it were, the master of ceremonies for the first capitalist state. Knowledge truly was power.

At the end of his life he declared that he would like to have 'another touch at metals', but his work was done. It was perhaps in that spirit that he refused to be given the last rites; he remained self-sufficient to the grave. He said that all his life he had been 'only like a boy, playing on the sea shore' while beyond him, undiscovered, lay 'the great ocean of truth'. But Newton was being unusually modest; he had, after all, recreated that truth in his own image.

16 October 1997

112

The Genius of Shakespeare
Jonathan Bate

Shakespeare's Sonnets
Edited by Katherine Duncan-Jones

The fact that Jonathan Bate's exemplary account of Shakespeare owes as much to quantum theory as to Edmund Kean is testimony to the true genius of his subject; the illustrious dramatist was both lightning and quicksilver, with so fluid a personality that he changed himself as often as he changed the world and with so mobile a wit that it accommodates itself to every age and every country.

Every age and every country also knows the story. William Shakespeare was the product of a county grammar school, where he was the scholar most attentive to the arts of paraphrase and rhetorical elaboration. At the beginning of his career he was ridiculed by university hacks, until he found a patron and began to out-Latin the Latinizers with poems such as *Venus and Adonis*. Then, in Bate's words, 'he invented the *profession* of dramatist' in order to gain secure command of a company of actors.

He was a man of great fluency, in every sense, able both to take advantage of unexpected situations and to create opportunities for himself. The general portrait, taken from contemporary anecdote, is of a man 'who thinks quickly and likes to tease'; more significantly, perhaps, he 'loves to act a role'. This is the author of plays comical, historical and tragical – sometimes all three at once, with pastoral or demotic interludes added for light relief.

That is why the notion that the sonnets are, in some sense, autobiographical, is wholly anachronistic. The achievement of Shakespeare is both more complicated and more paradoxical. The poems were written for a specific person as well as a local audience of intimates, while at the same time incorporating all the elements of literary game at the heart of the sonnet enterprise. Bate also makes the intriguing suggestion that 'Mr. W. H.' is a misprint, and that the recipient of the sequence was Southampton. It is a further token of Shakespeare's unknowability, of course, that Katherine Duncan-Jones should disagree. In her cogent and scholarly introduction to the 'Arden' edition of the sonnets, she argues that the verses were written much later than Bate supposes and that Pembroke is the dedicatee.

Both writers concur that Shakespeare turned to poetry when plague closed the theatres, but Duncan-Jones goes on to suggest that the sonnets were written in the reign of James rather than Elizabeth and thus reflect a genuinely homoerotic culture. Their misogynistic and devious passion does seem to have shocked the poet's more orthodox contemporaries, one of whom wrote in a margin – 'what a heap of wretched Infidel Stuff'.

One of the pleasures of Bate's book, in fact, is its account of the ways in which the phenomenon of 'Shakespeare' has been interpreted. An essay on the 'authorship problem', for example, demonstrates that the only problem lies with those who persist in believing that the man from Stratford could not possibly have written the plays attributed to him. A number of unlikely candidates have been brought forward to prove this interesting hypothesis but, as Bate suggests, 'actors know from the inside that the plays must have been written by an actor'. This is the key: Shakespeare, like other great artists, was a master of many parts and characters. Even when he wrote his last will and testament, he was still on stage. He was, as it were, 'warming up' God for the big scene.

The feverish energy devoted to proving that Bacon, or Elizabeth I, or A. N. Other, wrote the famous works is itself significant. In its most absurd manifestation it embodies the cultural ignorance of those who believe that no grammar school boy from the provinces could write great drama. There is in fact a case for saying that, within the literature of England, those at the 'lower' end of the class spectrum have always created taste. But it also suggests that the fluency and prolificity of the plays can barely be identified with one human being. The aspiring claimants to Shakespeare's pen are an indication of his own protean nature.

They also lend poignancy to Bate's suggestive remarks on the 'collaborative' nature of his genius. He was a jobbing dramatist who would be commissioned to add a scene or two to another play, revise the work of others, or interpolate a few lines. His was also collaboration in another sense. The foolish mistake plagiarism and pastiche for lack of originality, but Shakespeare himself stole or borrowed from any source available; almost 'all Shakespeare's plays', according to Bate, are 'rewritings of one kind or another'. Shakespeare is at his greatest when he is least original; the 'peculiarity' of his genius, to paraphrase the very subtle argument of this book, lies in theatrical complication without any definite conclusion. In a wonderful insight Bate associates the mobility or theatricality of feeling within Shakespeare's characters to the bewildering ease and fluency of the dramatist's own passage through the world.

Those who believe that literary scholarship has become the preserve of arcane theorists, or mawkish specialists, may be surprised by Bate's work. *The Genius of Shakespeare* is a wonderfully written and thoroughly enjoyable account, instructive and plausible in equal measure. The theme of this diverse book is diversity itself, and the range of essays here serves only to confirm the quixotic and disparate nature of Shakespeare's achievement. He has been described both as a Tory and a Marxist-Leninist; he has been derided as a chauvinist, and celebrated as a feminist. In truth he is radical and reactionary all at once, belonging to every age and to no age; he believed in everything, and in nothing.

So Bate is able to invoke contemporary scientific theory in order to explain how Shakespearean drama 'may have two contradictory meanings' at the same time. We must apply Heinsenberg's principle of uncertainty to *Macbeth* or *Twelfth Night* in order to understand that they 'mean' nothing except in performance. They are always on the point of being interpreted. We may then recognize that, in Bate's own words, they comprise 'a field of forces in space-time' as well as 'a vast collection of games'. Play, after all, is the thing.

30 October 1997

113

Beginnings: Intention and Method
Edward Said

Professor Kermode once wrote *The Sense of an Ending* and now, for the first time published in England, Professor Said counters with *Beginnings*; the poor lay author is often more concerned with the middle, however, which can prove far more intractable. Beginnings are wilful, and endings are resigned; the novelist or historian learns, along the way, that individual will or imagination cannot in the end triumph over the ineluctable laws of narrative and language.

And that, in one sense, is Said's theme. He is concerned with the nature of narrative itself, and in particular with the strange history of the novel; it began in the eighteenth century with a sense of procreative life but, by the twentieth, had acquired a carapace of constrictions and ambiguities which left it gasping for breath. Said suggests that 'the novelistic form was displaced by a later form in which discontinuity, dispersion and rarefaction are the essentials'; there has been a great transition from the classical principles of truthfulness and continual progress to modern notions of indeterminacy and plurality. The text is no longer authoritative; it has become vulnerable.

It ought to be clear, even from this somewhat generalized summary, that *Beginnings* was written some years ago. Said started work upon it in 1967, and the book was published in America eight years later. That is why the terms seem, perhaps, over-familiar. Yet the book is more than a simple exercise in literary theory. Said is right, for example, to emphasize the 'aboriginal human need to point to or locate a beginning'. It can be found in the very first story of that great egg from which life spilled out after being hit by a hammer; this was the earliest of the 'big bang' theories which have exercised the imaginations of magicians and scientists alike.

The whole question of origins is in any case complicated by contemporary theories which no longer require that the past should be anterior to the future; in the field of scientific experiment no such presumption can be made. It is in fact widely assumed that a future situation can affect the events that precede it, which is very close to the mystical belief that past, future and present exist eternally together. It is all very puzzling for the philosopher, but of immense interest to poets and novelists.

It is in fact the merit of *Beginnings* that it prompts such speculation. The book itself might be considered part of the Franco-American school of literary criticism, which was conducted at a very high level of generality and with a great deal of self-conscious word-play. There are times when this is appropriate and pleasing – Said's close reading of Gerard Manley Hopkins provides quite the best account of that poet's activity – but there are also occasions when it seems that a fistful of abstractions have been thrown into the air only to land where they may.

It is a young man's book, filled with the passionate versatility of a highly intelligent and gifted scholar who is attempting to create patterns of significance out of his multifarious reading. It resists criticism to that degree, since the impulse which brought it into the world was so private and so pure. But since Professor Said has presumably agreed to its republication it cannot remain immune from the kind of critical insight which he himself applies so successfully.

It is dated in the sense that it belongs to a very definite phase in the theory of criticism; the sixties and early seventies represented a period of astonishing fertility and inventiveness in the work of Foucault, Derrida and others. The main impetus came from France, but the theorists of that country were soon joined by eager academics from America and elsewhere. They attempted works of criticism which might accommodate everything; with language itself considered to be the true fabric of humankind, the student of language became the late twentieth-century equivalent of the medieval scholastic who believed that by steady concentration one might reach towards the mind of God.

There was one important corollary. The more fashionable and intelligent critics then came to believe that they were also artists, and that in some way their texts would be able to replace – or at least be equivalent to – the writing of the novelists and poets whom they professed to study. Two heroes of the literary establishment, Pound and Joyce, had contrived a literary language in which everything could be dissolved; in turn critical theorists manufactured their own language which might perform the same task. The academic was no longer the one who taught because he could not 'do it'; the academic became the creative genius. That is what Said implies when he suggests at one point that 'the classic novel goes on today in the form of the critic's enterprise'. He prefaces this remark by conceding 'It is probably too much to say that . . .' but it has been said, and the intention is clear enough.

It could not last. The critical texts of any period are always the least remembered. It is of course too late to return to the old canard that one kind of writing is superior to another – that the poem is superior to the novel, the novel to biography, and so forth. A great biographer is more dramatic than a mediocre playwright, and an interesting novelist is more accurate than a poor historian. That is no longer the point. One of the most important conclusions of recent critical activity lies in the sure knowledge that all writing is one. Instead one can only apply a pragmatic, if somewhat monosyllabic, test. Good criticism is not as good as good fiction or good history. That is all there is to be said.

It is perhaps best to return to what Said calls 'the beginning enterprise' and the origin of this review. *Beginnings* is a clever and intriguing work which can still be read with interest, if not always with pleasure; the aim of all discourse is to create a new order out of that which has already been written, and *Beginnings* fulfils that task. It should be on the shelf of anyone still intrigued by twentieth-century literary theory.

22 January 1998

114

Truman Capote

George Plimpton

From his earliest years he had the voice of an expiring dolphin; when excited, he would squeak. He gloried in 'butterscotch hair', and always looked half his real age – until the end, that is, when he looked no age at all. When he was in high spirits he would leap into the air, arms outstretched, and scream, 'I'm beside myself!'

He knew instinctively how to divert, and to amuse; he always considered himself a 'freak', to use his own word, and decided to supplant nature with nurture. Even when he was an infant he was an *enfant terrible*. Some said he resembled an elf or pixie but, if so, he was always a pixie with a whim of iron. Somehow he managed to escape his natal origins in the South and, at the age of eighteen, to become a copy-boy in the offices of the *New Yorker* magazine. From that time forward he conducted his life, in the words of one of the contributors to this entertaining memoir, 'like a carefully planned military campaign'.

His first, vaguely homosexual, novel was more than a scandal; it was a success. In fact it could be said that *Other Voices, Other Rooms* represents the best fiction he was ever able to write. He had a good ear for casual speech, only partly tempered by a somewhat ornate if not exactly purple prose. As soon as he was acclaimed as a genius, he travelled to Paris. Here he was introduced to various interesting parties solely on the grounds 'that person was so-and-so in Proust'. The delicate connection between society and literature was one Capote never forgot.

He may have been an only child but the more difficult familial problems came relatively late; just after he had enjoyed his first success, his mother committed suicide and his father was in turn committed to Sing Sing for embezzlement. It is said that these events 'haunted' him for the rest of his life, but there is very little evidence of this. Capote was a singular human being – Norman Mailer believes that he knew he led 'a special life' – and he is not likely to have reacted (if he reacted at all) in any orthodox way.

It is not hard to find that taste for the 'special'. He demanded to be the single most important human being in everyone's existence. Like many good novelists he turned his own life into a fabulous story, and fictionalized all those who accompanied him on the way. He always wished to be in command; he created scenes, manipulated people and engineered 'situations'. It was appropriate, then, that he was an extremely good and persistent liar, creating such interesting and entertaining fabrications that eventually he himself came to believe them. There were close friends, however, who noticed that he always put on dark glasses when he was about to lie; they were known as 'the shades of truth'.

That propensity may mark passages of his most famous book, *In Cold Blood*, which narrates the history of a particularly unpleasant multiple murder in western Kansas. It was, according to one of the investigators of the case, essentially a work of fiction dressed up as fact; instead of being a non-fictional novel, as Capote claimed, it was an exercise in fictional journalism. He was unhappy that it won no prizes, however, and instead of writing another book he gave a ball. From all accounts it was a rather gruesome affair, although most of the participants had the good sense to wear masks.

Someone once described him as a 'caramelized tarantula', but the sweetness was more than skin deep. He was very good with the innocent and the vulnerable, for example, perhaps because they represented the best part of himself. But he also demanded constant attention, and achieved fame with a potent mixture of guile, ambition and wilfulness. He aspired to the fashionable world, even though he knew that its inhabitants respected wealth more than character, celebrity more than talent; he spoke once of 'the glare of life', by which he meant its artificial brightness.

It is hardly surprising, then, that he turned against the powerful friends whom he had once courted. When he published *Answered Prayers*, a thinly veiled account of the more unsocial activities of those in 'society', he was dropped. The telephone no longer rang. He stayed in his bedroom, crying, with the curtains closed. He began to drink heavily. There was another reason for his unhappiness. He believed that he could turn gossip into literature, but the book was not well received. It is in fact a flimsy thing, marked by febrile and facile writing; although it is short, it seems prolix. And, as one contributor to this volume suggests, 'in America, there is no room for failure'. A writer is only as successful as his last book. Capote knew this better than anyone, of course, and he fell into despair.

He did not drink because he had lost a few friends – there were plenty more where they came from. He drank because he knew that he could no longer write well. As soon as he lost touch with his genius – if that is what it was – he began systematically to destroy himself. The last years were truly dreadful; his brain shrank to half its size because of the daily ingestion of booze and pills. When he was urged to stop before it was too late, he replied, 'Let me go. Let me go. I want to go.'

It is the virtue of this book, composed primarily of oral reminiscences from various 'friends, enemies, acquaintances and detractors', that Capote can be seen and heard at first hand. There are so many different voices, just like those at the parties which he gave remorselessly, that he comes alive from a hundred different vantages. He should, however, be given the last word – the artist like the criminal and the neurotic, he once wrote, 'have unpredictability and perverted innocence in common'. It is too long for an epitaph, but it may serve as an appropriate epigraph for this engaging and entertaining narrative.

19 February 1998

115

Cole Porter: The Definitive Biography
William McBrien

Cole Porter's countenance was variously compared to that of a rabbit, a leprechaun and a bullfrog; like those three creatures, also, he was quick, watchful and hard to capture. Although this biography describes itself as 'definitive', therefore, it is hardly the last word.

He came from a wealthy family in Indiana, but his first ambition was to be a circus performer. He was a natural showman who, instead of riding elephants or becoming a bearded lady, learned to play the piano very well. He was also something of a mother's boy – his first song was dedicated to her – but he seemed quite happy to leave Indiana for pastures new. At Yale he 'wore salmon-coloured ties and had his nails done' but, despite his personal eccentricities, he was acclaimed even then as a musical 'genius'. He wrote songs, and performed them with panache.

He was enlisted towards the end of the First World War and, fortunately, was dispatched to Paris where his military career remains something of a mystery. The only clue is to be found in a song he wrote in 1919, 'I find that life's not what it used to be / When I had a uniform on'. In the French capital, however, he encountered classical music and found a wife – both of which he kept at arm's length for the rest of his life. It has been claimed that his music is in the spirit of Poulenc or Rameau, but in fact it is much closer to Gilbert and Sullivan played 'with a difference'.

On the death of his grandfather he became a multi-millionaire, but that did not change a life already cosseted by grand hotels, liners and servants. The 'society' of Europe congregated at the Porters' various palazzi, as did those artists who could pick up the scent of money across a continent. Whether he himself was an artist or not was still an open question: he was afraid of failure, and so preferred to appear in public as a wealthy dilettante. He dawdled away most of the twenties but then, in the latter part of that decade, he wrote such songs as 'Let's Do It' and 'What Is This Thing Called Love?' In the thirties he triumphed and indeed, in the eyes of a certain select band, he *was* the thirties.

Unlike most lyricists his words are neither banal nor predictable and, in the best of his songs, technical efficiency is combined with inventive fluency to an exemplary degree. He wrote about love from a thesaurus and a rhyming dictionary, but at least the brevity and obliquity of his songs contrast favourably with his long and supplicatory letters of passion to various boy-friends. His public profile was as hard as a diamond but, in private, he was as messy as overripe fruit.

Like many rich people he seemed determined to find unhappiness, and he continually fell in love with unsuitable young men. Yet never has a homosexual passion inspired so many popular songs – those who listened on the wireless or the phonograph to 'Every Time We Say Goodbye' or 'Night and Day' or 'I've Got You Under My Skin', could never have guessed that they were written to the latest passing marine, lifeguard or masseur. That latter song is supposed also to commemorate a drug habit, which suggests the somewhat louche environment in which Cole Porter was most at ease.

The biography itself is written in a rapid, excited and somewhat breathless style as if Mr McBrien were continually introducing Cole Porter to a group of charming friends. There are in fact so many names, celebrities and social occasions in its pages that it sometimes reads as if it were a glorified guest-list interrupted by Porter's lyrics. The presence of Lady X or the Duke of Y only completes the picture of fake enchantment which Porter himself seems to inspire.

That enchantment wore a little thin when, in 1937, both of his legs were crushed by a falling horse. He said afterwards that he composed a lyric while waiting for help, but that was an example of the sang-froid which he developed into an art. For the rest of his life he was in constant and often alarming pain, but he rarely showed it. Then in the forties his physical suffering was eclipsed, perhaps, by 'a series of flops and bad reviews'.

His career was rescued by *Kiss Me Kate* in which he brushed up his Shakespeare and produced a work that was, in the opinion of Auden at least, better than the original, *The Taming of the Shrew*. This was followed by *Can Can* and *High Society* but the litany of successes did not necessarily lift Porter's spirits. He was too rich, too jaded, and he had known too many people: when you are on top of the world, for the first time you notice how small and inconsiderable it is.

In the fifties he began to suffer from the nervous stress which never left him, and to exhibit symptoms of 'insomnia, loss of appetite, black moods and fits of temper'. The death of his wife was followed by the amputation of his leg, and in both cases he began to suffer from phantom pains. He said little and wrote nothing, sticking compulsively to a routine of living while all the time wishing for death. It is, in a sense, a model of selfishness – even though there are many who testify to his warmth and generosity.

He remains, then, like everyone else, something of a puzzle – but one which this biography does not necessarily resolve. His secretary once remarked that 'almost no one became familiar with Cole Porter'; the same, perhaps, might be said of Mr McBrien who has produced a curiously opaque version of its subject. As Cole Porter himself once wrote, 'So Near and Yet So Far'.

5 November 1998

116

Servants of Nature

Lewis Pyenson and Susan Sheets-Pyenson

In Samuel Johnson's great dictionary the first definition of 'science' is simply 'knowledge'; the history of how it has decayed into a paranoid and destructive system of specialized applications is the history which this volume attempts to trace. It charts the course by which what was once the 'servant of nature', to employ Francis Bacon's phrase, became the usurper and maligner of nature.

It must be noted at once that contemporary science is not an all-encompassing reality. It is a system of beliefs competing with other systems. It is an enterprise in time and is, in other words, an activity which changes direction or shape and sometimes even goes into reverse. One of the strengths of this volume, in fact, is the extent to which it illuminates how science alters according to the country or culture in which it is practised. Certain cities encourage certain types of scientific methodology; throughout the seventeenth and eighteenth centuries, for example, London and Paris were engaged in internecine warfare for pre-eminence in experimental matters, with London encouraging pragmatic applications. And the authors of this book suggest that the nineteenth-century invention of the 'campus' and the 'graduate school' in the United States created a suitably enclosed and hierarchical environment for research.

In fact science has for most of its existence depended crucially upon institutions, generally male-dominated, and thus has become an aspect of patriarchal society. The culture of learned societies was co-opted by the state and became that of 'official institutions' which supported 'the forces of rational enlightenment, progress and modernization'. Measurement itself becomes co-opted as a state activity – 'The state established measures of assets, animate and inanimate,' according to the authors of this book, 'better to control them' – and thus the concept of precision was directly related to acquisitiveness and power. The authors once more suggest that 'measurement signalled industry and improvement'. The introduction of uniform clock time, with the use of mechanical clocks, regimented life in ways unknown to any previous generation.

There are other very interesting chapters in this almost encyclopedic survey. The connection between science and Protestantism, for example, is firmly made. It is true that the founders of the Royal Society, including Sir Isaac Newton, were practising alchemists and astrologers – and it is also true that this aspect of early experimental science has remained obscured in most histories of the subject. But the history of science in the last decades of the seventeenth, and the early decades of the eighteenth century is wholly implicated in the Protestant ethic. One great intellectual historian has suggested that 'Puritanism, and ascetic Protestantism generally ... played no small part in arousing a sustained interest in science.' The rejection of scholastic authority, the sustained examination of God and nature beyond the corrupting interpretation of priests, the faith in human perfectibility – all blossomed in a consuming reverence for science and technology.

In similar fashion individual 'cabinets of curiosities' became collections, which then turned into state-funded museums where the taxonomy of knowledge was displayed; the temples of the nineteenth century, 'monumental and imposing', which evoked 'connotations of dignity, antiquity and permanence', when in fact they were organized upon distorted and temporary misinterpretations of the world. In this context it is interesting to note that in the 1870s one or two brave souls dared to question the truth and purpose of Darwinism – that, in the words of one opponent, it was quackery designed 'to refer all effects to the same cause, – before being silenced by the scientific establishment. The social order and the scientific system have become so clearly implicated with each other that they cannot now be separated. There is no such thing as 'pure' science, only that which has become the 'servant' of the state rather than of nature.

There is a very interesting chapter here on the relationship between science and slaughter. It poses the question, 'Why should warriors have a professional interest in abstract knowledge?' to which the only possible answer is that abstract knowledge is an instrument of power and of oppression. Abstract knowledge has no perpetrators and no victims; it represents a supposedly impersonal force which can effortlessly master the world. The authors note how physicians conduct a 'war' against disease while bomber pilots master the guidance of their missiles with 'surgical precision'. The principal medical officer in the United States is known as the 'surgeon-general'.

This is in certain respects not an easy book to read; the level of cliché is high. Writers thunder, sands shift, struggles are deadly and tomes are unwieldy. But if ever there was an occasion to divorce style from content, *Servants of Nature* represents it. It is a challenging, and necessary, book.

29 April 1999

117

The Arcades Project

Walter Benjamin

The human aspect of this extraordinary narrative, perhaps in deference to the book's theoretical content, has been buried in an appendix. But, in true homage to Walter Benjamin's memory, it is the first matter that should come to light. The German critic and essayist was living in Paris when the Germans invaded France in 1940; in flight from the occupying power Benjamin chose to cross the border between France and Spain by a desperate route over the Pyrenees. He was ill, with a disease of the heart, but he took with him a manuscript in a large black briefcase. 'It is the manuscript that *must* be saved,' he told a companion on this fateful and perilous journey. 'It is more important than I am.' Undoubtedly it comprised his last book.

He managed to reach the border, and the apparent safety of a small Spanish town; but, soon after his arrival, he was told by the local authorities that he was to be expelled and sent back to France. Benjamin then committed suicide yet perhaps with some relief or consolation that at least, as his guide said, 'his manuscript and he were out of reach of the Gestapo'. The briefcase, and the manuscript itself, were never seen again. It has been suggested that he gave them into the care of a travelling companion, who forgot or mislaid them. Or they may simply have been discarded after his death, as part of the detritus of war. In any event his memorial, as he thought of it, has not survived.

Yet here, in *The Arcades Project*, is a kind of restitution. This lengthy volume incorporates all of the materials which Benjamin had collected, in the last thirteen years of his life, for a study of *les passages* in Paris; these were the covered shopping arcades, constructed out of iron and glass, which in the words of his translators he considered to be 'the most important form of the nineteenth century'. The narrative is in the shape of 'convolutes' or chapters of notes which include quotations, extracts, letters, reflections and brief essays upon subjects which range from photography to theories of knowledge, from modes of lighting to dolls and exhibitions. It is, in effect, a new kind of history; it is writing as montage, designed in Benjamin's words 'to discover the analysis of the small individual moment the crystal of the total event'.

The 'event' itself is no less than everything, since it incorporates the change in human consciousness wrought by nineteenth-century industrialization. We may consider here Benjamin's wonderful, and characteristically Germanic, remark that 'knowledge comes only in lightning flashes. The text is the long roll of thunder that follows.' *The Arcades Project* is the reverberation of that thunder in a thousand different directions. Yet it is by no means an incomplete or provisional work. Its errancy and discontinuity are an integral aspect of its overriding structure, in fact, since Benjamin seemed intent upon what his translators describe as 'the transcendence of the conventional book form'. Much of his writing is concerned with what he called 'the commodification of things', from which came his fascinated attention to the primal rhythms of Parisian shopping, and what could be more of a commodity than the book itself?

So in oblique and elusive form Benjamin elucidates what he describes as 'the phantasmagoria of capitalist culture'. The Parisian arcades become the high altar of high capitalism, where in sometimes solemn and sometimes playful manner he observes the sacred rites of mass production. He is concerned, for example, with the diminution of the 'aura' around every created object and the estrangement of the crowds which seek gratification in purchase. Thus he remarks that 'with the establishment of department stores, consumers begin to consider themselves a mass (earlier it was only scarcity which taught them that). Hence the circus-like and theatrical element of commerce . . .' He notes also that 'fashions are a collective medicament for the ravages of oblivion. The more short-lived a period, the more susceptible it is to fashion.'

A 'phantasmagoria' also has elements of dream, however, and in part *The Arcades Project* resembles a dream narrative with strange disjunctions and fugitive associations. Yet it is not the dream of one individual alone; the quotations which he has collected from works of travel, or of history, or of philosophy, make up a collective unconscious in which the nineteenth century and the early twentieth century speak to each other. He considers 'the world of nineteenth-century things as if it were a world of dreamed things', according to one of his interpreters, but who is the dreamer? It is humankind, passing from one phase to another of its restless sleep.

In order fully to comprehend the life of a great metropolis such as Paris, however, it is necessary to create a narrative which reflects the conditions of the city itself by means of suddenly seized detail and a fine if quixotic randomness. So Benjamin is as interested in the shape of an umbrella, or a scrawled notice pinned up by a workman, as he is in Marxist concepts of production or the latest aesthetic theory. Baudelaire (upon whom there is an extraordinary chapter here) once wrote of the 'religious intoxication of great cities', and in Benjamin's words there is a hint of his drunken exuberance when faced with the sheer multiplicity of sensations and ideas which beckon to him.

We might also recall here Baudelaire's other reflection that 'the child sees everything in a state of newness; he is always *drunk*.' Benjamin, too, is very like a child. It is as if he were seeing historical reality for the first time, and in this primal or pristine state all its significant and generally obscured characteristics are revealed. Everything is stripped bare by his gaze.

It was perhaps fate or destiny that consigned the black briefcase and its contents to oblivion, since it is hard to imagine any formal narrative doing justice to the new kind of written history which Benjamin has fashioned. This posthumous volume suggests that, in its incomplete and fissiparous state, his reflections are themselves an unflawed mirror for the world which he was attempting to explore. He seems to have retrieved everything, and anticipated everything. His friend, Gersham Scholem, once declared that Benjamin's suicide also represented 'the death of the European mind'. *The Arcades Project* suggests that this was not too great a hyperbole.

30 December 1999

118

The Total Library: Non-Fiction, 1922–1986
Jorge Luis Borges Edited by Eliot Weinberger

With his mind and imagination filled with the literature of the world, Jorge Luis Borges walked endlessly through the streets and alleys of Buenos Aires. He loved his native city, every corner of it; it was the nutshell from which he could view infinite space. There were occasions, too, when he glimpsed intimations of eternity within its fabric, so that within a specific urban scene he transcended time. From this local experience many of his general perceptions sprang. This was Borges the man.

Borges the legend is another matter. He will forever be associated with the supposed labyrinth of literature; he is the guide or seer who appears, as if in a dream, to lead the votary forward. In a short essay here entitled 'Dante and the Anglo-Saxon Visionaries' he notes the close affinities between the visions of certain seventh-century Englishmen and those of the Florentine poet, with the unstated suggestion that they derive from a common source. In his cyclical and phantasmagoric prose, every story is assumed to spring from some unknown original. The Argentinian writer's blindness has ancient associations with prophecy, too, so that he seems to envision writing yet to come as well as that which has already been.

This is a remarkable collection of his non-fiction, moving from an account of *Citizen Kane* to a description of the *Timaeus*, from

Layamon to Flaubert; here are film reviews and book reviews, essays and lectures, taken from a writing life of more than sixty years. Many of them are very short, but brevity is no impediment to genius. His editor, Eliot Weinberger, notes that in Spanish there is no word for non-fiction, a lacuna which has interesting possibilities for those who believe that the arts of writing are indivisible. Weinberger also notices that many of Borges's stories were first presented to the world in the guise of 'essays', which in turn suggests that his work may be conceived as one project. Why should his contributions to newspapers or women's magazines be of any less consequence than his published fables? A visionary is also a prodigal, since visions themselves belong to everyone.

Certainly Borges visits insistent themes within all of his published writing; there is his central preoccupation with the grand illusion of time, in which capacity he has anticipated the work of contemporary scientific theorists by several decades. There is the same fascination with the more wayward or arcane writers of the nineteenth and twentieth centuries. There is the interest in dreams; like the tenuous difference between 'fiction' and 'non-fiction' eroded in his writing, his interest in such matters effaces the boundaries of sleep and waking so that in his account all human life takes on the elements of a perpetual haunting.

The essay itself is not an Anglo-Saxon form; there have been great essayists in the English language, among them William Hazlitt and Washington Irving, but the medium has characteristically been considered to be the effusion of an essentially journalistic nature. The work of Borges suggests, however, that the spirit of the essay is at once comprehensive and unassuming. Where else but in this volume, for example, could one find mentioned in a single sentence 'Lana Turner, David Hume and the heresiarchs of Alexandria'?

Yet the essay is so personal and almost conversational a form that, to trust its efficacy, you must trust the voice behind it. It is a matter of tone. Despite his range of reference, for example, Borges himself is never guilty of obscurantism or assumed learning; his brevity is a positive inducement to clarity, while in no sense does it distort the truthfulness of his perceptions. He is witty and elaborate, in turn intimate and magisterial, with a playfulness that does not preclude but rather proves utter seriousness of purpose. That is why he understands Oscar Wilde so well. A lecture here upon his blindness is measured and exact, but in its intensity it can be said to rival Milton's sonnet upon the same theme.

In his writings during the Second World War he castigates anti-Semitism and German aggression with the same fervour that he extols the virtues of England. Part of that love, however, sprang from his belief that the country and its culture were suffused with tokens of the supernatural. He concurred with a Byzantine historian that the nation consisted of two parts, 'one with rivers and cities and bridges, the other inhabited by snakes and ghosts'. Perhaps he understood England better than the English themselves.

Borges's erudition is truly bewildering, in fact, and can only be explained upon the supposition that he has spent his entire life among books; he is the human being as reader, as definite and as marked a category as that of warrior or saint, for whom all the activity and pleasure of life derives from the experience of words. Yet these qualities are not in themselves enough to explain the sheer delight in first coming upon these essays and reviews, many of which have never before been translated into English; Borges has taken so much pleasure in reading that he has been able effortlessly to reproduce that pleasure for his own readers.

There are many extraordinary excursions and diversions. He is fascinated, for example, by the phenomenon of G. K. Chesterton and the detective story. He is half in love with Edgar Allan Poe, whom he considers to be the unacknowledged master of all contemporary writing. He adores the screen-writer, Ben Hecht, and describes William Beckford's *Vathek* as a masterpiece of diabolism. He admires Ray Bradbury, whose *Martian Chronicles* is described here as revealing not some alien planetscape but 'the long empty Sundays, the American tedium, and his own solitude'. In one essay he says of Joyce that 'he is less a man of letters than a literature'. We may without hesitation apply the same description to Borges himself, with the codicil that his is the literature of eternity.

27 January 2000

119

Hawksmoor's London Churches: Architecture and Theology

Pierre de la Ruffinière du Prey

In the first sentence of his prologue the author remarks that architecture may on occasions 'suggest that time has stood still'. In this grave and numinous context he then compares the eighteenth-century London churches of Nicholas Hawksmoor 'with that of Christians in the Near East some thirteen hundred years earlier'. This is the solemn analogy which he pursues throughout his narrative.

Yet Du Prey's study also offers an ample theological and architect-ural context for Hawksmoor's work. There has been a tendency among novelists to present Hawksmoor's achievement in a dim or shadowy light, with allusions to the more occluded aspects of *prisca sapientia* or ancient wisdom. But Du Prey places the architect amongst an enthusiastic circle of scholars and divines who wanted to recapture the optimism and simplicity of the early Christians. In a world of plague and fire, regicide and civil disorder, all seen as tokens of some great and final alteration, they sought the solace of primitive religion. The politics of the period were also congenial. In 1711 an Act was passed to facilitate the building of fifty new churches in the suburbs of the capital, the inhabitants of areas as diverse as Stepney and Deptford having previously been denied the consolations of religious worship. This is where Nicholas Hawksmoor stepped in.

There is a sketch of an area in Bethnal Green where he has drawn 'The Basilica after the Primitive Christians'; here is a church and graveyard, with an area for baptismal immersion and a vestry for 'holy Vessells', all emanating from 'ye purest times of Christianity'. The drawing contains an enclosure 'to keep off filth – Nastyness & Brutes', while the dark crypt would be used as a 'School for ye Charity Children'. Yet the oddest aspect is the one least frequently mentioned – that buildings modelled upon those of Tyre or Halicarnassus should be set down in Bethnal Green.

Thus in post-Reformation and Anglican England there grew a strange desire to imitate the churches of the earliest Christians, who worshipped before Rome was mighty, in the belief that 'the places of

worship themselves would bestow greater holiness upon the worship-
pers'. This is a wonderful supposition, with the presumption that stone
itself can become an object of veneration. Here may be heard, then,
solemn echoes of an original purity not unconnected with splendour
and magnificence.

Nicholas Hawksmoor, chosen with James and Vanbrugh to build
certain of these new churches, was obsessed with the history of
architecture no less than with architecture itself. He studied the mass
and monumentality of pagan masterpieces; he admired the simplicity
and symmetry of early Christian temples. A copy of *De Architectura* by
Vitruvius has been discovered with the inscription 'Nic: Hawksmoor
At Sr Chr: Wren's in Scotland Yard'. He had been a pupil of Wren's in
his office as Surveyor of the Royal Works. There also survives a
drawing, by Hawksmoor, of the Mausoleum at Halicarnassus; he was
inspired by the elaborate words of Vitruvius to recreate the seventh
wonder of the world. He then employed it later as a model for the
steeple of St George's, Bloomsbury, which was subsidized by the brewer
to the royal household and which can be seen behind the drunken
inhabitants of Hogarth's *Gin Lane*. The portico of that church was in
turn based upon the temple of Bacchus at Baalbek, thus lending a pagan
authority to the generally inebriate atmosphere. Is all this chance? There
is no such thing as coincidence in London.

Hawksmoor never saw any of these ruined monuments; he never left
England but, according to Du Prey, he 'wrote about Baalbek as if he
knew it personally'. This is the formidable and astonishing aspect of
his architectural genius: he had the power of clairvoyance and,
brooding over old volumes and travellers' tales, could see the ancient
piles once more rising before him. An obituarist noted that he 'could
give an exact account of all the famous buildings, both ancient and
modern, in every part of the world'. In particular he was fascinated by
the Temple in Jerusalem, built by Solomon at divine command. No one
knew its outlines but in the seventeenth century many plans were
produced out of the Old Testament and the Book of Revelations. So
the altar of Hawksmoor's St Mary Woolnoth, in the centre of the City,
has 'twisted Solomic columns'.

In the church of St Alphege in Greenwich, too, Hawksmoor created
pedestals which in the words of Du Prey 'intentionally recall ancient
sacrificial altars' with metal lamps contributing to 'the image of smoke
issuing from burnt offerings'. Du Prey relates it to the early Saxon
habit of converting pagan temples into churches, but Hawksmoor's

imagination was still desperately strange. There is mention of the fact, for example, that he was obsessed with mausoleums. It has also been suggested that the six churches which Hawksmoor designed for the riverine suburbs were 'an interrelated group'. With their 'massive bulk' and 'soaring height' they 'beckon' the inhabitants of Wapping or Limehouse to enter their mysteries. The effect was described by the architect himself as 'Gothick' where pagan and Christian motifs are mingled as profusely as gargoyles and saints.

One additional fact lends strength and structure to the argument. While rebuilding St Mary Woolnoth Hawksmoor discovered the remains of an ancient temple and, according once more to Du Prey, 'sought a way to celebrate a spot hallowed by such a long tradition'. He decided upon a cornice like that of the Roman temple dedicated to Mars Vindicator while the rustication of the church itself 'resembles the stratified layers or earth in an archaeological excavation'. So time and stone are joined in a mutual embrace. This book is a celebration of Hawksmoor's genius, but it also provokes reflections of a more general kind.

5 July 2000

120

England: The Making of the Myth
Maureen Duffy

There have been several recent books upon the theme of England, and of Englishness, among them Michael Wood's *In Search of England*, Jeremy Paxman's *The English*, Paul Langford's *Englishness Identified*, Roger Scruton's *England: An Elegy*, and Peter Vansittart's *In Memory of England*. The reasons for these books are not far to seek. The dissolution of the UK by government fiat, with the consequent assertion of Welsh and Scottish identities, has advanced England's own self-consciousness. The expansion of the EU has also prompted or promoted a new interest in the national culture. There is nothing wrong with this development; a nation without an identity is a nation without a memory, and a nation without a memory is not a nation at all.

Maureen Duffy has embarked upon her own task of retrieval by reconstructing the 'myth' of England. Of course it comes under many different forms and disguises. She invokes Britannia, for example, before resurrecting the spectre of Albion. For many centuries England was considered by its historians and antiquarians to be the promised land; in the seventeenth century Milton repeated the claim which was then confirmed in the eighteenth century by William Blake's poem, commonly known as *Jerusalem.*

There have also been many myths of origin and identity: Brutus the Trojan, Arthur the Briton and Joseph of Arimathea among them. The fact that none of these legendary figures was English at all – that race came from an area known as Angeln, north of what is Schleswig-Holstein – has not affected their place in national mythology. One of the curiosities about Englishness itself is that it has been created out of assimilation and adaptation; it has borrowed its resources (usually from Europe) before calling them its own. The language is a polyglot mixture of dialects while the race itself was best described by Daniel Defoe in *The True Born Englishman* as 'Your Roman-Saxon-Norman-Danish English', to which other nationalities have added their contribution. That England also has many names leads Duffy to confirm its 'confused identity' which needs to be upheld 'by the repeated affirmation of the national myths'.

She begins at the beginning: a skeleton was found in Cheddar Gorge at the start of the last century; it was dated to the eighth millennium BC but in 1996 its DNA was matched with that of a schoolteacher who lived in the neighbouring village. Ten thousand years had passed, and yet the organic link remained. Duffy suggests other continuities – that the first English heretic, Pelagius, promulgated in the fifth century a doctrine of a 'pragmatic "English" character'; ever since, English learning and inquiry have been of a practical nature. The first chroniclers of England describe it as an island of mists and ghosts; ever since, the literature and art have been striated with dreams and visions.

The English came and conquered this ghostly island, but their identity was first formulated by an obscure monk in Northumbria. The Venerable Bede composed *The Ecclesiastical History of the English People* in AD 731, and at a single stroke created a national myth and history.

Duffy devotes much of her narrative to the Anglo-Saxons, since it was from them that most elements of Englishness derive: the love of place, the sense of the sea, the antiquarian imagination, the interest in biography and books of travel. Of the greatest figure of that period, Alfred, Duffy claims that he represented 'the English tradition of irony, eccentricity, and muddling through'. But he embodies other qualities also. He was a great administrator, and it has been said that England is a deeply governed country with institutions and legal customs dating back to the ninth century.

But Alfred's 'muddling through' is only part of the truth, since the English of his period were also known for their fierceness and fatalism. Even in defeat, the war-song insisted, our courage must be the stronger. But this was also accompanied by a propensity for violence which was noticed by foreign travellers from the twelfth to the eighteenth centuries. Today's football hooligans might be seen as thoroughly English in sentiment and intention.

There are more salubrious connections. Duffy makes the point that Churchill's wartime speeches were not couched in contemporary English 'but in the vocabulary, rhythms and periods of the previous century'. The antiquarian tendencies of the English were mocked by Goethe, but they have always been part of the native genius; they have reappeared in contemporary English literature, for example, where the 'historical novel' has been revived.

Duffy also makes the point that E. P. Thompson's celebrated study was entitled *The Making of the English Working Class* in order to celebrate 'our very English version of socialism'. This embodies an important truth, since the English tradition of libertarianism is an ancient one.

England: The Making of the Myth is in some respects a potted history, but there are passages and elements here of absorbing interest. Never has there been a period when it was more necessary to recognize the nature of national identity – even if only to mourn its demise.

21 February 2001

III
Lectures, Miscellaneous Writings, Short Stories

Lectures

121

The English Novel Now

One night about eight years ago now, I suppose, I was having dinner with some friends at the top of a very large apartment block in New York. My host was a novelist and literary critic; his wife wrote long, theoretical articles about painting in several of the more fashionable art magazines. There was a large Warhol print on one wall of their dining room, of Marilyn Monroe, I think, matched by an even larger Rothko on another. They were a very New York couple.

After dinner my host took me on to his balcony. The city below resembled a vast, illuminated insect. 'This,' my host informed me, as he waved his hand over Manhattan, 'is the centre of the world.' I was very young at the time and saw no good reason to disbelieve him; indeed, during this period of the early seventies most cultural observers would have acquiesced in his statement as a mere matter of fact – in every area of creative work it seemed that New York, and the vast engine of America which fuelled it, were pushing forward the boundaries of aesthetic expression and artistic experience. A litany of names could have been, and often was, recited like an aesthetic creed: Jasper Johns, Andy Warhol and Frank Stella had already beaten out wide paths for themselves; minimal art, earth art, information art and conceptual art were all crowding in upon one another. And in the novel, which one might define as the elaborate conscience of the American race, there were Saul Bellow, John Updike, Joseph Heller, Philip Roth. There was John Cage's music, Merce Cunningham's dance, Claes Oldenburg's monumental sculptures.

For an Englishman, it was peculiarly difficult to be anything other than slightly awkward and apologetic when confronted with this great expanse of energy. There had once been something in England called 'the movement', there had been some 'angry young men', but one might as well have been discussing the merits of Wyatt and Surrey, it all sounded so distant. There was W. H. Auden, of course, but he was then resident in New York, and there was David Hockney – well, Hockney was living in Los Angeles. It seemed that America was the new empire and that those of us who had the good fortune to share its language were in the position of itinerant minstrels and scholars, finding patrons wherever we could.

Looking back now upon that period, almost a decade later, one is struck by the immensity of the claims which were put forward for American culture. But what is still more striking, and more to the point, I think, is the paucity of the actual achievement which emerged from it. The cultural hegemony was derived from fantasies as seductive as the then myth of American military supremacy, and it all now seems as distant and as remote as sky-writing, which we read once, before it dissolves. But one is struck also by another fact, and one that seems to me to have gone largely unrecorded. Over the last ten years, there has been a renewal of strength and self-confidence among English writers and artists. They have, as it were, come out from that shadow which their contemporaries in America once cast, and are producing work of a power and substance which, on that balcony in New York, I would not have thought of as being possible. Any interpretation of this reversal of roles (although it goes deeper than mere role-playing since it touches upon the heart of our respective cultures) is bound to be a difficult one. We are still too close to the phenomenon to see it clearly, or to see it whole. But there are certain preliminary observations to be made.

There is, first of all, the question of the collapse, or the evident decay, of American culture in its modernist and internationalist guise, a collapse which will provide certain clues to the renewal of our native culture here in Britain. Just as the landing of a man on the moon was considered to be the apex of American scientific and technical achievement, so the American avant-garde, equally far out, as it were, was the focal point of that nation's artistic supremacy. It was thought that the dissolution of old forms and the assiduous pursuit of certain fashionable certainties were the constituents of a new and powerful art. The critics talked enthusiastically about 'deconstruction', 'metatext' and any other code-word they could lay their hands or their typewriters on. And yet their notion of the avant-garde was a peculiarly rootless one. The aim was to astonish rather than to convince. It was based not so much upon an understanding of cultural history as upon a willingness to flout or ignore it.

Now, such attitudes are possible only in times of affluence – when art dealers and cultural foundations, to take two of the more eminent examples, have a superfluity of money. The manifestations of the avant-garde during the sixties and early seventies were the equivalent of those redundant luxury goods – toasters covered in jewels, fur-covered refrigerators, and so on – which were available in the more fashionable department stores. In the sixties also, the Vietnam War lent a certain piquancy to the situation. There was a kind of angry energy, a sense of being in a powerful empire, which the avant-garde writers and artists were able effectively to channel in order to assert their own, equally ferocious, claims to primacy. The art of the period did not, in other words, struggle, or even *have* to struggle, with its environment; prevailing social and economic circumstances were simply the armchairs in which it rested. Their art reflected, in that sense, the spirit of America.

But now that spirit has vanished with inflation, with an awareness of the limits of imperial power, and other symptoms of the current American malaise. And, as a result, the aspirations of the avant-garde now seem merely grandiose. I recently attended in London a perform-ance of the Merce Cunningham Dance Company. Their truncated gestures, the self-consciously abstract sets, the deliberate disharmonies of music and taped voices – all seem stale now and somewhat dated. There is nothing solid, nothing convincing there. For similar reasons, minimal art and information art, the last exotic flowering of visual experimentation in New York, have now been abandoned within ten or fifteen years of their creation. Contemporary American poetry now lies breathless and inert among a jungle of state-funded small presses and little magazines. There has been the same slackening, the same purposelessness, in every area of the American avant-garde.

In England, however, there was no distinctive avant-garde in the seventies: the principal reason being, perhaps, that none of our artists was able to float easily upon the surface of a successful consumer economy. It was difficult to imitate our American contemporaries, since their vague and self-conscious exploration of 'alternative form' could hardly be taken seriously at a time of great social and economic unrest. Instead we turned in upon ourselves. We were forced to confront an economic decline which seemed to be a symptom of some larger national distress. Modish aesthetic theories are particularly ill-equipped to help writers and artists who are surrounded by decay and by a kind of helpless self-abnegation within the nation itself. But out of this struggle with local circumstances, with the idea that our society and in fact our whole social history might have to be re-examined, came an art which was strong and readily identifiable. One example may provide an illustration of what I mean by this. Until quite recently, the British film industry was generally regarded as negligible, if not entirely moribund. But within the last few months, at least three new British films have been released, *Rude Boy*, *Radio On* and *Breaking Glass*, which incorporate a peculiarly intense and consistent vision of the society in which we now find ourselves. We may argue about the merits of these three films, but there is no doubt that they share an identifiable and convincing tone. They evince a raw energy, a kind of grittiness, an attention to social detail, to the more painful and perplexing areas of British society. There is in them, too, an absence of sentiment and of the glossy heroics which are now all too frequent in the American cinema. I've chosen film here as my example, but I could equally well have taken contemporary British art and poetry, both now enjoying an extraordinary revival, in order to make a similar point.

Here, too, we have clearly defined and concentrated work, showing a disciplined attention to the local characteristics of form, of texture, of language, rather than to some fashionable or glossily abstract state-ment. It is as if writers and artists in England were now attempting to rediscover a sense of identity within their own work, which, like our national identity, has to be reformulated and redefined under the pressure of events.

In this context, the development of the novel in England and America during the seventies is of particular interest. The most distinguished American novelists – Saul Bellow, John Updike, Philip Roth, Joseph Heller – seemed at one time to be using a language that was larger and freer than our own. Like new Elizabethans, they employed the language as a melodic instrument, creating elaborate structures out of thin air. It was as if they had a more comprehensive and more humane vision of life than our narrow, domestic sagas allowed us. And theirs was indeed at one point a genuinely expansive writing, but, in the same manner as the American avant-garde, they were in fact living off the fat of the society – a society they looked to not as observers or as critics, but only as clients seeking financial support. They wanted to become writers-in-residence, professors of creative writing, and so on – and many of them in fact did so. But if you live off fat, you are destined to become overweight. Their large concerns became grandiose, their language turned into a flat rhetoric which concealed far more than it revealed.

Some of the most recent American novels, Heller's *Good as Gold*, Updike's *The Coup*, John Barth's *Letters*, to take three of the more prominent examples, seem to me to be hollow, written at a forced pace, preoccupied with literary special effects, and unable to deal with human beings in other than generalized and stereotypical terms, a literary equivalent, if you like, of *Apocalypse Now* or *Kramer v. Kramer*. You would not know, reading these books, that American society had actually changed profoundly over the last ten years.

There are, no doubt, many and complex reasons for this ineffectiveness and this decline, but one stands out as being of particular relevance to any understanding of our own literary culture and its new strength. It concerns the nature of the American language itself. That language tends characteristically towards the abstract, moving away from the specific to the general at every opportunity. I am not referring here to the political neologisms of the Watergate era, when lie turned into 'mis-speak', and so on, although these were a symptom of the prevailing condition, but rather to the nature of the society itself. It is both too large and too multifarious to create a recognizable idiom, a vernacular if you like. It is also too heavily dependent upon, and also entranced by, certain concepts and principles – contemporary technology being, I suppose, the most obvious now. It is too dazzled by such things to allow much space in its language for the workings of human agency. It is a language of power, one in which reality is seen as a phenomenon which can be easily manipulated and controlled. I remember on a trip on the Long Island railway (it must be about three years ago now) being handed a notice which read in part: 'By giving our train service personnel an improved appreciation of your service expectations, and by sharpening their consumer contact skills, we hope to reduce frictions.' It meant simply that the railway staff had been asked to be more polite to travellers, but the nature of the language used suggests that the human beings involved were simply soft machines which needed to be reprogrammed. The American novelists who live within this language, and whose perceptions are determined by it, are uniquely ill-equipped to deal with human motives and responses, and as a result they are also unable to present any convincing account of their own human society. Their language becomes an imperialist syntax, co-opting all available realities and transforming them into the same bland shape. The prose of contemporary American novelists is like a veneer upon a painting, so thick that the human figures are distorted and unrecognizable beneath.

In England, none of this has occurred. The vernacular remains strong, and our novelists, far from turning to abstraction, have used a harder and more direct English in recent years. This is only the context, of course, and by no means a necessary condition of good writing, and it has in fact been said of mainstream British fiction that it is too domestic, narrowly class-bound in its preoccupations. Now it is certainly true that in most English novels there is a deliberate smallness of scale, a smallness at least when compared to the broad expanse of the American novel. But it seems to me to be a smallness which is full of resource. In effect, it means the absence of heroics, a refusal to countenance rhetoric as a means of describing reality. In novelists as different as Alan Sillitoe and Beryl Bainbridge, Francis King and Angus Wilson, there has been a genuine attempt to register the actual reality of our contemporary circumstances, a reality which is not, and in fact cannot be, described in any other form. It is as if our national identity were being redefined. Like the raising of a great ship from the sea bed, it is being done slowly, consistently, and with a meticulous attention to detail.

I'm not suggesting here that there is any easy correlation between economic circumstances and cultural ones, but it can be said with some confidence that the peculiar and distressing circumstances we have lived through, and in fact which we are still living through, have changed our notion of ourselves in radical ways. Conventional wisdom is seen not to be wisdom at all. English novelists have assisted in this process by, as it were, stripping the veils of the language – reality is now presented as uncomfortable, as being demanding, and as a result it has become less open to conventional habits of narration and description.

That is why much recent fiction in England is filled with sporadic violence, with confrontation, with the harsh ironies which our social history has inflicted upon us. Three novels occur to me at once: Beryl Bainbridge's *Injury Time*, Jack Trevor Story's *Up River* and Francis King's *The Needle*. In each of them we are continually being made aware of the oddness of the ordinary, the menace and brutality which lie behind the conventional political and social worlds. You might, I suppose, call it the new realism – paranoid realism. It could be said that such writers have made a compact with smaller truths, but their truths are human truths and they evoke our society with a rare clarity, as if it were being seen for the first time. Their fiction is an exploration. Characteristically, American fiction is a statement.

These impressions are not, I hope, chauvinistic ones. I'm not attempting to suggest that British writing and British culture in general are now the most elaborate and invigorating on the planet. I have not, for example, discussed here the culture of the European mainland, nor have I dealt with those writers who use English in a different idiom and from the vantage of a different society. My point has been limited to that special relationship between English and American culture – a relationship in which, in recent years, we were always thought to be the inferior partner, but a relationship which has now changed in the most fundamental way.

On the other side of the Atlantic I see decay and I see rhetoric; here I see renewal and self-confidence. It is as if we were learning to say to ourselves, and our writers and artists were saying for us: look, we have come through.

The Listener, 15 January 1981

122

The Englishness of English Literature

One has to say at once that this is not a fashionable subject. I can think of only one full-length study of a remotely comparable nature, and that was written some thirty-five years ago by a German emigré. Of course I mean *The Englishness of English Art* by Nikolaus Pevsner, and I have been foolhardy enough to adapt the title of that famous work in order to see if I can, however tentatively and inconclusively, repeat his analysis of English forms in a completely different context. I want to see if I can find Hogarth's line of beauty, that long gentle double curve which Pevsner saw as characteristic of English art, in English literature. No doubt because he spent so much time travelling across the English countryside, he believed climate to play a large part in the formation of national character and thus of national culture; it is not so odd a suggestion in fact. Milton himself surmised that 'the sun ripens wits as well as fruit', and of course in the eighteenth century it was a conventional piece of cultural wisdom from writers as eminent as Montesquieu that England was 'warm enough' for poets and musicians, but still too damp and cold for painters to flourish.

I don't wish to add anything to that debate, since climatology has become almost as unfashionable as theology, but nevertheless Englishness itself remains very difficult to talk about. It has become almost embarrassing. Perhaps this has in part to do with a supposed reticence, and it is also compounded by the native English distrust for wide generalizations of an inconclusive nature. But in the last twenty or thirty years there has also been something close to a political or social embarrassment; there is no longer much guilt about erstwhile English imperialism or colonialism but, nevertheless, the fear of appearing 'nationalistic' has led to a certain reluctance to espouse the virtues of Englishness at all. In addition the apparent decline of English influence has on occasions promoted the belief that there may be nothing much left to celebrate or to preserve.

It was not always so. In fact the attempt to define Englishness – the attempt to recover and to describe a native English spirit – is almost as old as English culture itself. One thinks of the sixteenth-century debates about the foundation of this country, in which various antiquarians and historians disputed the claims of Brutus to that high honour or speculated about the presence of an original giant race which survived the sinking of Atlantis. One thinks of the eighteenth-century interest in the Druids and in Stonehenge, as emblems of some lost English inheritance. And then one thinks of the mid-nineteenth-century fascination with an indigenous past, with the establishment of the Early English Text Society and the Ballad Society. The importance of England and Englishness was in fact once the great theme of English poetry. It is well known that Milton was projecting an epic on English and Arthurian lines before he started work on *Paradise Lost*, while poets as diverse as Spenser and Morris, Blake and Tennyson, have been fascinated or obsessed with the idea of writing truly English epics.

But no more. No longer. All that has gone and, as I remarked just now, Englishness is not a fashionable subject. But it is not just a question of reticence. It is also a question of ignorance. I am in particular referring to the historical and cultural ignorance of those who are involved in the creation and presentation of our culture – writers, novelists, critics, poets, newspaper reviewers. There is for example among some of them a shallow kind of internationalism, commonly associated with the Enlightenment in the eighteenth century and with socialism in the twentieth, which looks upon national traditions and national cultures as something to be ignored or even actively discouraged. But as T. S. Eliot once remarked, the more truly native – even parochial – a literature is, the more universal it can become. It is one of the most perceptive critical points which Eliot ever made, and I strongly believe that a literature must be imbued with a powerful local presence before it can aspire to any kind of unique status. The works of William Blake and Charles Dickens, those two Cockney visionaries, might be brought into evidence to support that belief. And I could put the same point differently, I suppose, by noting that there is no such thing as international writing – even though I have seen the phrase blazoned in some of the more fashionable literary pages. If it did exist, it would be the literary equivalent of airline food – acceptable to all, but interesting and palatable to none.

But the concept of Englishness has also been attacked from another direction. I am tempted to say from an academic direction, but its provenance is wider than that. For just as English writing can be displaced by some bogus internationalism, so it can also be challenged by the creation of new ahistorical categories of writing – black writing, gay writing, feminist writing. I have no particular quarrel with the creation of these disciplines (if they are disciplines), only with the fact that the idea of a national literature is subtly displaced in the process. You would think, from the remarks of certain writers and reviewers, that real culture began on the day they were born. Again it is a question of ignorance, but it also reveals a more important failure of nerve. In some quarters, for example, there is still that general obeisance to American culture which has been so characteristic of the decades since the end of the Second World War. It would not be too hard to find intelligent men and women who know the entire work of John Updike without having read a word of John Milton, or who extol the virtues of Saul Bellow while knowing nothing of Spenser or Skelton. And this of course is a serious error: it may sound revolutionary to say so, but you can learn more about our culture today by reading Tom Paine rather than Tom Wolfe, and by reading Milton rather than Bellow.

For I believe that there is such a thing as the English spirit, the English genius, the English tradition. But if there is what might be called a *genius loci*, how is it ever to be found within English literature? Is there some equivalent to Hogarth's painterly line of beauty? I do believe that there is a strong central activity which can be reaffirmed, but there are many different ways of understanding it. It would be perfectly possible, for example, to elaborate upon the argument which Bishop Percy advanced in one of his editorial comments in *Reliques of Ancient English Poetry*. 'It is worth attention,' he wrote, 'that the English have more songs and ballads on the subject of madness than any of their neighbours.' One might connect this with the madness portrayed in Jacobean drama, with the extraordinary success of eighteenth-century English graveyard poetry, and with the less than literary fact that in the nineteenth century London was known as the suicide capital of the world. Is 'The Mad Song' an English invention? I suspect not but, in any case, there is no point in being prescriptive about such matters. There is little value in trying to establish the constitutent parts of some grand national tradition in the Leavisite manner, or in trying to construct some enclosed hierarchy of English values and beliefs. Certainly I would not like to adopt some literary variant of a Little England posture, and there is to me nothing more depressing than the English poetry and fiction of the fifties and sixties which opted defiantly for the small scale and the domestic in the face of French experimentation and American energy. I am, I hope, talking about something larger. I am talking about lines of force which eddy through the language. I am talking about something which begins, if you like, at the beginning.

So where should we begin? Where can we still find patterns of continuity, or even certain national characteristics which appear striking or significant? One might start with the English epic, that tradition which is to be found in Hardy's *The Dynasts* as much as Spenser's *The Faerie Queen*, in Keats's *The Fall of Hyperion* as well as in Milton's *Paradise Lost*. It is to be found in Tennyson's *The Idylls of the King*, in Browning's *The Ring and the Book*, in Blake's *Jerusalem*, in Wordsworth's *The Prelude*, in Byron's *Don Juan*, in Shelley's *Prometheus Unbound* . . . the list could be multiplied. But although epic can appropriately be called an English tradition, it can hardly be described as an English form. Everyone knows that the work of Homer and Virgil were the models to which the epic poet aspired, but I would make this one nationalist proviso. The most customary subject for the English epic was the 'Matter of Britain', largely concerned with Arthur and the famous table but also encompassing the nature and origin of the country itself. There are some wonderful passages in *The Faerie Queen* where Spenser clearly puts on the robe of an English Virgil and sings of

> . . . mighty, Albion, father of the bold
> And warlike people, which the Britaine Islands hold.

And then of course Blake enlists not only the epic but also the biblical tradition in order to justify his belief in the English as the chosen race.

> All things begin and end,
> On Albion's Ancient Druid Rocky Shore.

But of course this is the kind of thing that embarrasses us all these days, and I will say only this about the epic form: insofar as it is a way of celebrating historical continuity, and of course thereby celebrating a language which can be used on so large a scale, we can detect a particular English interest in, and affection for, the epic form. To use a modern term, it provided the right kind of national image.

But where else can we find reflections of that image? One might turn to the ballad tradition, which has its roots in the twelfth century, but like the epic it is a form and interest shared by many other cultures. One might turn to the tradition of English pastoral poetry, where in fact I would locate another enduring source of English verse – in the management of the euphonious line, that line of harmonious open vowel sounds which you can hear all the way through Wyatt

> From these hie hills as when a spring doth fall,
> It trilleth down with still and suttle course . . .

And Hopkins:

> I have desired to go
> Where springs not fail . . .

And Auden:

> How will you answer when from their calming spring
> The immortal nymphs fly shrieking

I suppose that particular cadence might be the equivalent to Hogarth's line of beauty in English painting, but it seems also to bear some relation to those soaring melancholic harmonies which are to be found in English music from Byrd and Tallis to Britten and Vaughan Williams.

This is perhaps just uninformed speculation on my part, but I believe I can be less hesitant about another example of the continuity of English literature, although it is to be found in an apparently unlikely place – I mean in the tradition of the journalism of 'low life'. We can trace it from the Elizabethan pamphleteers, Nash and Greene, through John Gay in the eighteenth century, into the nineteenth-century compilations of Henry Mayhew and G. A. H. Sala, and then of course into our present century with George Orwell and his successors. In addition this particular interest among English writers is matched by the characteristic gift among English artists for the caricature of low or common life – Cruikshank, Rowlandson and of course Hogarth all thought of themselves as wholly and almost defiantly English artists engaged in a peculiarly native art. It is also interesting to note in this context that Hogarth was one of the original members of the Academy of Ancient Music, which specialized in arranging performances of early English music. And it should be remembered that Hogarth was one of the chief propagandists for a school of national historical painting. Here we find an exponent of Englishness who had such confidence in his own native genius that he looked for signs of it everywhere.

So perhaps we also can range a little wider, and here I want to enlist again the assistance of Nikolaus Pevsner. He was very perceptive indeed about the English interest in what he called 'architectural historicism'. He put it very well in his second chapter or, more strictly speaking, second lecture entitled 'Hogarth and the Observed Life'. 'England,' he wrote, 'was the first country to break the unity of interior and exterior and wrap buildings up in clothes not made for them but for buildings of other ages and other purposes.' He quotes as examples a school built in a Gothic style, and a gentlemen's club constructed on the model of a Renaissance Italian palace. Now this sounds reasonably close to what has in recent years been termed 'post-modernism'. Far from it. It is quite clear that this is not some recent cultural development, but something which has always been close to the heart of the English genius. If I may quote Pevsner once again, he notes that in the sixteenth century English 'funeral monuments were self-consciously made to look medieval'. In prose, we have Walter Savage Landor's *Imaginary Conversations*, in which he became Sir Isaac Newton, Thomas Middleton, Lord Chesterfield and so forth. There is little point in multiplying examples, but this is true English historicism. I suppose it might also be related to the English antiquarian tradition, which was once such a joke in the rest of Europe – there are those lines in *Faust*, spoken by Mephistopheles, in which he asks

> Are Britains here? They go abroad, feel calls
> To trace old battle-fields and crumbling walls . . .

But in this context it is important to recognize what Pevsner called the 'self-conscious choice of a mode of expression', the formal or playful use of a historical style which he placed very firmly at the heart of the English sensibility itself.

Of course it is another aspect of that cultural blindness or ignorance to which I alluded before when the label of 'post-modernism' is attached to such a familiar and ancient tradition. In passing, I suppose one might glance at that once popular faith in the 'deconstruction' or 'reconstruction' of a literary text by some ideal reader. It has been treated as quite a fashionable or at least novel preoccupation, but of course such an idea is as old as civilization itself – at least our civilization, because it has its roots in the process of biblical exegesis. If I may quote one authority on the Book of Revelation, it was a 'celestiall theatre' or 'holy labyrinth' in which the reader was forced to find himself and to reintegrate the text with his own spiritual life.

Well, enough of this. It is too easy to score points off contemporary follies and we need only agree, in the context of this discussion, that the interest in the styles and languages of the past is an intrinsic feature of the English literary inheritance. So at this point I would like to stop skirting around the edges of my theme, and approach closer to the centre. There was one work of English fiction which two or three years ago most impressed and affected me when I was about to embark upon one of my own novels, *English Music*, and it is probably well known to all of you – it is *The Arcadia* by Sir Philip Sidney. It can, I suppose, be designated as a sixteenth-century prose romance but what has always intrigued me is the multitude of forms and devices which Philip Sidney employed. His narrative is interrupted by letters, songs, sonnets, theatrical dialogues in the form of eclogues, while the story itself moves from pantomime to tragedy, from melodrama to magical fantasy, from the depiction of battles to the invocation of pastoral. I might have mentioned *Tristram Shandy* in the same context, of course, and noted the fact that Dickens drew upon this kind of multiple narrative and even gave it the name of 'streaky bacon'. We have here then something which at least *might* be part of a recognizable English tradition – it may be very minor but it is also very noticeably there, even though I doubt if you will find it in many of the critical histories or critical studies of our literature. It might even be said to have gone underground.

At this point, before we embark upon the sticky subject of critical history, I would like to make a very brief diversion. Perhaps we can agree that, if there is a broad division between human beings, it is between those who hold a secular view of the world and those who entertain a religious notion of life and death. Of course there are degrees of faith and degrees of scepticism, and problems arise when they become confused with one another. That is why I would like to suggest only tentatively here that a dispossessed or displaced Protestantism – what might be called a secular Protestantism – has dominated twentieth-century literary criticism in this country. There are many examples but the names of F. R. Leavis and Raymond Williams are still fresh in our minds. Their achievements are significant and substantial – no one could doubt that – but there seems little doubt that the themes and beliefs which they explored in their reading of literature were largely taken from the values of a Protestant or Dissenting culture.

They praised the communication of lived experience, the concrete expression of moral truths, the subtleties and complexities of the individual consciousness – individuals who were of course necessarily part of a larger moral community. And they explored these concerns with a vocabulary and emphasis which effortlessly recalled the values of a Protestant hermeneutics. It is as if they were looking for confirmation of their erstwhile religious values within a context other than that of religion. For a certain kind of romantic or melodramatic vision, for high-spirited heterogeneity, for theatricality, for spectacle, for pantomimic humour, they had little if any time. And yet I am convinced that it is in these somewhat neglected areas, if anywhere, that we will actually find a true English sensibility at work.

Let me take the case of pantomime. Max Beerbohm has written that Christmas pantomime is 'the one art form that has been invented in England ... an art form,' he added, 'specially adapted to the English genius'. Charles Lamb extolled the virtues of 'the clownery and pantaloonery of these pantomimes' which, in one of those flashes of extraordinary insight of which he was capable, he compared to 'the grotesque Gothic heads that gape, and grin, in stone around the inside of the old Round Church of the Templars'. The Gothic connection is actually very apposite, as we shall see, and at least Lamb was wise enough to take the form itself very seriously indeed. But that wisdom has not come naturally to our more distinguished literary critics and literary historians. Where are the critical studies of pantomime, this true English art form? Where are the texts and the concordances? Let me put it more personally. We have all been asked to study, or are at least obliged to know about, the work of Robert Browning – that expert monolinguist, parodist and dramatic rhetorician. But how many of us know about his near-contemporary Dan Leno, whose dramatic monologues are more interesting and certainly more comic than anything in *The Ring and the Book*? He was the great star of the London halls, known as the 'funniest man on earth'. Of course he died young, as most music hall artistes did; he was worn out by alcoholism and periodic bouts of insanity, but not before becoming justly famous as Mother Goose, as the Railway Guard, as Sister Anne in *Bluebeard* and a hundred other extraordinary characters. His monologues are now quite forgotten – but I bring him to your attention now because I truly believe that he was a great English genius.

The theatricality displayed by the pantomime and Gothic art is an intrinsic aspect of the English genius. It is a theatricality in which pathos and comedy, tragedy and farce, are combined. Of course it is not the theatre of Racine; it is much closer to the theatre of Shakespeare. And it is a theatre which, in England at least, is not necessarily confined to the stage. Certain cases are self-evident. In Milton's dramatic verse, also, there are pervasive and continuous echoes of Shakespeare. But there are also more surprising examples of this English theatricality. I have been struck, for example, by the extent to which Blake's Prophetic Books mirror the Gothic dramas performed during his lifetime at the London Patent Theatres.

As I said before, the songs of the pantomime and the music hall may have more significance than has previously been recognized. It is a subject about which much more could be said but I would only add one point here – someone might usefully be employed in writing a book about the way in which changes in acting, scenery and even stage lighting have affected fiction and poetry as well as the drama itself. At this point, though, I would like to make a slight pantomimic jump.

We all know how the drama was in origin a form of religious ritual, how in this country its beginnings are to be found in Mysteries and the Miracle Plays and how its deepest source probably lies within the Catholic Mass itself. We also know how certain forms of Protestantism were as deeply opposed to drama as they were to Catholicism. As one theatrical historian has put it, at the time of the Reformation, 'Prompt-books of Roman Catholic origin and orientation were confiscated and burned, wardrobes were sold and scenic gear turned to other uses or left to decay.' Now I suggested earlier that the characteristic voice of English criticism seems to represent a form of secular Protestantism and, in this historical context, it is not hard to understand why that same criticism has tended to ignore the pantomimic, the theatrical, the scenic and the spectacular. Could it not be that, in so doing, they are also ignoring the buried traditions of a once Catholic England?

Let us try and imagine what kind of culture might emerge from such a tradition. Let us imagine, for a moment, that there had been no Reformation. I think we can agree that Catholicism tends to emphasize the significance of authority and historical tradition, whereas Protestantism emphasizes the moral value of individual experience. It is the difference between the quests of Spenser's Redcrosse Knight and Bunyan's Christian. Similarly Catholicism is a religion of ritual, spectacle and symbolism, whereas Protestantism is more concerned with the exigencies of the solitary conscience and the individual's relationship to God: it is not a long step from *The Pilgrim's Progress* to

The Prelude, and the connection between Protestantism and English Romanticism has often been made. The Protestant tradition is one which has characteristically also emphasized the uniqueness of the individual genius, and the exclusivity of individual creativity. Chatterton was, as he knew well enough himself, born at the wrong time.

So let us fantasize then about a Catholic culture. It might well have returned to an older tradition of creativity which is based upon imitation – until the late sixteenth century originality in English literature was not seen in terms of private fabrication but in terms of the individual adaptation and reinterpretation of the best literary works in existence. As Chaucer puts it in *The Parliament of Fowls*,

> For out of olde fields, as men sayeth,
> Cometh all this new corn from year to year

We might also expect this hypothetical culture to be far more interested in the possibilities of linguistic ritual, in a certain kind of sonority and cadence combined with a highly disciplined attention to formal variety and display; it might also be interested in spectacle, and in certain forms of historical exposition within the broad framework of an authoritative tradition. It might also be concerned with the symbolic re-enactment of certain visionary truths.

But this is the odd thing. Isn't this theoretical culture very much like the one which Nikolaus Pevsner considered to be uniquely and inalienably English – this interest in adapting previous styles, this 'self-conscious choice of a mode of expression', this belief in variety and display as elements of true invention, this sense of the individual artist dependent upon a historical or spiritual tradition? He found it everywhere within the English sensibility and, significantly, traced it back to a specifically Catholic source. At one point he describes the illuminated manuscripts of the Middle Ages, and notes the peculiar fact that narratives of the most sacred nature were counterpointed by illustrations in the margins which were, in his words, nothing more than 'grotesque caricatures' of the narrative itself. They were called 'babooneries', these irruptions of the comic into the sacred, and, according to Pevsner, 'if one tries to trace the baboonery to its source, one finds that it originated in England'.

Quite so. But if this is part of the culture of Catholic England, it is also something we find in what Charles Dickens called the 'streaky bacon' effect of his narratives. It is in Sidney's *Arcadia*. It is in the advertisements placed on Reynolds's Great Theatrical Booth in August 1730, when he announced 'a medley of mirth and sorrow' as well as a puppet show which would be 'comical, tragical, farcical, droll'. It is everywhere. It has been described as baboonery but let us call it, more politely, heterogeneity. It lies in a characteristic mixture of forms and styles, in the alternation between tragedy and comedy, in the unwillingness to maintain one mood for very long, in the manipulation of form for theatrical effect. It is not something which you will find celebrated in the traditional histories of English literature; it is not part of Leavis's 'Great Tradition' or Williams's description of novels as 'knowable communities'. But if we cannot find it in the twentieth century, perhaps we can go back a little and recall what Voltaire wrote in his *Letters Concerning the English Nation*, published in the 1730s –

> It seems that up to now the English have only produced irregular beauties . . . Their poetical genius resembles a closely grown tree planted by nature, throwing out a thousand branches here and there and growing lustily and without rules.

This is precisely what Stendhal meant, also, when in *Racine and Shakespeare* he contrasted the two dramatists and questioned the French passion for the unities of time and space.

It is for this reason that Gothic literature has always seemed to me to be, of all types of fiction, the most thoroughly English in inspiration and execution. We have heard the word before on this occasion – Charles Lamb used it in connection with the pantomime, and Pevsner employed it to describe a particular type of English historicism. There is no time now to investigate the debt which writers as dissimilar as Charles Dickens and Emily Brontë owe to the Gothic novel, or to pursue its modern reincarnation in the English murder mystery or detective story, but it is worth noting that in its consummate use of sensationalism and artifice Gothic literature always hovers on that ambiguous edge between comedy and tragedy where, as we have seen, the English genius seems happiest to reside. It is an innately theatrical form, in other words, which depends upon a congregation of moods and styles. As one prologue to a Gothic play of the late eighteenth century put it, 'it is a drama of mingled nature, operatic, comical and tragical'. One might say the same about almost all of the English works I have discussed here. One might say the same about two other great

English artists of more recent date – Havergal Brian, in his monumental *Gothic Symphony* (one sees how that word keeps on recurring)
created what one musicologist has called the 'mood of contradictory,
simultaneous parts'. And in Stanley Spencer we have an English artist
with a unique ability to mingle the sacred and the profane with all the
gusto of his medieval predecessors. The work of Spencer has its own
'babooneries'.

It is possible, then, that in observing these various English writers
and artists, and in drawing out some of the less acknowledged
connections between them, we are approaching some definition of
English taste or English sensibility. I am almost tempted to refer this
hybrid art to the hybrid nature of the English race. As Defoe put it in
The True Born Englishman:

> From this Amphibious Ill-born mob began
> *That vain ill-natured thing,* an Englishman . . .
> By which with easie search you may distinguish
> *Your Roman-Saxon-Danish-Norman* English.

Of course I realize that I may have overstepped the line in my
argument, when I suggested that these English works from Sidney to
Havergal Brian, from the Gothic novel to Stanley Spencer, represent
the powerful but unacknowledged presence of the old Catholic culture
within our nation – on an ordinary level, of course, very few of the
writers and artists whom I have been discussing had even the remotest
connection with the Roman Catholic Church as such. But perhaps
there is a different kind of inheritance, and a different kind of
continuity. In this university Rupert Sheldrake has completed some
remarkable work on the subject of 'morphic resonance', and in his
book entitled *The Presence of the Past: Morphic Resonance and the
Habits of Nature* he has suggested that '. . . a person may for some
reason tune in by morphic resonance to a person who lived in the past.'
Rupert Sheldrake went on to suggest that we must 'think of the past
pressed up, as it were, against the present and so potentially present
everywhere'. I suppose in this lecture I have been considering the
possibility of something we might call chronological resonance. Just as
it seems possible to me that a street or dwelling can materially affect
the character and behaviour of the people who live within them, is it
not also possible that within our sensibility and our language there are
patterns of continuity and resemblance which have persisted from the

thirteenth or fourteenth centuries and perhaps even beyond that? And is it not possible that, in outlining what I consider to be a buried Catholic tradition, such a pattern can be seen to emerge?

And here I come to my central belief. The Englishness of English literature is not some literary construct, some museum of the past, some enclosed hierarchical order – the very heterogeneity at the centre of the English sensibility suggests that it is in no way exclusive. I am trying to describe a line of force which is the very life and breath of the sentences we are writing now. I am trying to chart the passage of English literature through time, creating its own patterns and energies. Some might think of this as constricting but for me it is liberating – as liberating as the return home after a long period in another country. There is such a thing as homesickness, after all: it is the need for belonging, for continuity, for the embrace of the city or street from which you have come. But what greater or more enduring home can we have than our language? So when I talk about the Englishness of English literature I am not referring to some impersonal tradition. I am talking about something very close to us.

I would like to end by quoting from Byron's *The Prophecy of Dante*:

> We can have but one country, and even yet
>   Thou'rt mine – my bones shall be within thy breast,
> My soul within thy language . . .

For I do believe that there is such a country, such a national literature, and to lose sight of it would be to lose sight of our own selves.

University of Cambridge, Leslie Stephen Lecture
22 October 1993

340

123

London Luminaries and Cockney Visionaries

Dan Leno, the great pantomime dame, comic and music hall star, known as 'the funniest man on earth', died in London on the last day of October 1904. 'I defy anyone not to have loved him at first sight,' Max Beerbohm wrote,

> the moment he capered on the stage with that air of wild determination, squirming in every limb with some deep grievance that must be outpoured, bent but not broken, faint but pursuing, incarnate of the will to live in a world not at all worth living in.

So Beerbohm described him. But the truth is that Dan Leno did not live for very long. He played Mother Goose just once too often and this small, nervous, excitable man died of exhaustion.

He had been born just forty-four years before, on a spot now covered by St Pancras railway station, but on the occasion of his funeral many thousands of Londoners lined the streets of the city. They were mourning a man who had represented for them their lives and their condition; in his role as a shop-house waiter, a grass widow, a grocer's assistant, a lady of the old school, or simply 'One Of The Unemployed', he came to symbolize all the life and energy and variety of the city itself. I like to think of him as being buried beneath one of the great halls where he performed – the Old Mo in Drury Lane, the Panorama in Shoreditch, the Cambridge in Bishopsgate – while above him roars for ever what Thomas De Quincey called 'the uproar of unresting London'. Now of course Dan Leno is quite forgotten. His name and reputation have been literally swallowed up by the silence of the grave.

So why now, at the end of the twentieth century, should I wish to resurrect him? Why should I want to call him back to a city – his city – which seems to have changed beyond all recognition? I do so precisely because it has not changed. He would recognize it well enough. He would recognize the faces of Londoners, always so familiar to him. He would understand their expressions, their gestures, their moods. Of

341

course there have been, and will always be, modifications. I have lived here all my life, as many of you have done, and I have witnessed the developments, the rebuilding, the violence, the riots, the whole continual process of urban existence. It is that process I want to define tonight: I want to talk to you about those London luminaries and those Cockney visionaries who in their art have expressed the true nature and spirit of this place. I want to describe those artists, poets, dramatists, novelists, actors who have recreated all the variety, the energy and the spectacle which this city expects and demands of its inhabitants. They have expressed the horror, too, for this also has been one of the dark places of the earth.

The truth is that London has always been a shadowy and merciless city. It has been built upon the imperatives of power and money rather than the needs or aspirations of its inhabitants. For many thousands of years – literally thousands – it has been a city of commerce and trade. It has attracted the poor and then crushed them in its progress since, as the old prayer of the London alchemist puts it, 'it is the city of gold, it is the city of fire, it is the city of death'. Plenty of gold has been found here, but there has also been much fire and much death. London has sucked up waves of immigration. It has presided over riots and repression. Sometimes it even seems to me that the city itself creates the conditions of its own growth, that it somehow plays an active part in its own development like some complex organism slowly discovering its form. Certainly it affects the lives, the behaviour, the speech, even the gestures of the people who live within it: Dan Leno understood this, and so I place him in the line of great Cockney visionaries. He understood the spirit of London, the genius of London, and that is what I want to talk about tonight since I believe that nothing fundamental has changed.

Let me tell you a true London story. There is a certain street I know well – an ordinary street of offices and shops, much of it redeveloped over the last ten years. I will call it City Lane, to protect the innocent. I happened some months ago to be reading a newspaper when the name of this particular locality caught my attention: it seemed that the police had visited an establishment there because of certain sexual or pornographic activities. This surprised me because City Lane is an utterly staid and nondescript place. But it is also a very ancient street – I knew that – and on an instinct I looked at my old maps and topographical descriptions of London. And there was City Lane described, in the fourteenth century, as being notorious for its brothels and stews of vice. So here, you might say, is a continuity.

Let me provide you with another example. The streets close to the British Museum, in particular Great Russell Street and Great Queen Street, have for many centuries been the home of occult or radical spiritual groups. The Theosophical Society had its headquarters opposite the museum, while the Order of the Golden Dawn met in Great Queen Street – that is also the street where the headquarters of the freemasons was first established in the mid-eighteenth century and where, as you may know, it remains to this day. The Swedenborg Society is a few yards away, opposite Bloomsbury Square. You will find perhaps the most famous occult bookshop in England, the Atlantis Bookshop, in Museum Street while only a few yards away stands Equinox, the astrological bookshop, in Neal Street. These are the patterns of habitation, and patterns of inheritance, which seem to emerge from the very streets and alleys of the capital. Areas like this are reminiscent of what Henry James said of Craven Street, that narrow thoroughfare which runs down from the Strand towards the river – he said that it was 'packed to blackness with accumulations of suffered experience'.

We must not think of time as some continually flowing stream moving in one direction. Think of it more as a lava flow from some unknown source of fire. Some parts of it move forward, some parts of it branch off and form separate channels, some parts of it slow down and eventually harden. Recently I joined a group of enthusiasts who were actively searching for the first playhouse ever built in London – ever built in England. It is to be found in Shoreditch, near New Inn Yard. And in their enthusiasm for the old landmarks, for the ruined stones beneath the present street level, for the remains of the past, I saw the spirit of the city reasserting itself and I felt a sense of exaltation. It is as if the past and present were then locked in an embrace, like lovers. Perhaps this is more visionary than realistic but, then, what is the use of a writer who has no vision? That is why I feel impelled to talk about London, about the place from which I have come – which has formed me and in whose life I myself can live. I am talking about a sensibility and a culture which has persisted for many centuries.

It is not an easy subject to discuss, I admit, because the cultural traditions of London have largely gone unrecognized or unacknowledged. When I was obliged to study literature as a young man I was told, for example, that there was no real theatre in nineteenth-century London except for a few rather grotesque Shakespearean revivals. But if someone had just scratched the surface they would have found penny gaffs, music halls, patent theatres, blood tubs, Gothic dramas, pantomimes, the routines in the song-and-supper rooms and in the free-and-easies.

Let me take another example. For many centuries there has been a tradition in London of what were called monopolylinguists – in other words comedians or actors who play a number of quick-change parts in the course of one performance. In the eighteenth century Samuel Foote had a comic routine, 'Tea at the Haymarket', which affected writers as diverse as Samuel Johnson and William Blake. His successor in the early nineteenth century was Charles Mathews, who so impressed and influenced Charles Dickens that the novelist discussed him endlessly. In 1831 he had seen Mathews play Miss Mildew, a lady dressed entirely in white, and he never forgot it: we know what happened to that dear old creature when she re-emerged, as Miss Havisham, many years later. And the successor of Mathews was of course Leno himself, whom Dickens also met and admired.

But you will find nothing of this particular and native London art form in any of the standard reference books, even though it is one that has carried on into our own time in the routines of impersonators and stand-up comics such as John Sessions or Jack Dee, who may or may not be related to the great Doctor Dee. In the same fashion modern street theatre and contemporary buskers are the direct descendants of the running patterers and ballad singers of the last century who haunted the streets of the city. You may think I have been talking about the past, but all the time I am talking about the present. I am describing what is all around us still, if we cared to see it.

Let me mention one last example of the London spirit that goes unrecognized. In my university days we were encouraged to read the poets of the late nineteenth century – Johnson, Dowson, the early Yeats, and so on. They were the strange fruit in that hothouse known as the *fin de siècle*. But, for real pathos and diversity, the scholar or critic should turn to the tunes of the London halls. These are songs that still retain enormous power and feeling – who could fail to be moved by verses like 'My Shadow Is My Only Pal', or 'When These Old Clothes Were New'? Who could fail to be amused by 'Why Don't We Have the Sea in London' or 'Don't Stick It Out Like That' or 'I Don't Suppose He'll Do It Again for Months and Months and Months'? If

London could be turned into an allegorical personage in some neoclassical extravaganza, it would be heard singing these songs. They are powerful because they are charged with the real presence of place, just as much as the dark stones of London Wall or the steel surfaces of the Lloyds Building. These are the true melodies of London, and only a very blinkered culture can afford to ignore them.

I call them true melodies because they come very close to the kind of theatricality that I believe to be an intrinsic and necessary aspect of the London genius. They possess that spirit of place. When I talk about theatricality, however, I am not necessarily talking only about the theatre – I am talking about a particular London sensibility that derives its energy from variety, from spectacle, and from display. I am talking about a sensibility in which pathos and comedy, high tragedy and low farce, are effortlessly combined. The two greatest London novelists, Henry Fielding and Charles Dickens, were steeped in that sense of life. Of course they were both practising playwrights as well as novelists but, what is more important, their fiction is saturated with the conventions of the theatre. All his life Dickens haunted the penny gaffs and the small playhouses; when he was a boy, it is very probable that he acted in them. So although it is possible to read the death of Little Nell without laughing, it is impossible to read it without realizing that Dickens had already seen it done on the stage.

Then there is that other great Cockney visionary, the painter Turner. He was born in Maiden Lane, as you know, just off Covent Garden, and many critics have analysed his debt to theatrical scenery as well as the great London dioramas. He said himself that he got his inspiration for one of his greatest paintings, *Ulysses Deriding Polyphemus*, from a pantomime song in a little piece of stage business called *Melodrame Mad*. Turner could even quote the verse:

> I sing the cave of Polypheme,
> Ulysses made him cry out,
> For he ate his mutton, drank his wine,
> And then he poked his eye out.

The influence of the music hall, you see, is everywhere.

In passing I would like to mention another Cockney visionary, William Blake. He was born in Broad Street, just by Golden Square, and only left London once in his life. He really had no need to go anywhere else: he saw, literally *saw*, the universe here. Perhaps we all

can, if we look hard enough. I have called them Cockney visionaries –
Dickens, Blake, Turner. I could have chosen others but I wanted to give
you the benefit of a novelist, a poet and a painter to suggest to you a
particular London spirit that entered them and a particular London
presence that surrounded them.

But I am not, as I said before, talking about a dead or irrelevant past.
I am trying to disclose a definite pattern of continuity. The small
playhouses of previous centuries are now reincarnated, in our own
time, in venues like the Bush and the Gate, the Hampstead Theatre, the
Tricycle Theatre in Kilburn and the Warehouse Theatre in Croydon. In
the same way I am not talking about dead authors. I am also describing
modern London novelists such as Angela Carter, with her wonderful
understanding of urban pantomime, of Michael Moorcock and his
historical panoramas of London, of Iain Sinclair and his explorations
of London mythology. I am invoking a living inheritance that has
everything to do with the spirit of place and with the nature of the city.

Since I have mentioned some contemporary London novelists,
perhaps I may be allowed a very brief passage of autobiography. I was
brought up on a council house estate in west London. It was the very
best start in life I could possibly have had because somehow, from an
early age, the city became the landscape of my imagination. You don't
have to be brought up in a grand house to have a sense of the past, and
I truly believe that there are certain people to whom or through whom
the territory – the place – the past – speaks. I often wondered where my
novels came from – or, rather, I knew where they came from, but I
never understood why they took the form which they did. I am always
being accused of mixing the comic with the serious, of creating
theatrical caricatures, of treating fiction as if it were some kind of
intellectual or cultural pantomime. This puzzled me because I really
couldn't help myself. It just happened. Now, at last, I know why it
happened. I was coming into my inheritance.

And what else could it be but the inheritance of these Cockney
visionaries, Blake, Turner and Dickens? All of them were preoccupied
with light and darkness, in a city that is built in the shadows of money
and power; all of them were entranced by the scenic and the
spectacular, in a city that is continually filled with the energetic display
of people and institutions. They understood the energy of London,
they understood its variety, and they also understood its darkness. But
they are visionaries because they represented the symbolic dimension of
existence in what Blake called 'Infinite London' – in this vast concourse

of people they understood the pity and mystery of existence just as surely as they understood its noise and its bustle. They were all, by the way, dismissed by contemporary reviewers as being out of touch with reality – can you imagine it? Turner and Blake were derided as madmen, while the mature Dickens was condemned as a feeble remnant of his younger self. I am sure that the judgement of contemporary reviewers is very much higher, although sometimes just the tiniest shadow of a doubt crosses my mind.

It has often struck me, for example, how for centuries there has always been one sure distinction within London culture. There has always been a journalistic and intellectual establishment which likes to think of itself as being fashionable or even enlightened. It constitutes an informal circle of what might be called *bien pensants* – or, in the cliché of our day, the politically correct. These are the people who parrot whatever the conventional wisdom might be, and support the shallow-minded artists who reflect it in their work. But in London there has always been a stronger and more significant tradition – it is that of the energetic, individualistic and unfashionable artists who, more often than not, turn out to be native Londoners. They may be right-wing reactionaries or apolitical anarchists, but they always reject the values of the standard intellectual culture and, as a result, they are discounted, or attacked, or marginalized. It happened to Blake, it happened to Turner, it happened to Dickens in the last half of his literary career – which of course is enough to say that these establishment attacks are not only foolish but ultimately unsuccessful.

I will tell you what the newspaper critics disliked about the Cockney visionaries. They disliked precisely those qualities which were essential to their vision of the great city. They disliked their energetic display. They disliked the variety they provided. They deplored Turner's 'visionary absurdities' and 'crude theatrical blotches' – just as they condemned Dickens's theatrical caricatures. They also condemned Dickens for mixing the tragic with the comic, just as they despised Blake for mixing the spiritual with the material. They detested what is an essentially Cockney vision. Dickens called it the 'streaky bacon' effect, and revelled in it. That is why he can go from the pathetic death of Paul Dombey to the farcical comedy of Toots in the space of a page. But let us choose a phrase other than 'streaky bacon'. Let us call it heterogeneity. It is what Dan Leno managed when he went from the tragedy of the unemployed to the comedy of the waitress in a moment's change. It is what happens in that great city novel, Pierce

Egan's *Life in London*, which moves rapidly from verse to philosophical speculation and dashes from topography to an operatic score.

Again I make no apologies for going back so many centuries, because they are as close to us as tomorrow or yesterday. They are close to us because we still live in a city where the extremes of the human condition meet, where one emotion or mood is quickly succeeded by another, where comedy and tragedy are to be seen side by side. This is the true London sensibility, and I want to explore it one stage further. Some thirty-eight years ago Nikolaus Pevsner gave a very interesting series of lectures on *The Englishness of English Art*, and he located one of the enduring features of English style as 'historicism', by which he meant the interest of English artists and architects in the self-conscious use of past styles and in experimenting with the details of various historical periods. But when we talk about stylistic variety, display, heterogeneity, we are discussing something close to what I have outlined as the London genius – perhaps that is why Pevsner chose so many examples of London architecture in order to make his point. He talks about Holloway Prison conceived as a Gothic castle, and of Wren's church of St Mary Aldemary in Queen Victoria Street which is an amalgam of fourteenth- and seventeenth-century aspects.

I would like to mention one of my own favourite architects, Nicholas Hawksmoor, who could create two sets of designs – one in Baroque, the other in Gothic – and allow the appropriate authorities to choose according to taste. It is reminiscent of the work of Thomas Chatterton, who committed suicide in a street near the Grays Inn Road – in the middle of the eighteenth century he wrote authentic medieval ballads. And so here we have another continuing London tradition, this experimental and self-conscious use of past styles. Of course these days it is called post-modernism, as if it never existed before, but one of the features of contemporary cultural journalism seems to be a great ignorance of the past.

And that brings me back to the central point – that the real continuities and traditions of London, the real spirit of place, are characteristically overlooked or forgotten. But I am not adopting some variant of London jingoism. This is not quaint Cockney pride of the old sort. The central point is that this variety, this heterogeneity, is of more than just historical interest – it means that it can include and empower anything that strays within its bounds. That is why London writing is always open to new themes and concerns – in our own time this has included black writing, gay writing, feminist writing. I could mention here Caryl Phillips, or Neil Bartlett, or Jeanette Winterson, whose identities as strikingly individual writers are strengthened by their association with London. I am not talking about one exclusive inheritance, in other words, or some form of private property; I am describing an open sensibility which is continually being regenerated. The city has to a large extent been created by successive generations of immigrants, from the Huguenots to the Bangladeshis, and in the same way its variegated and heterogeneous culture has been maintained and strengthened by the successive arrival of first generation Londoners. And that of course is the true strength of an old city – within its very texture and structure it incorporates a diversity of human moods and actions, events and responses. It is strengthened at the same time as it strengthens those who become a part of it.

That is why this London sensibility, this sense of place, is also very much at the centre of London painting by artists who may have been born elsewhere. There is indeed what the painter Kitaj has described as a 'School of London' and it is represented by Kitaj himself and by such painters as Auerbach and Kossoff as well as those of a younger generation – what their work shares is a sense of great energy and exuberant painterliness, combined with a unique ability to divine the mythic and the fabulous within images of the contemporary city, and an extraordinary attention to colour, sensation and the narrative possibilities of urban life. Frank Auerbach has painted the streets of London or the area of Primrose Hill over and over again; while Leon Kossoff has his own vision of Hackney and Bethnal Green and Kings Cross. These painters have for me the same intensity and almost hallucinatory vividness which Turner brought to the Thames and to what Ruskin called his 'whole compass of the London world'. Here too there is a continuity, and in the great art schools of Camberwell, the Slade, St Martin's, Goldsmiths and the Royal College it is being celebrated and maintained.

I believe I am describing London in almost a religious sense, although I cannot be sure what particular religion it is. Someone once said that cities are always pagan places, and there is a great truth to that. I have been talking about the theatrical presence of London culture and the dramatic roots of the London genius, for example, and it is well known that the theatre itself has its origins in Catholic ritual. But it may even go beyond the Catholic Mass and the old Catholic culture of London. When we contemplate Dan Leno dressed up as Mother Goose, we may be considering something very pagan indeed.

349

And there is another point here, too. The London visionaries I have been discussing are not necessarily ethical or moral artists. They are not necessarily concerned with the minutiae of the human psyche, or with debates about values and beliefs. They tend to favour spectacle and melodrama and the energetic exploitation of whatever medium they are employing. As city writers and artists they are more concerned with the external life, with the movement of crowds, with the great general drama of the human spirit. They have a sense of energy and splendour, of ritual and display, which may have very little to do with ethical judgement or the exercise of moral consciousness. That is why the more intellectual critics, for example, hated Dickens so much. These Cockney visionaries have a very powerful sense of the sacred, but in the darkness of Dickens's novels or in the light of Turner's paintings there may be something as pagan as Mother Goose. You remember that when Turner died, not far from here, in Chelsea, his last words are supposed to have been, 'The sun is God.'

There is an irrepressible energy and exuberance here which seems to me characteristic of great London artists, as if they always knew that they were part of something much larger than their own selves. When William Blake lay on his deathbed, in a small courtyard off the Strand, he died singing. But these are not fashionable notions now. There is a great problem in talking about truly religious artists – of being a religious artist – in a predominantly secular world.

But nevertheless there is a continuity here, and there is an inheritance which we can all share. In my own case I have noticed when writing in the voice of Chatterton, or Hawksmoor, that the sentences seemed almost to form themselves in some simulacrum of the London period I was describing. In my most recent novel, *The House of Doctor Dee*, I have tried to invoke my own vision of the continuing city – that is why some of it is set in the sixteenth century – but I knew, as I was writing these passages, that the speech, the behaviour and the beliefs of sixteenth-century Londoners were exactly as I described them. I do not believe this to be an act of mediumship or divination – except in the sense that one is divining the historical patterns of London speech or London writing that lie just below the surface of our contemporary language.

We seem to have come a long way from Dan Leno and his death in the October of 1904, worn out by his life in the halls and on the pantomime stage, dazed by his fame, cooked by gaslight, and destroyed by insanity. But he was also a Cockney visionary, just as much as Turner or Blake or Dickens, and I think this great chronicler of the streets and trades and cries of London would have understood perfectly everything I have tried to say tonight. I hope that you have understood it, too, because the truth is that if we lose sight of our city – if we lose sight of our inheritance – then we lose sight of our own selves as well.

LWT Lecture, Victoria and Albert Museum.
7 December 1993

124

William Blake, A Spiritual Radical

The subject of this talk is Blake, but it may not be the Blake whom we all know. It may not be the Blake of 'Jerusalem' and 'Tyger Tyger'. Instead I want to take you into what was for me, before I began this biography, unknown territory. I want to talk to you about spiritual radicalism. I want to talk to you about a London which is as foreign to us today as Marrakesh or Delhi. I want to talk about a revolutionary city once filled with magicians and prophets and visionaries. Blake described it as 'Spiritual Four Fold London eternal'.

Let me begin at the beginning. William Blake was born within a family of hosiers. It is a very honourable trade, of course, but it also has an interesting history. Hosiers or cloth-makers, their counterparts, have always been connected with spiritual radicalism. We learn in the fifteenth century of Lollard heresy, particularly in the cloth-working villages of Buckinghamshire, Essex and Kent. Thomas Cromwell was the son of a cloth-maker. William Tyndale came from a family of cloth-workers. The phrase 'man of the cloth', popularly applied to clergymen, in fact described travelling preachers.

What did this family of spiritual dissenters read to him but the Bible? The cadences and images of that book haunted him for the rest of his life. What did he see around him as a child, too, but visions of the Bible – of prophets, of angels, and of God himself who peeped at him through the window of Broad Street. London became for him a biblical city, a city of revelation and apocalypse, the home of a true spiritual art. That is how it was that this son of a hosier, this son of religious dissent, was to create a poetry and an art as intricate and as elaborate as anything to be found in Michelangelo or in Dante.

But why on earth should hosiers be spiritual dissenters, then? It is meditative and solitary work. It is done in silence. It is the same atmosphere as that of the cobbler; and shoemakers, too, have a history of radicalism. There is a famous book on radical shoemakers called *Lives of the Distinguished Shoemakers*. There is in fact a theory, first suggested to me by that great London historian Raphael Samuel, that radicalism itself may spring from this type of intense and silent labour. It is well known for example that blacksmiths tended to be very orthodox, very conservative, and it is generally believed that this is because they drank far too much because of the heat, and were surrounded by so much noise that they could not hear themselves think. But it was certainly solitary, perhaps meditative, artisans who characteristically did become radicals. We have to recall here, for a moment, that Blake himself – the son of a hosier – became an engraver. This is also a work to be performed in silence and in isolation, and at a later stage we will discuss the extraordinary spiritual history amongst the practitioners of that particular craft as well as among its companion trade of printing.

But let me first turn to Blake's spiritual history. Go back with him to Westminster Abbey where, as an apprentice engraver, he walked among the tombs of the great dead. It was for him a time of revelation – again and again in his art he returns to the images he first glimpsed there. The faces of the dead appeared to him in vision. The canopies of their tombs are to be found in his art, together with the bosses, the sculpted foliage and the panels of the abbey. And out of this emerged the last great religious artist in England.

What do we see in his work, after all, but the belief in spiritual form, the divine outline traced with love and reverence? In works such as *The Three Maries at the Sepulchre* and *On the Morning of Christ's Nativity* we see the extraordinary devotion of his nature. May I mention that this is also very close to a Catholic art? Blake had a great reverence for the past, and for the cultural inheritance of the nation, and we ought to remember here that England was a Catholic nation for a thousand years before it ever became Protestant. Is it not possible that by those acts of divination and intuition which came so naturally to him he tapped into our forgotten inheritance?

Remember that he once saw a vision of monks in the abbey. Remember that he once told Samuel Palmer that, of all forms of government, papal government was best. He was probably referring here to the papacy of Julius II, that great figure who wished to be buried by the tomb of Nero, the Pope who donned armour and led his troops in battle. It was he who must have inspired Baudelaire when he said that as a child he wished for one of two things – he wished either to be a comic actor or a military pope. But Julius II was also the great patron of Michelangelo and, in espousing a papal government, Blake is looking back with longing to a time when there was a public spiritual art, a national religious art to be seen on frescoes and in statuary.

But his devotion also has deeper and darker sources. We know the great images of Blake's art and prophecies – Los with his mallet, the beaked figure in *Jerusalem*, the hermaphrodites in the margins of *The Four Zoas*. Now what do we find in the stone gargoyles and hidden images of medieval churches but the figures of the famous mallet god, of beaked figures and of hermaphrodites? These are in turn taken from the pagan past of Europe, which early Christians adopted – and Blake in turn, by an act of divinatory imagination, has found them too. He said in the catalogue to his exhibition that he had been transported back to the great cities of an inconceivably remote past – it may be that he meant it more literally than we realize. At this point, of course, he began his own spiritual journey. But before we go with him, let me take you on one of my own.

Blake was in many respects a Cockney, a Londoner of a recognizable type. What kind of radical is it that is born in Infinite London, as Blake put it? What does it mean to be 'radical' in any case? I conferred with my dictionary, and found that one of the original meanings of the word is 'native heat' or the properties intrinsic to any particular body. What then is the 'native heat' of Londoners? Those of you who have ever travelled on the Underground – I rarely do since at my age I find it too exciting – may think you know. But it also has characteristics that are rather less palpable.

I have recently been reading Thomas More and John Milton as well as Blake. More and Milton were born within a few yards of each other – Milk Street and Bread Street respectively – but there is one particular quality which they also share with Blake. That is the capacity for abuse of the most disgusting kind. We have More telling Luther, 'If you extend your filthy mouth far open someone should shit in it' (not the language of a saint, perhaps, but the language of the city); and we have Milton telling various ecclesiastical dignitaries to 'sit upon a stool and strain, nothing but dirt and filth comes from you'. And then we have Blake: 'If Blake could do this when he rose up from shite, What might he not do if he sat down to write.' So there is a certain scatological tinge to the vocabulary of Londoners.

Blake was also an artisan, of course, and London artisans have always been prone to radicalism and dissent. They were almost forced to, you see, since they were always discriminated against by the established authorities. In fifteenth-century London even the indigenous artisans, outside the network of the guilds, were officially termed 'foreigners'. I mentioned printers, and to invoke that name is to invoke the whole history of London radicalism. But it leads to another aspect of London, and the nature of radicalism within it.

There is a wonderful story by the writer, Arthur Machen, in which he describes an area of Stoke Newington where, on occasions, an enchanted landscape can be glimpsed and sometimes even entered. Few people have seen it, or know how to see it; but those who do can speak of nothing else. Machen wrote this story, 'N', in the early thirties but now, at the end of the twentieth century, we are beginning to realize that there are other enchanted areas in London which remain visible and powerful to anyone who cares to look for them. You may think we have strayed very far from Blake's spiritualism, but in fact we have only made the slightest detour.

I was recently asked to write an anniversary tribute for a newspaper called the *Big Issue*. I cannot remember now what kind of anniversary it was, but as you know the *Big Issue* is devoted to the needs of the homeless and the unemployed. I bought a copy from a charming young person on the street and, lo and behold, I discovered that it is produced and published along the Clerkenwell Road, just a few yards south of Clerkenwell Green. Where, you might think, is the enchantment here? Well, in the eighteenth century the printers of Clerkenwell were denounced by the authorities for distributing 'seditious and blasphemous literature'. In a house on Clerkenwell Green itself, Lenin edited and published a revolutionary journal (known in translation, as *The Spark*); that house is now the Marx Memorial Library. There is, then, a continuity.

The enchantment is one of place and of time; it is as if an area can create patterns of interest, or patterns of habitation, so that the same kinds of activity (indeed often the same kind of people) seem to emerge in the same small territory. Consider the case of Clerkenwell once more. The first of the Tolpuddle Martyrs to return to this country was greeted on Clerkenwell Green by a large crowd. The group of political radicals known as the London Corresponding Society met in Clerkenwell. The Chartists, in part protesting against unemployment, began their marches from Clerkenwell Green. John Wilkes, the radical whose slogan was 'Wilkes and Liberty!', was born in Clerkenwell; the great visionary who lived among the artisans, Emmanuel Swedenborg, died in Clerkenwell. Wat Tyler, leading his vast army of the dispossessed, stormed the priory of Clerkenwell – just a few yards east of the offices of the *Big Issue*. So it is possible to see how, in this pattern of time and continuity, the *Big Issue* has itself found its true radical home. And of course the coincidences begin to multiply. We read in the sixteenth-century chronicle of John Stow that the London cloth-makers, our old radical friends, paid £14 each year to the churchwardens of Clerken-well.

Let me mention another group of religious dissenters here in passing, the Lollards. It is known that in the fifteenth century, they found refuge and fellow sympathizers in Coleman Street in the City. But then two centuries later we hear of Puritan loyalists taking refuge in safe houses after the Restoration – and where do they go, but Coleman Street?

So we must see Blake living within what he called 'Infinite London'. He wrote this while he lived in South Molton Street – in middle age he was still very close to his birthplace in Broad Street. Like all true Cockney visionaries, like Dickens, he never moved very far within the city itself. 'I behold London,' he wrote, 'a Human awful wonder of God.' His spiritual radicalism was very much part of this city, and it is worth recalling the conditions in which spiritual and political radical-ism flourished in late eighteenth-century London. It was a most extraordinary time of change and turmoil. There has never been a period in the history of London when there were so many political clubs, debating societies, dissenting groups, underground newspapers. It was a time of great religious enthusiasm, of course, with the lives of John Wesley, Joanna Southcott and Richard Brothers as the single most important examples. We have to think of a city, and of a culture, filled with radical and even revolutionary intimations. The established order of the eighteenth century was indeed coming to an end, assaulted again and again by the new industrialism, the new commercialism, the stirrings of popular or at least freeholder democracy. There was the American War of Independence. And then of course the French Revolution. We must remember, too, that for most of Blake's lifetime Britain was at war. But for him something else more important was going to happen. He believed that the old order, 'Old Corruption', might be broken apart and that the process of spiritual regeneration might begin.

Then look again at London itself. In the late eighteenth century this city was the single most oppressive urban conglomeration on the face of the earth. It was also the richest city on earth. It had some of the most pernicious slums. There were many riots – by butchers, by bakers, not perhaps by candlestick-makers but certainly by coal-porters and silk-weavers. There were occasions, like the time of the Wilkes riots and the Gordon riots, when the city was more or less under the control of the mob. Blake himself was caught up in one great riot, and watched Newgate being burned to the ground and the prisoners freed. He also knew the conditions of London from very close at hand. Round the corner from his house was a parish workhouse. It was supposed to house three hundred of the poor, but it was severely overcrowded. One contemporary report speaks of 'the stench hardly supportable, poor creatures, almost naked, and the living to go to bed with the dead'. In fact Blake's father supplied linen to that workhouse, and it is not too fanciful to imagine the young Blake delivering it at the door. So the poet of London really did know what he was talking about. He was a London radical because he knew what London was actually like. But what of his colleagues and contemporaries?

It is often assumed that Blake fell in with a group of radicals who worked with Tom Paine, the author of *The Rights of Man*, and who were associated with the newly formed Society for Constitutional Information. Blake could then be viewed as a London radical of a recognizable type. But the fact is that there is no evidence at all to suggest that Blake was closely involved with these people or groups. He may have met Paine on one or two occasions, at the house of the bookseller Joseph Johnson, but there is no record of the fact. He was certainly never a member of any of the radical associations of the period. It is a pertinent fact that he remained apart from them. 'I must create a system, or be enslaved by another man's,' is the declaration of one of his prophetic characters, and that more or less represents his own stance in the world. It informs his artistic experiments, the nature of his Prophetic Books, his very being in the world.

Now the conventional radicals of the period, like Paine and Joseph Priestley and Mary Wollstonecraft, were unitarians or deists, believers in what Wollstonecraft called 'rational religion'; they were also materialists and progressives who implicitly or explicitly denied the importance of historical tradition. All of these things Blake abhorred: he believed in divine inspiration, in the presence of angels, in the paramount importance of historical and cultural inheritance. They in turn would have seen an artisan of eccentric views, if they bothered to see him at all, a journeyman engraver who could be very difficult in company – sometimes very assertive, sometimes quiet and self-absorbed. We will not find his particular form of spirituality, then, among these people. We will have to look elsewhere.

Let us start with Blake and his wife sitting naked in the garden of their house in Lambeth. It is a story told by one of his few patrons, and indeed one of his few friends. 'At the end of Hercules Buildings there was a summer house. Mr Butts calling one day found Mr and Mrs Blake sitting by this summer house, freed from "those troublesome disguises which have prevailed since the Fall".' This is a mid-Victorian way of saying that they were not wearing any clothes. 'Come in!' cried Blake, 'it's only Adam and Eve, you know!' This has generally been dismissed as anecdotage, but that is to miss one of the central aspects of Blake's radicalism. He is reported declaring, towards the end of his life, that 'the Gymnosophists of India, the ancient Britons, and others of whom History tells, who went naked, were wiser than the rest of mankind pure and wise – and it would be as well if the world could be as they.' Blake and his wife can in fact be seen within the context of an entire history of English radicalism. The Ranters were believed 'to preach stark naked many blasphemies', and the Adamites went naked in order to practise promiscuous sexual intercourse. The Quakers went 'naked for a sign', in accordance with the twentieth chapter of Isaiah, and antinomians in general considered nudity to be a representation of primeval innocence before the Fall as well as an emblem of 'the naked truths' of the Gospel. Blake was for a while deeply impressed with the writings of Emmanuel Swedenborg, and Swedenborg's own interest in sexual magic is related to his belief that 'nakedness corresponds with innocence'. There was also the late eighteenth-century doctrine of Nareism, in more intellectual circles, which associates the practice of nudity with the liberation of female sexuality. That sounds very modern but, as we all know, there is nothing new under the sun – especially when you have no clothes on. But before we start to speculate about what was so twentieth-century about Blake and his contemporaries, we might care to wonder what remains eighteenth-century about us.

So Blake's sexual radicalism has its antecedents, but there was nothing which entered that wide and wonderful imagination without being strangely changed. When we talk about his radicalism, we have to remember that it was an amalgam of various sources and ideas, taken from ballads, pamphlets, books, conversations and of course from the resources of his own genius. And so we will find, in the margins of one of his most extraordinary and beautiful poems, *The Four Zoas*, a number of drawings which it would be an understatement to call erotic. I will not go into details, but it suffices to say that there are pictures of homosexuality, transsexuality, child sexuality, oral intercourse, anal intercourse, dildoic excess, and any number of what the Victorians called phalloi.

An innocent might describe this as pornography, but it is nothing of the kind. It is part of Blake's religious awakening, an aspect of his radicalism far removed from the *bien pensant* pieties of Mary Wollstonecraft or Joseph Priestley. The image of the hermaphrodite, for example, which he draws both with male and female sexual organs, is for him a literal emblem of that time before the sexes were divided and human faculties thereby distorted or degraded. We recall also his wonderful phrases, 'He who desires but acts not breeds pestilence' – 'Exuberance is Beauty' – and 'Energy is Eternal Delight'.

He was in fact fascinated by the phallos, the male member, too, and of course he knew well enough the contemporary speculations by prurient old scholars like Richard Payne Knight that that particular thing or object was the centre and source of many primitive religious cults. Here again Blake makes his own leap and, if we leap with him, we will find ourselves in the world of late eighteenth-century magic. There is a famous remark scribbled by someone in the margins of one of his letters – not many people bothered to keep them, by the way – and the remark is, 'Blake, dimmed by superstition'. A friend also referred in another letter in a somewhat patronizing way to Blake's immersion in 'dim incredulity, haggard suspicion and bloated philosophy'. The writer of this letter, Thomas Butts, was a Swedenborgian and therefore to contemporary eyes at the nuttier end of the religious spectrum. For him to talk of 'dim incredulity' and 'haggard suspicion' suggests something very nutty indeed. So what was it?

Well, to begin with, Blake believed in magic, both white and black. He believed for example that a rival artist had been able to destroy or deface one of his own drawings by 'a malignant spell'. In a little poem he describes one of the rituals of such a spell – 'and turned himself round three times three'. I would demonstrate it for you now, but it would make me even more giddy than I am already. But we can go a little further, at least by suggestion. One of his friends was the painter Richard Cosway – for a while they lived around the corner from each other. (That is something else to remember, by the way, about London radicals and London radicalism. It was a much smaller city where radicals would know each other by sight, even if they had not been introduced.) Cosway actually described Blake as a man 'of extraordinary genius and imagination'. I suggest that he said this because he knew, or thought he knew, one of the secrets of Blake's art. Now the point about Cosway is that, apart from being a fashionable painter, he was also a magician and mesmerizer. There are reports of various erotic ceremonies, of the taking of drugs and elixirs, of a belief in the manipulation of the world spirit. Mesmerism itself was considered to be a magical practice. Sexual magic was popular among occultists of the period.

There is another point. Many of them also saw visions. There were the Ancient Deists of Hoxton who talked of spirits and of prophecy. One rather acerbic contemporary noticed that 'any visitor not in the habit of hearing supernatural voices, or not informed of the common occurrences of the day by the ministration of Angels would have been treated as a novice.' It should also be made clear that such people tended to be artisans or small shopkeepers, from the same class as Blake and his family. And of course the point here is that Blake himself heard voices, saw spirits and conversed with angels. He had seen visions since the age of four, and they surrounded him continually. But he was not necessarily alone: there were groups of Londoners, living close by him, who espoused a similar sense of life.

What else did these Hoxton visionaries discuss? Well, for a start, they reviled Newton and Newtonianism. This is something which we are now beginning to understand better at the end of the twentieth century, perhaps, but certainly through the eighteenth century there were groups of people who were opposed to the official science of the period – who despised materialism and rationalism, and who believed that Newtonian physics was simply wrong or invalid. We recall Blake's lines, 'May God us keep, from Single Vision and Newton's sleep.' They were also the people who tended to distrust industrialization and commercialism, which were of course the true fruits of science.

If you read any of the pamphlets attacking these activities, you will get some idea of the occultism which suffused certain London radical circles in this period. One such pamphlet was entitled *Proofs of a Conspiracy Against all the Religions and Governments of Europe carried on in the Secret Meetings of Free Masons, Illuminati and Reading Societies*. These occult gatherings were also associated, in the words of the anonymous author, with 'the mystical whims of J. Behmen and Swedenborg' – both great influences upon Blake – 'by the fanatical and knavish doctrines of the modern Rosycrucians – by magicians – Magnetizers – Exorcists'. We can also add to the litany from another pamphlet: 'Alchymists, Astrologers, Calculators, Mystics, Magnetizers, Prophets and Projectors of every kind'. And that, in fact, is exactly the radical milieu in which we may place William Blake. People read Boehme just as he did. People read Paracelsus. It was a way of trying to hang on to some kind of reality beyond the world of the manufactory and the workhouse.

One or two other points come into view here. Someone once pointed out to me that Blake's work often included the symbols of freemasonry. It sounded a strange idea but, in fact, I looked at the painting described to me and there was indeed all the symbolism of the freemasons. I am not suggesting that he was a member of that group – far from it – but I am suggesting that he was open to the claims and symbols of a group of people who believed themselves to be possessed of ancient wisdom. Another example may suffice here. The visionaries were linked to the mesmerists and alchemists of London, as I related, but what else do these practitioners have in common? They share a belief in the fundamental unity and restoration of the spirit. For the mesmerists it was a question of manipulating the world spirit within the human body. For alchemists the transmutation of base metals into gold was an emblem of the restoration of the imagination and divinity within the alchemist himself. This is the message of Paracelsus, whom Blake read. And what do we find in the very curve and cadence of Blake's prophetic books but the need for the restoration and regeneration of the Divine Man, Albion, the primal human being? His is the first great epic concerned with what we now call the struggle between psychological faculties – like the magician, the alchemist and the mesmerizer, he wished them to be restored to their ancient and innate harmony.

It was an ancient wisdom, perhaps. But it was also a modern wisdom. It was Blake who first made the connection between thwarted sexuality and violence, a revelation not vouchsafed to us until the beginning of this century. It was also Blake who first made the connection between phallocentric sexuality and the established Church. But there are small points as well as large ones. We know the introduction to *Songs of Innocence* when the piper is requested to 'Pipe a song about a Lamb . . . Piper pipe that song again'. Well, in AD 680 the first English poet, Caedmon, was visited in a dream by a spiritual messenger who requested him to 'sing me a song . . . you shall sing to me'. I was reading in Erasmus only the other day of those prophets who were so inspired (and he gives this as the prime example) that they drank oil in mistake for wine. What do we learn in Blake's biography but of the time when he drank walnut oil in mistake for something more alcoholic? Small events, as I say, but God, as well as the devil, is in the detail.

But Blake was not only a visionary and a prophet. He was also a great artist and, if we look, we may find a tradition of artistic radicalism to which he was partly attached. It will not explain him. He is too great a genius to be understood merely in terms of his origins or his associations. But it may help to bring him forward once more as a living Londoner. Let us think of a friend of Blake who shared his profession. William Sharp, the engraver, became a theosophist and then a Swedenborgian. Later he became a disciple of Richard Brothers, the self-styled Slain Lamb of Revelation and the founder of that movement known as the British Israelites. But Sharpe was not only a Swedenborgian and a spiritual radical – he was also a member of the Society for Constitutional Information who engraved a banner with the title 'A Declaration of Rights'. He was, like Blake, a radical in every sense. I have already noted that engravers, like printers and hosiers, tended to become radical by some process of osmosis. Perhaps engravers became radicals, too, precisely because of their professional skills: they knew that the reality of images and symbols was made, not given. And what can be made can also be unmade. Another example of what one might call the artist as purveyor to the people rather than to the establishment is Philippe de Loutherbourg, the great scenic designer and inventor of the very popular Eidsophusikon – a sort of interior *son et lumière*. He was also a Swedenborgian and a freemason. He was a mesmerist and magnetic healer, as was Cosway the painter. Do you see what an extraordinary nexus of belief and practice and politics grew up in this city two hundred years ago? Now it has almost faded from view – it was not considered serious by the Whiggish historians of the nineteenth century – but it was there. Perhaps I might say, it is here.

And what was it, then, to be a radical painter or a radical engraver? Remember that these people were not exponents of salon art or portrait painting; they were engaged in the engraving of prints which would have a wide circulation, and of images which would have a large public audience. And what we see emerging in their work is something close to patriotic radicalism or nationalistic radicalism. Recall that it was the radical demagogue, John Wilkes, who first proposed the establishment of a national gallery of art in London. And what are the images characteristically to be seen in the paintings and engravings of William Blake – the bard, the druid, the ancient of days, the liberated figure of one young man known in one version as 'Albion Rose'? Who or what is Albion? Albion is the ancient name of England itself, and it is one that Blake uses continually. And what was the call among the radical groups, but for the return to ancient English liberties? That is why curiously enough, the great London antiquarians like Thomas Hollis were also radicals. We go back to the young Blake in Westminster Abbey – in that sacred place he saw the legendary history of England revealed. That was for him the primary spiritual revelation. The bardic figure is very important to Blake – not only because it represents the prophet and the visionary but because that figure is related to Celtic legend and the whole mythological alternative to eighteenth-century polity. The figure of One Man, the Divine Human, the leaping figure of Albion Rose is linked to the idea of the nation as some ancient living organism and not some hierarchy of functions or needs. That is why Blake is so concerned with Gothic art, and with the builders of the cathedrals: he was convinced that there was an English spiritual art which had been systematically stripped away by the rationalists and the scientists who organized the perceptions of the state. Innate 'Gothic' liberties were also considered as an alternative to the artificial faction politics of the eighteenth century. All these ideas were an integral part of the nationalistic and artistic radicalism of the day, and my point is that there was a whole fund or repertoire of images upon which they could draw. Looking at the Chartists and Fabians of a later date, I think it would be fair to say that these contemporaries and acquaintances of Blake represented the last great wave of nationalistic radicalism in our culture.

What is it that he wrote in 1808? He spoke of 'all his visionary contemplations, relating to his own country and its ancient glory, when it was as it again shall be, the source of learning and inspiration'. This was not the spiritual dissent with which Tom Paine or Joseph Priestley were associated. It was not internationalist. It was not progressive. It was not rational. It was touched with occultism, with sexual libertarianism and with a reverence for the past. It was, in fact, an emanation of this city we live in now. One thing we have to remember, you see, is that London has always been a dark city. For a thousand years – literally a thousand years – it has been built upon the imperatives of finance and commerce and power. It is the city where the extremes of the human condition meet. This is what Blake saw when he walked through the chartered streets, observing the marks of weakness and the marks of woe. And what was this radicalism of his contemporaries, with its interest in occultism and the resources of some great spiritual past? It was a way of finding alternative sources of power. It was a way of confronting the darkness on its own terms. It was a way, alas unsuccessful, of constructing a mythology as powerful as that which Newton had established.

Of course he did not succeed, but I believe that now, finally, his time may have come. He is at last beginning to be understood and recognized as a great visionary of the human condition, and a great prophet of our technological age. I do believe, also, that he will become the great prophet of the next millennium.

I will end with some lines from the poet himself:

Are these the Slaves that groaned along the streets of Mystery
Where are your bonds task masters are these the prisoners
Where are your chains where are your tears why do you look around
If you are thirsty there is the river go bathe your parched limbs
The good of all the Land is before you and Mystery is no more

Winter 1995

364

125

All the Time in the World
(Writers and the Nature of Time)

The question of past, present and future has not been solved in three thousand years. So I do not propose to attempt it on this occasion. It would be very unfair on those who ask the question – how long is a present moment before it flies in to the past? How long is a perception before it becomes a memory? Since I am a writer who has spent a considerable amount of effort, let alone time (if, that is, we know what time means), in trying to revive or restore the past in various novels and biographies, you might think that I would have even a tentative solution. I am sorry to disappoint you. There are cosmologists and others who suggest, in turn, that future events can determine those within the present. It is all very confusing. It is like being within the vortex of a vortex within a great whirlpool. To use Stevie Smith's phrase, we are not waving, but drowning. But these are really questions for philosophers or, if any still exist, metaphysicians.

I suggest that all writers can do is look towards that which is closest to them. To language. Language itself is like some model or simulacrum of time. Nobody knows where it came from, but everybody is afloat within it. It seems to occur spontaneously and naturally, where of course it can only be highly artificial. It is an impersonal force which creates the individual; it forms our perceptions and our expressions without anyone having a real grasp of its strength or complexity. It spans generations. It is a source of reconciliation and a source of confusion.

Let me give you an example of how it works. In my biography of T. S. Eliot I wished to quote from his intimate prose style, because it seemed the best way of conveying something of the inner nature of the man. Yet I had been forbidden by his estate from quoting any of his unpublished work, which included his letters, or from quoting more than a few fragments of his published work. So how was I going to evoke the texture of the man, and of his age? The best way of doing this was in fact by attempting to reproduce the cadences and movements of his prose within my own narrative – to introduce Eliot within the texture of the book. I hoped that this would have a subliminal effect upon readers so that they might say, 'I am here. Yes. I am seeing this.'

In my biography of Charles Dickens I wished to evoke the spirit of the novelist as well as of the Victorian period itself, and I did so by writing in a deliberately Dickensian fashion. I had thought of writing the life of Dickens as if it were a novel by Dickens, but in fact he had done that already. But I thought that by writing a biography which was both of the nineteenth century and of the twentieth century, then both ages might embrace.

With the biography of Thomas More the challenges were more complicated because it was not so much a question of reproducing a past, or of restoring a lost chronology, but of conveying the lineaments of a lost culture. With Thomas More in particular it was a question of recreating Catholic England with all its panoply and power. Now this was not as difficult as you might imagine. I have always thought and believed that there is still in England a buried but scarcely concealed Catholic culture. It seems likely from recent research that Shakespeare himself was a Catholic, for example, and so the inheritance still lives. Even as I speak Christmas pantomimes are being performed in a score of English cities, and they are the direct descendants of the miracle plays of the early medieval period. The death of Princess Diana elicited a response in itself not far from Mariolatry, where the image of the dead princess acted as a form of religious icon, like that of the Virgin Mary, provoking mass hysteria.

So the need in the biography of More was to elicit the basic emotions and needs of the buried Catholicism in an English audience, so that they might identify with or at least understand the figure and character of Thomas More. He was not after all the man for all seasons as portrayed in Robert Bolt's play – or rather he was that and much more. He was a devout scholar, wholly attached to the laws of God, of the Church and of his society. In that sense he wrote and thought like a lawyer. He was not some free spirit deciding upon the dictates of his conscience – he would have abominated the idea of the individual conscience – but rather a wholly pious man trying to reconcile irreconcilable laws. And of course he died for it.

In my novel, *The Last Testament of Oscar Wilde*, Wilde meditates upon the portrait of a Florentine prince which he had seen in the Louvre. 'I would like to return to that past,' he said, 'to enter another man's heart. In that moment of transition, when I was myself and someone else, of my own time and of another's, the secrets of the universe would stand revealed.' This is not too far from my attempt at writing Dickens's biography – where I wished to inhabit both the nineteenth and twentieth centuries simultaneously.

Well. I have admitted it. I have written biographies and novels. This can sometimes be the cause of confusion, and even backbiting by those who believe that one should stick to separate disciplines – as if there were any great distinction between them. In fact, as far as I am concerned, there is very little difference between the two. Let me qualify that. I have often said that the only difference between them is that the biographer can make things up, but that a novelist is compelled to tell the truth. That sounds paradoxical but it really is not so. You see, the biographer and the novelist both share the same techniques, and the same principles of composition. In fact they often share the same kind of research. The actual process of writing itself, at least as far as I am concerned, is also much the same. You focus upon a character, and you watch him or her moving through a sequence of events, scenes, tribulations, coincidences, locations, by which you hope to demonstrate some guiding theme or principle. You might say that one is real, and one created, but it really does not feel like that at the time. A biographical subject is real, and yet at the same time created; a fictional character is created, and yet at the same time real. The fictional ones are sometimes more real than any around you, and they can sometimes wrest the narrative out of the novelist's hands. I know. It has happened to me. If you are fortunate there is a beginning, a middle and an end. There are subsidiary characters. There is an eventual resolution. In both novels and biographies, of course, there is a story sometimes known as history.

When I say that the novelist is somehow bound to tell the truth, I mean that the power of the vision or the imagination must be strong and genuine enough to impress the reader with the force of reality itself. Now the biographer must of course aspire to the same happy condition, but the biographer also has certain commonly known tricks and devices by which he may conceal his ignorance or perplexity. It is quite easy, for example, to cover up a black hole of some months, when nothing is known, by simply ending one chapter and beginning another a little further down the line. If you have no idea about a certain subject's real motives or beliefs, you can simply quote a letter or an extract from published writings. These are not devices which are well suited to a novel. So in essence the novel is the more truthful form.

Well, you may think I have travelled some way from my main theme. But really it was only a small diversion. What I wanted to suggest to you was that my own novels and biographies are part of the same process. They are chapters in a single book which will only be completed at my death. In all of them I am concerned with that spectral and labyrinthine world where the past and present cannot necessarily be distinguished. Or to change the metaphor they represent a house with many rooms. In some it is a question of introducing the past to the present, and in others of introducing the present to the past. If they get on with each other, then we may introduce them to the future.

My most recent novel, *The Plato Papers*, which is not published in this country until next year, is set in London some four thousand years hence. I do not call it science fiction. For one thing, there is very little science within it. It is for me a way of understanding and recognizing the present through the medium of an inconceivably remote time. My novels and biographies, which are set in the past, are engaged in precisely the same activity. They are not historical novels, or biographies, in the sense that they are concerned only with the minutiae of past times. They also dwell in the present. They are written in the present, after all.

The question of Shakespeare is suggestive here. Can you imagine a sixteenth-century critic saying to him, why don't you write about current conditions? About Tudor social policy? About all the poor and wretched under your feet in the streets of London? Why do you write about ancient kings and ancient countries, about far off places and improbable fantasies? I am sure that if such a question was asked him, he would have been able to think of an answer. The point is that Shakespeare essentially wrote nothing but histories – almost all of his plays are set in some past or distant time – and yet he still managed to dwell upon the very foundations of the human condition. In other words he used the past to illuminate the present.

Now I am very far from Shakespeare. But I want to suggest to you, from my own slight example, other ways in which the past and present can effectively imbue each other. The novel I mentioned to you previously, *The Last Testament of Oscar Wilde*, was written in Wilde's voice – with, I hope, his own particular cadence and peculiar repertoire. It was from that book, in fact, that I learned how to deal with the biographies of both Eliot and Dickens. But this act of imitation instigated a curious process. By writing the novel in the language of the late nineteenth century it was possible, by some act of osmosis or symbiosis, for me actively to enter the perceptions of the period. And by so doing it was also possible for me to propel the reader in the same direction. It was as if an amnesiac had suddenly reacquired his memory. You see, all the previous structures of our language lie just beneath the one we are presently using, and if you reintroduce them you are able to open the readers' eyes to other realities and to other times which in similar fashion lie just beneath the one we are currently part of.

Now of course that may be simply a fruitful illusion. When the eighteenth-century poet, Thomas Chatterton, wrote medieval verse, that was an illusion too – although there were some who said that it was very great medieval verse indeed, and somewhat better than the stuff actually produced at the time.

In the research for my novels and biographies it became clear to me that every period has a different sense of time. Every period has a different past. In the medieval period, I discovered in my work upon More, there were several different times. In the records and chronicles ancient London customs were declared to be 'from time out of mind, about which contrary human memory does not exist' or an object will have been said to have been standing 'where it now stands for a longer time than any of the jurors can themselves recall'. These are ritualized phrases suggesting that the earliest measure of the past was human memory itself. But beyond the time measured by human memory there was sacred time – like that, for example, measured by the bells of London's churches. If I may quote for a moment from my life of Thomas More,

> The most sacred truths of the faith are given material reality, leading up to that moment when Christ himself becomes present at the altar. This was marked by the moment of elevation when the priest held up the host, become by miracle the body of Jesus. At that instant candles and torches made up of bundles of wood, were lit to illuminate the scene; the sacring bell was rung, and the church bells pealed so that those in the neighbouring streets or fields might be aware of the solemn moment. It was the sound which measured the hours of their day. Christ was present in their midst once more and, as the priest lifted up the thin wafer of bread, time and eternity were reconciled.

In this context of course there is no fundamental distinction between past and present, both are seen with the gaze of eternity. But in More's period here was also a form of communal memory, you might call it London memory. 'In the great hard frost . . . in the late dreadful storme . . . ever since the sickness year . . . two or three days after the great high wind' are common phrases. Other communal events were invoked to measure the movement of time such as 'In sermon time . . . at Exchange time when the merchants meet at the Royal Exchange' and so forth. And then there was the close observation of the passing light: 'about candlelighting in the evening . . . when it was duskish'.

These are intimate and human modes of evoking time. But when I was researching my biography of Blake I realized that quite another time was in operation. He often inveighed against the 'Watch Fiends', because in the eighteenth century according to one historian England 'led the world in the measurement of time'. It was the greatest centre of watchmaking in the world, too. In the same spirit eighteenth-century scientists regarded London as 'a potentially universal centre of calculation'. Then in a city based upon work and upon labour, time becomes an aspect of industry. Where before the watch had been an ornament or useful toy, it now became 'a measure of labour time or a means of quantifying idleness'. That is why the city became famous for its clocks, from that upon St Paul's to that within Big Ben in Westminster, and renowned for its clockmakers. The measurement of time, and the ingenuity of its artificial instruments, fascinated eighteenth-century Londoners; in a city always moving and always making, the attention to the processes of measuring time was also an attention to its own energy and greatness.

When I came upon the life of Charles Dickens it soon became clear that Dickens himself was obsessed with time. He was never late. He hated unpunctuality in others. He always finished each weekly or monthly part in good time. He insisted on walking for as much time each day as he worked. He timed his readings and speeches to within a minute. He was in other words a typical product of nineteenth-century time, when it became the central fact of social and economic life. The time signal ball at Greenwich, for example, regulated 'the time of all the clocks and watches in London'. A time current along the electric telegraph also standardized the time in the sixteen most important cities in Britain. With the position of Greenwich upon the meridian, Victorian London might be said to have controlled the time of the world.

Now the Victorians paid very little attention to the past. They were great vandals, destroying any ancient building which stood in the path of development. Their obsession with time did not suggest any interest in the past – far from it. They wished to master time, just as they wished to master the past. Their civilization was based upon forgetfulness and hurried business. Dickens had no sense of his own past, except as something to be controlled and transformed. But that of course meant that he had no sense of the present – to paraphrase one of his own remarks about himself, he was interested only in what he was about to do next. It was always tomorrow with him, never today.

And this in turn raises questions about the relationship between past and present – you really cannot understand one without the other. This is of course something which I learned in trying to decipher the life of T. S. Eliot. You all recall his famous lines –

> Time present and time past
> Are both perhaps present in time future
> And time future contained in time past.

It might be considered the epitaph of the present century. It was only through an understanding of his life, in fact, that I came to be conscious of my own interest in the matters of time past and time future. His own intimations and glimpses of his childhood in New England, set within the London of his present moment, together with his reflections upon the past masters of the language forming among themselves a living tradition, helped to shape my consciousness of the past as a living and formidable force. Perhaps that is what all the really great writers are able to do – by the strength of their language, containing within itself all the potential and power of the past, they are able to intimate that time itself is an illusion. Dante's great poem is as striking and as significant now as it was in the fourteenth century. Eliot's meditations upon time are as important now as they were when first written sixty years ago. They have conquered chronology. It is the one triumph to which I also aspire.

1999

Miscellaneous Writings

On *Notes for a New Culture*
Preface to the revised edition

This book was published in 1976, but it was in fact written some four years earlier. I was twenty-two years old at that time, and was attached to Yale University in the guise of a Mellon Fellow. It was one of those admirable fellowships which require nothing of their holders, since it was essentially a celebration of the connection between Clare College in Cambridge and Yale itself. And so, after the first shock of arrival in a perfectly foreign country, I found myself – for the first time in my life – with nothing whatever to do. I enrolled in a course on urban planning, but I do not believe that I completed it; I wandered around New York, which was only a short distance away by train; I spent many evenings at the various film societies of the university; in a phrase, I drifted.

But it is hard to resist the temptation of old habits, especially in a new environment, and it was not long before I found myself at a desk in the university library with a pile of books in front of me. I suppose I ought to admit at this point that I have a marked streak of blind acquisitiveness in my character: I have to discover as much as I can about any particular subject, whether it be thermodynamics or the iconography of Flemish painting, before completely forgetting about it a few months later. It may be the intellectual equivalent of bulimia. But at twenty-two you believe that you are capable of understanding anything (now, at forty-three, I realize that I know nothing) and so, in the library of Yale University, I decided to complete the study of aesthetics and literary criticism which I had tentatively begun at Cambridge.

It was not simply a theoretical pursuit. At this stage in my life I wrote nothing but poetry, and wanted only to be a poet: I saw no other future ahead of me, which meant that really I saw no future at all. I had met one or two other aspiring writers at Cambridge, and we found that by some miracle of what would now be called 'generational taste' we admired the same poets and were united in our hostility to the established or at least more prominent writers of the time. The work of Philip Larkin, for example, was considered second-rate to the point of feebleness – an opinion, strangely enough, which I have never felt the need to revise. But if we were keenly aware of mediocrity, we were all the more appreciative of excellence; the poetry of Frank O'Hara, John Ashbery and J. H. Prynne was the standard by which we measured all other contemporary literature. It is no accident, therefore, that these were three of the writers whom my book eventually came to celebrate.

Notes for a New Culture, in other words, was an extension of my interests in contemporary literature; the passages of history and theory were a way of extending, and confirming, what were instinctive judgements on my part. I am not implying that the historical speculations are therefore false or peripheral – only that, like most theoretical arguments, they arose from profound emotional commitments. In fact, on rereading this book after a gap of some sixteen years, I am convinced that its central argument is still broadly correct. And if anyone were foolish enough to study all of my later books in sequence – the biographies as well as the novels and volumes of poetry – I believe that the concerns, or obsessions, of *Notes for a New Culture* would be found in more elaborate form within them. I have since that time written at much greater length on certain of the writers mentioned in this volume, but my first opinions of Pound or of Eliot, for example, still seem the most accurate ones. I hold the poetry of Ashbery and Prynne in as much respect as I ever did; in fact, it has increased over the years. And, if I may indulge in a small bout of self-congratulation (if you cannot do so in a preface to one of your own books, where can you?), I believe that this was one of the first works published in England to analyse the writings of Lacan and Derrida. In that context, if in no other, I am pleased to have avoided the great waste of words devoted to 'post-modernism' which deluged fashionable criticism in subsequent years. Yet this book was also very much part of its time: it was written at a period of what seemed like national decline and decay, although, as I sat in the library at Yale, I suppose that anxiety about my own future helped to fuel my anger and concern. I remember writing it quickly, almost furiously, which will perhaps explain, if not justify, the absence of footnotes and acknowledgements. (At this late date, I cannot even remember the books I read.) I also made my fair share of mistakes but, even so, I believe that this book has the energy as well as the failure of all first things.

But if it represented my first attempt at prose, it also marked my debut as a 'serious' writer. When it first emerged from the press in 1976 I was literary editor of the *Spectator* – how I reached that eminence, after Yale, is a story too long to recount here – and I still remember the pride and delight with which I carried my six complementary copies from the house of my publisher, Alan Moore, to my bedsit in Shepherds Bush. But that pleasure was very swiftly dissipated. Many of the reviews were hostile, and each of my mistakes was lovingly disclosed to what I imagined to be an eager public. The experience was a useful one, in retrospect, since that first shock of rejection has largely immunized me against any subsequent attacks by newspaper reviewers; but, at the time, it was peculiarly painful. I put the book upon a shelf and, as the years passed and other books were written, I almost forgot about it.

The prospect of republication, then, filled me with some trepidation; it seemed that a youthful indiscretion was about to be repeated. But I hope, and believe, that I was wrong: I might have been able to add a few clarifications to this account, but there is very little that I would now willingly omit. I have removed a few of the more obvious errors (others no doubt survive), but the book remains largely in its original state. I think this is what my younger self would have wanted.

London, 1993

I27

On *T. S. Eliot*

Perhaps I should begin with a confession: the first, and only book I have ever stolen was T. S. Eliot's *Four Quartets*; it was a small blue paperback which I came across by chance in one of the smaller bookshops along the Charing Cross Road. I was then twelve years old, and can clearly remember sitting and staring at it, first in bewilderment and then in determination.

If I was going to be a poet (a vocation which twelve-year-olds then favoured), I would have to understand these words and cadences. The figure behind them was remote, so remote that for me he need not have existed. But I am convinced that it was this childhood incident which led me to undertake, twenty years later, what seemed to be an impossible if not ridiculous enterprise. I decided to write the life of T. S. Eliot and, in so doing, place that bewildering poetry in the context from which it originally sprang.

The commission to do so had come quite unexpectedly, and I rushed towards it without any consideration of the possible difficulties in my way; in fact, I was not then aware of any such difficulties but my ignorance proved to be my strength. It was not a happy period. I half-expected the world (or at least that small part of it concerned with literary matters) to cheer me on my way; not at all. 'You've put your head on the block this time, haven't you?' or 'I'd wish you luck but you'll need more than luck' or 'It could ruin you', were a few of the kindlier comments I received.

It seemed that I was about to undertake a task equivalent to that of a stuntman who carries a grand piano across a high wire, with the vast abyss beneath him. I do not know much about stuntmen, but I imagine that only will and determination see them safely over to the other side.

I wrote to Mrs Eliot explaining my intentions; but, since she is bound by her husband's wishes that there should be no biography, she could offer me no help. Faber and Faber, Eliot's publishers, were charmingly oblivious to my pressing need to write such a book and they also declined to help. I then began writing to those who knew Eliot: many did not reply, and those who did tended to do so in a cool or non-committal fashion.

I had made it clear, in my letters, that I wished to write as serious and as scrupulous a biography as I was capable of; but it soon became clear to me that my attempt was being seen as nothing short of desecration – at best I was a misguided idiot, at worst a gossip. I was neither: I simply wanted to write an honest account of Eliot's life and, although I was not about to worship at his shrine, I was certainly not going to vandalize it. But how could I explain that to his friends and colleagues, if they would not see me?

It was at this point that I telephoned my agent and, with the lucidity born of despair, asked him, 'How can I write a book without any material?' In the course of a long conversation in which he mentioned Johnson's *Lives of the Poets*, and other luminous biographies, he said to me in effect, 'Don't be a fool. You're still the best person to write this book. You'll find what you need.' It was clear that I was not expected to turn back, just because I had seen a few hurdles strewn across my path, and the torment of the biographer (a subject under-employed in literary fiction) now filled me.

My next step was to allay such torments in the most appropriate place, the Reading Room of the British Museum. For six months I read everything even remotely connected with Eliot; I acquired that pallor which George Gissing ascribes to those 'who live in the valley of the shadow of books'.

It is difficult to wade through the volumes of Eliotic scholarship which, when seen *en masse*, provoke grave doubts about the nature of academic life. Eliot became variously the Symbolist, the Christian, the Philosopher, the Sceptic, the Modernist and eventually, the Guru whose most fleeting remarks were analysed with a seriousness usually only applied to Holy Writ. The major problem was that they made Eliot seem so *boring*, a plaster image of a man around which various candles were being lit.

But then I began to read contemporary memoirs about the man himself, some of them in volume form, some of them hidden away in obscure publications. And a quite different Eliot emerged – a young man, nervous, difficult, proud, exhibiting a kind of hyper-sensitivity which left him almost defenceless against the world. And there was another man – the bank clerk and later publisher, who fulfilled his obligations and arranged his tasks as if by so doing they might form a carapace in which he might hide. And then there was the older man – stooped, deathly pale, ill, unable or unwilling to derive much pleasure from his fame.

There was also the fourth man, who emerged after his second marriage to Valerie Fletcher; he became a joyful and optimistic septuagenarian who considered taking up dancing lessons. Where was the key to unlock all these doors, so that the various images might meet and, in that meeting, become the complete person?

Quite by chance I entered the Manuscript Room of the British Museum; out of curiosity I looked up the entry on Eliot and found there his correspondence with some friends, the Schiffs, which he had written during the early years of his marriage to Vivien Haigh-Wood. For the first time I could hear his own voice – and it was the voice of a man both considerate to his friends and attentive towards his wife, and yet of one who felt himself to be fighting an unequal battle against circumstances. The contemporary memoirs which depicted a difficult and nervous young man suddenly began to cohere, for I had found their centre in Eliot himself.

I had previously ignored the possibility of finding such letters, believing them to be safely stowed away for the use of researchers in the next century (or even the one following that); but it was at this point that I decided to write to every university in England and America, asking them for information about any Eliot material which was contained in their archives. I expected very little, but the response was overwhelming. From Texas, Princeton, New York, Yale, California, Cornell, Arkansas, Virginia, Maryland, and many other places the answers came: yes, they did hold Eliot letters and documents, and I was quite at liberty to see them.

And so I travelled, using most of my relatively small advance in what had now become a personal quest for what Hugh Kenner has called 'the invisible poet'. What I discovered is now in my biography: the fact that I could not quote or even exactly paraphrase, the material which I uncovered mattered much less to me than the fact that I had, as it were, seen him at first hand and was able at last to turn him into a living figure – sometimes a baffling and bewildering one, but one in which I had found a coherence of personality and a consistency of aim.

It has been suggested to me that, because my biography is 'unauthorized' it must therefore be at a disadvantage. I do not doubt that there are omissions, or that on occasions I have misinterpreted other people's memories, but I do not doubt, either, that this is the first coherent account of the man and his work. No biography can ever be 'comprehensive', for the art of the biographer is necessarily inconclusive: the most important events in a man's life may be revealed to no one; the letters may be designed to conceal rather than to reveal certain matters; contemporary memoirs are of their nature unreliable. The art of the biographer is, in that sense, one of interpretative scholarship – to avoid the fictional excesses which mark the biographies of putative novelists, and to eschew the pale parade of facts which are sometimes forced to pass muster for a 'life'.

During the eighteen months of my research, I believe that I came to understand the man, and the forces that shaped him; and, by doing so, to lead myself and others back to the poetry with a finer perception of the crushing forces which formed it. If I have failed I am quite happy to lay my head on the block (academics make good executioners); if I have succeeded, I will have done something to bring the 'invisible poet' into that light where he emerges as a more substantial, more complicated and more human figure than his admirers or critics seem to have understood.

The Times, 15 September 1984

128

On *Hawksmoor*

Inspiration is a curious phenomenon, but I suspect that most examples of its invasive power are really only manifestations of desperation or of physiological necessity: one of my own novels may illustrate this unromantic premise. In hubristic fashion I had decided that I would begin it upon a certain date some weeks ahead – perhaps significantly, it was Monday, 1 April – and noted the fact in my diary, even though at this point I had not the slightest notion what or how I was to write.

As the weeks passed and no ideas occurred to me, it seemed that I had been foolish or vainglorious to expect my imagination to operate on this form of remote control. And then on Sunday, 31 March – the day before I was scheduled to begin – the theme and story of the novel emerged fully ordered in my head. Clearly this was not coincidence: inspiration, on this occasion, was a mechanism for fulfilling my expectations.

But this apparently efficient faculty can work in different ways: in my most recent work of fiction, *Hawksmoor*, the 'inspiration' behind it was really a principle of organization which served to animate otherwise disparate materials. Since childhood, I had been interested in the less salubrious areas of London – Wapping, Spitalfields, Limehouse – and in the air of dilapidated gloom which they embody: if there is such a thing as the landscape of the imagination, then these darker parts of the city represented mine. Their history, too, fascinated me and it seemed, as I walked from St Anne's Limehouse, to St George's-in-the-East, Wapping, that each street was an echo-chamber of the past in which contemporary voices mixed with those long dead.

But if these areas of London were my imaginative preoccupation in those days, my theoretical interests were soon of quite a different order: in particular, when I was at university, I was most intrigued by that period at the end of the seventeenth century when the 'New Philosophy' (which one might define, in shorthand, as embodying scientific rationalism and a belief in human progress) seemed about to displace a set of older and more complex cultural allegiances which vigorously tried to resist the threat.

There was really no connection between my London pilgrimages and my academic interests: and neither of them, in turn, would seem to have much relevance to a novel which two years ago I completed and then abandoned (the discarded book was a study in human extremity, in which the novelist himself must be presumed to be mad). But then inspiration, or rather the principle of organization, touched me: a story, the plot of *Hawksmoor*, emerged without my conscious design and in the rise and fall of that narrative all of the elements I have previously discussed came to cohere.

What emerged was a story half-situated in the early eighteenth century and half-situated in the twentieth; it is concerned with the activities of a certain eighteenth-century architect, and the investigations of a contemporary detective who discovers that 'time' is perhaps an ambiguous or uncertain dimension. As a result, I do not know if *Hawksmoor* is a contemporary novel set in the past or a historical novel set in the present.

Of course 'historical novel' is a term which is still employed by most writers only hesitantly, largely because it has earned such a bad reputation. It is generally considered to be a debased form, not unconnected with 'romantic fiction'. But the curious fact is that historical fiction, if we mean by that novels set largely or wholly in the past, is enjoying something close to a creative revival, with examples very recently from novelists as diverse as Graham Swift and A. N. Wilson, Barry Unsworth and Beryl Bainbridge.

It seems to have happened, almost by chance (although there is no such thing as chance), that a good deal of the more significant English fiction is now set in the past; not a dead past, to be described like a tapestry or an illuminated manuscript, but a past which still touches us because it embodies the secrets both of the historical process and of time itself.

My own attempt, in *Hawksmoor*, was to recreate an earlier period in a convincing and substantial manner. In a previous novel, *The Last Testament of Oscar Wilde*, I discovered that I had a minor but useful ability to reproduce different styles of written prose – in that book, it was the prose of the late nineteenth century. In *Hawksmoor* I decided that the most evocative way of introducing the early eighteenth century was to write in eighteenth-century prose and, as far as I was capable, to make it indistinguishable from the real prose of that period. So I read, and studied, until I satisfied myself that I could write the earlier prose as freely and as instinctively as I wrote contemporary English: I hasten to add that the narrative was not created *ab nihil*, of course, since I borrowed phrases or passages from the original sources where it seemed appropriate to do so.

There was something peculiarly pleasing about reclaiming the past and making it part of a living design, however, and in the process something else happened: by interweaving chapters of eighteenth- and twentieth-century prose, I discovered that their vocabulary and syntax began both to reflect upon and to interpret each other; *Hawksmoor* was a mystery story of detection and revelation, but part of that mystery seemed to reside in the nature of language itself.

As a result two worlds were created, related and yet still apart. Just as the structure and vocabulary of eighteenth-century writing still inform our own, so the past in the book seemed to inform and to animate the present; just as twentieth-century prose is both more capacious and yet more standardized than that of the eighteenth century, so the world which modern prose described in my novel seemed more noticeably to reflect that ambiguous condition.

The specific implications of this are of concern only to the readers of *Hawksmoor*, but there is a larger point which might tentatively be made here. It is possible that innovation both in the language and structure of the novel might be accomplished by means other than conventional stylistic experiment on modernist or even post-modernist lines – and that, by incorporating an awareness of the historical process within fiction, the possibilities for a new kind of 'realism', quite removed from ordinary social or psychological observation, are considerably enhanced. It is an interesting prospect.

The Times, 23 September 1985

129

On *First Light*

How does any novel begin? *First Light* was so much part of my own concerns and attitudes that it is almost impossible now to disentangle the strands of its origin. Certainly parts of it emerged from my own favourite pastime – idly looking out of the window.

I live for some of the time in a cottage on the side of a valley, at that mysterious point where Dorset and Devon meet, and over many months I have been looking from the window of my study across the valley, and speculating about the race which once inhabited this region. Far, far, back. Who were these early inhabitants, who lived in the neolithic encampments to be found all over the area, and who perhaps helped to build the stone circles which are also to be discovered here? Why did they build their circles in stone, and why did they take their bearings from the sky? What did they *see* in the sky? In our time we trace waves of energy emanating from some inconceivable moment of origin, and we detect such fabulous phenomena as 'black holes'. Did they see waves, too – did they believe themselves to be embarked upon a vast sea? And what creatures did they recognize in the sky? So it was that *First Light* slowly filtered down to me.

For these matters fascinated me. I have always been interested in the nature of time, and the presence of even the most remote past in the landscape through which we move every day and which we call our own. I have always believed, too, that if there is any harbour for the dead, and any meaning within the world, it is to be found in the process of time itself. Perhaps that is why Dorset has always seemed to me to be an especially interesting place – of all the areas of England it is perhaps the most continuously inhabited, from the remotest period of human settlement. There is a continuity there; a kind of haunting. And, in *First Light*, the story began to circle around the discovery of an ancient tumulus and its inhabitant.

Of course I read everything I could about that remote past – books by archaeologists, by palaeontologists, by economic historians. But the evidence is scattered or hard to interpret, and the central mysteries remained. No one really knows much about these people, our ancestors. Our own origins are lost in darkness and all our learning really amounts to no more than stories told in the dark. Wonderful stories, sometimes – about stone cicles which become observatories, about ritual sacrifice, about an international order of wise men. But stories, nevertheless. I put some of them within the narrative because novelists, too, often need stories to explain a world which is otherwise unfathomable.

But even as I was writing *First Light* I became aware of another mystery – for some time I had been reading accounts in books and the more specialized magazines of those discoveries being made in the areas of quantum physics and cosmology, since the scientific exploration of these two intimately related areas – the infinitely small and the infinitely large – represents the most exciting development in our period. And what had been disclosed in the course of these explorations? More mysteries. More mysteries of origin. The closer matter is examined, the more incomprehensible it becomes. Electrons move in all possible trajectories at once, and appear in two places at the same time. The spin of a subatomic particle follows the random choice of the scientist, as if he were literally creating the universe as he went along. Or perhaps it might be said that the universe always fulfils our expectations – the stars adopt the pattern which our theories predict they will take. Once we have conceived of the miraculous possibility of 'black holes', then they come into existence and wait patiently for our observations. In that sense scientists also have to be fabulists, magicians, storytellers – with the authority to make sense of a universe which seems literally inexplicable.

That is why in *First Light* an observatory springs up on a moor not far from the excavations of the ancient site and why the astronomer there, Damian Fall, suffers a kind of breakdown when he comes to believe that

in each generation the heavens become a celestial map of human desires, reflecting the most recent theories concerning the nature of matter and the history of the universe. What were the theories of Kepler, of Ptolemy, of Copernicus, of Einstein but stories – stories lasting only for a brief period before being replaced by others? And what did all their knowledge really demonstrate? Merely that the stars took on the shapes which we chose for them. They became the image of ourselves. Perhaps there were no stars and no planets, no nebulae and no constellations; perhaps they merely came into existence in recognition of our wishes and demands. And if there came a moment when no one on earth was studying the heavens – no child looking up in wonder at the stars, no radio telescope directed towards the distant galaxies, no astronomer sitting in the observatory – what then? Was it possible that the heavens would then disappear?

And so in *First Light* the mysteries of the universe and the mysteries of matter became associated for me with the mysteries of our own origins upon the earth. The dunes and tumuli of Dorset were filled with as many secrets as the cosmos. The ancient neolithic shape within the chamber grave is as much a part of us as the cosmic trace elements to be found in our bodies. But of course these are themes which cannot really be discussed in analytic prose and can only be disclosed through the medium of fiction or of poetry. That is why, in *First Light*, the archaeologists at the excavation and the astronomers in the observatory seemed in the end to represent two fields of force which touched each other at every point; why the discoveries within the ancient tomb affected the very sightings of the stars. That is why the story has a circularity like the circles of the sky and the circles of the stone monuments. As always the characters emerged as I wrote, starting to talk so loudly that I could only listen and take down what they had to say – the inhabitants of the region, the scientists, the lost people who haunt ancient sites, the invading hordes from London, all of them in turn affecting each other.

It may seem paradoxical that I am trying with difficulty to trace the origins of a book which is at least in part about the nature of origin – but even this is part of that endless pursuit towards certainty or meaning in which all of us are engaged. That is why the book is in part a comedy, for the impossibility of finding that goal is matched only by our assiduity in continuing the search for it. And that is why *First Light* is also a mystery, a pastoral mystery, for it is the mystery of our own selves.

The Times, 24 December 1989

130

On *English Music*

Preface to the Franklin Library Signed First Edition

I suppose that the search for English music began with my first novel, *The Great Fire of London*, in which I imagined an unsuccessful attempt to film Charles Dickens's *Little Dorrit* in contemporary London. It has been pointed out to me that, ever since, my novels have been concerned with the relation of the past to the present – and, in fact, with the possibility of some continuity in human affairs that allows the past actually to invade the present. Of course it never seemed like that at the time. I was just telling stories, and each of my books has first come to light as a simple narrative. Every novel is a fresh beginning and it is only afterwards, when the words have finally settled on the page, that the constituents of the same vision become apparent to me once again. I do not distinguish my biographies from my novels for precisely that reason; they are all part of the same process. It is not a question of simply reviving the past, but of recognizing that 'the past' is only that which we recognize or understand within the present: if my work has one central purpose, it is to restore the true face of the contemporary world by considering all the latent forces within it.

English Music, as with my other fictions, seemed to emerge quite by chance. For some time I had been hoping to write a novel largely concerned with certain sixteenth-century English composers – Byrd, Tallis and Dowland among them – but I could find no vital clues in their lives to assist me. The idea of old music remained with me, however, and in the peculiar way of such things it gradually attached itself to another stray notion. While writing my previous novel, *First Light*, a character suddenly emerged from nowhere; it was that of a woman so susceptible to books that she actually entered them and wandered through the landscape of other writers' imaginations. I had thought of placing her in a library, from which she would never escape. In the end I did nothing with the idea, but let it rest within my consciousness – until it was restored by contact with old music.

A third theme had, in the meantime, slowly been working itself out in a much more explicit form. I had always wanted to explore a father–son relationship in some detail, having begun the process in *Chatterton*, and the chance reading of the autobiography of a Victorian medium (while pursuing research on my life of Charles Dickens) reawakened my interest. The medium, Daniel Home, had a young son who is mentioned only briefly in the story of his life; but then I began to consider the possibilities. Did the son believe his father to be a genuine clairvoyant or a fraud and how, in either instance, would he react to him? So the main narrative of *English Music* emerged and, during the period that I was writing *Dickens*, I spent my idle moments in working out a plot which would take my particular father and son on their strange journey.

But the preparations were not complete, not yet. Originally I had planned a novel solely concerned with this familial narrative but late one night, as I lay awake, my earlier notions of old music and literary possession seemed to flash across and attach themselves to the new story. These things happen by instinct – they cannot be explained – but the result was clear enough. Suddenly the separate themes became stronger and deeper in combination; the story of father and son became part of a larger story, that of the generations which make up the history and culture of a nation. One of the central aspects of the plot lies in the extent of the son's own powers, which may or may not have been inherited from the father; but in *English Music* the question of inheritance is placed in a different context with the introduction of various English literatures of the past. How much is my own, and how much is borrowed or bequeathed?

I put the matter so personally, because *English Music* is not meant to be some objective or prescriptive account of English literature. It is a novel, not a lecture or work of criticism. It is simply a record of my own interests and obsessions, lying somewhere within this story of a father and a son whose lives are caught up in a vision. I hope it is a vision you will be able to share.

London, 1992

131

A Manifesto for London

For many centuries London has been the greatest of all cities. When its citizens walk along Cheapside, or Wood Street, they are treading on an area which has been continuously occupied for two thousand years. Do Cockneys realize that their accent and intonation stretch back for at least five hundred years? These are perhaps incidental features of the city but they serve to emphasize one great central fact – London is a unique historical phenomenon. It has always been an independent city, standing against the demands of crown and state. It has always been an open city, revived and enlarged by centuries of foreign immigration – it is well known that anyone who resides in London for a year or so becomes, by strange alchemy, a Londoner. Who would not want the chance to restore the history and magnificence of such a city?

This is not special pleading on my own behalf. There was some speculation in the press that I might be persuaded to stand as the new mayor, but the idea is absurd. No political party in their right mind would have me, and I am hardly a 'household name'. But the notion of a writer, or imaginative artist, as mayor is an arresting one. I do not believe that this great city wants a retired politician, or an exalted business manager, or an over-ambitious urban planner. It requires a man or woman of imagination, even of vision; it needs someone who understands its past and can envisage its future. It requires someone who is steeped in London, who knows the East as well as the West, who knows its dark as well as its enlightened aspects. London needs a true representative, in other words, who reflects its variety as well as its energy, its practicality as well as its theatricality. Let us imagine that Victor Hugo had become Mayor of Paris, or that Charles Dickens had been minister for London in a nineteenth-century government. Would they not have changed the entire tone and temper of their respective cities?

I am not placing myself in the company of those gentlemen, of course, which is one of the reasons why I will not stand as mayor of London. But since I am meant to be an imaginative writer, I can at least provide an imaginary manifesto. Here are a few not so modest proposals.

The southern parts of the city have been scandalously neglected and misused. A programme of public works, including proper rail transport, should be introduced to counter the blight which still affects Bermondsey, Deptford, and areas further afield. The resources of the Thames have been squandered, as well, and I would at once commission Richard Rogers to restore the river as the centre of the city's life.

The waste places of London should also be revived; the area around Kings Cross, for example, should be remodelled with St Pancras Old Church (one of the most ancient sites of Christian worship) at its centre. All empty or derelict land, anywhere within the city, should be converted into parks or into playgrounds for children.

No building over eighty years old should be demolished without a special licence. In my own backyard, literally, Islington Council is planning to knock down a wonderful fabric of old warehouses in order to create a new street. It ought to be prevented from doing so. It is true that the history of London has been the history of vandalism and rebuilding, but I have now come to believe that it is necessary to preserve rather than to rebuild. The only exception may lie among the tower blocks on the council estates of Hackney and elsewhere; if some way can be found to rehouse their inhabitants with decency and dignity, then the large blocks should be demolished.

There is a case to be made for free public transport in the central areas of London, as well as a ban on parking in that central zone. Cycle paths should also be installed within those areas. The Millennium Dome should be given to the Museum of London, and in that space should be created a great public monument to the city. Public art should also be encouraged, and artists like Rachel Whiteread should be commissioned to install works in the squares and thoroughfares of the city. A tax of £5 should be levied on each tourist (collected as a hotel tax) and the revenues spent on refurbishing public buildings.

London is an infinite labyrinthine city and, in order even partially to understand it, its history should be made part of the curriculum of every London school. It is now also a megalopolis, a world space to be surveyed by satellites, but attention should be given to the inner rather than the outer areas. The historic trend has always been outward, in suburbs or in 'ribbon development', but the citizens must reclaim their old territory. It would be wonderful, for example, if people returned to the City itself so that the ancient centre was inhabited once again. These are not changes to be achieved within the space of three or four years, perhaps, but the mood and appetite for such a transformation can only be established by a mayor who has the authority of one who speaks with the real voice of London. Step forward . . .

The Times, 10 January 1998

132

Frank Auerbach: Recent Works

Introduction

I hate leaving London. I don't think I've spent more than four weeks abroad since I was seven. (Frank Auerbach)

As you come up the Hampstead Road you pass, on your left, the site of the school where Charles Dickens was once a pupil. There is a house a few yards further where George Cruikshank, the great cartoonist and caricaturist, lived and worked. Turn left there and you enter Mornington Crescent, a terrace of houses erected in the 1820s and now in a state of some dilapidation. Clarkson Stanfield, the great marine painter, was once here. Spencer Gore had his studio here. Walter Sickert, a painter with whom Frank Auerbach is sometimes compared, lived at number six. If you proceed a little further you can turn into a narrow street, and see some letters scrawled in white paint – 'To the Studios'. This is where Auerbach has worked for the last forty years. Mornington Crescent itself has that air of mournful shabbiness which is characteristic of the sadder remnants of the early nineteenth century but, perhaps as a result, it exerts a powerful fascination over the solitary observer. It is, as Henry James said of another London street, 'packed to blackness with accumulations of suffered experience'. And perhaps that is what Auerbach means when he says that in his own work he wishes 'to emphasize what was more permanent . . . massive substance . . .'

Auerbach has also said of London that it 'has always cried out to be painted, and not been', but throughout his own artistic life he has attempted to give it form and expression. Characteristically he has chosen two or three patches of territory – Primrose Hill, Mornington Crescent itself, and the ground beside his own studio – and he has described the process of transference and divination which can then take place. 'Also there is a kind of intimacy and excitement and confidence that comes from inhabiting the painting and knowing exactly where everything is . . .' That is why he so vividly suggests the soft and sombre brightness of this particular part of north London, which sometimes seems to glow with the iridescence of decaying things, and why in the charged textures of his paint he is able to evoke the striated and granulated stone of the streets and houses among which he works.

In Auerbach's magical paintings of Mornington Crescent, by night and by day, one senses both the exultation and the exaltation of an artist finding himself and his true subject within the immediate presence and energy of London. He himself has spoken of 'fullness and perpetual motion' in certain art of the past; this is also the condition of the great city, which itself provides the context for the substance and speed of Auerbach's own painterly activity. There are times when his vivid brush-strokes have the explosive vitality of the graffiti scrawled upon the walls around him, as if the perpetual anonymous voices of Londoners had entered his paintings.

Perhaps this explains his ability to suggest the occasional desolation of urban life. Of course he would be right to dispute any direct reference on his part – his job is really to deploy his chosen medium as inventively and energetically as possible – but it is hard not to look at his portraits and sometimes glimpse what that great Cockney vision-ary, William Blake, in a poem simply entitled 'London', described as 'Marks of weakness, marks of woe'. There are occasions when the sitters seem to enter an almost comic complicity with the artist, but certain of his studies of human figures are invaded by an unmistakable sense of sorrow, resignation or isolation. They may have just been cold, or uncomfortable; but it also seems clear that, in their intense and furious proximity to one another, artist and sitter have managed to conjure up some spirit of the place itself. It is intriguing to remember in this context that many of Sickert's most haunting interiors – in particular that extraordinary study in desolation, *The Camden Town Murder* – were painted just around the corner from Auerbach's own studio. That murder in Camden Town took place very close to Mornington Crescent itself, and there is a still closer connection with the night of the city – Walter Sickert's landlady always claimed that Jack the Ripper had once lodged in Sickert's own house.

Perhaps that is one of the reasons why Auerbach has also remained an essentially figurative painter, despite the blandishments of international fashion; he is alert to the possibilities of a specifically London narrative of change and continuity, of building and destruction. And is it possible to see in the very tactility of Auerbach's paint, once so thick and now so redolent of the layers of colour beneath the immediate surface, the levels of the city itself? That this is not an altogether fanciful comparison is suggested by Auerbach himself, who has described his need 'to excavate the subject', just as he paints with delirious precision the excavations and building sites of London. There is always 'the image underneath' which must be brought to the surface through many layers of paint; but these images of excavation also suggest the city's eternal compact with the present and with the past, as its builders channel through the soil and clay like paint, tunnelling down towards some dark forgotten origin. In fact the whole nature of Auerbach's artistic activity is a simulacrum of the city's life, with his incessant revisions and accretions, with his scraping down of the surface of the board or canvas to make a fresh start. In order to locate the inner form and vitality of his subject he must act like a London workman – 'I tend to set up an image and destroy it many times a day ... putting up a whole image and dismantling it and putting up another whole image, which is physically extremely strenuous.'

But this endless process of change and becoming is also connected with Auerbach's interest in time and continuity; there are few works of his which are not at some level concerned with the changing moments of human perception, and with the need to give form to that chaos which surrounds us. In the three complementary studies, *From the Studios*, for example, it is possible to find materials for a city meditation – the persistence of some unchanging identity through time or, perhaps, the gradual acquisition of identity through the process of change as if the area which Auerbach depicts is some complex organism slowly discovering its own form. Blake called it 'Infinite London' and, like Auerbach, he hardly ever left it; he did not need to do so because he knew that he could find the materials of eternity there. That is why one of the characteristics of the great London artist, also, is the ability to divine the mythic and the fabulous within images of the contemporary city – and indeed, Auerbach has remembered how he 'scattered my mythological properties over the [Hampstead] Heath'.

But there is another aspect of Auerbach as a London artist. In his youth he was devoted to the performers of the music hall, in Camden Town and elsewhere, and in particular to the comic routines of such artists as Max Miller. It is an interest, of course, which was shared by Walter Sickert, George Cruikshank, Charles Dickens and other of his Mornington Crescent forebears. He was attaching himself to a very old London tradition, in other words, and his sense of urban character or personality must have been affected by his experience of the great Cockney comedians. The theatre has always been a potent source of inspiration for London artists and in Auerbach's portraits, in particular, it is possible to detect the presence of an extraordinary and intense theatricality. Some of his subjects display a Hogarthian life or vigour, itself deeply rooted in the sense of London spectacle and display, but on occasions some of them have the look of exhausted harlequins. Auerbach is well known to use the same sitters repeatedly and perhaps, looking upon these vivid or melodramatic shapes, we might be reminded of the old pantomimic cry from the London halls, 'Here we are again!' Auerbach has himself described the task of the painter as resembling 'the way that an actor would don a character or become a part', and it is the perfect phrase for suggesting the fact that London art can have a peculiarly theatrical appeal in which mind, matter and spirit are joined together in a ritualistic consummation. But this is also another way of emphasizing the sheer visual pleasure to be derived from Auerbach's painting, that almost physical sensation of being stunned by gesture and dazed with colour. If one were to enter the world of Auerbach's paintings one might become lost, as if it were a city, among the incandescent forms and the brilliant colours; it would be as if the sombre architecture of Piranesi had suddenly been afflicted by St Vitus' dance.

Just as it seems possible, then, that a street like Mornington Crescent can materially affect the life or the art of those who dwell beside it, so it is possible that within the city and its culture there are patterns of response and patterns of sensibility which have persisted for many centuries. That is why I have invoked the names of Turner and Blake, great Cockney visionaries who seem (for the moment) so distant from Auerbach, as well as Sickert and Hogarth who stand in a more direct relationship. There is a London art, and there is a London vision. It is an art of theatrical variety and display, of extremes constantly being married together, an art of exuberant painterliness which has all the energy and momentum of the city itself.

And then, finally, there is the *Tree in Mornington Crescent*. It is an extraordinarily poignant image, but not because this tree is in any sense struggling to survive in an alien environment – that would be a romantic illusion, and not one to be foisted upon Auerbach. It is in fact a pure London tree, a tree grown out of the peculiar city soil. I do not know if I have seen this particular tree, but I know its history and its setting. There are eighteenth-century reports of just such trees in the northern parts of London, and they give very similar descriptions. The trunks of these trees were always covered by a greenish moss or down, because of the humid foggy air, and their delicately coloured moss could be rubbed off with the hands. At last, after more than two hundred years, that particular variety of London tree is finding expression.

New York, 1994

133

Thomas Chatterton and Romantic Culture
Edited by Nick Groom
Foreword

It is enlightening, and somewhat heartening, to learn that Thomas Chatterton is at last being taken seriously as a poet and dramatist. He was so prodigal of his genius that he attached the names of others such as 'Rowleie' to it; and, in the same manner, he has survived a variety of literary incarnations ranging from eighteenth-century fraudster to Romantic icon and post-modern avatar. His supposed suicide has of course assisted this process, although there are those who believe that it was not self-murder at all. It was, perhaps, an accident that created the 'legend' of the poet to be seen lying upon a narrow bed in Henry Wallis's painting.

In reality he is more interesting than any of the stereotypes fixed to his reputation and his work. He pursued that antiquarian passion, for example, which seems inseparable from the native genius and the moment of his revelation in the muniment room of St Mary Recliffe's in Bristol, whether legendary or not, must stand as one of the most important scenes in English literary history.

Chatterton believed that the past, and the language of the past, might be made to live again. He was, in a very real sense, correct. By writing in the impassioned cadence and ornate vocabulary of the fifteenth century, he was able to move beyond the restricting imaginative climate into which he had been born. He was not a Newtonian, or a Lockean; he was a visionary who understood the world in terms of myths and legends. That is why he was so admired by William Blake, for example, as well as those other eighteenth-century writers and artists who were quite out of sympathy with prevailing poetic and painterly customs. It is a mistake to assume, therefore, that Chatterton was 'discovered' by Wordsworth or by Coleridge. His visionary importance had already been vouchsafed to an earlier generation who were equally distrustful of the materialist culture – and materialist aesthetic – emerging around them.

But if Chatterton remains an example to those who reject the mores of their age, he also possesses a further significance. In renewing the literature of the medieval period, and in a sense actually creating it, he was invoking a tradition which in *The Englishness of English Art* Nikolaus Pevsner described as an inalienable aspect of the English sensibility. For many hundreds of years the artists and writers of this country have used a mixture of historical styles as a form of ludic comprehension of the past. It has nothing to do with some 'post-modern' examination of narrative; it is connected, instead, to the enduring consciousness of the nation. We seem to have come a long way from Thomas Chatterton himself, the 'marvellous boy' who found within himself the living presence of the past, but in fact he can stand as the one great genius of historical restoration and renewal in this country.

1999

134

Perfume: The Story of a Murderer
Patrick Süskind

Patrick Süskind's novel is a book of smells – the odours of history, in fact – and on the first page eighteenth-century Paris is anatomized into its component stinks. In its most fetid spot, beside a mephitic cemetery and beneath a fish stall, the hero of *Perfume*, Jean-Baptiste Grenouille, is born. But the point, the miraculous point, is that he has no smell at all. He is an orphan whose absence of body odour turns him, also, into an outcast – both damned and blessed, pariah and magician.

Grenouille himself is haunted by smells. He recognizes the odours of separate stones and of the varieties of water, he can locate even the most tremulous perfume from miles away; he can separate the simplest stench into its various elements – that of a human being, for example, being composed of cat faeces, cheese and vinegar. As a child and young man, he survives as an outsider only through some stubborn instinct – deciding 'in favour of life out of sheer spite and sheer malice' – but this means that in eighteenth-century France, in an age of 'reason' and a time of 'progress', he is a barbaric intruder. For him, this is a world stripped bare of its more elegant trappings and organized around the one fundamental principle of smell.

His sole ambition is to become the greatest perfumer of all time; in order to conceal his own lack of odour he creates a perfume that 'did not smell like a scent, but like a *human being who gives off a scent*'. He can even manufacture perfumes that create an exhalatory illusion, a phantom object lingering in the air. But his ambitions are fatal: not only does his company prove mortal to those who take him in, but there are precious scents that reside only in certain favoured human beings and must, like blood, be sucked out.

At first one specific human scent haunts him, and he kills the young girl who has the misfortune to possess it; only thus can he rob 'a living creature of its aromatic soul'. This murder precipitates his odorous, malevolent lusts, but before he instigates further deaths he becomes apprenticed to a Parisian perfumer and concocts scents never before known on this earth. Then he vanishes into the wilderness for seven years, in a region of no smell where his own personal power seems greatly to increase, and on his return to civilization he resumes his fatal career. Several young girls are murdered by him, stripped of their scents and left as odourless corpses. He is an olfactory vampire – Noseferatu. Eventually he is captured and tried, but once more his inhuman powers assist him. The novel begins as a historical document and ends as a metaphysical mystery.

That this is in every sense an olfactory novel gives a striking sensory immediacy to the fiction itself. *Perfume* is a historical novel but one in which the sheer physicality of its theme lends it an honorary present tense. And if Grenouille is the hero of the novel, his obsessions are also its informing presence. Just as he has difficulty with words 'designating non-smelling objects, with abstract ideas and the like', so the novel itself creates an elemental world in which such abstract matters are only of token significance. The nose is defined here by a priest as 'the primitive organ of smell, the basest of the senses', with its powers springing from 'the darkest days of paganism'; but it flourishes in Grenouille, even in an age of 'enlightenment', and the unspoken message of *Perfume* is that it flourishes still. The point about genuine historical fiction is that it is primarily concerned with the contemporary world. This is not a historical romance but a meditation on the nature of death, desire and decay.

The idea behind the book is actually a simple one, Grenouille being a conflation of Dracula, Charles Maturin's Melmoth the Wanderer – that damned soul of early nineteenth-century fiction – and the assorted inhabitants of Gothic literature. Mr Süskind's fastidious but sonorous prose (and John E. Woods's translation from the German is a marvellous piece of work) bears a striking resemblance to that of Oscar Wilde in his more sentimental moments, and *Perfume*, with its languorous catalogue of scents and its interest in the aesthetics of horror, is strangely reminiscent of *The Picture of Dorian Gray*.

Of course, certain writers are drawn to the past precisely in order to explore such interests; history becomes, as it were, an echo-chamber of their own desires and obsessions. But this cannot be conveyed by some easy trick of style: the generally debased standard of historical fiction springs from the fact that most novelists think it sufficient to create approximately the right 'atmosphere'. But the important things are the details. Without details nothing can live, and one of the pleasures of reading *Perfume* is the unmistakable sense that Mr Süskind has deftly employed the fruits of what must have been long and arduous research into the more arcane aspects of eighteenth-century French life.

This is Patrick Süskind's first novel – he is also a playwright – and the fact that he has turned at once to historical fiction suggests the current revival of that genre. The point is that it represents a way of abandoning the constrictions of conventional naturalism without falling into the familiar trap of a self-conscious 'experimentalism' or 'modernism'. It accommodates a realism that has nothing whatever to do with ordinary social or psychological observation, but that retains the strength of a fable. As a novel of character or incident, *Perfume* is at best tentative, therefore; but as a disquisition on sensibility and as an instrument of historical analysis, it is both well conceived and carefully sustained. Just as Grenouille can manufacture a perfume that infallibly conjures up the same response in anyone who senses it, so Mr Süskind creates words that provide a satisfying illusion of another time. Grenouille the perfumer becomes a kind of novelist, creating phantom objects in the air, but Mr Süskind himself is a perfumer of language. This is a remarkable debut.

New York Times Book Review, 21 September 1986
Originally published in the *New York Times*

135

Oscar Wilde

George Meredith once described Oscar Fingal O'Flahertie Wills Wilde as 'a mixture of Apollo and a monster'. And if Oscar Wilde was indeed a *monstre sacré*, he had all the right credentials. He was born in Dublin in 1854, the late child of an eccentric father and an equally eccentric mother, a nationalist poet who called herself Speranza; he went in easy stages to Trinity College, Dublin, and Magdalen College, Oxford, before arriving at his destined home in London. He was a poet but his youth was combined with cleverness, and he realized that self-publicity might count for more than mere achievement. If he did not walk down Piccadilly with a lily in his hand, as the parody of him in Gilbert & Sullivan's *Patience* suggested, he did at least create the atmosphere in which such a floral parade might have been thought likely to occur.

Wilde was an aesthete only until he grew up, however, and it was in the late 1880s and 1890s that he began his serious work – his stories, his criticism, his one notorious novel and of course his plays. Yet even as he composed those dramas, which will last as long as the English language itself, he was beset by rumours about his private life that eventually transformed him into what he described as 'the pariah dog of the nineteenth century'. It was a brilliant career: he went from poetry to prose, from prose to drama and then from drama to prison. He always did the unexpected so that, although he was not forgiven, he was certainly never forgotten.

But even before that fall which in some distant region of his consciousness he seems positively to have longed for, he was something of a puzzle to his contemporaries. To some he was a saviour (literally so, since on occasion he seemed to possess the gift of healing), whereas to others he was perilously close to becoming an Antichrist. In appearance he was unmistakable – as one contemporary noted, he looked like a Roman emperor carved out of suet. But as soon as he opened his mouth, any unfavourable impression was dispelled – when he spoke, the delicately rounded sentences, the orotund expressions, the epigrammatic flashes of lightning, all worked together to render him an unparalleled conversationalist. Those who knew him best also remarked on the sheer buoyancy of his spirits. Certainly his letters are unique, filled as they are with an exuberant and exhilarating wit; as Borges has said, 'The fundamental spirit of his work is joy.'

But it was not just the bravura of his self-expression that gave him such a hold on his contemporaries. It was something much more profound and perhaps more dangerous, for, if he was a genius, he was one because he came to embody the obsessions of his own period. He said of himself, 'I was a man who stood in symbolic relations to the art and culture of my age,' but it was both his blessing and his eventual tragedy that the age itself might most aptly be termed *fin de siècle*. Since we are now entering an equivalent period, perhaps we are in the best possible position to understand that joy in artifice and parody, that celebration of style and pastiche, that mockery of previous values, which such a time seems to encourage. In Wilde's lifetime the end of

'Victorianism' (and all that it had come to represent) was in sight, but nothing had come to take its place: it was a time of spiritual, moral, social and artistic chaos, when even the most formidable conventions and the firmest convictions began to crumble, to slide and eventually to dissolve. In many ways it was a worn-out society, theatrical in its art, theatrical in its life, theatrical even in its devotions. It happened to be Wilde who defined both the conscience and the consciousness of the artist at a time when all other values were thrown into doubt. Indeed, it was from the wreck of those values that he tried to save the concepts of beauty and of pleasure. He knew Walter Pater just as he understood Ruskin, and he incorporated them into what he considered to be a finer philosophy of life. Only the Puritans, whom he hated but whom he also understood, might call this 'decadent'.

In fact, one has only to read his criticism – and essays like 'The Critic as Artist' and 'The Decay of Lying' are as fine in their way as the finest of his plays – to see how serious a critique of his age he actually provided. His most inspired role, beyond that of dandy or Uranian (the nineteenth-century expression for those whom less sympathetic contemporaries called sodomites), was that of the aesthetic philosopher: this was, you might say, a discipline he knew by heart, and in his deceptively simple and unarguably witty formulations he fashioned a vision of the world as subtle as that of Pater, as devastating as that of Schopenhauer. 'The truths of metaphysics,' he said, 'are the truths of masks.' He was often (and wrongly) accused of insincerity, but he pre-empted this charge when he declared that 'insincerity is a method by which we can multiply our personalities.' In his disavowal of conventional ethics he is thoroughly Nietzschean. 'Those who see any difference between soul and body have neither,' he remarked. 'It is only shallow people who do not judge by appearances. The mystery of the world is the visible, not the invisible.' Both art and conduct became the supreme reality, therefore, and there were times when he did not attempt to distinguish between the two. There were even occasions when he declared that his only concern was to turn his own personality into a work of art – although, in a climate so hostile to the pursuit of personal perfection as that of England, such an art was bound to turn into one of open defiance. 'I was a problem,' he said with one eye on Victorian society and the other on the legal system, 'for which there was no solution.'

Essentially he remained an alien, and it was in this uncomfortable but necessary position that he was able to see English life very clearly.

Shaw said that Wilde was a 'very Irish Irishman', and although he told Yeats that 'we are a nation of brilliant failures' Wilde himself belongs to a long line of successful Irish dramatists – among them Congreve, Sheridan and Goldsmith. Yet of all of them, perhaps, he was the one who was least at home in England. Just as in his drama he exposed the hypocrisies of late Victorian life – and there is no more damning indictment of that society than *The Importance of Being Earnest* – so in his life his fondness for boys and drink scandalized those who believed themselves to represent public morality. No attitude could be more alien to the English 'mind' than Wilde's comment that 'I have never learned anything except from people younger than myself' and his belief in 'that inordinate passion for pleasure which is the secret of remaining young'.

But more importantly, it was a mistake for him to show the English in his dramas that their ideals were illusions, their understanding mere folly: it was only a matter of time before they turned on him. He had been their entertainer for a while but he soon became the figure in a fatal pantomime, to receive blows from the harlequin's wand and kicks from the clowns. He had dallied with them too long; he had grown too accustomed to 'society' even as he mocked it. It was thoroughly appropriate, therefore, that his splendid career should be ended by a Marquess and ruined by a visiting card. Lord John Sholto Douglas, the Marquess of Queensberry, dismayed by Wilde's association with his son, Lord Alfred Douglas, left his card with the message 'To Oscar Wilde posing as a somdomite' (*sic*). Wilde sued Queensberry, lost, and was himself put on trial for consorting with minors. He longed for fame, but in the end he was destroyed by it. He ran willingly to his destiny, but he forgot that he could become its victim. He was the ox fattened with flowers, but only for the sacrifice.

Yet his fate is in some ways still the least interesting thing about him, just as his earlier poses did him a signal disservice. At least he realized the latter: 'To the world,' he said, 'I seem, by intention on my part, a dilettante and a dandy merely – it is not wise to show one's heart to the world.' But there was one other paradox on which he rested his case, even in the well of the Old Bailey itself: 'Art is the most serious thing in the world. And the artist is the only person who is never serious.' So it is that although he turned conversation into an art, and his personality into a symbol, his real achievement lay elsewhere. Indeed there is a sense in which Oscar Wilde was the greatest artist of his time. Some of his poems, most notably *The Ballad of Reading Gaol*, have survived the work of more single-minded versifiers; he invented the art of modern criticism, just as he reinvented the art both of the parable and of the prose poem for a modern audience; as a letter-writer he is unequalled in his century, and no one can read *De Profundis*, a letter he wrote to Alfred Douglas from his prison cell, without being almost as moved by it as he was; with *Salome* he created symbolic drama in English; *The Picture of Dorian Gray* has been described as the only French novel ever written in English; and of course he brought comedy back to the London stage. The nineteenth century was on its deathbed and still he managed to make it laugh at itself.

And so he wrote drama for society, philosophy for his equals, epigrams for everyone. Above all he was a self-proclaimed 'lord of language' – a master of style, and in every sense a modern master since many of his lessons have yet to be learned. But Oscar Wilde may be supposed to have the last word even here. 'If one tells the truth,' he once wrote, 'one is sure, sooner or later, to be found out.'

New York Times Book Review, 1 November 1987
Originally published in the *New York Times*

136

The Essays of Virginia Woolf
Volume Two: 1912–1918
Edited by Andrew McNeillie

'One short choppy wave after another' was the phrase Virginia Woolf used to characterize the regularity and brevity of her reviews in the *Times Literary Supplement*; but even in the turbid waters of journalism, there are occasions when the wind is at her back, her thought unfurls itself, and she sails calmly towards the open sea. Hers are not the reviews of a critic, in other words, but of a writer: in the six years covered by this second volume of her collected reviews and essays, Woolf completed her first novel, *The Voyage Out*, and was working on *Night and Day*. She had just entered her thirties but was not yet well known and, as other writers have discovered, one of the nervous ailments that precede success is the need to review as much and as often as possible. The years of her worst mental trouble during this period were not productive (there were long episodes of illness in 1913 and in 1915) but in 1917, for example, she wrote some thirty-five separate pieces.

The editor of the *Times Literary Supplement* at first seems to have given her books about women, and especially about women novelists – not unnaturally in the circumstances – but, as Virginia Woolf soon demonstrated, a good writer can discuss practically anything with perfect self-assurance. The first review in *The Essays of Virginia Woolf* concerns the biography of a philanthropist, while the last discusses *The Method of Henry James*; in between there are reviews of guidebooks, anthologies, memoirs and even children's books.

The earlier reviews are solid, not to say professional: it is clear that Woolf did her homework and, for example, she took care to know about all previous biographies of Jane Austen (then mercifully a finite number) before embarking on the review of the newest one. But even in the most workmanlike of pieces one senses the novelist looking deeply into the pages of these books in order to catch some glimpse of herself in them, some reflection of her own art in the art of those she praises. Even the subjects that one would think might be uncongenial to her – Thoreau and the English travel writer Richard Hakluyt, for example – give her the opportunity of airing her own preoccupations in public or, as she put it, of slipping in 'some ancient crank of mine'.

In the later reviews the oddity of the 'cranks' is gone and, in her commentaries on writers as disparate as Swinburne and Conrad, she is systematically expounding the artistic principles that inspire her own work. Of course there is no formal announcement of her interests – the letters and journals go much further towards providing that – but even in these necessarily brief contributions her predilections become clear. Though she rarely mocks or satirizes the work of the generation immediately preceding her own (one of the easiest things in the world to do), she is implicitly hostile to the nineteenth century, at least in its more solid mid-Victorian aspects. She inclines to the belief, as she puts it in one of her reviews, that 'there is a form to be found in literature for the life of the present day,' and this is a form that she discovers in modern prose rather than in poetry or drama. In these reviews also – specifically in those of the great Russian novelists, who emerge here as her single most potent source of inspiration – she charts her preoccupation with the knots and loops in mental imagery and a style that, partly as a result of her own work, has since become better known as 'stream of consciousness'. In that sense the novelist and the reviewer cannot be separated.

Neither can these reviews be separated from the cultural life of their time and, although it would be absurd to suggest that English writing has collapsed in the last seventy-five years, it is perhaps true that Virginia Woolf's graceful but elaborate prose would not now be welcome on the desks of many literary editors. Certainly it would be difficult for any contemporary reviewer to deploy her range of allusions – a fact painfully emphasized by the number of footnotes that Andrew McNeillie, the editor of this volume as well as the previous one, feels obliged to append to each review. Woolf's little shafts of lightning now come trailing clouds of detail.

But no doubt one ought to take one's cue from Virginia Woolf: she was a kind reviewer, at least in the sense that she looked for the best in everything rather than labouring over the worst. This was partly because she was herself notoriously fearful about reviews of her own work, and so she perhaps practised a form of sympathetic magic – she praised others in the hope, rather than the expectation, that she in turn would be praised. In fact, she was often so careful not to give offence that she kept her real opinions to herself – she informs us in a letter that she thought Edward Marsh's memoir of Rupert Brooke 'one of the most repulsive biographies I've ever read', but she allowed only the mildest of reproofs to percolate through into print.

As a result, she lacked the acerbity of T. S. Eliot and the grandiloquence of Pound, both of whom took to reviewing with metaphorically slavering jaws. And, unlike these two famous contemporaries, she made no attempt to assemble a literary theory out of disparate critical remarks. Her judgements tend to be couched in the form of striking individual perceptions, and yet by these means she often gets to the heart of the matter – she explains how *Jane Eyre* is so powerful that 'if we are disturbed while we are reading, the disturbance seems to take place in the novel and not in the room.'

In addition, Virginia Woolf possessed a sense of humour, however desperately won, and this volume is filled with what can only be described as a comic spirit – an individuality all the more remarkable when one remembers that these reviews were printed anonymously and were to a certain extent forced to comply with what was then the standard authoritative mode of the *Times Literary Supplement*. And so this book emphasizes the lesson Virginia Woolf herself suggests in a review – 'To be able to write such criticism is so rare a gift that one is inclined to doubt whether it is ever done save by the poets themselves.' Or by novelists. There are some beautiful essays here (notably those on James and Dostoyevsky) and many memorable ones; but each of them has that steady glow of purposefulness and attention that issues from a writer who not only loves literature but also knows herself to be, on occasions, capable of writing it.

New York Times Book Review, 27 March 1988
Originally published in the *New York Times*

137

Marcel Proust
Edmund White

Crazy Horse
Larry McMurtry

It is perhaps significant that the first two Penguin Lives – a new but not necessarily innovative series of short biographies – are written by novelists rather than orthodox biographers. *Marcel Proust* by Edmund White and *Crazy Horse* by Larry McMurtry are widely separated in theme and culture, but they bear testimony to the fact that biographical narratives can aspire to art rather than to history. These relatively inexpensive volumes are more than Auden's 'shilling life', which 'will give you all the facts', primarily because they are both works that issue from imagination and intuition as much as from scholarship and research. That may give them a chance to survive.

Other novelists have crossed the boundary into biography – Graham Greene on the Earl of Rochester and Evelyn Waugh on Edmund Campion are two notable twentieth-century examples – but there has been a general lack of enthusiasm for the enterprise. It is often supposed that a writer of fiction should stick to his or her trade, but the reasons are not obvious. Of course there are differences between the two forms. In novels one is forced to tell the truth, for example, whereas in biography one can invent more freely. This will sound like a paradox only to those who do not practise either art. In fiction the accuracy and coherence of the imaginative narrative must be strong enough to impart a vision of truth to the reader, in biography the devices and tricks of historical narrative are so abundant that it is much easier to disguise lack of knowledge or loss of comprehension. Biography is the art of concealment; fiction is that of revelation.

But there are also obvious similarities between the two forms. Biography and fiction are both concerned with human narrative; they require a central character and a coherent plot, as well as a strong engagement with place and motive to drive the developing story. Indeed it is possible to envisage the moment when biography and fiction – or history and fiction, to put it more grandly – cease to be separate and identifiable forms of narrative but mingle and interpenetrate each other. That is why the idea of the 'short biography', embodied in this Penguin series is one way to capture a presiding truth or vivid impression in much the same manner as a short story might. Edmund White here explores the pathology of a man who was passionate and yet oblique, rhetorical and secretive, sentimental and yet clear-sighted, innocent and depraved – a great writer condemned as a *flâneur*, and a gossip who wrote a masterpiece. It requires the skill and intuition of an imaginative artist to make these aspects cohere within a single and living portrait. Larry McMurtry, on the other hand, evokes a period and a culture rather than one man – a moment when the forces of the burgeoning American state destroyed whole tribes and indeed a whole civilization, of which the Sioux warrior Crazy Horse remains the single most potent emblem. A longer biography might not have been able to address the issue with such vigour and clarity.

Short biographies have always been popular – starting, perhaps, with *Lives of the Caesars*, by Suetonius – and the fashion has continued into the nineteenth and twentieth centuries with series like *Great Lives, Modern Masters* and others. Oscar Wilde was scathing about the *Great Lives* series in particular – 'formerly we used to canonize our great men, now we vulgarize them' – but in fact these series of biographies have commanded the learning and imagination of some remarkable writers, among them G. K. Chesterton on Blake and Rose Macaulay on Milton, E. H. Gombrich on Leonardo and Sacheverell Sitwell on Mozart.

The present Penguin series, edited by James Atlas, has projected a wide range of subjects, from the Buddha to Marlon Brando, Chekhov to Martin Luther King. It is a tribute to the ambition and catholicity of the project that such a choice is possible and testimony also to the heterogeneity of contemporary culture, but it ought not to be forgotten that in biographical narrative the writer rather than the subject is paramount. If this again sounds paradoxical, perhaps it ought to be recalled that the only biographies that have survived the encroachments of time and forgetfulness are those that have been written well. Who now remembers the factual and detailed accounts of Charlotte Brontë, after Elizabeth Gaskell's wonderful if often inaccurate narrative? All nineteenth and twentieth-century scholarship and research upon Samuel Johnson are nugatory beside Boswell's account. Many long biographies, particularly those by Anglo-Saxon academics, are stuffed with facts and with research; but they are about as interesting as telephone directories and are equally transient. Scholarship is not necessarily art. Only well-written biographies survive because, by the alchemy of charmed language, the truth they reveal is the one that lasts. So Edmund White, in his biographical account, proceeds by evoking memorable scenes – from the moment when the young Proust stopped in front of a rosebush and stared at its flowers for so long that it seemed as if 'his entire being was concentrated' to his last night on earth, when he dictated one final sentence: 'There is a Chinese patience in Vermeer's craft.' White has a novelist's eye for the telling detail or the remarkable phrase and, like Proust himself, concentrates upon the minutiae of the past so that it might live again. He has a wonderful sympathy with his subject, adduced in such reflections as 'Proust fancied that so long as he failed to begin his life's work, his life would go on.'

If there is a weakness, it is a tendency upon White's part to assert the gay life and consciousness of Proust. It is perhaps understandable in a novelist and critic who has written extensively on gay themes, but in a subtle and unintentional way it diminishes Proust's significance. One of the secrets of the biographical art lies in the extent to which the biographer can intuit the personal stirrings of the individual consciousness. It is not a question of admiring, or liking, the subject of the narrative. It is a question of making him, or her, live upon the page. To introduce a somewhat anachronistic term such as 'gay', with all its late twentieth-century connotations, is to avoid making that act of personal, intimate sympathy that a great biography requires.

That is perhaps also the central problem with Larry McMurtry's biography of Crazy Horse. He writes of 'the Crazy Horse legend', concerning a man whose character and beliefs have retreated from the memory of mankind, and whose activities are surrounded by 'assumption, conjecture and surmise'. The nature of biography then changes, and becomes a history of symbolic truth rather than of a human being. Since 'the man and the way of life died together' it also becomes the narrative of a lost civilization in which man and myth become inextricably aligned. So Crazy Horse remains a figure trapped in a history that he himself only partly understood, and the narrative must essentially remain at the level of supposition rather than of truth.

McMurtry is good at the less intimate moments, however, when he suggests that mutual incomprehension between white settlers and Indians led to sporadic and at first inconclusive warfare. And this apparently objective story is striated with the gleams and intimations of the novelist shrouded within the biographer. 'They had been marching since the middle of the night,' McMurtry writes of Custer's ragged troop. 'A lot of them were so tired that they could barely lift their guns. For them it was dust, weariness, terror and death.'

This is fine writing, and suggests once again that history and biography can best be restored by the creative imagination. This central point needs to be restated, for writers as well as readers. The truest biographies are those that are most engaging and inventive; style precedes fact. But if biographies, like fiction, are fluent narratives concerning the lives of human beings, they are also irradiated with historical speculation and cultural interpretation. Biographers must therefore learn as much from the masterworks of the past as any poet or novelist, since biography itself is the great transcript of human life.

New York Times Book Review, 10 January 1999
Originally published in the *New York Times*

138

Walter Pater: Lover of Strange Souls
Denis Donoghue

He had the appearance of a pork butcher and the manners of an anchorite. He tried never to look anyone in the face, and spoke only upon subjects that did not interest him. If Walter Pater had not existed (and some of his contemporaries were undecided on the point), then Oscar Wilde would have had to invent him. In fact, it might be said that Wilde did invent him – or, at least, completed the process, by claiming Pater as the spiritual progenitor of what became known as Aestheticism: art for art's sake; art aspiring to the condition of music; art, even, as sin. Wilde, from his prison cell, described Pater's *Studies in the History of the Renaissance* as the book 'which has had such a strange influence over my life'. Denis Donoghue, in his critical biography *Walter Pater: Lover of Strange Souls*, similarly claims that Pater 'set modern literature upon its . . . course' and, as a result, 'is audible in virtually every attentive modern writer'. But to most of Pater's peers he was a somewhat over-refined Oxford tutor who lived with his cat and was cared for by his two sisters. Such were his reserve and his diffidence that for Henry James he was 'the mask without the face'. He is, then, an interesting case.

Pater was born in 1839, in the riverside district of London's East End known as Shadwell. His father, a doctor who treated the poor, died when Walter was two, his mother when he was fourteen; it sometimes seems that half his family died during his childhood, so that by the time he reached the age of proper schooling he was possessed by a sense of fate as colourful as what he once called 'Othello's strawberry handkerchief'. But Pater displaced his suffering in ritual: he had an instinctive taste for what was then known as Decorative Gothic. He fashioned flowers out of sealing wax and had a passion for anything white. He was, according to one of his more feline biographers, 'fond of organizing little processional pomps' – a phrase that might also be used as a description of his writing.

He was educated at King's School, Canterbury, where he wrote a poem suggestively entitled 'The Chant of the Celestial Sailors' – one that was revealing, but not in the expected way. A small footnote in a privately printed volume states that the poem 'describes rather his waning ideas of heavenly progress'. His heavenly ideas waned very quickly indeed, and by the time he arrived at Oxford as an undergraduate he had no more faith in Christianity than in Ovid's *Metamorphoses*. At university, he had the misfortune to be considered ugly but intriguing. He was described as 'the Caliban of letters' or, more esoterically, as a woodcut from Charles Lamb's *Satan in Search of a Wife, by an Eye-Witness*. A wife was the last thing Pater wanted, however, and he searched instead for academic preferment. He never succeeded in becoming a clerical fellow, for obvious reasons, but he was eventually given a classical fellowship at Brasenose College, Oxford.

Brasenose had a reputation for 'hearties' – athletic young men with more profile than prose style – and nothing could have suited Pater better. The poet A. C. Benson, who shared his tastes, put it nicely: 'That a man should be ardently disposed to athletic pursuits was no obstacle to Pater's friendship, though he was himself entirely averse to games; it rather constituted an additional reason for admiring one with whom he felt otherwise in sympathy.' Pater disliked ugliness of any kind and even admitted, 'I would give ten years of my life to be handsome.' He took defensive action and grew a moustache, which only made matters worse. He confessed that he could read Poe only in Baudelaire's translations, because 'he is so rough', and, according to his first biographer, Thomas Wright, 'even Goethe did not pass butcher's shops more rapidly'.

At Brasenose, Pater lectured on philosophy, usually without mentioning any particular philosopher, and his private quarters contained little beyond a bust of Hercules (which he termed a 'coquetry') and a bowl of dried rose leaves. He was, a contemporary observed, 'one of the first of Oxford dons to bring a carefully studied taste to the arrangement and decoration of his rooms'. He was to inhabit them for the next thirty years, but it cannot be said that his university life was an unmitigated success: he never received any other lectureship or professorship, and was relegated largely to the company and comfort of undergraduates. 'Well,' he would say to them when they brought him essays, 'let us see what this is all about.' But what, they must have wondered, is Mr Pater all about? He had a high receding forehead and eyes that were bright but perhaps a little too close together; his moustache looked as if it had been chopped with a pair of pruning shears. He wore a frock coat very correctly, but he sported an apple-green tie, which in some eyes, at least, was equivalent to wearing a dress.

Pater's predilections, however, were fully revealed only in his prose. In his first published essay, on the subject of Samuel Taylor Coleridge, he fretted over that poet's 'excess of seriousness' – this in 1865, the year that Matthew Arnold's *Essays in Criticism* extolled the virtues of a high moral ground. Pater had attended Arnold's lectures as an undergraduate, and amid all that sweetness and light one can imagine him whispering, 'Life should mean less than this.' His second essay was a celebration of Johann Joachim Winckelmann, the eighteenth-century German scholar who had pursued Hellenism in more than a scholarly sense. Pater adverted, rather coyly, to Winckelmann's 'romantic, fervid friendships with young men', which 'perfected his reconciliation with the spirit of Greek sculpture'. The essay was unsigned, according to the custom of the *Westminster Review*, where it appeared, in 1867, and so Pater escaped the opprobrium of those who might see his own aesthetics in an equally florid light. The following year, he wrote an essay on the poetry of William Morris in which, searching for a conclusion, he composed a sentence that will last as long as the English language itself: 'To burn always with this hard, gem-like flame, to maintain this ecstasy, is success in life.' Again, he had written anonymously. His particular flame was meant to burn unseen.

But then he made a decision that marked, as he said of the title character in *Marius the Epicurean*, his only finished novel, 'the discovery of his possession of "nerve"'. The essay on Winckelmann and the conclusion to his essay on Morris were revised in 1873 as a final note to *Studies in the History of the Renaissance*, a volume that touches upon the strange life of Pico della Mirandola and the delicate works of Joachim du Bellay, among others, to define what Pater called 'the powers and forces of pleasurable sensations'. Here Pater stood revealed. There was no one passage or perception that could have been used in evidence against him, but the generally perfumed atmosphere of the book left his more stolid contemporaries uneasy. The style is overwrought, wanton and ethereal. Pater dissolves in raptures over images of male beauty, whether they are constricted in 'dainty, tight-laced armour' or covered in chains 'like scalding water on their proud and delicate flesh!' And in one of the most famous passages in all art criticism, on the *Mona Lisa*, declaring her to be 'older than the rocks among which she sits', Pater conjures up vampires, Leda and

St Anne. This was hardly the classical or Renaissance culture to which the Victorians wished to become accustomed. Rather, it was a world of pagan reveries, where the cult of the beautiful and the worship of physical perfection represented the true pieties. Pater talked of 'sensations', of 'pleasure', of 'ecstasy'. There were times when he even mentioned 'suffering'. It was all too much.

You should go to *Studies in the History of the Renaissance*, in other words, not to learn anything about the Renaissance but only to understand Walter Pater. He once explained to Wilde that the art of prose was more difficult than that of poetry, and, in fact, the chapters of *The Renaissance* are not so much essays as prose poems. He composed them very slowly, on sheets of ruled paper, leaving spaces between the lines, to be eventually filled in with words; he was always searching for that perfect sentence which would mean everything or nothing. The book is part scholarship and part fiction, part biography and part criticism – what he called, in one of his more medieval moments, a 'cantefable'.

Its publication was immediately followed by rumours of strange sins and even stranger beliefs. 'I wish they wouldn't call me a "hedonist",' he complained to the poet Edmund Gosse. 'It produces such a bad effect on the minds of people who don't know Greek.' The term 'homosexual' had yet to be revealed to the world, but Pater was generally considered to be one of those 'Uranians' or 'urnings' who wore their green carnations 'with a difference'. He was even made a character in a comic novel, where, under the name of Mr Rose, he is said 'to talk of everybody as if they had no clothes on'. He was more strongly affected by the controversy than he ever cared to admit, though, and was afterwards said to look 'like a man pursued by the Furies'. Denis Donoghue quotes a contemporary report of Pater's becoming 'old, crushed, despairing', which adds, 'This dreadful weight lasted for years.' It was a question of the world's trespassing upon what he called 'reserve'. Of his own sexuality he never spoke, and there is no reason to suppose that he ever engaged in a sexual act involving anyone other than himself. We might remark of his homosexuality much as Dickens's dying Mrs Gradgrind whispers: 'I think there's a pain somewhere in the room . . . but I couldn't positively say that I had got it.' Pater had thought to hide himself in the sinuosity of his prose but instead had become trapped by it.

Donoghue, in his wonderful study of Pater's languid strangeness, offers a persuasive argument for considering him the precursor of the

modern movement in English letters. *The Renaissance* suggests that he
was the first English writer deliberately to distance himself from the
world of orthodox morality – to elaborate what Donoghue calls an
'adversary life' in a period 'when official life was deemed to be
bourgeois, Protestant, imperial, male, and heterosexual'. But, of
course, this cultural perception must rely upon a persuasive reading of
Pater's temperament, and here Donoghue brings to his academic
discernment the divining skill of the novelist. *Walter Pater: Lover of
Strange Souls* begins with its subject's death and ends with a beginning,
as Pater inaugurates the modern age. It is a biography, but one in
which the biographical facts become material for exegesis, and do not
stop with mere report. Where Thomas Wright, in his 1907 biography,
spends some 140 pages discussing Pater's early years, Donoghue
manages to dispatch them in twenty. This is a 'brief life', to use one of
Donoghue's phrases, but it is immensely suggestive: in a number of
short chapters, which read like elegies, he elucidates Pater's fiction and
essays with subtlety and genuine sympathy. He sees Pater to have been,
for example, 'withdrawn as if it were a matter of principle from
anything that presented itself for attention'. This hits precisely the right
note. Pater avoided what the world would probably call 'significance'.
He hesitated, always unsure, but he lived in the space of his hesitations
and exulted in his uncertainty. His philosophy, if that word can be
used, is perhaps best comprehended not as Aestheticism but as a
strange mixture of scepticism and idealism, celebrating the sensational
moment while at the same time trying to derive some visionary
understanding from it. In the process, he cast up a mist of words in
which 'intensity', 'experience' and 'impressions' can be glimpsed in a
fitful light.

The reaction to *The Renaissance* so terrified and subdued Pater that
he published only a handful of articles over the next twelve years.
Upon the reissue of *The Renaissance* in 1877, he removed its famous
conclusion on the ground that, he later said, 'it might possibly mislead
some of those young men into whose hands it might fall'. Two 'might's
here were not mighty enough, and he went on to say, 'I have dealt
more fully in *Marius the Epicurean* with the thoughts suggested by it.'
He is referring here to the 1885 novel that was the hothouse fruit of his
twelve years' exile, the saga of a lonely soul in his journey through
various forms of belief. It was a critical success, and was acclaimed a
tour de force. Yet it has not worn well. It is neither poetry nor prose
but some withered offspring of the two. It is filled with ornate

meditations and contrived descriptions, but at its best it reads like Mrs Humphry Ward at her worst. After its publication, Pater settled in London for a time, and, emboldened by its success, he wrote more essays, attempted some short fiction, and even, on occasion, gave public lectures. The last were not very public, however, because of his unnaturally restrained manner. 'Did you hear me?' he asked Oscar Wilde after one event. 'We overheard you,' Wilde replied.

All these labours eventually made up a collected edition of some eight volumes, but what, in the end, are we to make of it? Donoghue is such an astute critic that through the alchemy of his prose Pater becomes a much finer and stronger writer than is generally supposed. There are occasions, of course, when even Donoghue has to accept the poverty and prolixity of his subject's 'thought'; he confesses that aspects of his theory 'are not clear to me', and at times he comes across 'a confused sentence'. The fact is that Pater is confused about most things; he rejected the moral certainties of Arnold and of Ruskin, but he could not create an adequate critical vocabulary from his own impressions. As a result, he is at once vague and over-emphatic. His essays intermittently approach the condition of Muzak – a delicate cacophony of unfinished sentiments. Much of his work also approaches meaninglessness, in the same spirit as the long silences with which habitually he decorated social conversations. That he positively seems to enjoy not saying anything at all is an aspect of his fear of self-revelation, or commitment. Reading Pater is like listening to Wilde through a conch shell.

As Donoghue puts it, 'he was always shy in intellectual matters and shrank from engaging on equal terms with the personages of scholarship and rhetoric.' But there are times when reserve becomes a form of cowardice. His greatest labour was self-censorship, and his greatest fear was of literary reviewers. In revising an 1876 essay entitled 'Romanticism' thirteen years after its publication, for example, he deleted Whitman's name and replaced a reference to Baudelaire with a reference to Hugo; the allusion was more discreet. On other occasions, he excised any passages that suggested the delights of Greek friendship, and omitted anything to do with 'the life of the senses'. In middle age, he recoiled from such prose as if he had unexpectedly touched someone's flesh. And this cowardice was part of a larger withdrawal from the world. It was said by many of his contemporaries that, somehow, he shrank into himself during his middle age. His light was one that failed. That is also true of his work; as has been the case with many Oxford dons, his youthful sensibility was preserved in amber. Neither his art nor his personality ever developed beyond that point; if they had, he might have become a real artist – or, at least, a real essayist, in the tradition of Lamb or Hazlitt. That is why his true heirs were perhaps not Joyce and Pound, as Donoghue suggests, but Harold Acton and the Sitwells.

When the news came of Pater's death, in his fifty-fifth year, Wilde asked, 'Was he ever alive?' And, indeed, his life, as one looks back on it, does seem to have been suspended on a very slender thread of events. Pater called death 'the last curiosity', and it is somehow appropriate that he should have been buried at Oxford during the summer vacation. Yet he left an apt legacy: within his endless hesitations, velleities and divagations he had found a prose style that was so exact a simulacrum of his life that it became a substitute for it. Only a single question remains unanswered: How does one burn with a hard, gem-like flame?

New Yorker, 15 May 1995

139

The Inheritance

I had been asked to write an article about tattooing – a difficult subject and one not quite to my taste, but I needed the money. The research, as always, was dreary: telephoning for appointments, trudging around tattoo parlours, thinking of new 'angles' and new questions, trying vainly to listen to the answers. 'Why did you choose this particular emblem?' 'Why torture yourself by having a crucifix picked out on your skin?' All I could drag out of the old scarred men, the tattooists, the pale teenagers were a few embarrassed grunts and monosyllables. I was beginning not to care.

One afternoon I was in the tattoo parlour of an operator known in the 'trade' as Happy Harry. He was trying to impress. 'There is one man who could help you, but he'll never see you. No one outside is supposed to know about him.' Harry's knowing look was beginning to irritate me. 'This is an important bloke, he just comes in for a session and then he's off.' The tap in the sink was dripping, mixing the garish residue of colours. The air was musty; it smelt of dyes long impregnated in the walls. I wanted to get away. 'So why is he so important?' 'I've never seen anything like it. His whole body's covered with them – portraits, snakes, women, the lot. But you'd never know – you'd have seen him in a suit.' Harry's face had a look of infinite craftiness when he emphasized the last word. 'When would I have seen him?' 'Oh you would have seen him.' Harry winked – it was a kind of 'us' as opposed to 'him' wink. I didn't quite know what to make of it. 'Famous, then, is he?' 'Ask no questions and hear no lies.' The knowingness was becoming overbearing. I made the ritual excuses and left.

Happy Harry phoned me a few days later. 'Listen, I've got a really good case coming to see me. He wants to have his tattoo taken off –

and it's a big one. It'll take all morning. Do you want to come and have a look?' Well, at least this was a new slant on what I now considered to be a rather sordid business. 'By the way, that gentleman I mentioned. He's very interested in what you're writing. He said he looks forward to reading it.' 'And what is this gentleman's name, so I can thank him for his interest?' 'You're not going to get me that way, my old mate. I'll see you next week.'

Happy Harry's parlour is in Borough, down the Marshalsea Road. I had read that some workers on a building site had just unearthed a Roman temple there, full of strange artefacts, but that isn't really my kind of thing. Whatever it once was, Marshalsea Road is now just another old, dark London street – a truckers' stop, a betting shop, a gym and some tenement housing. Harry's parlour was next door to the local social security office, one of those small government buildings which casts a shadow over its vicinity just as surely as if it were a cemetery.

Harry greeted me, as always, with a slightly false smile. 'Well, old son, come to have a look, have we?' Harry's client was a man in his mid-fifties; he was stripped to the waist, and his back was decorated with a large portrait of the Virgin Mary. The image had worn badly and had faded in parts. Harry was going to strip it off entirely. It was not a pleasant process, with all the tannic acid and caustic pencils, but Harry enjoys his work. He slowly covered the Virgin's face with white paste. He didn't like to be disturbed during these long and delicate operations, and so the parlour was formally closed.

Such procedures take a long time, and are accompanied by the unconscious noises of those who are wholly engaged in what they are doing – a low whistle from Harry, and grunts of pain from the enamelled victim. There was a tapping on the store-front window. 'Tell him to fuck off, will you?' Harry was absorbed. I went outside; a white-haired man had his back to the large window, and appeared to be studying the traffic which drove loudly past. 'I'm sorry, but the parlour's closed for the morning.' He turned around; he looked elderly and conventionally 'distinguished', and the face was familiar. 'Oh you must be the journalist. Harry has told me all about you. I'm very pleased.' So this was the man. The famous man in the suit. I smiled; he smiled. He walked past me and into Harry's 'operating' room. 'Good morning, Harry, we won't disturb you. We'll talk in the front.'

He led me through. His manner, despite the strange circumstances of our meeting, was perfectly easy. We sat down on a cheap modern sofa, beneath various photographs of Harry's more colourful clients.

'Well, Mr Lambert, I hear you are writing about this peculiar subject.' He gestured at one of the pictures on the wall above us. 'You may think an industrialist is out of place here. Do you?'

'No, not particularly. No more than anyone.' I knew now why he seemed familiar – the man was Alistair Hardy. He was the chairman of a large nationalized company, a familiar 'face'.

'Tattooing is a strange pastime, and it has many strange adherents. I suppose you could say that I was one of them.'

There was a television dealer's across the street, and from Harry's shop-front window the same scene was displayed in varying degrees of garish colour, on fifteen or sixteen screens.

'Did you come here to talk especially to me, Mr Hardy?'

'In a way yes, and in a way no.' The tone again was familiar, confiding. 'I want to talk to you privately, if you understand me. I don't want to be mentioned in anything you care to write, but I may be able to help you none the less.'

Hardy was wearing a dark suit, the cuffs of his white silk shirt hovered just below his wrists, perhaps just a quarter inch too low. His plain tie had been carefully knotted. What had been Harry's description – 'portraits, snakes, women, the lot'? Hardy was saying something about the need for concealment, propriety. I had been looking at him, but had not listened to what he was saying.

'And so will you join me for lunch, Mr Lambert? Harry is happier working alone.'

I am not at my best in restaurants. It is difficult for two people to find each other sufficiently interesting for an entire meal. I drink too much, and smoke other people's cigarettes. But Hardy's ease was infectious. We had gone to a rather seedy Italian restaurant just south of the Thames; the waiter was watching a small television set in the corner of the 'bar', and paid us little if any attention.

'I was first tattooed at the age of fourteen – it was a small butterfly – although I can remember being interested in such things from much earlier on. It seemed such a natural thing to do, to decorate my body. My mother saw the device and was horrified; my schoolfriends laughed at me. Only then did I realize that it was something I would have to continue in secret, my only audience myself and naturally, the tattooist. I suppose it would now be called an "obsession",' he used the word as though he had extracted it from some alien vocabulary, 'but every tattoo I acquired seemed to call forth another, needed to be complemented. From the age of nineteen I decided I would acquire one new tattoo each year. I am now fifty-eight, but I've kept to it.' I noticed that he pulled at his cuffs as he spoke, but this seemed to be a theatrical rather than a nervous gesture. He wasn't tense, he wasn't even diffident, he was addressing me in a curiously parental, affectionate manner. He talked about his public career, and the need for him to conceal the designs which now covered his entire body. Only his wife and his doctor, outside the tattooing fraternity knew. Only in death would he be revealed, and the prospect seemed to please him.

'I don't know how you feel about such things, Mr Lambert, but I have never believed that human beings are confined to one life. You know this too, don't you? I look upon my double nature as a kind of test. I suppose I have been initiated.' This is not the kind of thing one tends to hear from industrialists, and I must have seemed a little surprised.

'You know, I have never discussed this with anyone before.' He seemed to be continually offering me something which I could not yet grasp, a gift which was as yet invisible.

'Neither have I.' He laughed; it was the kind of laugh which acts as a signal, and we both rose. The Italian waiter grudgingly abandoned some television soap-opera, and showed us out into the dank streets of south London. Hardy left me by an underground station, but not before another of his bland surprises. 'I have a small flat in London, where I stay sometimes. I would like you to see my collection before you write your article. It might amuse you.'

Hardy telephoned me three days later. 'Are you free on Wednesday evening?' I wasn't but he made it sound as if that was the last and only day which he could manage. I agreed to visit his flat, or hide-away, to witness the unveiling of his 'collection'. He lived off the King's Road – which seemed an appropriate enough place to see Hardy's secret, or at least covered, life. There is something wilful and uncaring about that part of London, and it could harbour Hardy's mysterious collection just as easily as it could encompass the smiling public man.

He lived on the top floor of a rather grand Georgian house. The flat itself was small but uncluttered: a few magazines, some stereo equipment, some innocuous-looking books. Hardy looked as though he had just come out of a board meeting – the carefully pressed suit, the silk shirt and tie, the same rather engaging briskness. He was not very interested in small talk. 'Not even my wife has seen this collection, Mr Lambert. It has taken me some years to build, but in its way it is the best of its kind in the world.' He moved towards a small ivory cupboard, in a corner which I had not noticed, which had fierce-looking gargoyles carved on its sides. He unlocked it, and behind the white doors were a series of compartments or drawers – each of these, too, was locked. He opened them, painstakingly, and handed me a number of files and transparent packages – containing engravings, photographs, drawings.

It was an extraordinary collection; quite how extraordinary I was not to know until later. Even at first glance I could see that here was a record of tattooing on a scale I could not possibly have envisaged. The backs of natives were emblazoned with the marks of the sky and the planets, there were portraits of kings and queens with tattoos (on their arms, their thighs) of extraordinary obscenity, engravings of corpses with cabbalistic tattoos so fresh that they could have been painted at the point of death, of unnamed men and women mapped with religious emblems, of scarred children. It was as if I had wandered into a planetarium, and seen the stars in the middle of the day. 'Perhaps you can understand something of my fascination with the subject, Mr Lambert' – Hardy was looking at me with an expression of intense interest – 'and how, in a way, it has taken over the whole of my private life.' And, in a sense, I did understand: tattooing, I could see from the engravings themselves, was a secret art which could bless or maim its devotees. I imagined that Hardy thought himself blessed.

We talked for a while. It turned out that Hardy devoted a considerable amount of time to the study of the uses of tattooing in 'primitive' religion. The North Library of the British Museum was as private as his flat, and he could pursue his researches unnoticed and undisturbed. But time, because of his public duties, was limited. He looked at me as though demanding some kind of response; I got the impression that time was the one thing he didn't have enough of. The rest of his conversation was unfathomable. 'The body of the tattooed man is in some way free from fault, according to ancient practice. By undergoing external suffering which transforms the physical body, the tattooed man receives blessings when he passes into another life. Of course, you know, Mr Lambert, that life goes on – in one way or another. But I have discussed this with you before.' I remembered the engravings of the corpses, tattooed with hieroglyphics. 'And now,' he said, 'I'm afraid I must leave you. There are some people I must see.'

And yet there was still one question which I wanted to ask him. 'I believe that you are, yourself, elaborately tattooed.' 'I have been told so, although I'm hardly up to their standards' – he gestured towards the ivory cabinet. 'But you are, all the same, something of a rarity nowadays, aren't you?' 'Yes, I suppose you could say that.'

It was then, finally, that I understood the joint interest which had brought us together. It was something which neither of us had cared to say, until now. 'May I photograph you? After all, your face needn't be seen.' I had been taking pictures to accompany the article, but nothing (as I thought) on this scale. 'Yes, Mr Lambert, I believe you can.'

That night, I dreamed that I was participating in a ceremony, the nature of which was mysterious to me. All I knew was that it must not end – not because it was enthralling but because the final act, the culmination, would be too dreadful to witness. I found myself behind some gates. There were many people on the other side, walking away across a bridge. My hands could just fit through the metal railings of the gate, but it would not open. I stood there like a suppliant, my white and unmarked hands on the other side.

Hardy phoned me a couple of days later. 'Well, Mr Lambert, where are we going to indulge your hobby?' His tone was familiar although hardly ingratiating. It was as if we were old acquaintances, fixing a date for dinner. I had felt slightly ill at ease about photographing Hardy, but his tone dispelled my anxieties about the whole business. We agreed that, since I had a certain amount of photographic equipment which might have to be used, he should come to my flat.

We arranged to meet the following evening, for, as it were, the final unveiling. I had by now almost forgotten the article I was preparing – Hardy had taken over. I was intrigued (more than intrigued) by the fact that he had secretly marked his body over a great number of years: a private system of signs with their own internal coherence – a coherence, I hoped, which my camera might disclose: but somehow I doubted it. The ease with which he accepted my request to photograph the tattoos suggested that he did not expect their mystery, if that was what it was, to be vouchsafed to me or my lens. But in this I was to be proved wrong.

It was the early afternoon and in my eagerness, or nervousness, I was already preparing for that evening's encounter. I was shifting the furniture around the main room of my flat when the front-door bell rang. It was Hardy. He was leaning against the wall, his face was flushed. 'I feel very hot,' he muttered, almost to himself, as he walked in. 'This is a very hot day.' He seemed preoccupied, and paid very little attention to his surroundings or, for that matter, to me. He sat down on a chair by my desk. 'Did you want to be photographed now, Alistair?' It was the first time I had used his Christian name. 'Yes, yes, can you do it now? I must get on with it.' I was a little alarmed by his behaviour; it was as if he were taking part in something with which I had nothing to do. 'I am very hot.' As if preparing for the photographs, he took off the jacket of his suit and let it drop to the floor. I took out my camera, and began adjusting it. He looked out of the window, started to remove his tie, and then stopped. He stared out of the window for a minute or more. I pretended not to notice, and carried on with my preparations. 'Why is it so hot?' He seemed to be addressing himself to the sky. I didn't answer. And then, quite suddenly but at what seemed an infinitely slow speed, he toppled on to the floor and lay there in a crouched position.

For a moment I thought he had fainted – his tie was half off, and his hands folded together. I knelt over him, felt his pulse, and there was no movement. His heart, too, had ceased to beat. I was surprised, now, by my own reaction, how calm I felt. He had died, I imagined, of a heart attack – how and why, I didn't know. It would be necessary to call an ambulance, although he was already dead. Would it be necessary to call the police? And, if so, what story would I tell them? Perhaps just the truth – that he had come here to be photographed. And then something else struck me – why should his death prevent me from completing our task? He had made his way to me in the last moments of his life – he had entrusted me with his secret, had befriended me, and had now died in my presence. Surely such things are done with a purpose. I recalled the pictures, in Hardy's collection, of the chieftains in death, their bodies emblazoned with ritualized marks and symbols.

I removed Hardy's tie altogether, and unbuttoned his shirt; his chest was dominated by the tattoo of a plant, or bush, which was also a human face. His arms were covered with branches, which were also snakes. I turned him over with some difficulty. On his back was depicted a scene of three women, who seemed to be in mourning, and beside them was a casket picked out in gold.

I undressed Hardy completely, and began to photograph his body – as one image, and then in sections. I knew that I had very little time, and that I would soon have to call for help. It was all over in a matter of minutes. It took some time to dress him again, to order his tie and trousers so that they looked relatively intact. I then called an ambulance and ran down – taking care to appear breathless – to rouse the porter. I knew what to say to the police: that Alistair Hardy had come to be interviewed, that it was to be 'off the record' and in the relative privacy of my flat. I hoped that they would suspect nothing (indeed there was nothing to suspect) – and, so it proved, I was right.

The ambulance men came within a few minutes, tried to revive him but, predictably, failed. They removed his shirt, as I had done some minutes before, but they seemed quite uninterested in the tattoos beneath. In any case, faces look curiously impersonal in death and they did not connect this particular body with the public figure of Mr Alistair Hardy. The next morning two policemen came. They had already found my name in his appointments diary, and were satisfied with the explanation I gave them. It seems that he had had a massive coronary attack – unusual at his age, but not unknown. They did not mention the tattooing. I next saw Hardy's face in the obituary columns.

I phoned my editor and, with appropriate apologies, I confessed that I couldn't make any headway on the proposed article. Perhaps on some other occasion . . . By now, however, I had developed my photographs of Hardy; they showed him as relaxed in death as he had been in life. I had not, under the circumstances, done a bad job – the tattoos themselves were clear and sharp. But they still puzzled me – they seemed to represent a code which I could not quite decipher.

Five weeks later I received a letter from Alistair Hardy's widow. It was to the point: 'My late husband left instructions that you should inherit the photographic collection which he kept in London. I have instructed our solicitors to act accordingly.' The cabinet arrived a week later.

I opened it at once and went through the material, but there was too much to comprehend in one session. I looked again at my own photographs of Hardy, and understood what had previously eluded me; they were indecipherable in themselves. The tattoos had puzzled me because they were incomplete. They belonged with the collection. It would take many years to collate and interpret the wealth of material with which Hardy had presented me at the point of his death, and in any case the secret which he offered me might still be beyond my power to grasp. The only thing to do was to begin at the beginning. I looked through the pictures one more time, and then phoned Happy Harry. I suggested the design of a tattoo which I wished to have placed on my chest. He agreed to work on me the following morning.

Spectator, 22 December 1979

140

A Christmas Story

'. . . the army of spirits, once so near, has been receding farther and farther from us, banished by the magic wand of science from hearth and home.'

J. G. Frazer, *The Golden Bough*

Kevin returned home from the hospital in a state of mild imbecility; his wife, Claire, had been about to give birth for the past twelve hours and he had not slept or eaten as he waited. He blamed the delay upon his mother-in-law, Vera, whose presence always seemed to reduce his wife to a kind of nursery torpor. And it had been Vera who had eventually ordered him away.

'Kevin darling,' she had said, patting her hair into shape (for the occasion she had tied it behind her head in a bun as if, Kevin thought, she were a nurse in a field hospital), 'Kevin darling, do go home. We can manage perfectly well.' It was the voice of the professional organizer; it never varied at weddings or at funerals, at christenings or at cocktail parties. He had been hearing it all his life and, as usual, he obeyed.

The telephone rang and he was so tired that he gazed at it incuriously before going towards it. 'Kevin darling.' It was Vera again, her voice higher so that it seemed both more peremptory and more triumphant than ever. 'It's a boy! It's a lovely boy!' He said nothing in reply but when he replaced the receiver, those words still echoed in his head as he noticed how warm it was for the early autumn.

He had been hoping that, before Christmas came to end another year, he might have a child – it seemed to represent his real purpose in the world, a duty he felt bound to undertake. But now that it had happened it was more like a wonderful gift – a gift both to him and to Claire but, more mysteriously, also their gift to others. He took the telephone and danced with it in a small circle. 'It's a boy,' he whispered. 'It's a boy!'

The memory of that first exhilaration did not leave him until they returned with the baby. Then he saw how pale and tired his wife was, how bright and plump his son – in that respect, at least, the infant already resembled Vera whose energy had redoubled as that of her daughter began to fade. In sympathy with Claire, Kevin began to feel very tired as well. 'Is there,' he said, 'anything I can do? Shall I boil some water?'

'Kevin darling, what on earth would we need boiling water for? This isn't the nineteenth century. Why don't you be a poppet and see to Claire's things?'

'I only thought . . .' He looked inquiringly at his wife, who was presenting the child to Vera. Then she said, 'Mummy's got it all arranged.'

The telephone rang and, in his confusion, Kevin picked it up without saying anything. There was someone talking faintly at the other end, and he heard the word 'joy' or 'toy' before putting down the receiver. 'There must be a crossed line,' he told them, almost apologetically, but they were not listening to him. Vera was holding the baby in the air while Claire gazed at it solemnly. So my child, he thought, has become one more reason why they can ignore me.

The dusk of early winter cast its thin gloom over Kevin as he tried without success to read Benjamin Spock's *The First Year of Baby's Life*, and when the telephone rang he rose to answer it with a certain relief; his mood of pleasurable anticipation changed to one of incredulity, however, when he heard Vera saying softly but quite distinctly, 'It's a boy. It's a lovely boy . . .' It was the fact that she was whispering which really disturbed him. 'Vera?' The dialling tone returned and he was already blushing when he called her back. 'Vera?'

'Kevin, angel, I'm already out of the door. Tell Claire to wait.'

'Did you just talk to me?'

'Of course not. Why should I talk to you?' But she added: 'Is there anything the matter with the baby?'

'No. Nothing's the matter. I'll tell Claire to expect you.' When he put down the telephone he crept to the foot of the stairs, and listened intently as his wife whispered to the child.

As the rockets of Guy Fawkes' Day exploded above his head Kevin hurried home through the darkness, worried in case his wife already missed him. When he opened the front door he heard the telephone ringing. He raced towards it and with his coat half-falling from his shoulders, picked it up to hear Vera shouting at him, 'It's a boy! It's a lovely boy!' With a sudden rush of anxiety he slammed down the receiver and stood panting in the middle of the room.

He climbed the stairs slowly, as if in pain, and found Claire lying on the bed beside the baby's cot. 'I thought it must be you,' she said without rising to greet him. 'What were you doing?'

He was still breathing heavily. 'I think I was talking to Vera.'

She immediately raised herself into a sitting position and piled the pillows around her. 'Oh, what did Mummy want? Did she get that book on breastfeeding?' He was about to explain what in fact had occurred when a bell rang – for one moment Kevin thought it was the telephone again, and gave a start which was perceptible to Claire. But it was the front door, and when he went down to open it Vera was waiting for him on the threshold, dangling some keys. 'Oh Kevin darling, can you be an angel and get Claire's book from the car for me. You can't miss it.'

'Of course.' He could not look at her, but stared down at his shoes as she passed in front of him and went upstairs to her daughter. With a nervous gesture he examined his watch: it was now 6.15. And when he returned with the book he lingered in the bedroom doorway to scrutinize Vera; she was laughing, her head deliberately thrown back as if the world were being asked to witness her good humour, but she seemed neither ill nor deranged. And yet she must have telephoned him just before coming to the door. 'There, there,' she was saying now as she took the infant from its cot. 'Come to lovely Vera. She could eat you, you're so gorgeous.' And the baby, apparently fascinated by this sudden access to his grandmother's face, stuck his tiny fingers in her open mouth.

It was an evening in late November. Kevin was turning on the television at six o'clock when the telephone rang; and as he watched the screen fill with light, casting vague shadows upon the walls, he picked up the receiver and heard Vera shrieking. 'It's a boy! It's a lovely boy!'

'Vera, I'm sorry if this is a joke but . . .'

'It's a boy! It's a lovely boy!' To Kevin the voice now seemed hysterical, with an additional ferocity which both alarmed and angered him. He was about to shout back in panic when he looked up and saw Vera's face at the window, her mouth flattened against the glass and rendered a luminous grey by the light from the television. He dropped the telephone. 'Let me in, darling!' she was saying. 'Your bell isn't working!' He stared at her. 'Kevin darling, have you gone deaf?' And as he looked at her grey mouth he wondered whose voice it was he had heard, a voice which in memory no longer seemed human at all.

A week later, at the same time, he heard it again; he had thought of little else except those disembodied sounds, and he wanted to test his theory, that Vera had somehow arranged a recording. He was quite calm but, when he picked up the receiver, his calmness disappeared. 'It's a boy! It's a lovely boy!' He remembered what he had to say. 'Can you repeat that, please?' There was a slight pause. 'It's a boy! It's a lovely boy!' So there *was* someone there, listening to him, hearing his quick breathing and the sudden intake of that breath. He put down the telephone and hurried upstairs: for some reason he now feared that some terrible harm might befall either Claire or the child.

She looked defiantly at him as he entered the bedroom. 'Mummy told me to rest, so I'm resting. It's good for my milk.' But she was clearly puzzled. 'Are you all right? You look as if you've seen a ghost.'

'It was the phone.'

'Anyone I know?'

'No. I don't think so.' The baby gave a fat gurgle of satisfaction from the cot beside her.

He went downstairs and in order to calm himself, noted down the time and day of this latest call. But he did not need to look at his own scrawled handwriting to know that the telephone always rang at six o'clock on Tuesday evenings. This was the time when Vera had originally called him from the hospital with news of the birth. And who could have known that? Only Vera and Claire, naturally. He put his hands to the sides of his head. Then he thought, perhaps the baby knew . . .

When the following week the telephone rang again he snatched up the receiver and shouted, 'Who are you? Who put you up to this?' There was a pause, almost out of politeness, and then it began again, 'It's a boy! It's a lovely boy!' It seemed to Kevin that these harmless words had become threatening, even sinister, like an incantation designed to raise the dead. The voice seemed about to break into laughter: he could not bear the thought of that, and slammed down the receiver just before Claire entered the room. She looked at him curiously, and in that moment they realized how ill at ease they had become with each other.

'I thought I heard voices.'

'It was the phone.' He dared not look down at it, but pointed his finger.

'Oh? I didn't hear it ring.'

'They rang off quickly,' he replied without thinking about what he was saying.

'Who were *they?*'

'Oh I don't know. Just the usual.' She said nothing, but he noticed that she was biting the inside of her mouth as she stood uncertainly in the middle of the room.

When she left him, he sat down sighing – only to spring to his feet with the thought that perhaps the telephone had never rung, that the voice was only within his own head. All at once he saw himself as the centre of an illness which might infect his wife and child. He went over to the telephone and began minutely to examine it; he did not know what he was looking for, but he wanted to feel its weight and bulk in his now trembling hands. Then suddenly it rang again and with a yell he dropped it to the floor; from the spilled receiver he could hear Vera's voice oozing out. He wanted to scream abuse at it but instead he carefully picked it up, holding it a little way from his ear.

'Kevin poppet. What *is* the matter? What was that bloody noise?'

'Nothing.' He cleared his throat. 'It's just the phone.'

But apparently she had not heard him, since she began hurriedly to discuss the arrangements which she had made for them all at Christmas. Oh God, he thought as she talked at him, will I be able to endure all this until Christmas?

On the following Tuesday, at six o'clock, it rang again; but he remained seated and would not answer it. Claire and her mother were shopping for presents, and the noise of the bell seemed to fill the house. But he sat very still.

When at last it stopped he went to the cupboard under the stairs, took out a can of paint, a brush, and then began solemnly to daub the telephone until it was entirely blue – a bright blue. For some reason this exercise calmed and satisfied him. It had become a battle of wills, the next round of which would be fought on the following Tuesday, which was Christmas Eve.

They were all sitting together on that day, Vera rocking the baby in her arms, Claire watching her, and Kevin pretending to doze. At six o'clock, the telephone rang. He looked up at them quickly to see if they had heard it, too, and when Claire muttered, 'Now who can *that* be?'

he got up from his chair in relief. 'It may be for you,' he said to his mother-in-law, 'Why don't you answer it?'

'Don't be silly, darling, with a baby?'

'Could you get it then, Claire?' He coughed. 'I've got a frog in my throat.'

She glanced at her mother before slowly picking up the telephone. And then there came the voice again: 'It's a boy! It's a lovely boy!' Kevin stiffened and stared down at his infant son, not daring to say anything. But Claire laughed. She handed the receiver to her mother. 'Oh Mummy, it's you!' Vera listened as the baby tried to grasp the telephone and the voice came again. She laughed also, but clearly she was abashed. 'I didn't realize,' she said, 'how *military* I sound. I'm sorry.'

Kevin was astonished at their response, and even more so when his wife walked forward to embrace him. 'What a wonderful Christmas present! I knew you wouldn't forget baby's anniversary! Is it like a singing telegram?'

'No.' He didn't really know what to say. 'Not exactly.'

Vera was smiling at him. 'So that's why you painted the phone. We thought you were going dotty, darling.'

And Kevin laughed with them, for all at once he realized that the voice had been neither menacing nor inhuman. His suspicions had been absurd; the only evil had resided in his own fear. It was Vera's voice, but, somehow, it had never left the telephone and had become an echo of that joyful mood he had experienced at the first news of his infant son. 'So you don't mind?' he asked his wife.

'Why should I mind? I was waiting for you to show some sign.'

'Sign?'

'You know.' It was her turn to become abashed. 'About little Tom.'

Tom was laughing now, and Kevin took him from Vera's arms to hold him up to the light. The two women rested the telephone between them, listening once more to the refrain. 'It's a boy! It's a lovely boy!' as Kevin realized that these words also represented the spirit of Christmas itself. And at each Christmas they returned.

The Times, 24 December 1985

141

The Plantation House

There was nothing wrong with the hotel, as far as he knew. It was situated on the west coast of the small island, and his old-fashioned wooden balcony looked out upon the Caribbean. There were many areas here he had always wanted to visit, many caves and forests about which he had read before he came, but he could not bring himself to leave this place. He sat for hours above the sea, and watched the variations in the colour of the water and the sky – emerald, azure, cobalt, ultramarine, even violet, shimmering all around him so that he seemed to be enclosed within some crystal cabinet. All he could hear was the steady beat of the surf somewhere beneath his feet and slowly, as he sat here in the early morning or the late afternoon, he could sense his mind being emptied of any other thought; he contemplated nothing but the blue expanse before him. Occasionally a small green lizard or brightly coloured bird would share the large balcony with him, enjoying the shade, and he was happy to have their company. He knew that growing old could be a lonely matter, even here, but as he looked out upon the sea he became reconciled to all the changes taking place within him – or, rather, he considered them of no account beside the continual movement of the waters.

There was one spot which induced in him a more than usual restfulness; over the left side of the balcony hung the slender branches of a palm and, if he moved his chair beneath them, he could watch the Caribbean through a canopy of vegetation. He could also see the sky like a patchwork of blue through the green, and it was for him such an image of repose that he found himself able to sleep whenever he sat here. It was as if the pattern of the leaves, together with the beating of the surf, laid some strange enchantment upon his senses. At such times the island truly possessed him.

So, gradually, all his cares were lifted – even though he was, in many respects, a disappointed man. Edward Stanton was a travel writer, one of those mild but desperate people who find their only true relief in unfamiliar surroundings; he had spent his life moving on from place to place, never feeling quite at home anywhere, until now he found that he was growing old. His sister had been his closest friend, but she had died five years before. In fact it was she who introduced him to the island, and her memory had now brought him helplessly back; they had stayed at this same hotel and, invaded one cold London evening by a sudden sense of loss, he had decided at once to return here. Nothing could reinstate her familiar bright presence, however, and now he was alone with the birds and the lizards.

In the evening he walked through the gardens of the hotel to the small restaurant, past the orchid trees, the ginger lilies and the jasmine. As always, the garden was filled with powerful scents, which seemed to him like some echo of the sleep which overpowered him on the balcony; the blue and yellow blossoms glowed in the dusk as if they concealed some secret fire. Was that not one of the myths of the island, that there is a fire within all things? The restaurant was situated on a veranda which had one side open to the sea and, ever since his arrival, he had sat at a small table from which he could watch the curve of the surf illuminated by the lights of the hotel and hear the thin cries of the fruit bats as they soared through the mild air. The hotel had once been an old plantation house, one of the first built here by the English settlers in the seventeenth century; where the original owners had cleared the forests and planted tobacco or cotton, there were now lawns and gardens. The house itself had been extended, in the nineteenth and twentieth centuries, but the disposition of the central living quarters no doubt remained much the same. He entered the 'cocktail area' where the guests waited before being taken on to the veranda, and a young woman sat there before a piano. She was playing Mozart: how odd, he thought, to hear European music in this tropical setting. Yet perhaps this was the music which later generations of settlers used to play, when they sat after dinner in the plantation house.

'Are you all set?' A waiter had come over to him, ready to take his order; he asked for soup and fish, as he always did, and then chose a bottle of wine.

A few moments later another waiter appeared by his table. 'Are you all fixed?'

'Yes,' he replied, 'I'm fixed.'

'How are you enjoyin' your evenin' so far?'

'It's fine. Very pleasant.'

'Oh yes. Everythin's good tonight.'

After the meal he rose to leave, and almost slipped on the polished marble floor of the restaurant. He saw his shadow swaying wildly for a moment and, for that moment, he thought: this is the most real thing about me, my shadow. He returned slowly through the garden, amid the mournful chirping of the crickets, and stopped to admire a bank of pink hibiscus. Something clattered at his feet and darted away: he jumped back, alarmed, as he watched a large crab scuttling sideways into the shadows. There was no reason to be afraid, not in this perfumed garden, but he felt the sweat pouring down his face. He walked on, trying to be amused at his own nervousness (after all, a man in his late sixties!), and came up to the swimming pool. It was illuminated at night, and he saw the water rippling under the impress of the warm breeze; then he glimpsed something else in the corner of the pool. He had the impression of something floating in the water – no, not something, but a head and a truncated body suspended just below the surface. He turned away in horror but, for an instant, he thought he had seen the body of his dead sister floating towards him.

He turned back, and the dark shape had gone. It must have been a trick of the light, or of the shadows of the palm trees around the pool. Yet it had seemed so real. He walked quickly back to his room, and locked the door behind him.

It took a few minutes for his fear to dissolve. He went on to the balcony, back into the warm Caribbean night; the sound of the insects had grown more insistent, and he could make out the shape of two lobster boats floating close to the shore. No, there was nothing to fear. This was a welcoming island which by some powerful act of sympathy was occupied only by friendly inhabitants: this was what he had always thought, at least, although there had been occasions when he sensed a certain reserve or even hostility beneath their comfortable, cheerful manner. But there was nothing really hidden, nothing which did not dwell under the sun. The shape in the pool had been an absurd illusion and, not for the first time, he considered reducing the amount he drank each night.

He was tired, as exhausted as he had ever been, but for some reason he did not want to sleep. Not yet. Instead, he decided to prepare something for the article which he would have to write in order to justify his time here. The essential facts were easily comprehended and for that reason did not seem to him to be particularly important: the tropical island of St David, 30 miles long and 15 miles wide, with some 100,000 inhabitants, principal industries being tourism and sugar . . . and so on. He was more intrigued by the history of this place, which was characterized by a violence quite at odds with the calmness and even languor of its present setting.

The island had originally been inhabited by the native Caribs, or Indians, who were extirpated by the first English settlers in the middle of the seventeenth century; the men were burnt or hacked to death, while the women and children were pushed out to sea on open rafts. The English had then cleared the thick forests which covered the island by a technique known perhaps unhappily, in the light of their previous conduct, as 'slash and burn'; farms or plantations were then established, which were soon stocked by slaves transported from West Africa. The rest of the story followed a similar pattern of injustice and terror – violent conflicts between the white inhabitants and whatever governor the Crown imposed on the island, as well as sporadic slave revolts which were quelled with extraordinary and even gleeful ferocity. In 1839 the slaves were granted their freedom by an act of British policy which was at first resisted by the white inhabitants, for by now the black population greatly outnumbered the descendants of the settlers. And then, in the middle of the twentieth century, St David was given its independence under a native government.

So much for the known past – and yet, for Stanton, it seemed as amorphous and illusory as the shape he thought he had seen suspended in the pool. How did such a history explain the two dominant emotions of that day – his feeling of exhaustion and his sense of menace? Or could they be related in some way which he did not yet understand?

He had once visited the capital of the island, Milltown, with his sister; it was in the year before her death, and already she had shown signs of the illness which would eventually prove fatal. But the first sign of Milltown had given her some unsuspected energy.

'Isn't it extraordinary,' she said, 'how much it resembles an ancient town?'

'Ancient?'

'It's like eighteenth-century London.'

She was excited, almost exuberant, at this unexpected vision of the past.

He looked at the painted signs hanging in front of the shops, at the ruined interiors of the wooden buildings which hung over the narrow thoroughfares, at the projecting balconies, at the men and women shouting out their goods as they strolled through the streets, at the piles of rubbish discarded in alleyways. Yes, she was right – this was as close to an eighteenth-century town as anyone was likely to find.

'But what about the factories?' he said. 'And the refineries?'

'Don't be ridiculous, Edward. The core remains the same. We still remember our childhood, don't we?' He did not understand what she meant by that but, together, they wandered through the crowded streets of Milltown – past the wizened old women in their brightly coloured dresses, past the vegetable stalls, past the young men loitering on corners, past the donkey-carts and the old-fashioned bicycles. His sister seemed to revel in the life all around her, but he was filled with a growing sense of unease as the sun rose higher in the sky.

'Oh look,' she said. 'Have you ever seen a name like it?'

And she pointed to the painted street-sign before turning off the thoroughfare into Fever Lane. It was a narrow track, lined each side by rotten wooden shacks where the poorer townspeople lived, and he did not particularly want to enter it. But his sister had marched ahead of him, as she always did. He followed her down the lane, and then stopped abruptly when she halted – a few yards ahead of her an old man, dressed entirely in red, was sitting on a mound of refuse. He was swathed in different varieties of red rag and upon his head was a red turban, which came down just above his eyes. He seemed to be laughing, and then he pointed a wooden stick at her. She staggered back and Stanton hurried forward; he helped her to sit upon the remnants of a stone wall but, when he looked up, the old man had gone.

'It must have been the heat,' she said. 'I'm quite all right now, Edward. Don't fuss.'

This was his real memory of Milltown and, a year later, his sister was dead. Now he lay upon his bed and listened to the thud of the surf, like the beating of some vast drum.

On the following morning he woke, as usual, to the sound of a cock crowing in the courtyard of the hotel. Under the light of dawn the sea had become very still, although he noticed several small craft in the distance. He left his room and began walking through the gardens to the veranda once more, where breakfast was always served. Two gardeners were pointing towards the interior of the island and talking loudly to each other, but they lowered their voices when they saw him approaching. He could not have understood what they were saying, in any case, since the native demotic was particularly difficult to grasp; it always sounded to him like some distorted amplification of a Devon accent, but this was perhaps because he knew the original settlers had sailed from the south-west of England. When he passed the swimming pool he thought he saw movement and quickly looked away; but he knew that he had to master his sensation of horror, and once more turned to face the water. There was a young man within it, swimming lazily backwards and forwards.

He was the first to arrive in the restaurant, and he drank his coffee while surrounded by the small blackbirds which screamed defiance at the waiters trying to protect the bread and the sugar. What was that nursery rhyme which his mother used to sing to him? Four and twenty blackbirds, baked in a pie? He had always thought of them as essentially English birds and here, in this alien setting, they seemed more menacing; they were more starkly defined against the bright colours of the island, and therefore more dangerous. And perhaps they were eaten still – eaten by the islanders to ward off their threat. It was as if everything here was designed to conceal or keep back the darkness, and now he was joined by two or three other hotel guests who wore garishly coloured shirts and shorts in instinctive deference to the general brightness which surrounded them. In England, or America, they no doubt wore the dark suits of lawyers or businessmen: here they felt obliged to rival the tropical flowers. Stanton finished his breakfast with a vague sense of oppression, as he looked out at the shifting blue expanses of the sea. Then he went back to his room and slept.

It was evening before he finally managed to rouse himself from a heavy, dreamless slumber. And what a beautiful evening it was as the sun slowly descended into the shimmering water, as a mild breeze fluttered in the white and yellow sails of the small sailing craft, and tossed the leaves of the palm trees which fringed the shore. But he looked at all of this in bewilderment, so dazed was he by a sleep which had lasted all day. He had never done such a thing before, except when laid low by a fever, and with something approaching pity for himself he ascribed it to his advancing age. Then he got up from his bed, and began to prepare himself for dinner.

He was always given the same table; it was on the open side of the veranda and from here, if he wished, he could look out at the Caribbean. But he also sat at the end of the restaurant, with his back against a wooden pillar, and from this vantage he could survey the other tables – indeed that was why he had chosen this table in the first place. He was an observer of life now; having seen his ambitions fall down in flames around him, and having calculated on another ten or twelve years of life, he had quietly accepted his role as a spectator of other people. He was not a religious man, and had no thought of any kind of existence after death; this is all there is, he would say to himself, and I might as well see as much of it as I possibly can. So he travelled still.

'How are you makin' out with your evenin'?' It was the wine-waiter who, as always, approached him with a list at which he never glanced.

'It's a fine evening. I'll have number 20.'

He was distracted tonight. He scarcely bothered to notice what he was eating, and he gazed out across the water as if he half-expected something to emerge from its darkness. From time to time he would glance at the other guests but he had been staring into the darkness too long: his eyes were blurred slightly, and the outlines of the others were curiously indistinct. He looked down at the shadows on the polished marble floor, in order to refocus his vision, but they also seemed to be shifting around; in fact, even as he stared at them, they seemed to change their shape and motion. Was he having a stroke? Was he about to fall to the floor and mingle with the shadows there? He passed a hand across his face, but it did not feel like his hand at all. When he opened his eyes again and looked up, the hotel guests, the waiters, the plants, all had gone. He was no longer sitting down; he was leaning against the wooden pillar, but the veranda was now quite changed. Where there had been white chairs and tables there were now some pieces of plain wooden furniture, and the floor felt different beneath his feet: the marble had gone, and in its place he saw planks of dark mahogany. But this was only the first change. Everything had become smaller, but also more intricate, more substantial, more intense; it was as if a bright light had suddenly been turned on inside a small space. He felt more alive than he had ever done before, and as a result he entered a different relationship with all the objects around him; they seemed to come closer to him. They seemed to be part of him.

The piano was still there. No, not a piano. It sounded like a harpsichord. And someone was playing it – playing not Mozart, but some English country dance. The music stopped, and he watched as a young woman got up from behind the instrument and walked slowly across the veranda; she gave no sign of noticing his presence, although he could see her clearly. She gripped the wooden rail of the balcony, bowed her head, and began to sob. Something was wrong here;

something had happened in this place. And yet what place was it? He was in the old plantation house, but he was gradually becoming too large for the space he occupied. He felt as if he were somehow suspended, hanging over the room like a cloud through which the young woman would surely pass. He did not know if he could bear the sensation and then, suddenly, he heard the sound of a man or creature screaming.

He put his hand across his face, and no time had passed at all; he was sitting in the restaurant, as usual, about to drink the coffee which had just been placed before him. The other guests were beginning to drift away after their meal, but he stayed where he was – he did not, at that moment, know if he would be able to rise and walk away. What had happened? He could not believe that he had really seen anything at all, so strange had the sensation been, but he was aware of some alteration within himself; he was no longer considering the reality of the plantation house which had once stood here, or of the young woman who had once played the harpsichord. He was thinking, instead, of his childhood. All at once several scenes and images from his own past had risen up before him and, for the first time in many years, he could recall in perfect detail the faces of his mother and father. Then he remembered that terrible scream. He left the table and walked back through the gardens, but the perfume of the flowers reminded him of his mother's perfume, and he was astonished to feel tears coming to his eyes. He passed the swimming pool on his way to the room, and made a conscious decision to look into its water; but there was nothing there.

He amused himself, the following morning, by tracing the actual shape of the plantation house which had once been erected on this site. It was part of what had been known as the Greatorex Plantation: he knew that only because there was a map of the place hanging on the wall in the main reception. The situation of the rooms was still clearly visible upon it, and he could see how the terrace and the veranda had remained approximately the same – at least they were in the same position as the original wooden areas constructed in the seventeenth century. He could also make out the presence of several other older rooms within the structure of the hotel; there had once been a kitchen or parlour at the back of the house, and this was now an office where the hotel accountant worked. There had been a dining room where the hotel bar was now located, and two other reception rooms had been partly retained over the last three hundred years. It was curious how the living shape of the old house was still visible after so long a time, but one entry on the map puzzled him even more: the area of the garden now covered by the swimming pool was marked with a dark red cross, and a strange emblem which resembled the crude drawing of a human face.

He waited eagerly for evening, so that he could return to the veranda and sit at his customary table; he did not understand why he was so impatient to return, and perhaps did not care to examine the sources of that feeling, but he was the first to arrive for dinner. The manager of the hotel was there to greet him, to his dismay. She was a small woman, one of the few white natives descended from the original settlers, and she swooped around her establishment like the bats even now pirouetting in the dark air. She laughed easily with her guests; in fact she seemed to be laughing all the time, often for no apparent reason. The most neutral remark would be met by extraordinary amusement, as if the speaker were the wittiest person on the island, and she had a habit of repeating such remarks to anyone in the vicinity. But Stanton had once glimpsed her talking to her black staff, and there was no laughter then; her face had been distorted in anger, and she spat out the words to them. She was approaching him now, smiling in anticipation.

'You are the first,' she said.

'Am I? I suppose I was hungry.'

'You suppose you were hungry!' She laughed very loudly at this joke. 'Oh dear!'

'And I believe my watch is a little fast.'

'A little fast?' She seemed to curl up in laughter. 'No. Don't. Don't say another word. Enjoy.' A menu had been placed in front of him and, at that moment, she walked away to greet two other guests.

He had no appetite for his meal. As soon as he sat down at his familiar table, he was invaded by a nervous tension so acute he could hardly sit still. He wanted to jump up, to flee from this place, and it was only by concentrating upon the thin white line of surf beneath the terrace that he was able to remain where he was. Gradually, however, his tension abated. He had come to the end of his meal, and nothing whatever had happened. But what had he expected, in any case? Another hallucination? He was too old to indulge in such fancies. He rose from his chair in order to leave the veranda, when something pushed him down. Someone's hand had knocked him backwards. He fell against the wooden pillar, and fearfully put his hands against his chest where he had felt the blow. Had he in fact suffered some kind of heart attack? In that moment of fear and confusion, the world around him fled to the margins of his vision; but, when the first surprise had passed, he was standing once more on the veranda of the old plantation house. Although it was open to the sea there was such a suffocating smell of heat and burning here that he felt himself being deprived of breath; it was as if the past were a fire which would never be extinguished. He was not even sure that he was breathing at all, as he looked across at the young woman who was still in tears. She was wearing a red shawl, and he noticed some kind of silver chain around her neck as she leaned over the balcony. The echo of a scream was still ringing in the air when a middle-aged man, dressed in a brown jacket and white open shirt, came on to the veranda.

'He has enough fat,' he said. 'He will fry nicely.'

'Was it necessary to burn the creature?' She had quickly dried her eyes with a linen handkerchief before turning to face the man.

'What would you have me do? As a warning, yes, it was quite necessary. Do you wish to see us overrun?' There came the sound of a long, low moan that filled the terrace; for a moment the woman put her hand up to her neck in terror.

'Not the slave,' he said. 'The wind.'

Once again it seemed to Stanton that he was suspended somewhere around these people even as he listened to them; he had the strangest sensation that he had become the house, that he was arched over them in the walls and ceiling, and that this was why they could not see him. The young woman now walked straight towards him, as he leaned against the wooden pillar, and stopped no more than a few inches away from him; she was staring into his eyes and he watched her, immobilized with fear simply because she was not seeing him at all.

'I cannot endure this place,' she whispered. 'I cannot exist on this terrible island.' There was another scream from somewhere beyond the house; she turned, put her hands up to her head, and then fell on to the mahogany floor.

He was still staring down at the marble when a waiter approached him. 'Are you lookin' for somethin', sir?'

'No.' He was out of breath, as if he had been running for a long time. Then he sat down again, and noticed with surprise that his hands were trembling.

'What was this place before?' Stanton asked him suddenly.

438

'Before?'

'Before it was a hotel.' For some reason he became very angry with him, as if he were deliberately trying to conceal something.

'It was always the Greatorex Plantation. Can I get you somethin'?' Stanton shook his head and the waiter, with his usual placid, amicable smile, strolled away.

What is happening to me? What is going on? I am growing old. And old men dream dreams. Or do they see visions? He found himself thinking of his own past once again, since the young woman reminded him very much of his mother as she appeared to him sixty years ago. He could recall her taking him in her arms, and allowing him to touch the silver crucifix which she kept around her neck, but the rest was darkness . . . I am older now than she ever was. I am older than the young woman who fell in front of me, even though she may have lived centuries back. Is that why I can see them now? He did not linger in the garden on his return to his room; he walked straight back, and fell asleep at once.

The next day he awoke with a determination to find out more about the Greatorex Plantation. On several occasions he had passed, along the highway which led to the hotel, a sign pointing to 'The Department of Archives'; he telephoned for an appointment as soon as he could and, before the heat of the day grew too intense, he made his way there in a taxi. It was an unprepossessing white stone building among a group of other government offices but, as soon as he went inside, he sensed a change of atmosphere: for the first time since he had arrived on the island, he was surrounded by evidence of the past in documents, in deeds, in boxes of maps and plans, in estate books, in volumes of parish records. But he was not sure what he expected or even hoped to find, and hardly knew how to frame his request to the young man who came over to him.

'Do you have,' he said, 'any papers relating to the Greatorex Plantation?'

'And in what parish might that be?'

'This one. Cabbacott parish.'

'No problem. And what years are you goin' to be lookin' at?'

'I'm not sure. The seventeenth century. Perhaps the eighteenth.'

'So you'll be wantin' the earliest records?'

'If you have them.'

'Oh yes, sir, we have them. Take it easy, and I'll be right back.'

439

Stanton recognized the usual affable and courteous manner, but had he also noticed once more a certain reserve and even wariness? He could not be sure, but it seemed to him that there was a vague atmosphere of suspicion circulating around the island.

The documents were soon in front of him, but most of them were title deeds and complex legal papers about boundaries and rights. It had not been a large plantation, and the house had clearly been a dominant feature from the beginning; there had been the customary transition from tobacco and cotton to corn and sugar, when these last two were introduced in the late seventeenth century, and in fact there was nothing contained in these stained and dusty papers that seemed at all unusual. But then he noticed a parchment folded and tied with blue cord. He opened it as gently as he could, and realized at once that it was the earliest map of the plantation he had yet seen: the house was not yet marked upon it, but a series of lines and measurements suggested that it was about to be constructed when this plan was drawn up. And, yes, there was the same dark red cross which he had seen upon the map in the hotel reception: it was precisely the same spot, but there were some words beside it in faded brown ink. He put his face close to the parchment, smelling its age as he did so, and by degrees he was able to decipher the lettering. 'Here Stood the Idol.' He looked back with renewed interest now at the later maps; the cross was no longer there but on the same spot, on one map dated 1698, someone had drawn a circle with a legend beneath it – 'The Burning Ground'. Suddenly the sweat poured from his neck and forehead, and he put the old papers aside.

He was about to leave the room, when the young attendant approached him. He was smiling and holding a book in his left hand. 'I just knew there was somethin',' he said.

'What is it?' Stanton could feel the sweat drying upon his face, and looked away for a moment.

'This is about the Greatorex Plantation. It's all here, in this tremendously old book.'

He put the volume down on the table, and Stanton took it up. It was entitled *Great Newes from St David or A True and Faithfull Account of the Treachery of the Negroes against the English and The Happy Discovery of the Same.* He did not have to read far before he found the first reference to the plantation: the leaders of the slave revolt had, according to the anonymous narrator; 'bin in the possession of Mr

Greatorex upward of two years before entering upon their horrid conspiracy'. They had tried to suborn the other slaves on the plantation but a housemaid, herself a slave, had heard them whispering their plans and had informed her master. 'Whereupon the two treacherous negroes fled the plantation and, in their wildnesse, attempted to raise a general rebellion against the lawful possessors of this fruitful isle.' The revolt was not a success, however, and led only to the burning of a few wooden dwellings in Milltown and in the parish of Redlake; the two leaders fled into the inland forests but, after a matter of weeks, they were captured and led back in irons to their old master. 'Whereupon Mr Greatorex, being a gentleman of the utmost probity and justice, ordered his two slaves to be whipped until their skin hung about them in ribbons and then led them to certain wooden posts where they were shackled to one another and burnt alive. Many witnessed this scene, and laughed exceedingly when one of the condemned men called out, "If you bury me today, you cannot bury me tomorow."'

Stanton looked up from the book. He understood now the meaning of the legend, 'The Burning Ground', inscribed upon the map he had just examined; and he believed now that he had already heard the screams of those who had died there. But what was the significance of the dark red cross marked at the same spot, with the words 'Here Stood the Idol'? What had this to do with 'The Burning Ground'? He opened the book again, and went back to the beginning in case he had missed some reference or allusion to this mysterious idol. But he could find nothing – nothing, that is, until he came to the end of the volume and found two pages in italic print which were entitled *The History of the Greatorex Plantation before the Rebellion*. One passage immediately arrested his attention: 'And in this place also, when the clearing of the lush verdure began apace, Mr Greatorex came upon a stone statue of middling height which had bin carefully formed: thinking it no doubt the idol of the savages who had previously inhabited this island, he overturned it and broke up the stone so that no portion of the original remained. Having quite destroyed the demon, he praised God for His triumph on this island. Yet there were some curious pieces of pottery, vessels and such like, which Mr Greatorex retained as tokens of his removal of that barbarism.' Stanton closed the book. He did not greatly care for Mr Greatorex and he suspected, too, that he had deliberately burnt his slaves on the same spot where he had found the pagan idol. It would be a way of affirming his power, his control over the 'savages' – whether they were the native Caribs or blacks transported as slaves from West Africa. But what had happened to the relics he had decided to preserve as tokens of his victory? He had seen no sign of their presence in the hotel, and in any case it was unlikely that they would have remained in the plantation house for the last three hundred years. He got up from the table and took the book over to the attendant, who was standing by a window. He was staring into the large garden which surrounded the building and seemed to be looking into a bank of yellow Bird of Paradise flowers; but when he turned around, his eyes were curiously unfocused.

'Thank you,' Stanton said, holding out the volume.

'That's my pleasure.' At last he seemed to take in once more the presence of this old white man.

'There was one thing. There's a reference here to old native artefacts. Before the settlement. Do you know where they might be kept now?'

The young man laughed. 'I never seen *that*.' Stanton showed him the reference at the end of the book, and he laughed again. 'Did you ever hear that expression, you learn somethin' new every day?' He made it sound as if the phrase had just been coined that morning.

'Yes. I have heard that.'

'You should try the museum. This beats me.'

'The museum?'

'In Milltown. By the old church.'

There was only one museum in the town, and it did not prove difficult to find. It was a two-storey building with the shutters closed to protect its interior from the sun, and for a moment Stanton stood blinking in the unaccustomed darkness. The place seemed quite deserted, but after a short time he understood the chronological sequence upon which all the exhibits had been arranged. Two rooms on the ground floor held material from the nineteenth and twentieth centuries, while the rooms above contained objects from the earlier history of the island. At the top of the stairs, in fact, he found a long wooden cabinet with a handwritten notice pasted on the side – 'The Carib People'. And then he saw it. Beneath the glass there was an ink drawing of a statue, with a crudely represented face; there was a card beside it which explained that this was the 'Drawing of the idol known as Thanos, worshipped by the Caribbean Indians'. It was simple enough, a pillar of stone surmounted by a head, but there was something about the shape and size of this idol which seemed curiously familiar to him. Yes, this was very like the thing he had seen moving in the swimming pool of the hotel.

But that was not possible. It could not be. It was a trick of his memory. He looked more closely into the cabinet, keeping his eyes away from the ink drawing, and saw there three small objects carved out of red stone. Next to them was another card, upon which had been written, 'Some vessels or ornaments of the Carib people, which were found at the Greatorex Plantation in the parish of Cabbacott'. So these were the relics which Mr Greatorex had uncovered and preserved – except that they did not look like 'vessels' or 'ornaments' at all. All three of them were elongated into something resembling the shape of a pear, but they clearly represented faces; two round holes for eyes, an incision in the stone as a nose, and a small open slit for the mouth. They were such distinct faces that they unnerved Stanton; they seemed to be staring directly at him, or rather, *through* him just as the young woman had stared through him on the veranda of the old plantation house.

He looked across at the drawing of the idol and, with something like dread, saw that the same face had been delineated there. And there was something else, too: there was a blankness about the mottled red stone but the eyes and mouths had been cut in such a way that they preserved some sense of menace and even hostility. These relics of an old time were not necessarily at rest, and he was surprised that Mr Greatorex had ever taken them into the plantation house.

He returned to the hotel, chastened and uneasy after his morning's research; he had managed to discover the true history of the Greatorex Plantation, but it was not something that could safely be relegated to the past. The faces still survived in the museum but, more importantly, his own visions of the plantation house suggested that everything which had happened around this place – the discovery and destruction of the idol, the burning of the rebellious slaves – was somehow still here. He was about to reach the swimming pool when he heard a terrified scream; he ran forward in panic, and at once saw a dark shape paddling towards a young girl who was bathing there. Then the scream turned to laughter: it was a large dog which had jumped into the pool, and was now swimming happily towards the side. As soon as Stanton reached his room, he went out on to the balcony and gazed at the Caribbean.

For a moment that young girl had reminded him of his sister. No, it was the association of the girl and the dog; when they had been children, they had owned a black mongrel which had followed them everywhere. And as he looked out upon the waters, his past welled up again; it was as if the very blankness of the sea, and the calmness of this island, acted as a surface upon which the images of his childhood could more clearly be seen. All at once he could recall the atmosphere of the house in which he had grown up – the narrow piety of his mother's Christianity assailing him like the smell of wood-polish in the dining room, the terrible grief of his father at the time of her death. He had not thought of such things for many years – perhaps not since he had left home as a young man – but now, as he looked out at the shifting sea, he was filled with his father's old sorrow and his mother's superstitious dread. And he mourned, too, for his sister. All of them gone. Was that why he had become so open to the past, with his own gradually increasing sense of loss and solitude breaking open his experience of the world? What was it exactly that was haunting him? Am I afraid of the distant past, and of the savages, or am I afraid of my own childhood? And why am I so easily lulled to sleep upon this island? He went down to dinner that evening in a state of expectancy not unmixed with fear; he did not know what else there was for him to see, if indeed he saw anything at all. He ate his meal quickly and nervously, but once more managed to steady himself by gazing out into the darkness. Occasionally he glimpsed the silver circle of a fish leaping out of the water and turning over before it dived again into the depths, and he watched the swift movements of the bats as they pursued the insects and glided briefly from the darkness into the light. He drank some wine and, for the first time that night, he relaxed into his chair. It was possible, after all, that everything he witnessed had been the product of his own anxious imagination; he had heard of places where the climate or terrain provoked strange symptoms in visitors, and perhaps this was also true of the island of St David.

He put up his hand, to attract the attention of the waiter, when suddenly he heard all around him a whistling noise like the rushing of wind in a confined space; then it turned into a loud, prolonged and agonized scream. He was knocked back by a wave of heat and, when he managed to regain his balance, his eyes opened wide in horror. He was standing in a field beside the old plantation house, and in front of him two men were burning; only patches of their bodies were visible through the smoke and flames, but he could see that they were tied with iron chains to large wooden posts. They seemed to be shaking or breaking up inside the fire and, although he did not want to look too closely, it was not clear where the charred flesh and the charred wood of the posts had separated. He was overwhelmed by the cloying sweet savour, and then one of the men fell forward in his dying moments: his face emerged from the flames and Stanton realized that the visage of this man, burnt almost beyond recognition, had taken on the shape of the red stone faces he had seen. The eyes and mouth were no more than holes in an uneven surface, and fat from the man's cheeks had dripped down so that the whole face was unnaturally distorted into the shape of a pear.

Stanton lost consciousness and, when he awoke, he found himself lying beside the swimming pool with two waiters bent over him. For a moment, they might have been the remains of the slaves burned at the stake; he put out his hand in terror, and one of them grasped it. 'Are you all right?' the waiter said. His face, in the darkness, was that of the idol. 'Are you OK?' He helped Stanton to his feet.

'I want to go home,' he murmured. 'I want to go to my room.' The waiters stared at him as he hurried away; then they shrugged and, saying nothing, went back to their work.

He dreamed that night of the island, but it was somehow confused with his family home; the banana and the manchineel trees were growing in the garden of their semi-detached house in Exeter, while the bougainvilleas and allamandas flourished in the living room. His parents had changed also. 'Is everything OK?' his father asked him with a slow smile. 'Are you enjoying your evening with us so far?' Stanton woke up, terrified, and waited impatiently for the first intimations of dawn.

As soon as it was light he left the hotel and began to walk down one of the narrow, dusty roads that led to the interior. He did not know where he was going; he simply wanted to get away from the old plantation house, with the hope that in the quiet of the central region he might be able to resolve his disturbed thoughts. Yet the further he travelled, the more uneasy he became. Whatever he was trying to escape from, somehow, existed all around him: he thought he could see the face of the idol inscribed on the bark of the trees he passed, and he glimpsed it in the very pattern of the vegetation which surrounded him. The same eyes and mouth were on the leaves, along the stems, in the moving grasses, even on the beaten track of the earth which he now followed as he made his way towards the interior. It was in the very shape of the wind which brushed past him, crying, and, yes, it was also the face of an infant still in the womb. A map of the island had been fixed to a wooden board, for the sake of any tourists who might venture this way, and with a sudden shock of recognition he saw that the shape of the island was exactly the same as that of the stone relics. And there, too, in the dark areas marking forests and swamps he could make out the same eyes, the same nose, the same mouth. The island's face was upon the idol which Mr Greatorex had tried to destroy; it was the island itself which the Carib Indians had worshipped.

He knelt down upon the lush grass, and put his face in his hands. He could feel the trembling of the earth beneath him. Everything around him was moving now; it was as if the rise and fall of his lungs, the actual beating of his heart, were being reproduced in the rise and fall of the land around him and in the distant drumming of the sea. But was it not his body which was imitating the island, as he knelt upon the earth? These noises had always resounded here and, if he listened carefully, they would surely overwhelm him. He lay down and experienced a terrible melting fear when he realized that this – thing – was alive beneath him. He looked up for a moment, and the two mango trees in front of him seemed to be quivering in the heat; no, certain shapes upon them were trembling and shaking. He could see the two slaves tied to them, their bodies so burnt that they were the same colour as the bark. Then they were gone, and the trees were still again.

He did not know how many minutes or hours he had lain there on the dark brown earth, but it was long enough for the soil to have got into his mouth and underneath his shirt. He realized, from the position of the sun in the blank sky, that it was already late afternoon. He began walking while everything remained very still and, since the heat of the day had abated, he managed to make some progress. But progress towards what? He was no longer sure if he was returning by the right path, since the vegetation around him seemed much thicker and darker than anything he had encountered on his outward journey. After an hour or so in this difficult terrain, he came to the edge of a forest which spread in all directions before him. But surely no forest of this size remained on the island? It looked almost impenetrable, but everything of that kind had been cleared centuries back. He had no choice but to make a path through it, however, but it was so dark that for the first time on St David he felt quite removed from the influence of the sun. The shadows lay quietly upon the luminous green floor of the forest and he realized, with some fear, that other creatures must also take refuge here from the heat of the air and the passage of the days; there was a sudden movement among the shadows, and for a moment he thought he glimpsed figures darting between the trees. He stumbled forward beneath the canopy of the forest, with the smell of dank vegetation and rotting bark all around him. There seemed to be no end to this place but then, suddenly, he found himself stepping into brightness; he stood in the air, dazed by the light, until he heard the crashing of the sea somewhere in front of him. With his right hand he shielded his eyes from the glare, and saw at once that he had come out near the shore. But this was not a part of the coastline he recognized; it was thickly covered with vegetation, and seemed deserted. There was something about the prospect, in fact, which unnerved him; it was as if he had returned to the dream of his parents' house which had so alarmed him the previous night.

Then he heard voices. He could not understand what was being said, but he made his way in their direction. He walked along a dusty track between two rows of cabbage palms until he came out into a clearing where, ahead of him, stood a recently built wooden house with ornate balconies on the first floor. Something about it was familiar to him, but his attempt to remember was disturbed by the sight of a half-naked man running towards him with his arms outstretched. Then he looked towards the house again and, with a groan, realized to what place he had come. He was standing outside the old house. He was on the Greatorex Plantation. It was as if the familiar outlines of the hotel and its surrounding area had shrunk or, perhaps, as if the whole world was diminished. There was no sense of space here, and no sense of time. Everything was concentrated on this one moment of vision.

'Master! Master!' The man had come up to him, and knelt in the dust at his feet. 'She gone. Come now.'

He stared at the kneeling slave, and a change came over him. Something had happened to his wife, the young woman he had brought all the way from England. He kicked out at the slave, and rushed shouting into the plantation house. Usually he liked to hear the sound of his tread upon the newly laid mahogany boards – it gave him a strong sense of possession – but now the silence after their echo terrified him. 'Elizabeth!' What had been the words he heard her whisper last night? I cannot endure this place. I cannot exist on this terrible island. 'Elizabeth!' He ran out into the garden, where the ground was still covered with warm ashes from last night's burning, and looked wildly around. 'Elizabeth Greatorex!'

A house-slave came running out from the veranda towards him. 'She gone,' she said. 'She gone this morning.'

He could see the cart still in the stable beside the house. 'Did she take a horse?'

The slave shook her head. 'No horse. She go that way.' And she pointed back towards the forest.

He cursed her and ran in that direction but, as soon as he came under the dark canopy of the foliage, he knew how hard it would be to find her. This was a wild and desperate place; the forests had not yet been cleared and stretched for miles over fever-swamps and precipitous cliffs. He cursed out loud again, and stumbled through the dank undergrowth. From time to time he fell forward, his foot tripping on a root or fallen branch, and then he found himself being suffocated by the broad grass and the foul-smelling lichen which spread over the floor of the forest. But still he pressed forward, without destination or direction. 'Where are you?' he called out. 'In God's name where are you?'

It was then he saw it. He had come out into a small clearing among the trees, and it was there. There stood the idol, seeming to watch him with its hollow stone eyes. This was the idol he had found and destroyed when he had first cleared the ground for his tobacco – he knew its features well enough after swinging an axe through them. Yet here it stood again. He remained very still for a long time, watching it for the slightest sign of movement, and then he approached it slowly. Somehow he connected this thing with the disappearance of his wife, and he could bear it no longer – he started to run towards it, yelling at the top of his voice, and beat his hands against the stone. It was on fire and he pulled back the palms of his hands, seared by the heat, while at that moment he heard the sound of some creature screaming. It sounded like the agony of the slaves he had burnt the night before but then, with horror, he realized that it was his own scream. He did not know what to do, or to think. He put his raw hands to his face, and looked upward at the thick foliage which hid the sky. He turned in a circle, still looking upwards, and he thought he could see his wife's face forming among the trees. Somehow she was now part of the island, and with a cry he fell to the earth.

Stanton lay there, unable to move. He understood what had been happening, and that in this place he had gone through some transition.

With difficulty he raised his head: the clearing was still there, but the idol itself had been taken away. Three hundred years had passed since he had fallen here, and the forest was the same. What else had remained here over that time? What else had not changed? But he was no longer afraid; or, rather, he had crossed the threshold of his fear and now dwelt hopelessly within it.

He tried to rise from the ground, and realized that he was covered with dry earth and fallen leaves, and grass – he might have become some spirit of the island, taking its surface with him everywhere. And then he recalled how he had used to play in his own garden when he was a child – how he had once rolled in the mud, and how his sister had mocked him. 'Why,' she had said. 'You look like a proper savage!' He could hear her laughing still, and then he saw her part the leaves and walk towards him. His sister had returned to the island after all. Or was it Elizabeth Greatorex, grown old and hard like the idol itself? This woman came up to him, and helped him to his feet. 'You will be a savage,' she said. 'You cannot leave now. Like all of us.'

Within this forest the air was so humid and heavy that he could scarcely breathe at all. He dropped to his knees again after walking a few yards, just at that spot where the idol had been erected centuries before. He felt then that he was sinking into the earth. No, not sinking but drowning. The presence of the sea was all around him, and his knowledge of its infinite depths mingled with the perfume of the brightly coloured flowers and with the terrible waves of heat which passed over his head. He felt certain he was dying and, in that moment of understanding, he knew he was haunted – haunted by his childhood, and by the ghosts of the dead, but also haunted by the island itself.

When they found his body the next morning, he was curled up like an infant still in the womb. He had one finger in his mouth, but his face was fixed in an expression of amazement – with his open mouth, and staring eyes, Edward Stanton had taken on the blankness of a stone carving.

New Statesman and Society Christmas Supplement, December 1991

Index